Homicide

A Psychiatric
Perspective

Homicide

A Psychiatric Perspective

Carl P. Malmquist, M.D., M.S.

University of Minnesota
Department of Sociology
Minneapolis, Minnesota

Washington, DC
London, England

Copyright © 1996 American Psychiatric Press, Inc.
ALL RIGHTS RESERVED
Manufactured in the United States of America on acid-free paper
99   4 3
First Edition

American Psychiatric Press, Inc.
1400 K Street, N.W., Washington, DC   20005

Library of Congress Cataloging-in-Publication Data
Malmquist, Carl P.
      Homicide : a psychiatric perspective / Carl P. Malmquist.
         p.   cm.
      Includes bibliographical references and index.
      ISBN 0-88048-690-2
      1. Homicide—Psychological aspects.   2. Murderers—Mental health.
   I. Title.
      [DNLM: 1. Mental Disorders—psychology.   2. Homicide—psychology.
   WM 140 M256h   1995]
   RC569.5.M35   1995
   616.85′844—dc20
   DNLM/DLC
   for Library of Congress   95-11551
                                                                                CIP

British Library Cataloguing in Publication Data
A CIP record is available from the British Library.

CONTENTS

PREFACE

Many years ago, on first becoming involved in forensic psychiatric work and training, I became aware of the paucity of psychiatric materials dealing with the subject of homicide. To be sure, there were several insightful articles dealing with a particular kind or case of homicide, and a greater abundance of them dealing with the subject of insanity, but they did not offer an overall psychiatric perspective on homicidal behavior. Other disciplines, such as sociology and law, had an enormous bibliography of the subject with their own orientations. Bookstores also seemed perpetually filled with volumes dealing with popular crimes or murder mysteries. Yet these never seemed as intriguing as the actual cases I had personally examined on consultation. My approach was to determine whether any psychiatric problems existed and secondarily to become involved in reasoning about the complex legal issues presented.

Several things pushed this situation toward a book. During a conversation with my old friend, Jay Katz, M.D., of the Yale Law School faculty, it came out that I had personally evaluated over 500 individuals who had committed a homicide. He urged that I share such experiences, and not merely keep them for my own curriculum vitae or my classes. The next step was a conversation with my colleague, David Ward, Ph.D., a criminologist and chair of the sociology department at the University of Minnesota. We decided to create and teach a course entitled "Killing." It has been a popular course, and at first it seemed a logical step simply to create an anthology of articles on homicide. However, an anthology lacked a broader coverage of the topic that was based on clinical knowledge that one person could synthesize. It meant raising the types of questions that clinical and research psychiatrists would ask. This necessarily led to questions about the epidemiology of homicide, different diagnoses, descriptive diagnoses from the American Psychiatric Association's *Diagnostic and Statistical Manual of Mental Disorders,* and how to integrate certain psychodynamic formulations for understanding and explanation. All of the above corresponded to the period of increasing concern about serious violence in the United States. Different people from backgrounds, not only in psychiatry but in psychology, sociology, and law as well, wondered if there was a psychiatric textbook available that could give them some overall insights on how psychiatrists thought about the problem of homicide. I began to realize that there was indeed an audience for such a work. Only a few colleagues indicated that this was a subject outside the province of psychiatry proper. In my thinking, homicide does not seem any more outside the province of psychiatry than suicide, for which psychiatry has never hesitated in accepting the possibility of psychiatric contributions.

The subject of murder, in fact and fiction, is not likely to go away. In fact, the boundaries between real murder and novelized murder have become increasingly blurred in the media, such as the efforts to have some executions televised or videotaped for replay. My hope is that this book will shorten the search for other clinicians who have homicide cases, as well as attorneys, and that it will lead to an increase in articles and books in the field of homicidology.

In terms of ideas and fruitful interchanges, it would be impossible to list all the people from whom I have benefited through discussions over the years. Besides Jay Katz and David Ward there have been Paul Meehl, Alan Stone, and Yale Kamisar at the University of Michigan Law School, who introduced me to the intricacies of criminal law, and diverse philosophers have all been stimulating. I also express my appreciation to Kate Stuckert for her patience and assistance in the typing of this manuscript in its several forms.

INTRODUCTION

Clinical discussions about the nature of homicide and its perpetrators usually focus on the individual actor, viewing an individual perpetrator under the clinical microscope to gain an insight into the nature of homicidal aggression as it has been played out in that one person. Many chapters in this book are written from this perspective. However, too frequently, material from other disciplines that is significant to the topic of homicide is ignored, thus narrowing the knowledge base from which conclusions are made and limiting the validity of those conclusions. In this book, I have chosen to introduce data from other perspectives, which I see as crucial to fully understanding the phenomenon of homicide and perpetrators of homicide. The additional data are culled from the epidemiological approaches to homicide, in which information on the victims of homicide is emphasized, as well as from sociocultural approaches, in which diverse cultural and sociological variables and how they interact with other intrapersonal dynamics in any given perpetrator are emphasized.

Until quite recently, suicides seemed to arouse more concern and get more professional, public, and media attention than homicides. Surprisingly, the overall number of homicides per year in the United States is almost as great as that of suicides, even excluding all the aggravated assaults as "attempted homicides." The number of suicides is approximately 30,000 per year,[1] whereas the number of homicides is approximately 22,000–24,000 per year.[2] Now, with increased public concern about violence, there has been an increase of interest in homicidology to a level that equals that of suicidology. In turn, scientific interest has increased as well in terms of seeking a better understanding of this seemingly inevitable accompaniment of human existence. What has also emerged is the realization that homicide is a major public health problem.

The *Uniform Crime Reports* (UCRs), published by the Federal Bureau of Investigation, are a major source for data about the macro levels of homicide. *Homicide* is therein defined as the willful, nonnegligent killing of one human being by another person or group. It excludes deaths by negligence, attempted killings, assaults that lead to someone's death, and accidental deaths. *Justifiable homicide*—when a victim is killed while he or she is committing a serious crime or when a felon wanted by law enforcement agencies is killed—is also excluded from the definition.

Homicide is usually categorized as one of a group of serious violent crimes. In a practical sense, the concepts of aggravated assault and homicide are very close in that it may only be by a stroke of luck that violence against another person does not result in that person's death; the violent act is then legally classified as an assault and not as a homicide. For example, a gunshot wound that goes a few inches to the right side of the sternum, thereby missing the heart and major vessels, may allow the victim to survive, but, in all other respects, the ingredients of the act add up to homicidal behavior. In fact, some argue that most homicides are actually miscarried assaults with a gun in which the victim ends up being killed.[1] The converse argument is that assaults with guns are miscarried homicides in which the victim has survived.

Robbery is usually considered to be a violent crime, yet, despite the threat of force and intimidation that is present, it does not have the conceptual overlap that aggravated assault and homicide share. Even serious sexual assault, although it may have some overlap with homicide, has its own defining characteristics, just as a sexual murder is a subcategory of murder.

All of these violent offenses share the following characteristics:

1. The risk of physical harm is present, even though only homicide leads to death
2. The victim of such an act is placed in a situation in which a great deal of anxiety is present. This is true for victims of each of the violent crimes mentioned above, including survivors of attempted homicides.

3. There are long-lasting consequences for the perpetrator and the victim. Not only may the perpetrator be subject to a long sentence of imprisonment or execution, but the psychological sequelae may have long-range effects on his or her subsequent behavior as well. Although some victims of attempted homicide, aggravated assault, robbery, or sexual assault have minimal or no consequences, not everyone is so lucky. Some victims may experience consequences that are analogous to the long-range effect seen in veterans years after being in military combat; in fact, these side effects, whether from military or civilian settings, are currently assessed under the diagnosis of posttraumatic stress disorder.

■ References

1. Doerner WG, Speir JC: Stitch and saw: the impact of medical resources upon criminally induced lethality. Criminology 24:319–330, 1986
2. Ghosh TB, Victor BS: Suicide, in The American Psychiatric Press Textbook of Psychiatry. Edited by Hales RE, Yudofsky SC, Talbott JA (eds): Washington, DC, American Psychiatric Press, 1994, pp 1251–1271

CHAPTER 1

Epidemiological Aspects of Homicide

■ Historical Perspective on Rates of Homicide

Trends in deaths from homicides for the twentieth century reveal low rates early in the century, with a peak first reached during the economic depression years of the 1930s.[1] The rate dropped during World War II, followed by a slight increase in the late 1940s and early 1950s. By the end of that decade, the rate had dropped, but it picked up again in the 1960s with a steady climb. The peak rate of 10.2 murders per every 100,000 people was reached in 1980. During the 1980s, the homicide rate continued to be among the highest in the twentieth century in the United States. The above homicide rates are graphed in Figure 1–1.

In a report by the National Academy of Sciences,[2] it was noted that the annual risk of becoming a homicide victim had risen from 1 in 12,000 in 1987–1988 to 1 in 10,600 by 1990. The lifetime risk was much greater, as shown in Figure 1–2. The highest lifetime rate among the six demographic groups is for black males (see Figure 1–3). Their rate of 4.16 is equivalent to a 1 in 24.1 chance of dying by homicide. For American Native Indians, the risk is 1 in 57, whereas for white males and females the risk is less than 1 in 100. It must be emphasized that, despite the media's focus on killings of adolescents and young males, less than 25% of one's lifetime homicide risk is incurred by the time that person reaches his or her 25th birthday. Hence, the high number of black males dying by age 24 years must be seen in the context of the high homicide rate for black males at all ages.

Data from the 1990 *Uniform Crime Report* (UCR) indicate that a record number of 23,438 overall homicide cases were committed in that year.[3] However, such a figure by itself is relatively meaningless; it must be viewed in relationship to other time-measured variables to have any meaning. For example, an increase in population could lead to an increase in the number of homicides. This is what has led demographers to study longitudinal trends that include homicide rates. The overall rates can vary significantly over time. In addition, the data may be broken down into rates for various regions of the United States as well as detail the relationship of the people involved in the killing. For example, in 1990, the western United States appeared to supplant the South as the region with the highest overall level of violence.

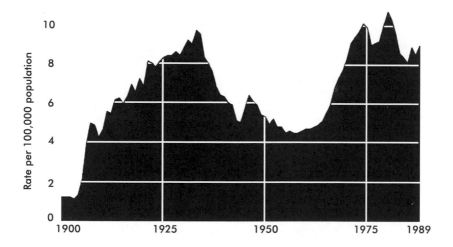

Figure 1–1. Homicide rates in the United States, 1900–1988.
Source. *Violent Crime in the United States.* Washington, D.C., U.S. Department of Justice, 1991.

■ Specific Epidemiological Aspects

Nine key epidemiological variables have been studied or raised as significant with respect to homicide: age, race, gender, socioeconomic class, method of killing, relationship between the victim and perpetrator (including cases that some interpret as being precipitated by the victim), the perpetrator's prior arrest, use of alcohol or other drugs, and temporal and ecological factors.

One caveat is needed before exploring the individual epidemiological variables. Epidemiological data reflect data on the victims but not on the perpetrators. This type of omission is interesting in its own right and perhaps signifies that understanding the mind of the murderer requires a clinical or criminological explanation. Thus, in an

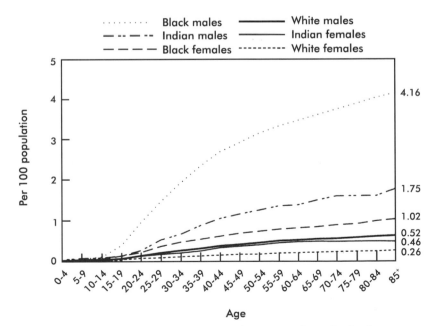

Figure 1–2. Cumulative homicide rates by race and gender in five-year intervals.
Source. Reprinted with permission from Reiss A, Roth J: *Understanding and Preventing Violence.* Washington, DC, National Academy Press, 1993, p. 63. Copyright 1993 National Academy Press.

operational sense, homicide rates can only give the numbers of people killed in any given population unit.

Many of the factors discussed below overlap, and no scientific presentation can make a claim that any one variable is the cause of a homicide. Instead, a workable model for determining factors leading up to a homicide must elicit significant background factors that, under certain precipitating circumstances, predispose an individual to commit a homicide. The inductive search for determining factors must be an empirical one in which the basic premise is that, for any one homicide, several factors are necessary but one factor is never a sufficient cause for that homicide. Such a position is compatible with considering the significance of personality attributes and given clinical diagnoses. It is also consistent with the position that, when legal questions arise regarding a person's responsibility for a homicide, no answer can ever be given simply on the basis of a diagnosis.

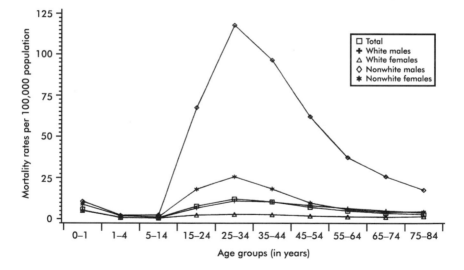

Figure 1–3. Age patterns of homicide rates by sex and race in the United States, 1900–1980.
Source. Reprinted with permission from Holinger P: *Violent Deaths in the United States.* New York, Guilford, 1987, p. 60. Copyright 1987 from The Guilford Press.

Age

With regard to the age patterns for homicide in the United States from 1900 to 1980, the highest rates occurred among individuals age 25–34 years. Rates for male victims are two to five times higher than rates for females victims across all age categories, except from infancy through early adolescence (i.e., to age 14 years), during which age the rates for males and females are comparable. Victim rates for infants are relatively high in general; the rates then decrease, with the lowest rate found among those age 5–14 years.

The age patterns noted above have remained consistent throughout the century for all gender and ethnic groups; whatever factors caused the increases and decreases in rates over the century seem to have operated for all. The fluctuations over time are operative irrespective of age, race, or gender for each group. Rather it is within these historical fluctuations that certain groups are at a greater risk for becoming a homicide victim based on their age, race, or gender. The one exception to this is that white female infants have had the greatest risk of all white females for dying by homicide in this century.

The significance of the age variable is seen in statistics for homicides committed by young adult males. The highest rate for violent crime overall occurs among black males age 18–20 years, or usually those right out of a juvenile court age jurisdiction.[4]

Race

The racial factor is reflected in fluctuations over time in general, but, again, rates for nonwhite homicide victims are higher than for white victims for every age group. Depending on the age group studied, the rate for homicides among nonwhite males can be as high as 10 times that for white males. It should be noted that most studies have focused on larger American cities. In a study of homicide in New York City, Tardiff et al. found that young black and Latino men were more likely to be homicide victims than men from any other demographic group.[5] In the subset who died within 48 hours, 31% were positive for cocaine metabolites, and 25% of their deaths involved firearms, which suggests a basis for the high death rate. In turn, these variables may be situational and related to poverty.

The significance of race in epidemiological studies of homicide cannot be ignored. Yet the deeper question is, What does it mean? Besides the national data noted above, other studies have documented that black people are involved at a rate far in excess of their numbers in the population. The studies are also consistent in indicating that such killings are overwhelmingly intraracial. Findings from Wolfgang's[6] early study in Philadelphia—in which it was reported that, based on 1948–1952 data, 73% of the offenders and 75% of the victims of 588 homicides were black—were consistent with those from Hewitt's[7] more recent study. Furthermore, the trend seems to be continuing. Data from the *UCR Supplementary Homicide Report* for 1990 indicated that most victims of single offender–single victim homicides (86% of white victims and 93% of black victims) were slain by an offender of the same ethnic group.[2]

These data are depressing and unremitting and cry out for an explanation as well as an amelioration of the situation. Black males age 25–34 years take the brunt of this public health problem.[8] When it is realized that blacks account for only about 12% of the United States population, but account for approximately 50% of those arrested for murder and 35% arrested for assaults, it is obvious that there is a problem that has so far remained insolvable. It can also be noted that, in terms of the years of potential life lost, homicide exerts a greater effect than many other causes of death, including suicide, because homicide victims are from a younger group on average. This in itself would make it a major social problem.

Several explanations have been offered for these findings. Traditional explanations have raised the possibility of social and economic inequality, lack of opportunity, racism, and discriminatory practices in the criminal justice system ranging from the point of arrest to sentencing. Some have argued that such disparities exist for minorities in diverse cultural settings outside of the United States as well. Yet, although all of these factors are relevant, in themselves they do not dispose of the question.

Consider the explanation of economic and social deprivation. It is raised as a correlate of homicide that can have some possible causal significance or possibly none at all. On looking at how these factors may operate, the concepts of poverty as a state of absolute deprivation and inequality as a relative deprivation are relevant. The result is that fewer economic resources are available for those in such a predicament. If the focus is on the relationship between poverty and homicide rates in large American cities, there is a consistent and positive correlation to all homicide rates. What is important is that this exists independently of variables such as race, region, or population size. However, various kinds of inequality do not show an impact on homicide rates, also independent of these same variables.[9]

Gender

According to data from the UCR report, 86% of homicides are committed by men, with 64% of these against other men, which means that 74% of all homicides (committed by men) involve men killing other men. The remaining 26% of homicides would be against women or children.

The predominance of males as victims begins from mid-adolescence to older adulthood. Figure 1–4 shows age-adjusted homicide rates by gender and race.

When gender-specific differences in homicide are studied in terms of victims or perpetrators, significances emerge. Kellermann and Mercy[10] analyzed UCR data on homicides of victims age 15 years or older that occurred in the United States between 1976 and 1987. Of the total of 215,273 homicides they analyzed, 77% were male victims and 23% were female victims. Although the overall risk of dying by a homicide was substantially less for women, their risk of being killed by a spouse or intimate was higher than for men. Kellerman and Mercy's analysis revealed that twice as many women were shot and killed by husbands or intimates than were murdered by strangers, even when counting guns and any other means used for killing.

Regarding perpetrators, in 80% of the cases, men killed nonintimate acquaintances, strangers, or victims of undetermined relationship, whereas women killed nonintimately related people in 40% of cases. When men killed with a gun, they most commonly shot a stranger or nonfamily acquaintance. When women killed with a gun, the victim was five times more likely to be a spouse, family member, or intimate acquaintance.

When the patterns for race and gender are looked at, an interesting variation emerges. Rates for men in the white and nonwhite categories are higher than for women in the corresponding racial categories. Rates for nonwhite individuals are higher than those for white individuals, partially based on the fact that homicide rates for nonwhite women are greater than those for white men. Holinger's[1] data revealed that homicide rates for nonwhite men are 5–10 times higher than for any other group. Data on homicides based on age, gender, and race are shown in Figure 1–3.

Separating the effects of race from that of gender may be difficult, and is complicated by the frequent connection between gender and killing. In Wolfgang's early study,[6] 82% of the perpetrators of killings and 76% of the victims were male. The race factor is also strongly connected to gender, as witnessed in the homicide offender rates being 41.7 for black males, 7.3 for black females, 3.4 for white males, and 0.4 for white females.

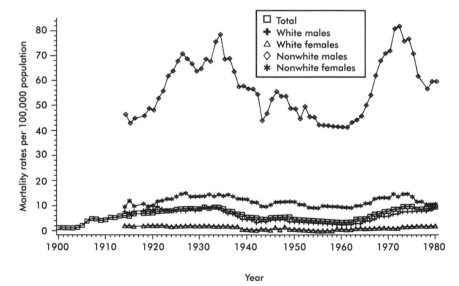

Figure 1–4. Age-adjusted homicide rates by sex and race in the United States, 1900–1980.
Source. Reprinted with permission from Holinger P: *Violent Deaths in the United States.* New York, Guilford, 1987, p. 58. Copyright 1987 from The Guilford Press.

From year to year, the UCRs do not show much annual variation in the arrest rates for homicide by gender, which is approximately 90% for males and 10% for females. However, such statistics cloak differences in the types of homicidal acts committed as well as the clinical differences in such acts. Bartol[11] noted that the 9:1 ratio is consistently found in studies for many major American cities, as well as for some cities in England and Israel. However, some intriguing cultural differences do emerge. In England, a far higher number of the victims are females (60%) than in the United States (25%). In an Israeli study[12] on Jewish homicides, 51% of Jewish victims were female, compared with 34% being non-Jewish. However, in absolute numbers, homicides are still less than in the United States, presumably because of the effects of alcohol, drugs, and crimes related to drugs (e.g., robberies).

Method of Killing

As to the method of killing, data from the UCRs indicate that most homicides are committed with a firearm, with the largest subcategory of firearm used being a handgun. Firearms are involved in about 60% of homicides in the United States.[13] In addition, there are an estimated 5.7 nonfatal gunshot injuries for every homicide.[14] However, the risk of death by firearms is skewed by a particularly high elevation among black male adolescents. In 1989, the ratio of individuals age 15–19 years who were victims of gun-related homicide was 7.5:100,000 for white males but 83.4:100,000 for black males. This is believed to be correlated with death by firearms, in which the fraction of homicides committed with guns peaked in those age 15–19 years, with 81% becoming victims by that means.[2]

The UCRs also indicate that knives or other cutting instruments are used second most frequently, followed by parts of the body (i.e., hands and feet used as weapons), then blunt objects, and, at the bottom of the frequency scale are more unusual measures, such as poison, drowning, arson, or explosives.[13]

A comparison of the risk of death versus a nonfatal injury during family and intimate assaults reveals that the use of a firearm is 12 times more likely to result in a death than nonfirearm-associated events.[16] Therefore, firearms play a significant role not only in homicides committed by men but also in the context of family and intimate assaults where there is access to such a lethal weapon.

Relationship Between Victim and Perpetrator

Although the victim-perpetrator relationship in homicides is often one of family ties or intimate relationships, the number of homicides committed by strangers has increased significantly in recent years. As characterized in the UCRs, the majority of homicides occur in the context of what is referred to as *primary homicides,* with *primary* referring to a death that occurs in a relatively spontaneous fight between people who know each other. According to the UCRs, 16% of perpetrators and victims are members of the same family, and another 40% are friends, neighbors, and acquaintances. Only 13% of homicides occur among strangers. In 30% of the cases, the police cannot determine whether a prior relationship existed between the perpetrator and the victim. This may be because they cannot discover who the perpetrator was, or because there is a lack of evidence to make any connection. It is at least possible that more people are being killed by strangers than heretofore. For homicides, there is a 70%–75% "clearance rate" (an arrest) with a high rate of reporting in that few homicides are never reported to authorities. It appears that about 50% of homicides stem from an argument, whereas another 25% occur under the influence of alcohol or drugs.

The above discussion leads to the broader topic of how an epidemiological approach conceptualizes perpetrator-victim relationships and their potential for heightening the possibility of a homicide. One approach has been to use a victim-precipitation model, which has been criticized as blaming the victim. In an alternative approach, the focus has been on the diverse and complex interactional variables in relationships or situations that can have a violent ending.

The victim-precipitation model looks at the ways homicide victims played some role in their own future death, focusing on situations such as arguments in bars, or disagreements between spouses and lovers that escalated into increasing taunts, insults, or physical contact. In later reconstructing the situations from the available facts, it often seemed that what had pushed matters toward homicide often began with a trivial event or exchange. The presumption in such theorizing is that the individuals, although not necessarily intimates, were interacting with each other, and therefore the killing would not be seen as part of a model for killing by a stranger. This model would not be applicable to killings occurring in the context of robberies or burglaries.

In an interesting approach that parallels many psychiatric theories of interpersonal violence, criminologists look at the type of interactions between individuals that eventually lead to a death. The difference between this theory and earlier theories about victim-precipitated homicide is the realization of how a homicidal outcome is a "situated" transaction that could easily have many possible outcomes. Frequently, a situation escalates into violence because neither participant allows the other the opportunity to back away while still saving face. These escalations are not the stuff of dramatic television portrayals, nor the act of a deranged killer who could later plead not guilty by reason of insanity. Instead, these types of killings arise in the give-and-take of ordinary transactions between people and comprise a frequently found framework in which homicide is enacted.

Psychiatry's major contribution to comprehending how these seemingly commonplace behaviors lead to homicides is in terms of understanding personality vulnerability and functioning and the impact of painful emotions on human beings. These painful emotions are evoked in the course of interactions in which sensitivities or misinterpretations are played out. In some situations, certain personality disorders or traits predispose the individual to overreact or misinterpret. For these people, the sway of emotions then surges to the surface and erupts into some impulsive action. The actors might be spouses or lovers who argue and then progress to shoving and slapping and then to the use of fists, objects, or weapons. Name calling or taunts are frequent. In some cases, it might be a child's disobedience or the endless crying of an infant that elicits feelings of helplessness in the adult who then reacts to the child's behavior as a provocative challenge that must be handled. At a crucial juncture, the point of no return is crossed.

Luckenbill has broken down these various types of interactions into a series of stages.[17] Stage one is where the future victim performs some type of act or verbalization that is interpreted as an attack on another's activities or their self-esteem. Seen from a psychiatric perspective, this initial stage would reflect the individuals' tendencies to distort or overinterpret. For example, individuals with paranoid or borderline personalities would be among those likely to overreact. Stage two is an attempt to confirm the meaning of what the potential perpetrator has heard. Other people may be turned to for their interpretation; in fact, it is interesting that a majority of such confrontations occur in the presence of others. By the time stage three is arrived at, the perpetrator is at the point of responding, often by challenging the intended victim or demanding a halt to or retraction of certain statements. Threats may emerge. Stage four is the counterresponse of the intended victim, who at that point does not back off. Stage five is the emergence of violence, either abruptly or after the perpetrator seeks out and obtains weapons. Stage six involves the reaction of the perpetrator after the killing, such as fleeing or being restrained by others.

In this framework, many variables are operating, and indeed are necessary, for the predicted final outcome to occur. One necessity is the occurrence of an intense interaction in which others are usually present, but in which no one intervenes. The ready availability of weapons as a part of a high-risk lifestyle may also be an operating variable. Such a milieu is typically present in places like bars, entertainment clubs, or street corner confrontations. Note that up through the first four stages of this model, various outcomes are possible.

Perpetrator's Prior Criminal Offenses

Although the juvenile files are sealed in many states (because juvenile offenses are classified as civil and not criminal, barring a waiver to adult criminal court), it appears that most people who commit violent offenses as young adults are not encountering the law for the first time. The median age of those committing homicide is age 29 years.[18]

Such data are not to be interpreted as saying that most juvenile offenders go on to become violent adult offenders. This is not the case. The data indicate that, of the 33%–45% of males in the United States who were once detained by the police or arrested as juveniles, the majority of them (approximately 65%) were arrested only once or twice and have no subsequent adult record. What these data mean is that a small number of juvenile offenders persist in committing crimes into young adulthood, and that those juveniles who engaged in serious crime at an early age formed a subgroup of individuals who are likely to engage in serious violence, such as a homicide, in their 20s. Thus an early age at onset of delinquent behavior is seen as a good predictor for committing chronic and serious criminal acts as an adult.

When a juvenile's early offenses include violent offenses (e.g., robbery), his or her probability of committing serious crime as an adult is increased. A third predictor variable in the juvenile offender is repetitive property offenses. Delinquency convictions before age 16 years and repeatedly being sentenced to juvenile correctional facilities are two other significant variables.[19] When these variables are taken together in a weighted, summative manner, the probability that juvenile offenders will commit a violent offense—including an increased possibility of committing a homicide—as an adult increases.

An often-asked question involves the significance of a person's past criminal acts and activities to that person's tendency to commit homicide. In Wolfgang's study[6] of 588 homicides, two-thirds of the perpetrators had prior arrest records. It was revealing that most of these arrests had not been for trivial offenses, nor even for property offenses, but for offenses against people that usually had been violent.

The psychiatric significance of these data is that they indicate these perpetrators had unresolved conflicts that involved aggression and had failed to contain that aggression. It can be hypothesized that these conflicts are replayed in later acts of violence against individuals and culminate in a subsequent homicide. Although criminological researchers have not studied just what these psychological or social conflicts might be, this hypothesis points to the need for parallel lines of inquiry. It would also be significant to determine which intervening variables contributed to the remaining one-third in Wolfgang's study later committing a homicide, or whether they were just "lucky" in that earlier personal violence did not lead to arrests.

Role of Psychoactive Substances

Alcohol or other psychoactive drugs are mentioned so frequently in connection with various incidents of violence, including homicide, that the specific role they may play is often not discussed. In fact, the words *alcohol* and *violence* are often used together as though they are inseparable, with an implication that alcohol causes the violence. This belief has become almost dogma among many in top political positions and has been reflected in legislative and community decisions involving fiscal distributions. The preconception is that alcohol facilitates the release of aggression. This position is usually based on data and figures that indicate a high percentage of violent acts are perpetrated by individuals under the influence of alcohol, even though in many cases the blood alcohol level of perpetrators has not been taken and this connection has been made solely based on observations. The same thinking applies to other drug usage in which, despite the varying effects of different drugs, the suggestion is that the person imbibed or took a drug shortly before a homicide occurred. Accurate tests to confirm or disconfirm the connection between homicidal violence and alcohol use would need to compare data between perpetrators who have ingested alcohol or psychoactive substances with individuals who have ingested similar substances but have not acted in this manner; they would also require control of variables such as when and where the drinking took place.

In the absence of any definitive studies of these factors, there are a large number of studies suggesting a relationship between psychoactive substances and homicide on a biological or sociological level. In Holcomb and Anderson's study[20] of males charged with first-degree murder in Missouri, the authors found that 55% of the perpetrators had ingested drugs, alcohol, or both at the time of the killing. Mayfield[21] found that 57% of convicted murderers studied had been drinking at the time of the killing. Greenberg[22] reported that alcoholism was diagnosed in 20%–40% of convicted murderers. A similar figure was noted in a California study of females arrested on homicide charges: 51% had been drinking at the time of the killing.[23] Results from such studies support the generalization that about half of homicides occur under the influence of drinking. What they do not bring out sufficiently is that, in many of these situations, the perpetrator and victim have both been drinking. In Wolfgang's study,[6] only the perpetrators had been drinking in 11% of the homicides, only the victims had been drinking in 9%, but both the perpetrators and victims had been drinking in 44%. Subsequent studies support a figure of close to 50% for the percentage of victims who had been drinking at the time of their death.[24]

However, despite the common assumption that alcohol, in amounts that are not sedative, increases one's potential for aggression, the action-reaction relationship is not a linear one. The outcome depends on a host of variables, such as the cultural setting, genetic vulnerability, neuroendocrinological factors, other drugs that may have been taken, and immediate precipitants. Hence, the mechanism for how a violent endpoint occurs is not entirely clear. Some studies find little evidence of a simple direct relationship between the psychoactive effects of drugs or alcohol and aggression.[25,26] The pattern of drinking may play a role, such as in the more concentrated style of drinking prevalent in the United States, rather than the spaced drinking style prevalent in some European countries.

The suggestion of a type of alcohol-facilitated, episodic dyscontrol syndrome arises. Yet results from studies in Scotland[27] and the Bordeaux region of France[28] have indicated that 55% and 51%, respectively, of those convicted for murder had been drinking at the time of their offense.

One persistent source of controversy is the extent to which someone carrying out a homicide under the influence of alcohol is responsible for that act. This, in turn, is connected in part with a belief system, neither proven nor disproven, that alcoholism is a disease. The inference is that individuals who are biologically vulnerable to the effects of alcohol should not be seen as responsible for their violent acts committed under the influence. This type of reasoning has been subjected to a critical appraisal by Peele.[29]

In addition, not everyone subscribes to the theory that the loss of inhibition that would be accounted for within a biological disease model of alcohol use is the crucial variable in assessing personal responsibility for behavior. Instead, proponents of social learning theory, buttressed by cognitive psychology, have focused on the learned expectations of what alcohol supposedly permits one to do. Hence, if the expectation is that when someone drinks, his or her control over personal impulses will be lost, then it is more likely that he or she will lose control. Bartol has summarized the debate from this social-cognitive perspective, in which the consumer's expectations of the effects of alcohol act as a crucial variable to how he or she will behave when drinking.[11]

On the other hand, no one can doubt that alcohol has physiological effects on the nervous system. A correlation exists between low cerebrospinal fluid concentrations of 5-hydroxyindoleacetic acid, a serotonin metabolite, and impulse control problems.[30,31] Also, the results of genetic work on alcoholism and antisocial personality have raised questions about whether there is some overlap among those who carry one or both diagnoses.[32] There also appear to be differences between males and females with regard to the connection between alcohol consumption and violent behavior that may be related to different social expectations.[33]

The debate concerning alcohol use and violence may primarily be over what is the prime influence on the violent behavior and whether alcohol is the necessary variable in an event culminating in violence. In a carefully designed research project involving all violent acts witnessed by or perpetrated on a random sample of citizens in a single town, Pernanen found that alcohol was involved in 54% of those acts, but that the effect of other factors on the violent outcome varied even more than alcohol use by the victims and perpetrators.[34] Some studies have demonstrated the missing effect by giving alcohol or substances purported to be alcohol to study subjects under single-blind conditions.[26,36] The researchers then observed the effect of the subjects' believing they had drunk alcohol as well as the context in which that alcohol had been drunk on the subjects' behavior. There are limits on how far the cultural setting can influence behavior if the amount of alcohol continues to be consumed. Eventually, higher cognitive processes (e.g., attention, concentration) do become impaired. In the end, it is the combined effects of the pharmacological, situational, and cognitive factors that determine the outcome: feelings of being threatened, provoked, or insecure; intrapsychic components (e.g., depression, anxiety); and the influence of alcohol can all contribute to an act culminating in homicide.

A similar critical appraisal could be done for the effects of psychoactive drugs on an individual's potential for extreme violence. In one study, 81% of 275 homicide victims were tested for benzoylecgonine, the major metabolite of cocaine. Forty percent of the victims tested positive for this metabolite, a number much higher than that presumed in earlier studies.[37] Although marijuana or opiates may inhibit violent behavior, phencyclidine, LSD, and amphetamines are also seen as increasing the potential for violence.

Temporal and Ecological Factors

Uncontrollable, environmental factors. In one case, a man called a rival, threatened to kill him, and announced that he was driving to this man's home to carry out his threat. The police were called and were waiting for him, but the man never arrived. Meanwhile, a different police squad was called to help retrieve a car that had skidded off the highway into a snowbank. In the car was the man who had made the threats, with a loaded shotgun by his side; only because of environmental factors was he rendered unable to progress further on his mission. This rather mundane example of an impediment to a homicide illustrates the idiosyncratic variables affecting whether a homicide occurs.

Seasonal, time-of-day, and other periodic factors. Seasonal factors have been studied to determine the incidence of violence, including homicides, by calendar month. Chertwood indicated that most homicides occur in the summer, although the month with the highest homicide rate is December.[38] These high-rate periods may simply reflect periods in which there are greater interpersonal contact and social mingling (i.e., summer with its long days and good weather, December with its many holidays).

Similarly, the day or time of day most likely for the occurrence of a homicide has been noted.[39] Saturday evenings and early Sunday morning appear to be the prime time, which would seem related to the most common time that people are exposed to each other.

The search for periodicity in homicide has led to recurring biological factors in homicides. One phenomenon referred to is "premenstrual frenzy," which is discussed in Chapter 2 under the topic of premenstrual syndrome. Humans' fascination with the moon has never diminished, even though astronauts have now walked on the moon. In mythology, stories, and song, profound powers have been attributed to the moon. "It is the very error of the moon; she comes more near the earth than she was wont, and makes men mad," as Shakespeare expressed it in *Othello*.[40] The reasoning is that the human body responds to the moon much in the same way as does the sea, especially considering the fact that the body is made up of 80% water, like the earth. The influence of the moon would also be induced via changes in the geophysical environment in weather, earthquakes, and electromagnetic fields. One investigation from this perspective in Dade County, Florida, showed a correlation between the lunar phase cycle and homicides and revealed that homicides peaked during a full moon.[41]

■ Cultural Variables

In addition to discussing different homicide rates within different social groups in a particular society, it must be recognized that cultural settings also influence homicide rates. This is true even when making comparisons among industrialized countries, let alone between industrialized and less industrialized countries.

Within the industrialized nations, the United States has the highest murder rate of any other country; Japan and Austria have the lowest rate. Some economically developing nations, such as Mexico, do have higher homicide rates than the United States.

The homicide victim rate for most industrialized countries is usually below 3:100,000. However, for the last several decades, the homicide rate in the United States has been more than twice that figure, falling somewhere between 5:100,000 and 10:100,000. When the rates are broken down in terms of age groupings, the disparity in the rate in the United States compared with European countries becomes even more glaring. Again taking males age 15–24 years, the homicide rate for the United States is 21.9:100,000, which is more than four times the next highest rate of 5:100,000 for Scotland,[42] and significantly higher than most European rates, which lie between 1:100,000 and 2:100,000. As far as can be determined from existing documentation, the murder rate in the United States in the twentieth century has never been as low as 3:100,000. It is informative to compare the numbers of homicides in cities of comparable size in different countries, as is done in Figure 1–5.

Explanations of this striking disparity vary widely. One is that Americans are more tolerant of aggression and violence, including violence with firearms, which are considered to be ever present in American society. (See discussion above of gun-related homicides in section on "Method of Killing.") Another theory is that American society does little to discourage physical aggression among its young male population. Still other theories stress the effects of the media and network television violence on America's tendency to be a violent nation. The conclusion of some researchers is that the United States is a society that promotes and accepts the extremes of personal aggressive violence, but is hypocritical about other standards, such as sexual deviance as witnessed in discriminatory treatment of those with diverse sexual practices.[43]

■ Sociological Variables

Changes in Lifestyle as Increasing Risk for Victimization

Some researchers see the question of who is likely to meet their death by homicide as a subquestion in the context of a broader, sociological one: Why is there more crime and violence in modern society, when material conditions for living are comparatively better than in preceding historical periods (an interpretation of history with which not all agree)? Those who view these questions from a lifestyle approach see the quality of people's lives and interactions with others in modern society as not being improved and consider the acquisition of more material goods as irrelevant. In fact, there are those who argue that a milieu for an increase of violent behavior has been created, referring to variables such as the following, among many others:

- The breakdown in family structure
- Increased number of families in which both partners work at jobs outside of the home
- Minimal time at home

Comparison of Homicide Rates—U.S. and Great Britain

Population	City	Number of Homicides
7,000,000	New York City	1,582
	London	67
863,000	San Antonio	162
	Birmingham	31
730,000	San Francisco	114
	Leeds	22
540,000	Cleveland	124
	Liverpool	14
400,000	Miami	148
	Manchester	16
380,000	Tucson	41
	Bristol	11
282,000	Birmingham	88
	New Castle	8
229,000	Anchorage	17
	Barsley	3

Comparison of Homicide Rates—U.S. and Japan

Population	City	Number of Homicides
7,000,000	New York City	1,582
	Tokyo	111
1,000,000	Dallas	347
	Hiroshima	14
725,000	San José	39
	Chiba	9
500,000	Indianpolis	63
	Amagasaki	11
450,000	Kansas City	116
	Funabashi	5

Comparison of Homicide Rates—U.S. and Denmark

Population	City	Number of Homicides
470,000	Atlanta, GA	186
	Copenhagen	18
290,000	Tampa, FL	79
	Aarhus	1
235,000	Santa Ana, CA	32
	Odensen	3
200,000	Mobile, AL	47
	Aalborg	0

Comparison of Homicide Rates—U.S. and France

Population	City	Number of Homicides
2 Million	Houston	408
	Paris	156
800,000	Baltimore	240
	Lyon	66
375,000	Tulsa	40
	Toulouse	10
350,000	Charlotte, NC	53
	Nice	21
320,000	Newark, NJ	113
	Nantes	12

Figure 1–5. Homicides in cities of comparable size in the United States, Denmark, France, Great Britain, and Japan.
Source. *"Do Guns Work? The Effect of Strong Firearm Laws on Homicide Rates in Other Nations. The Police Chief* 55:36–37, 1988.

- The increasing number of meals people eat out
- Increased numbers of people living in a state of concomitant isolation
- The fact that social lives are increasingly becoming centered outside of the home
- The pursuit of such entertainment and a social life based on endless shopping malls that are open 24 hours a day, 7 days a week

As a result, people are placed in locations where they can more often become targets of violence. More perpetrators are then stimulated to capitalize on the more readily available targets.[44]

Implicit in the above theory is that anything that increases the contact between human beings will increase the risk of a homicide. If, because of contemporary lifestyles, people are on the move more often, they are consequently more exposed to the possibility of violence. Hindelang et al. posited a theory on what increases a person's risk of being victimized by way of more contact with people under certain conditions.[45] As a common example, there is the increased risk of violence accompanying roles certain people play, such as a single person being more likely to go to diverse places and be exposed to unknown people more frequently. It is not only that individuals do more things alone, and that they do them alone more frequently than before, but also that they expose themselves more to the different phenomena and contexts that this lifestyle provides (e.g., bars, clubs), which in turn increases their risk of becoming a victim of violence.

Another factor increasing the risk of homicide is one's place in the social structure. For example, a cab driver going on "runs" into a drug-infested part of a city increases his or her risk of being killed, just as a college student's dabbling in selling drugs does. Constraints of race or social class operate within this framework. Of course, a person may try to set limits on these activities by avoiding certain exposures, but, depending on the above factors, certain risks may be unavoidable depending on one's circumstances.

There has been some research to specifically test these hypotheses. One group evolved an index called the *household activity ratio,* in which married households in which the female spouse worked and households headed by a single adult with children were studied in proportion to the total number of households of all kinds. The former group was seen as being in a higher risk category for being a homicide victim; in fact, the ratio provided by comparing the first two groups with the total households in the entire United States for 1947–1974 had a positive correlate with the rate of homicide.[46]

A variation on this theory is to see the ratio between the first two groups and the total households as signifying economic inequality, which, in itself, can lead to an increase in homicides.[47] With regard to households in which both partners work, that household has double exposure to risk in that both partners leave the home each day; with regard to households headed by a single adult, members of that household are more likely to have a lowered socioeconomic status and be exposed to poverty-like conditions and its accompanying offshoots, with such economic inequalities then placing that household at a greater risk for homicidal violence.

In an analysis of individual homicides in New York City, the impact routine activities have on the rate of stranger-committed homicides was confirmed.[48] According to this theory, if males are away from home more than females as a part of their daily routines, then they are more likely to become victims of homicides, a tendency that was confirmed in the New York analysis. Continuing with this hypothesis, white individuals would then be more likely than other races to become victims of stranger homicide because their jobs are more likely to take them farther from home or require travel.

The Subculture of Violence

The essence of the theory of a subculture of violence is that certain subgroups in American society hold values that are conducive to violence and that the socialization process in those groups not only accepts but promotes such behavior. The initial formulation of this theory was not restricted to homicide but rather was applied overall to criminal behavior in which such behaviors were seen as being learned. Through interactions with individuals who approve of crime, norms develop that are conducive to crime within certain subgroups. For example, a subgroup may be more tolerant of violence and likely see it as a legitimate means for the expression of aggression or violent tendencies. If a homicide results, this is seen as unfortunate for both parties, but simply an inherent risk in the way life is lived in the subculture. Such an outcome is not seen simply as two individuals interacting, but a reflection of some social groups more often resorting to violence that in turn increases the likelihood of homicide.

The exposure of members of these subgroups to violence can be intense, from the enormous violence witnessed on television and in films to the subculture's connection of male identity with expressions of violence. There is also the awareness that weapons are readily available for those who believe they need to "even things up" to express their aggression. Going along with the acceptance and promotion of these values is the hypocritical policing of sex and magazines, music, and television in society, which gives a strange mixture of messages in which sex is seemingly regulated but violence promoted.

One hope for members of this subculture is that the violence will be channeled into other options (e.g., competitive athletics among these groups). Another hope is that those who are observers and vicarious participants in the subgroups can mitigate the degree of their own need for direct aggression.

Of course, the linchpin of the theory that a subculture of violence leads to increased homicides is that those subgroups who have high rates of homicide actually do possess a different set of norms with respect to violence. The reverse—that high homicide rates validate such a culture—cannot be argued; rather, independent empirical validation of the theory is needed. Measuring attitudes toward violence is difficult; even then, expressed behavior may not match verbalized values. For example, almost no one directly states that he or she approves of violence, let alone the killing of someone (with the exception of those involved in political and ethnic cleansing). Rather, it is the covert way in which different attitudes toward violence are expressed that would distinguish one group from another. As a result, it is not easy for groups or individuals to be classified into being part of a subcultural group or not. It is more likely that they could be classified along a continuum. One group may approve of a good deal of criminal behavior and stand in opposition to many societal values, yet only approve of certain selected killings. In between may be groups that have a mixture of values, some of which may be conducive to violence and others not. On the other end of the continuum may be a group that has values approving of more minor antisocial behavior, such as white collar or bureaucratic violations, but sees a homicide that results from such activities as outside the accepted norms. Such continuums exist for groups as well as individuals within the group.

Strain Theory

Contemporary proponents of the subcultural theory have made many different arguments from those mentioned previously. These proponents rely on a *strain theory,* in which it is hypothesized that, when individuals cannot achieve their goals (e.g., monetary gains) through legitimate channels, they are more likely to resort to crime. When involved in frustrating situations, people are at increased risk to act out their anger and rage. The original writings within this theoretical framework stemmed from the well-known sociologist, Robert Merton.[49] Subsequently, his work went in various directions, such as focusing on the different goals people pursue, the barriers in achieving such goals, and how and why some individuals operating under strain resort to crime.

Responses other than resorting to criminal or violent behavior can ensue. For example, with regard to juveniles, delinquency and violence can be conceptualized within this framework as a form of rebellion.[50] Subsequently, interactions with other "strained" individuals may provide a social support setting and increase the likelihood of delinquent behavior becoming criminal behavior, in which violence comes to play a part.

A recent addition to the criminal law has been the category of hate or bias crimes, in which the perpetrator's state of mind and motivation toward the victim are the key. The very same act, such as a homicide, is distinguished from a "parallel" crime simply by virtue of the requisite mental state accompanying the act. Thus, a bias homicide would be if the person killed were selected based on discrimination or racial animus. In 1990, the Federal Hate Crime Statistics Act provided that offenses in which violent attacks, arson, intimidation, and property attacks are based on "manifest evidence" of prejudice based on race, religion, sexual orientation, or ethnicity were to be kept track of by the FBI. The purpose was to aid in the identification of criminal acts in which bias was present. By 1994, a crime bill directed by the U.S. Sentencing Commission to promulgate guidelines to enhance penalties for such offenses. Many states have adopted similar legislation to enhance penalties for acts that would receive a lesser penalty otherwise. However, determination of the motive in such cases may be difficult and involve a search involving complex interpersonal dynamics. Inasmuch as psychiatrists involved in intensive psychotherapy with patients often grope for motivational understanding, opening up such an inquiry in courtrooms may be confusing.

More recent versions of strain theory have emphasized motivations not simply linked to an interference in achieving monetary goals, but with more immediate or short-term goals, such as popularity, status, or some specific visible signs of status, such as cars or clothes. Such a shift allows the theory to fit more than lower socioeconomic groups, because the strain of not achieving goals can be applied to goals sought at many social levels. Focusing on goal attainment rather than strain for being frustrated in a certain social class then becomes the underlying principle.[51]

Other Theories

Others have argued that the strain theory is not sufficient to explain certain subcultures of violence. A revision has been offered that some individuals in groups selectively endorse, as well as distort, values of the dominant culture. Matza and Sykes stressed that, in some subcultures, the values of toughness, excitement, and pleasure seeking—values taken from the culture at large—are emphasized.[52] Within the context of these prioritized values, violence and homicide are more likely to emerge from the increased risk taking and impulsivity that may be present. Because members of these subcultures see these values exploited in society at large, such as in criminal law procedures or in how some businesses operate, they feel they are justified in adhering to these values, even if it leads to homicide and the exclusion of other values promulgated by society.[53]

■ Felony Murders

In some epidemiological studies, the concept of primary homicide (again, meaning a death resulting from a more or less spontaneous confrontation or fight between individuals or even groups) has been distinguished from the category of *felony homicides,* meaning killings taking place in the context of another felony (e.g., robberies, sexual killings, executions, violence between rival gangs, murders planned to achieve a certain goal [e.g., one gang sending a "message" to a rival gang]). Although the number of felony homicides is significantly less than the number of primary homicides, with some estimating their prevalence at only about 20%, they receive much more attention in the media than primary homicides because of their dramatic aspects and because they have greater appeal in terms of being fictionalized. When homicide rates began to increase in the 1960s, the proportion of felony homicides also increased. The result was a drop in the clearance rate for homicide because of the increase in these types of felony homicides, which do not have as high an arrest rate.

Those who have studied felony homicide often see it as an impersonal and predatory type of murder in contrast to murders committed in the heat of passion by intimates. In a classic work discussing felony homicides, Dietz listed their distinguishing characteristics:[54]

1. They are usually enacted by experienced, habitual, or career criminals.
2. The planning and premeditation of a felony homicide are critical parts of the act.
3. Felony homicides may involve multiple victims and multiple offenders.
4. Victims may be forcibly or physically restrained.
5. A specific antecedent (e.g., a relevant argument), as may be present in homicides between intimates, is often lacking.
6. The role of the perpetrator of a felony homicide is hypothesized, tested, and incorporated or rejected as part of the self-concept of the perpetrator.

Robbery homicides are the most frequent type of felony homicide; a bank robbery is only one example of this. Dietz[54] hypothesized that robberies occur in distinct stages. First is the planning stage, which usually occurs within a few days of the actual robbery. Sometimes those planning the robbery may specify killings during the robbery, but in other cases not all those to be involved in perpetrating the robbery are informed of this aspect of the plan, whether it is conceived that a killing will occur as a direct consequence of the plan or only as the need arises. One pattern may be that two or more of the group members are informed about the intended killing or make the decision they will do so if needed, with the other members acquiescing in such a decision. The victim or victims are usually regarded as someone impersonal or someone undeserving of respect. During the posthomicidal period, the members may talk about a killing that occurred in the course of a robbery, and, in some cases, joke about it.

Other variations on felony homicides occur within the context of planned executions, contract killings, or revenge killings, and are related to street gangs or planned killings between rivals in organized crime. In some of these situations, a professional, referred to as a "hit man," is hired to do the killing.

Although technically considered felony murders, homicides committed during a sexual assault differ in many aspects from these types of felony homicides (see discussion of sexual killings in Chapter 10 of this book).

It should be noted that the concept of felony homicide has also acquired a series of legal meanings connected with cases of who might be tried for a homicide. As this concept was initially conceived, the accomplice of the perpetrator of a homicide taking place during a bank robbery would also be charged with homicide. That concept has now been expanded so that the person driving the getaway car from a robbery in which a homicide was committed, even though he or she was not present at the killing, would be legally charged with felony homicide. As a further expansion of this concept, if a bank security guard kills one of the bank robbers in the course of the felony or attempted felony, the other members of the group attempting to carry out the felony could be legally charged with being responsible for that death.

Apart from sexual killings, psychiatric issues are much less frequently raised with this group of felony murders than in the primary type of homicide among intimates. This is because those involved in organized gangs, be they juvenile gangs or more advanced criminal organizations, or else those controlling the gang, do not wish to explore the intricacies of their psychiatric state at the time of the offense. Such inquiry is not part of their group ethos. Second, their own self-concept is such that they do not wish to be thought of as being deviant in a psychiatric sense, which would be unacceptable, even though social deviance is acceptable.

■ Multiple-Victim Murders

Mass and serial murders have gained increasing publicity in the United States. Whether they are in fact more prevalent in recent years, or whether American society is now simply becoming more aware of these types of killings through improved detection and investigation, is not clear. The Bureau of Justice classifies three types of multiple-victim murderers: serial murderers, mass murderers, and spree murderers.[55] It is estimated that there are approximately 3,500 multiple murder victims each year in the United States.

Serial Killings

A *serial killing* is defined by the FBI as the killing of several victims in three or more separate incidents over weeks or an extended period that can last for years. The names of several serial killers come to mind under this definition, each exemplifying different types of killings:[56]

- Jack the Ripper, who committed several sexual murders in nineteenth century England.
- Ted Bundy, suspected of killing up to 36 young women across the United States. His saga ended with his conviction in Florida for murdering 2 Florida State University female students.
- Jeffrey Dahmer, who killed adolescent males.
- Two men who ran a "little house of horrors" in Philadelphia where women were held in the house, abused, tortured, and eventually murdered and then cannibalized.[57]
- Various individuals who killed elderly people in rooming houses

or boarding home situations and then appropriated their pension or Social Security checks.

- Dorothea Montalvo Puente, in California, accused of killing nine people who were her tenants and burying them in the lush yard around her house.[58]
- Albert DeSalvo, commonly referred to as the Boston Strangler.
- David Berkowitz, who had the nickname of Son of Sam, and killed seven women.
- The Hillside stranglers of California, who were the cousins Kenneth Bianchi and Angelo Buono.
- Wayne Williams of Atlanta
- Henry Lee Lucas, who confessed to killing 350 people between 1975 and 1983. He subsequently recanted these confessions, which raised challenging issues about the veracity of these individuals and the difficulty in getting scientific data for profiling them.
- John Wayne Gacy, who sexually molested his male victims and was convicted of killing 33 people

Other cases that have been written about include those of Juan Corona, Herman Mudgett, and Wayne Henley.

Incidence of serial killings. The need for more valid data concerning the incidence of serial killings is quite obvious. The estimates for serial killers vary widely in terms of the number that are active at any one time in the United States. Estimates range from less than 100 to over 500, depending on the source. Problems in making these estimates include the low validity and reliability of official sources and the contamination of valid estimates by the mass media's tendency to overplay such a news-catching phenomenon, which is then followed by a sequence of panic reactions on the part of legislators and other policy makers.

Patterns seen in serial killings. One difficulty in understanding serial murderers' patterns is that they often drift around the country killing people, making it very difficult for them to be identified because their patterns are not picked up in one community. In addition, some serial killers select victims who are themselves drifters and not stable members of a community, and, in that sense, it is difficult to sort out the killer's pattern. The victims in these cases are often people on the margins of society themselves, such as people with alcohol or drug abuse difficulties who are living in public settings, runaway adolescents, children, or prostitutes. Because the victims may be strangers, the usual sources of information to detect the killer, such as members of the family or friends, are not available or produce almost minimal leads because the victims may have been gone from home for some time.

Other characteristics have been listed in an attempt to delineate more clearly the patterns of serial killers. The killings often occur at different times and seem to have no apparent connection to one another. Some serial killers wander about the country and pursue victims, whereas some are "geographically stable" and stay in their home locale, such as Wayne Williams in Atlanta or John Wayne Gacy in Chicago, and kill there. Some have said that serial killers wander simply to make it more difficult to catch them, yet not all serial killers do so. There is also a need to determine which subgroup of serial killers, if any, meet clinical criteria for different types of psychotic disorders. The understanding is that some of these individuals are in the midst of a full-blown psychotic disturbance (e.g., some type of schizophrenic disorder, a major affective disorder), whereas others show evidence of personality disturbances.

Serial killers display various behaviors in connection with their killings in terms of how they treat their victims (e.g., using blindfolds, attacking their faces, tying up the victim), dispose of their bodies (e.g., dismembering the body, placing the body in specific positions), how they "memorialize" the act (e.g., some take souvenirs from the victim or scene of the crime). Holmes obtained some information on these variables from interviews with serial murderers.[59] Blindfolds appear to have significance in terms of whether the perpetrator is comfortable enough to have the gaze of the victim fixed on them during the various types of assaultive behaviors that culminate in the killing; the perpetrator could use the blindfold on the victim or on himself or herself. It is hypothesized that attacks on the victim's face, particularly to blot out the eyes, may be a similar way of eliminating and controlling the shame that partially breaks through the perpetrator's defenses against affect. Similarly, it has been thought that oral sex in connection with these killings that is accompanied by blindfolding suggests a stranger-perpetrated offense, which relieves the perpetrator from having to view the victim as a fellow human being. The blindfold would serve little purpose with someone who is already known.

Use of weapons as part of the torture pattern may involve ritualistic aspects. If weapons are used, a serial killer usually selects one that requires personal contact between the killer and the victim because of his or her desire to touch or terrorize the victim, or because the act may be degrading in terms of the method used, such as strangulation, blunt instruments, and so on. Finally, if a dismemberment takes place, it is seen along the continuum of adding power and control over a powerless victim who is simply carved into pieces or repeatedly stabbed. Bondage occurs in a similar vein in terms of keeping the victim helpless or in a degrading position where they can be tortured or mutilated before disposing of the remains.

Again, different possibilities exist with respect to the manner in which the bodies of victims are disposed of, reflecting different types of serial killers. It is thought that serial killers who dispose of the bodies of their victims so they are not likely to be discovered would more likely be in the category of a lust, thrill, or power-control type of killer. None of the serial killers appear to be concerned about the families of the victims in terms of how relatives must live with unresolved anxiety and anguish surrounding the disappearance of the bodies. Because victims are seen as nonentities by the perpetrators, it does not cognitively register for them to put themselves in the position of the families of the victims. For some types of serial killers, great care is taken in disposal of the body because that is when they could be most vulnerable to discovery. Hence, some victims are buried on the perpetrators' property to minimize the risk of discovery.

Another phenomenon seen in some serial murderers after their apprehension is that they confess to far more murders than have actually been committed. The police may thus "solve" many unsolved cases in this manner. The dynamics of the individual who confesses to more serial killings than have actually occurred are interesting in that they touch on the murderer's narcissism and grandiosity.

In Table 1–1, a breakdown of homicidal behavioral patterns of male serial killers is provided in terms of victim selection, methods, and locations.

Characteristics of serial killers. It is difficult with the limited knowledge available to capture exactly what the characteristics of a serial killer are. One problem is that descriptions of serial killings vary among experts. Many workers in the field describe a serial killing as when one or more individuals commit a second murder or a subsequent number in which the victim is "relationshipless."[60] Others take issue with this requirement, allowing that a relationship might exist between the serial killer and some of the victims. Examples given are those of a professional person in a relationship to a client or patient who subsequently kills him or her, or a landlord who has a series of tenants that are killed over a period of time. (The possibility of people in more intimate familial roles carrying out killings [i.e., familicide] is

Table 1–1. Homicidal behavioral patterns of male serial killers.

Factors	Visionary	Mission	Lust	Thrill	Comfort	Power
Victim selection						
Specific		✕	✕	✕	✕	✕
Nonspecific	✕					
Random	✕		✕	✕		✕
Nonrandom		✕			✕	
Affiliative					✕	
Strangers	✕	✕	✕	✕		✕
Methods						
Act focused	✕	✕				
Process focused			✕	✕	✕	✕
Planned		✕	✕	✕	✕	✕
Spontaneous	✕					
Organized		✕	✕	✕	✕	✕
Disorganized	✕					
Spatial locations						
Concentrated	✕	✕				
Nomadic			✕	✕	✕	✕

Source. Reprinted with permission from Holmes RM, Holmes ST: *Murder in America.* Thousand Oaks, CA, Sage, 1994, p. 112. Copyright 1994, Sage Publications.

discussed below as involving a different conceptual basis than that present in impersonal killings.)

Most investigators feel that serial killings are not done for material gain, but perhaps are associated with a desire to have power over the victims. It may be added that the murders might be seen as primarily deriving gratification from the act of killing itself.[61] Other descriptions, instead of focusing on the killer's motive, stress that the killings may have symbolic value when carried out against victims who are perceived as being defenseless. Another theory is that the killings are the perpetrator's way of alerting others to the victims' plight; in essence, the victims are perceived as powerless and without status within their immediate surroundings (e.g., vagrants, migrant workers, children on the run, homosexual individuals, prostitutes, elderly women). More specific documentation is needed to determine whether there is, in fact, a selectivity in terms of victim selection going on with different serial killers.

Similarly, some serial killers see themselves as having a mission to rid the world of certain types of individuals. Although this borders close to the class of political killings, in which the killers are similarly motivated to eliminate a certain group of people, serial killers's victims are chosen simply on the basis of their own cognitive convictions that it is their duty to rid the world of undesirables or a particular class. This would appear to be the motive behind some of the killings in which prostitutes or homosexuals are selected as victims; friends of the perpetrator are often stunned to learn the identity of the perpetrator because he or she may come from an "upstanding background." These types of killings also present some overlap with the new category of hate crimes.

The group of "sadistic serial killers" who perpetrate erotized murders have their own characteristics in which there is often a connection with mutilation, torture, dismemberment, or other types of traumatic activity in connection with the killing. Such killings are not all sexual murders in an overt sense, for there is a type of hedonistic pleasure that can occur with some who perpetrate this type of killing. Some also become labeled cult killings. There is the possibility that neurotic conflict underlies the actions in these cases. Whether having total power over a helpless victim always conveys some type of neurotic basis is not at present a position that can be confirmed or disconfirmed.

A related question is whether there is a tendency for escalation in the serial killer's behavior (e.g., decreasing time between killings, escalating sadistic brutality in connection with the killings) or whether this only occurs in a subgroup in contrast to serial killers who do not escalate.

Role of fantasies. The role of fantasized images and objects connected with victim selectivity has specific psychiatric significance. There has long been a belief that the serial killer seeks out some type of idealized victim to pursue. Although this may be so in their fantasies, the records from serial killers indicate that what goes on is a type of depersonalization process regarding the victims selected. In their compulsion to carry out a homicidal act, a more generalized object will often do. In fact, the nature of the process is such that the victim selected is not only depersonalized, but viewed with some type of contempt or repugnance that seems to facilitate the violence being carried out. This degrading process of the victim was described by one serial killer as follows: "So, he mentally transforms them into hateful creatures, because, in the twisted morality of his own making, it is only against such that he can justifiably and joyfully inflict his manifestly hateful deeds of violence."[59]

Determining the origins and vicissitudes of the fantasies to carry out acts of violence in the process of gaining control over victims is a worthy clinical topic in its own right. Some of these fantasies emerge in nascent form in which they do not originally include the imagery of carrying out the homicidal act that evolves over time. Perhaps the fantasies are elaborations on certain actual experiences or are stimulated by "experiments" conceived in various types of movies or magazines. Some of this material may be integrated into actual sexual experiences or into masturbatory fantasies. A crucial shift occurs when the potential perpetrator begins to elaborate on these fantasies using actual people encountered, perhaps even rarely, in their daily life. Why, at a certain juncture, a small group of individuals begin to become discontent, if not anxious, about the frustrations of simply confining themselves to a fantasy level is a key question. At that point, the potential perpetrator plays out in his or her mind how the fantasized activity might actually be committed. This involves the distinct possibility that their control systems become less effective.

Once the potential perpetrator actually considers carrying out some type of violence against another human being, a crucial step has been taken. At first victims become depersonalized, and then they become viewed with contempt or anger. This seems to be connected with a process in which the potential victims are seen as people who are frustrating the potential perpetrator by not being available for the perpetrator's purposes when wanted. This defensive elaboration is crucial to the perpetrator's being able to carry out the type of violence anticipated, for if he or she recognized the victim as simply being an innocent person who has actually done no harm or wrong whatsoever to the perpetrator, it would be difficult for the perpetrator to carry through with the act.

There are also indications that, when it comes to the final enactment of killings in this sense, the act is related to a sense of utter hopelessness and despair. To a clinician, this may signify the possibility that a severe degree of depression is related to the act of killing. Thus it would seem that the perpetrator puts fantasies into action at the point at which there is an onset of a major depression, if not the threat of suicide. It is in response to the anger and rage they feel that perpetrators contemplate the final "solution," with the idea that things will be made better by acting out violent tendencies toward helpless victims—the actor survives at the expense of a person who is seen as being worthless and degraded. In that sense, the perpetrator's self-esteem is temporarily reestablished without his or her experiencing any personal feelings. In light of these proposed dynamics, there is also a possible explanation for the type of sadistic and degrading acts perpetrated in some cases to prolong the victims' suffering; such degradation allows perpetrators to view themselves as all powerful and the others as existing solely for the purpose of allowing someone who is superior to use them in such a manner. Hence, all manner of subjugating and torturing a victim may be seen as acceptable. Once there is relief from a state of utter despair and isolation by way of torturing or sadistically using a victim, the victim can be killed and disposed of like any other type of disposable object because the victim lacks any personal meaning.

Mass killings. A mass murderer is defined as one who kills three or four or more victims at one time as part of an ongoing killing event. Infamous names occur in this regard, each of which would warrant an investigative study in his or her own right.

- The worst mass killing in earlier times in the United States occurred in 1955 when an explosion on a passenger plane killed 44 people in California. It was later revealed that the son of one of the passengers on board the plane had planted a bomb to collect life insurance on his mother.
- In 1966, Richard F. Speck murdered eight nurses in Chicago.
- Also in 1966, Charles Whitman climbed a tower on the campus of the University of Texas and began shooting the people below. He killed 16 people and wounded 30. He was a former Eagle Scout, Marine, and engineering honor student.
- In 1983, 13 businessmen and gambling dealers were shot in a Seattle gambling club.
- In 1984, James Huberty entered a McDonald's Restaurant in San Ysidro, California, shooting everyone in sight, with the result that 21 people were killed and 19 wounded. He was eventually killed by police sharpshooters.
- Patrick Henry Sherrill, a mail carrier who was having trouble with his supervisors, opened fire in a crowded post office in Oklahoma in August 1986, killing 14 fellow workers and injuring 7 others before committing suicide.
- In 1991, another disgruntled postal worker killed three co-workers and wounded six more in Michigan.
- The worst mass murder in United States history occurred on October 19, 1991 when a single individual, George Hennard, entered a cafeteria in Killeen, Texas, with two semiautomatic pistols, killed 22 customers, and wounded 23 more. It was ironic that, the next day, the U. S. House of Representatives voted 247 to 177 to defeat a bill that would have banned 13 types of assault weapons and the high-capacity ammunition clips that make these guns so lethal.[62]
- On April 19, 1995, a bombing of a federal building in Oklahoma City killed 167 people.

Familicide. A variation on mass murder is the killing of an entire family by one member. I call this *familicide*. This type of mass murder has a different type of psychodynamic and psychiatric significance, as it involves an individual killing his or her own family members or loved ones en masse versus killing anonymous people. This distinction is not often made, which blurs an attempt to understand the psychiatric differences in such overt acts.[63]

Politically motivated mass killing. Another type of mass killing is political. The goal is to eliminate opponents or enemies of a regime or some adversarial group. The motivation can be to gain political control of a country or to enact a plan of genocide, such as was carried out by the Nazis in Germany and the occupied countries during World War II.

Medical mass murder. Using prisoners for purposes of experimentation, based on certain political or racial beliefs, is referred to as a medical mass murder,[64] again such as was seen under the Nazis. A variation on this are the cases reported from medical institutions or nursing homes in which an individual supposedly carries out acts of kindness or mercy killing by "putting away" the elderly or those with some disability. These are not acts done in terms of revenge or overt anger, but rather are seen by the perpetrators as altruistic acts. Sometimes the acts are carried out on those in the throes of a terminal disease through overdoses of lethal drugs.

Spree Killers

In spree murders, a killer goes on a rampage. The events may all be a part of a contiguous series of killings in which the rampage simply incorporates the killing as part of it. An example would be a series of armed robberies in which the perpetrators shoot and kill various people as they drive away. Other killings may take place in this context in terms of stopping at various places along the way subsequent to some type of felony and killing at those locations as well, such as at gas stations, restaurants, and so on. Perhaps an insight into contemporary society is reflected in the 1990s movie, *Thelma and Louise,* in which two women go on a rampage of violence and killing as they travel across the country. Bonnie and Clyde and Charles Starkweather are other examples.

■ References

1. Holinger PC: Violent Deaths in the United States. New York, Guilford, 1987

2. Reiss A Jr, Roth JA: Understanding and Preventing Violence. Washington, DC, National Academy Press, 1993

3. United States Department of Justice, Federal Bureau of Investigation: Uniform Crime Reports. Washington, DC, U.S. Government Printing Office, 1991

4. U.S. Department of Justice: Report to the Nation on Crime and Justice: The Data, 2nd Edition. Washington, DC, U.S. Government Printing Office, 1988

5. Tardiff K, Marzuk PM, Leon AC, et al: Homicide in New York City. JAMA 272:43–46, 1994

6. Wolfgang ME: Patterns in Criminal Homicide. Philadelphia, PA, University of Pennsylvania Press, 1958

7. Hewitt JD: The victim-offender relationship in convicted homicide cases: 1960–1984. Journal of Criminal Justice 16:25–33, 1984

8. Griffith EH, Bell CC: Recent trends in suicide and homicide among blacks. JAMA 262:2265–2269, 1989

9. Golden RM, Messner SF: Dimensions of racial inequality and rates of violent crime. Criminology 25:525–542, 1987

10. Kellermann AL, Mercy JA: Men, women, and murder: gender-specific differences in rates of fatal violence and victimization. J Trauma 33:1–5, 1992

11. Bartol CR: Criminal Behavior: A Psychosocial Approach, 3rd Edition. Englewood Cliffs, NJ, Prentice-Hall, 1991

12. Laudanu SF, Drapkin E, Arad S: Homicide victims and offenders: an Israeli study. Journal of Criminal Law and Criminology 65:390–396, 1974

13. United States Department of Justice, Federal Bureau of Investigation: Uniform Crime Reports. Washington, DC, U.S. Government Printing Office, 1989

14. Cook PJ: The technology of personal violence, in Crime and Justice: A Review of Research, Vol 14. Edited by Tonry M. Chicago, IL, University of Chicago Press, 1991, pp 1–77

16. Saltzman LE, Mercy JA, O'Carroll PW, et al: Weapon involvement and injury outcomes in family and intimate assaults. JAMA 267:3043–3047, 1992

17. Luckenbill DF: Homicide as a situated transaction. Social Problems 25:176–186, 1977

18. Riedel M, Zahn M, Mock LF: The Nature and Pattern of American Homicide. Washington, DC, U.S. Government Printing Office, 1985

19. Chaiken J, Chaiken M: Varieties of Criminal Behavior. Santa Monica, CA, Rand Corporation, 1983

20. Holcomb WR, Anderson WP: Alcohol and multiple drug abuse in accused murderers. Psychol Rep 52:159–164, 1983

21. Mayfield D: Alcoholism, alcohol intoxication and assaultive behavior. Diseases of the Nervous System 37:288–291, 1976

22. Greenberg DF: Methodological issues in survey research on the inhibition of crime. Journal of Criminal Law and Criminology 72:1094–1108, 1981

23. Cole KE, Fisher G, Cole SS: Women who kill. Arch Gen Psychiatry 19:1–8, 1968

24. Welte JW, Abel EL: Homicide: drinking by the victim. J Stud Alcohol 50:197–201, 1989

25. Bennet RM, Buss A, Carpenter JA: Alcohol and human physical aggression. Quart J Stud Alcohol 30:820–826, 1969

26. Lang AR, Goeckner DJ, Adesso VJ, et al: Effects of alcohol on aggression in male social drinkers. J Abnorm Psychol 84:508–518, 1975

27. Gillies H: Murder in West Scotland. Br J Psychiatry III:1087–1094, 1965

28. Derville P, L'Epee P, Lazarin HJ, et al: Statistical indications of a possible relationship between alcoholism and criminality: an inquiry into the Bordeaux region. Revue Alcoholisme 7:20–21, 1961

29. Peele S: Dispensing of America: Addiction Treatment Out of Control. Lexington, MA, DC Heath, 1989

30. Virkkunen M, DeJong J, Barko J, et al: Relationship of psychobiological variables to recidivism in violent offenders and impulsive fire setters. Arch Gen Psychiatry 46:600–603, 1989

31. Cloninger CR, Siguardsson S, Gilligan SB, et al: Genetic heterogeneity and the classification of alcoholism, in Alcohol Research From Bench to Bedside. Edited by Gordis E, Tabakoff B, Linnoila M. Binghamton, NY, Hayworth Press, 1989, pp 3–16

32. Secretary of Health and Human Services: Alcohol and Health: Eighth Special Report to the U.S. Congress. Rockville, MD, National Institute of Alcohol Abuse and Alcoholism, U.S. Government Printing Office, 1993

33. Wilsnack RW: Antecedents and consequences of drinking and drinking problems in women: patterns from a U.S. national survey, in Alcohol and Addictive Behavior: Nebraska Symposium on Motivation, 1986. Edited by Clayton P. Lincoln, NE, University of Nebraska Press, 1987, pp 85–158

34. Pernanen K: Alcohol in Human Violence. New York, Guilford, 1991

36. MacAndrew C, Edgerton RB: Drunken Comportment. Chicago, IL, Aldine, 1969

37. Hanzlick R, Gowitt GT: Cocaine metabolite detection in homicide victims. JAMA 265:760–761, 1991

38. Chertwood D: Is there a season for homicide? Criminology 26:287–306, 1988

39. Hagan FE: Introduction to Criminology, 3rd Edition. Chicago, IL, Nelson-Hall, 1994

40. Shakespeare W: Othello, in The Complete Signet Classic Shakespeare. Edited by Barnet S. New York, Harcourt Brace Jovanovich, 1972

41. Lieber AL: The Lunar Effect. Garden City, NJ, Anchor Press, Doubleday, 1978

42. Fingerhut LA, Kleinman JC: International and interstate comparisons of homicide among young males. JAMA 263:3292–3295, 1990

43. D'Emilio J, Freedman EB: Intimate Matters: A History of Sexuality in America. New York, Harper & Row, 1988

44. Maxfield MG: Lifestyles and routine activity theories of crime: empirical studies of victimization, delinquency, and offender decision-making. Journal of Quantitative Criminology 3:275–281, 1987

45. Hindelang MH, Gottfredson MR, Garofolo J: Victims of Personal Crime: An Empirical Foundation From a Theory of Personal Victimization. Cambridge, MA, Ballinger, 1978

46. Cohen LE, Felson M: Social change and crime rates trends: a routine activities approach. American Sociological Review 44:588–608, 1979

47. Carroll L, Jackson PI: Inequality, opportunity, and crime rates in central cities. Criminology 21:178–194, 1983

48. Messner SF, Tardiff K: The social ecology of urban homicide: an application of the routine activities approach. Criminology 23:241–267, 1985

49. Merton R: Social structure and anomie. American Sociological Review 3:672–682, 1938

50. Cloward RA, Ohlin LE: Delinquency and Opportunity. New York, Free Press, 1960

51. Agnew RS: A revised strain theory of delinquency. Social Forces 64:151–167, 1985

52. Matza D, Sykes GM: Juvenile delinquency and subterranean values. American Sociological Review 26:712–720, 1961

53. Matza D: Delinquency and Drift. New York, Wiley, 1961

54. Dietz ML: Killing for Profit: The Social Organization of Felony Homicide. Chicago, IL, Nelson-Hall, 1983

55. Bureau of Justice Statistics: Criminal Victimization. Washington, DC, U.S. Department of Justice, Bureau of Justice Statistics, 1987

56. Holmes R, DeBurger J: Serial Murder. Beverly Hills, Sage, 1988

57. Johnston T: A little house of horrors: murder in Philadelphia. Newsweek, April 6, 1987, pp 27–28

58. California jury weighs fate of woman in nine deaths. The New York Times, August 8, 1993, p 16

59. Holmes RM: Profiling Violent Crimes. Newbury Park, CA, Sage Publications, 1989

60. Egger S: Serial Murder: An Elusive Phenomenon. New York, Praeger, 1990

61. Heide R: A taxonomy of murder: motivational dynamics behind the homicidal acts of adolescents. Journal of Justice Issues 4:1–8, 1986

62. Rutherford A: Crime, Law Enforcement, and Penology. Chicago, IL, Britannica Book of the Year, 1992

63. Malmquist CP: Psychiatric aspects of familicide. Bull Am Acad Psychiatry Law 8:298–304, 1980

64. Proctor RN: Racial Hygiene Under the Nazis. Cambridge, MA, Harvard University Press, 1988

CHAPTER 2

Biological Factors in Homicide

■ Dilemmas in the Biological Perspectives on Homicide

A discussion of homicidal violence cannot proceed without first assessing work related to the biology of such extreme aggressive behaviors. The meaning of aggression itself is controversial because some writers confuse it with competitiveness and assertiveness. One approach is to use the term *aggression* only for behavior that has a component of intended harm. This permits an inquiry into the basis of such behavior in terms of the impetus toward harm.

Although general and developmental psychologists have stressed such factors as the role of frustration and social learning in aggression, the search for the inner source of such behavior has often been given short shrift. Several key questions are relevant when considering biological aspects of aggression related to a homicidal outcome:

1. Is there a common biological substratum with respect to acts of homicidal violence? If so, is homicide just one point, often reached by chance, along a continuum of violent expressions?

2. What is the extent of the current knowledge about the neurophysiological aspects of aggression and how these aspects are related to homicide?
3. How relevant—and how analogous—are the studies of nonhuman aggression and violence to the study of human homicidal behavior?
4. Are there any major limitations to the conclusions that have been drawn about human beings killing one another that can be drawn from naturalistic settings as well as from the artificiality of laboratory settings?

Some initial caveats should be stated with respect to the definitions and models of aggression that are used in experiments with nonhuman subjects, as such models might be quite different from those that are applied to humans in a separate milieu. It addition, it is oversimplistic to view nonhuman subjects' behavior as being programmed in a certain way based solely on genetic underpinnings; nor do sophisticated behavioral geneticists espouse such a reductionistic view. Instead, many environmental factors impinge on the behavior of both humans and nonhuman subjects, including their diverse types of social interactions with each other. There is also the role of ritualized and posturing behavior that animals engage in to different degrees. All these considerations need to be factored in before any implications about humans and homicidal violence can be drawn from animal studies. Beyond these asides, in this chapter I do not focus on nonhuman animal displays of aggression or violence in discussing the problem of humans killing.

It is commonly believed that biological factors operate in human beings in a dispositional manner—that is to say that they are predisposing factors that are seen as being necessary but not always sufficient in order for a violent outcome of homicidal proportions to occur. As such, these dispositional tendencies stand ready to trigger violent acts framed by environmental events. However, it must be noted that biological fluctuations within individuals can also heighten or lessen the potential for such behavior to be triggered at different times.

■ Early Theories of the Source of Aggression

Instinctual and Behavioral Theories

The search for an instinctual basis for aggression has an uneven history. In the early twentieth century, McDougall postulated that humans possessed a host of instincts that operated for acquisition, construction, gregariousness, flight, repulsion, curiosity, pugnaciousness, parenting, reproduction, desire for food, self-abasement, and self-assertion.[1]

Eventually, behaviorism became the reigning school of psychology in the United States through the 1950s. Believing that scientific validity could be proven only by observable events, behaviorists found McDougall's unprovable theory about an inner set of processes driving behavior unacceptable and replaced it with a drive theory based on external observable behavior, without reference to the inner state of a person. The emphasis on behavior as being primarily learned dominated psychological thinking at the time; it was felt that the idea of behavior being unlearned and inborn was not testable, and, being untestable, was therefore irrefutable, and hence not a legitimate part of the contemporary scientific domain. Environmental contributions were seen as always controlling behavior, beyond some basic motor patterns for reflexes.

Psychoanalytic Theories

Psychoanalysts have formulated general theories on the concept of instinct, focusing on questions such as the number and nature of the instincts, how they should be classified (e.g., energic aspects, libido theory), how they function, and how they could be transformed (e.g., instinctual vicissitudes). There was also a special theory of instincts referring to how instincts develop in any one particular person. Throughout the twentieth century, these theories shifted. Underlying the various theories was the idea that there was some built-in source for behavior that was distinct from the aim of the instincts or the objects on which they were played out. Originally, there was a division of instincts into the sexual and ego instincts. Freud later ascribed aggressive trends to the ego instincts.[2] With the addition of structural theory, aggressivity was no longer regarded as primarily attributed to the ego instincts. Rather, aggression and destruction were postulated as being independent instincts alongside the sexual instincts. It is beyond the scope of this chapter to go into Freud's speculations about a death instinct based on his need to explain how some behavior was not regulated by the pleasure principle but rather operated under the sway of a repetition compulsion.

Ethological Theories

In an entirely different arena of knowledge, European zoologists were laying the groundwork for studying instincts by way of ethology. Their methodology was to investigate animal behavior within animals' naturalistic settings. From studies of lower animals, it had become difficult to explain how all behavior operated simply on the basis of being learned. This is not to say that such behavior was immune from environmental influences, but rather that the genetic endowment of the animal was seen as interacting with the environment. The ethologists' reasoning was that instinctive behavior was genetically programmed, and therefore related to inheritable characteristics. Rather than referring to instincts, ethologists referred to innate behaviors that were specific to a given species.[5,6]

At times, confusion has resulted from the misrepresentation of the position that the phrase "inherited behavior" simply means that a group of genes can explain all behavior. This reductionistic position of viewing genetic endowment as being able to explain how aggression—up through acts of killing—unfolds is seen as omitting too many key variables. It is rather the interaction of genetic factors—the dispositional component—and environmental factors—the dispositional component—that is needed for reaching the potentiality of a homicide.

Much of Lorenz's and Tinbergen's early work, which involved concepts such as a "sign stimulus" and "fixed-action patterns," has been elaborated on by other investigators.[5,6] In more current research, it has been shown that complex, inborn behavioral patterns are activated by certain environmental stimuli that thereby function as releasers. Different species have different repertoires of fixed-action patterns. Whereas, in lower species, behavior is released by stimulation of certain command neurons, in mammals it is thought that there may be groups of cells that trigger preprogrammed motor acts. Command systems in turn may be responsive to certain sensory elicitors by innate releasing mechanisms. Although most of the studies of these concepts has not been with human subjects, let alone even mammals, they have provided a framework for thinking about the biological contributions to aggression in its diverse forms.

The transition from a behavioristic model to an impetus from within the organism has been by way of seeing the influence of genes on behavior. If behavior is regulated by neural circuits, then diverse proteins are required for the development of these circuits. The proteins are coded specifically by genes. Different genes may play a role, with some individual genes becoming more important than others. In essence, the genes are the key to producing the neural circuitry, but also to regulating behavior. This is because genes code the structural proteins that are necessary to maintain the circuitry, as well as the enzymes necessary for synaptic transmission. Genes are also seen as coding peptide hormones and modulations that can trigger or inhibit the discharge of behavior. (Peptides are neurotransmitters that affect specific neurons; these are discussed below.)

The complex question of what role innate factors play in determining human behavior remains. However, besides studies on the hormonal determinants of gender identity, four lines of evidence are presented in support of how some human behaviors can be affected by innate factors.[8] The first position is that human behavior, like that in other species, is mediated by genes. Consequently, to some extent, it is under genetic control. Second, certain emotional expressions are seen as having a strong innate component that cuts across different cultural settings. An example would be that of facial expressions in infants or adults, regardless of those individuals' home culture. Third, stereotyped motor patterns exist that resemble fixed-action patterns. Fourth, there appear to be certain complex patterns that require little or no learning. This is witnessed in humans who have had limited experiences of the environment or in the responses of blind infants who have not had any visual environmental input. In the remainder of the chapter, I focus on the biological—including genetic—factors that influence human aggression.

■ Genes and Violence in Humans

Genetic factors are being investigated for their role in diverse kinds of human behavior that have an influence on how aggression may be expressed. One difficulty in such work is separating the role of genetic influences from that of environmental influences.

Much of the genetic work in humans stems from the field of molecular genetics, in which techniques to localize, characterize, and clone genes that are believed to be associated with inherited diseases are used. By use of an oversimplified model, the steps used by molecular geneticists are as follows: First they locate a precise gene that can determine a genotype (i.e., the genetic constitution of an individual or group). Then they determine the products of a specific defective gene (e.g., alterations of some biochemical product) to reveal the biological mechanisms involved. The hope is that, through this process, the underlying pathophysiology of a certain disorder or condition will become clearer and assist investigators in reaching more valid clinical diagnoses. For example, genes for certain neuropsychiatric disorders (e.g., Huntington's disease) and certain metabolic diseases are typically cited as evidence for inherited diseases. It is hoped that these DNA methods can be extended to the study of mental illnesses and therefore yield a better understanding of the violent propensities that may accompany some of these illnesses.

Traditional approaches to studying genetic transmission have focused on the incidence and prevalence of disorders in families, twins, and adopted children, with the goal of separating genetic from environmental influences to the extent possible. This traditional model has been extended beyond the search for causes of mental disorders to those genes that simply express inherited traits through focusing on the similarities and differences in groups that have a similar genetic makeup. For example, if studies of monozygotic twins with certain traits who were separated at birth were later to reveal that both twins had an increased potential for violence in adulthood, perhaps even something as specific as homicidal violence, questions could be raised about the possibility of genetic influences on violent behavior. In the same vein, if one dizygotic twin separated at birth showed a comparatively lesser incidence of such behavior than the matching dizygotic twin, the same possibility would exist.

Family studies are the weakest line of evidence for genetic transmission because of the obvious loading of similar environmental variables in family rearing patterns. Unfortunately, this is the most prevalent model used for studies of mental disorders. For example, different studies on twins and adopted siblings point to genetic factors having some role in schizophrenia and certain mood disorders. In this connection, using adoption studies, investigators would not only look at the mood instabilities present in those with an affective disorder, but also investigate their violence potential in comparative studies. As another example, attempts might be made to connect the hereditary components in alcoholism with mood instabilities, and to go beyond that into the summative disposition to violence.

The complexities of investigating genetic components are increasing. For many diagnoses or conditions, researchers are still at the level of generating hypotheses, such as a single gene locus versus a multifactorial model involving polygenes in which environmental influences operate. At a molecular level, hypotheses involve the role of neurotransmitter enzymes and metabolites and how they can affect neurophysiological functioning. Even in dealing with diagnosable mental disorders or biological traits, such as schizophrenia or mood disorders, the results remain inconclusive. This ambiguity is even greater with traits related to violent behavior. The statistical models do not fit the data to the exclusion of other hypotheses.[9] The missing link would be data to show the coinheritance of an illness and a biological trait.

In studying genetic aspects of mental disorders and related traits, the current emphasis is on markers or genetic variations, with the goal being to localize genes. The hope is that molecular techniques can bridge the distance between a marker and a gene by identifying additional markers. Such work forms the basis for reports of linkage between diagnoses of bipolar affective disorder and genetic markers on the X chromosome, which suggests one form of a genetic bipolar illness. The complexities of the approach reveal obscure inheritance patterns and the fluid boundaries existing for many diagnoses.

■ Physiological Hypotheses of Violence

Because genetic theories of violence currently operate primarily at the hypothesis stage, physiology is often suggested as an explanation that can offer a more concrete explanation for aggression that can lead to the extreme of killing.

Seizures

Work with clinical populations in cases involving seizure disorders when a subgroup have been violent suggests one area for exploration. Early researchers speculated about the possibility of violent eruptions occurring in connection with temporal lobe seizures, positing some type of brain abnormality on an anatomical or physiological level. In the modern era, the search has turned to work on brain functioning for an explanation.

In the 1970s, some investigators studying a form of seizure now called complex partial seizures (also called temporal lobe, limbic, or psychomotor seizures) began to advocate the use of neurosurgical techniques to try to control such seizure activity.[10] The inference was that, if the seizures could be controlled, then associated sequelae of the seizures, such as violence, could also be controlled. However, surgical interventions of this type could not be carried out on large numbers of people without eliciting a large public outcry. Something inherent in the performance of surgical procedures on the brain for the purpose of altering behavior arouses both public and professional anxiety. Part of this concern is associated the fact that psychosurgery procedures on mentally ill individuals were less well regulated in the past. People also fear that permitting surgery of this type would allow future abuse of the procedure in attempts to control people by overdiagnosing complex partial seizures in those prone to violence. The difficulty in diagnosing such seizures because of unclear boundaries in the diagnosis also gives rise to fears that such a technique could be misused.

The fact that neurologists have been able to delineate diverse types of seizures, each of which might have different correlates for different types of violence—perhaps including homicidal violence—raises many potential diagnostic problems but also has implications for assessing violent individuals' behavior. In Table 2–1, the diverse types of seizures and their characteristics are represented, such as whether they are

Table 2–1. Classification of epileptic seizures

Generalized seizures (bilaterally symmetrical and without local onset)
    Tonic, clonic, or tonic-clonic (grand mal)
    Absence (petit mal)
        Simple—loss of consciousness only
        Complex—with brief tonic, clonic, or automatic movements
    Lennox-Gastaut syndrome
    Juvenile myoclonic epilepsy
    Infantile spasms (West syndrome)
    Atonic (astatic, akinetic) seizures (sometimes with myoclonic jerks)
Partial, or focal, seizures (seizures beginning locally)
    Simple (without loss of consciousness)
        Motor (tonic, clonic, tonic-clonic; Jacksonian benign childhood epilepsy; epilepsia partialis continua)
        Somatosensory or special sensory (visual, auditory, olfactory, gustatory, vertiginous)
        Autonomic
        Psychic
    Complex (with impaired consciousness)
        Beginning as simple partial seizures and progressing to impairment of consciousness)
        With impairment of consciousness at onset
Special epileptic syndromes
    Myoclonus and myoclonic seizures
    Reflex epilepsy
    Acquired aphasic and convulsive disorder
    Febrile and other seizures of infancy and childhood
    Hysterical seizures

Source. Reprinted from Commission on Classification and Terminology of the International League Against Epilepsy. *Epilepsia* 22:489, 1981.

generalized or partial, differences connected with age at onset, if they are primary or secondary, and the diverse settings in which they can occur. *Generalized seizures* are those that begin bilaterally; *partial seizures* have a localized onset, although they may evolve into generalized seizures of the partial complex type (here *partial* refers to consciousness being retained and *complex* to an impairment in consciousness). The potential for ambiguity in detecting violence from seizures in themselves from associated psychiatric phenomena are evident, which is magnified when there are legal issues.

Attempts to link temporal lobe seizures with violence. Early onset thinking about temporal lobe seizures was partially correct in that the electrical discharges for these seizures has been found to originate in deep, medially placed limbic nuclei in the temporal lobe consisting of the amygdala, uncus, and hippocampus. However, the limbic system is not all located in the temporal lobe, and other areas of the brain also affect emotion. It is interesting that some view the limbic system more as a philosophical concept than an actual discrete anatomical or physiological system.[12]

The epidemiological question of whether such people with seizure disorders actually have an increased tendency toward violent behavior has not in itself been satisfactorily resolved. Many times such a link has been implied in best-selling books or movies, such as Michael Crichton's novel, *The Terminal Man,* in which seizures spark brutal rampages.[13] However, authors of more recent studies did not find extreme violence occurring more frequently in the course of complex seizures.[14,15] One difficulty is that what has been categorized as violence is often a reflex set of behaviors carried out without any particular goal or purpose in mind. To further complicate the matter, some neurologists have posited that people with temporal lobe seizures may develop behavioral changes involving excess aggression, religiosity, changes in sexual behavior, and a preoccupation with writing or drawing (which some also think promotes creativity).

A different conceptualization interprets the problem not just as a seizure disorder but rather as a dysfunction in the limbic system that leads to episodic dyscontrol.[16] In one study of 500 patients referred for investigation of neurological disorders, including 17 cases referred for temper tantrums, none had a seizure disorder or episodic dyscontrol.[17]

Another approach has been to focus on seizure-prone individuals' interictal personality. It has been proposed that these individuals are more likely to be prone to violence between seizures rather than in seizure states and that such a predisposed personality shows traits of irritability and aggressivity that leave those individuals prone to having violent outbursts or to provoking others.

Difficulties thus abound in trying to achieve specificity in the association between complex partial seizures and violence. Some investigators have classified patients as showing increased aggressive behavior.[18,19] However, in these studies, varying definitions of aggression have been used, and in many of these cases these definitions fall far short of any type of serious violence toward people, let alone any homicidal violence. Whitman et al.[20] studied 83 children who were diagnosed with anterior temporal lobe epileptiform spike activity. The children showed elevated aggression scores on the Child Behavior Checklist.[21] Many variables had only a slight variance to predict behavioral disorder for generalized and partial seizures. Whitman et al. eventually focused on situation-centered variables instead of biological variables to try to predict behavioral disturbances.

In the early 1980s, Lewis et al. investigated psychomotor seizures in a group of 97 young offenders.[22] They believed there was an association between the offenders' seizure disorders and violence. Eleven of the youths were seen as definitely having psychomotor seizures, and 8 were thought to probably have such a diagnosis. The 11 had been seriously assaultive, with 5 described as having committed acts of violence during the seizures. Complicating the clinical picture, however, was the frequency of antecedent central nervous system trauma in the backgrounds of these youths. The group showed a loading of factors, such as complicated perinatal problems, head injuries, central nervous system infections, and histories of some generalized seizures of the grand mal type. Some also had psychotic symptoms, as well as a history of severe physical abuse. Given such a matrix of factors, which is often found in such clinical populations, attributing these youths' increased violence to complex partial seizures is like looking for a needle in a haystack.

In another study of a possible relationship between violence and seizures, Herman and Whitman[23] did not find any significant differences in the occurrence of violence between those who did and those who did not have seizures. Study subjects who had seizures were weighted on such variables as socioeconomic status, gender, age, and earlier developmental problems, much as in other studies. It was found that, apart from their seizures, these individuals had multiple problems, some of which may have originated in the subjects' deprived social environment and may have been connected with diagnoses of attention-deficit disorder with or without hyperactivity. Their problems took the form of coexisting restlessness, impulsivity, poor attention span, memory deficits, and so on. Some subjects' history of accident proneness or head injuries may also have left sequelae. Interpretations of the data were complicated by the study subjects' learning disabilities, soft neurological signs, and a variety of neuropsychiatric deficits that did not fit any one standard accepted diagnosis and may have included other diagnoses as well.

It is extremely difficult to sort out diverse factors such as those found in Herman and Whitman's study from what may be directly connected with the effects of seizures. The brain is not one discrete area, but instead encompasses the cortical area of the hippocampus, the frontal-orbital area of the cortex, and the cingulate gyrus. A high degree of connection exists between these limbic areas and the temporal lobes, and any hypothesized lesion need not occur in any one area. In fact, the seizure disorder is often ascribed to existing on a physiological basis leading to a dysfunction that is not specifically localized in any one anatomical area.

Many would also question the sensitivity of diagnostic instruments and practices to detect what might be associated with limbic seizures. Electroencephalograms (EEGs) are seen as too insensitive to detect abnormalities in subcortical activity, and neuropsychological testing cannot be relied on to differentiate such a diagnosis. Clinical practice relies on the old-fashioned diagnostic approach of history taking and trials on antiseizure medications in the absence of specific ways to validate the diagnosis. If the problems improve with medication, then the diagnosis is retroactively seen as being confirmed.

Thus conflicting views have emerged regarding the proneness of those with seizure disorders toward exhibiting extreme violence. At this time, it cannot be confirmed nor disconfirmed in principle that these individuals have such a vulnerability, except for citation of specific cases.

Possible linking mechanisms between seizures and violent behavior. Supposing for the moment that there is a connection between seizures and violence, how might a homicidal act occur in an individual during a seizure? The primary manifestations of a complex partial seizure begin with an alteration in the individual's state of consciousness, specifically described as a temporal aura spreading to the limbic system. Stages of impaired consciousness then occur, with degrees of loss of contact within the environment. Sometimes there is a focal onset that progresses to a loss of consciousness, or at times a loss of consciousness exists from the beginning. Automatisms may occur that appear quite integrated to an observer but for which the individual has postictal amnesia. The hypothesis is that it is during automatistic states that a violent act would occur. Possible automatisms are those involving movements or activities (e.g., chewing, scratching, walking, kicking, undressing) and those described as being responsive to stimuli in the environment (e.g., drinking, resisting movement by others such as when being placed in restraints). In addition, whatever behavior was occurring before the seizure, such as eating or walking, may be continued. These diverse behaviors occurring before and during a complex seizure make it difficult to attribute an act of aggression or violence to the complex seizure. In addition, automatisms sometimes occur after a seizure, and at other times in the postictal state. Attributing causation for the violence to a seizure is difficult because one would have to reconstruct the perpetrator's neuropsychological state at the time of the act after the act and without the benefit of contemporaneous EEGs or other measurements.

Interictal behavior proposed to be associated with an increased tendency to violence, assuming such a correlation has validity, may also be attributable to several possibilities: 1) the personality of the person prone to such seizures, 2) personality changes in reaction to being seizure prone, or 3) a hypothesized, undetected foci. Again, none of these possibilities can be confirmed or disconfirmed. Some hope that the ambiguity may be resolved by stereo EEGs, which involve surgical insertion of wire electrodes into the brain to monitor brain abnormalities. This is an interesting research approach, but it is not likely to attract many volunteers.

Psychiatric signs and symptoms connected with the seizures, whatever their cause, provide further complications. Autonomic nervous system involvement can show up in gastrointestinal, cardiovascular, pulmonary, or urogenital symptoms. Affective states of depression, pessimism, anxiety, or euphoria may prevail. A picture of confusion with memory alterations may impair the later recall of details. In some individuals, complex partial seizures evolve to a state of generalized seizures. Repeated seizures in themselves can induce brain injury and associated behavioral changes. Occasional electrical discharges or degrees of undetected discharge could be occurring.

From a psychological perspective, the tendency to violence could be explained by the individual's reaction to having seizures, which are, after all, a disease of the central nervous system. Often, a seizure-prone individual may have a comorbid diagnosis that involves schizophreniform- or paranoid-type personality features that are reflected in mood disturbances. The personality features most frequently referred to are hyperreligiousness, hyposexuality, hypergraphia, and circumstantiality. Auditory hallucinations and paranoid delusions can also occur. There is a need to determine if these symptoms are related to schizophrenia. To complicate matters further, the onset of psychotic symptoms may occur years after the onset of the seizures. In one study of 44 epileptic patients, 20 met the criteria for a schizophrenic disorder.[24]

Most elusive is the attempt to portray a "dyscontrol syndrome" as producing violence from lesions in the limbic system or temporal lobe in the absence of any observable seizures. This hypothesis suggests that there are epileptic types of discharges from the limbic system based on suggestive evidence from soft neurological signs, EEG abnormalities, attention-deficit disorders, and so on. It is a vague group of signs, symptoms, as well as diverse diagnostic possibilities exhibiting diverse types of dyscontrol in terms of frequency and severity. It appears to be a grouping not capable at present of being falsified as a diagnosis from its elastic boundaries when used in attempts to explain homicidal behavior.

It is likely that greater diagnostic specificity will be obtained in the future from EEG work along with more advanced brain imaging techniques. Although there have been large numbers of EEG studies attempting to detect significant brain abnormalities in individuals ranging from delinquents and psychopaths to murderers, major problems exist in interpreting these reports.[25] The methodological difficulties involve lack of controls, the subjective nature of scoring EEGs, lack of blind assessment of the records, lack of agreed-on criteria for defining abnormality, and lack of sensitivity to states of alertness of the subject. Perhaps the newer brain imaging techniques will allow greater specificity, such as pinpointing temporal lobe abnormalities in computerized tomography (CT). In one study of 87 patients with diverse psychiatric diagnoses who were referred for neuropsychiatric evaluation, both CT and magnetic resonance imaging scans were performed.[26] Twenty-three of the patients were diagnosed as having an organic mental disorder; significantly, the 14 of those 23 who had a history of frequent violent episodes showed lesions in the anterior-inferior temporal lobe, whereas the other 9 who were not violent did not show such lesions.

In summary, once a seizure-prone individual has carried out a homicide or serious act of violence, several possibilities arise.[27] One is that the act might have been caused by the seizure, although such violence as part of an ictal state is quite rare. Another possibility is that a type of cerebral malfunction may be the cause of both the homicide and the seizure disorders. Sometimes the violence may be associated with the confusion of a postictal state. Yet another possibility is that some types of psychological sequelae accompanying a seizure problem may foster resentment and accumulated rage, leaving the person prone to a homicidal outburst, or a mental disorder may have developed as a result of the seizure problem and may have played some contributory role in the homicide. Also to be considered is the background of psychosocial deprivation that can contribute to an individual's seizure proneness as well as to homicidal behavior. Furthermore, in some of these cases, patterns of violent or provocative behavior, whatever their source, can elicit reactive trauma and the possibility of resultant brain injury from such encounters.

Social and legal issues about seizures and violent behavior. The potential connection between complex partial seizures and homicidal violence raises complicated social and legal issues beyond those of proper medical diagnoses. The essentials for a criminal act are an *actus reus* (criminal act) as well as a *mens rea* (criminal mind or criminal intent). The latter involves the idea of an individual voluntarily choosing to commit a criminal act, in which case his or her behavior is seen as blameworthy. In the absence of such a choice, blaming and punishment would be seen as not only inappropriate, but unjust.

The possibility of a criminal act occurring in an ictal state raises questions about the perpetrator's volitional status. A more subtle consideration is whether an individual can be cleared of responsibility for interictal acts of violence, with the act being attributed to the "epileptic personality." However, in legal settings, questions are not posed in epidemiological terms. Instead, they involve the question of whether, in a particular case, an individual can validate the diagnosis of an epileptic personality, and whether the homicidal behavior can be encompassed under the seizure diagnosis. Then, depending on the jurisdiction, different types of legal questions arise with respect to an individual's capacity to control his or her violent behavior, conform his or her conduct to the requirements of the law, know the difference between right and wrong, and know the nature of the act carried out.

A legal distinction is made between an automatism defense and an insanity defense. The former is raised by way of a denial of homicidal responsibility because the *actus reus* is required to have been voluntary. A homicide occurring during an alleged seizure state could raise the question of whether the *mens rea* was negated because the perpetrator did not register the requisite cognitive or emotional states. A pure automatism defense would not necessitate proving the presence of a mental disease or defect. If successful, it would have a "not guilty" outcome, in contrast to a "not guilty by reason of insanity" outcome. Hence, it would bypass the types of questions raised in using an insanity defense, and the types of restrictions normally associated with a successful insanity defense, such as medical or court supervision. One interesting question would be the possibility of a later recurrence of the seizure and violence in the lack of such supervision.

Complex legal as well as psychiatric issues arise concerning assertions that voluntariness or its lack in conjunction with a seizure disorder exculpates a defendant for a homicidal act. It seems clear that simply making an assertion of a connection between a seizure disorder and involuntary behavior does not suffice for legal or medical purposes to establish a connection to the act of violence. Further, if there is medical documentation about such a seizure disorder existing, it may become legally significant when an issue of responsibility is raised. The need to validate the diagnosis by a competent neurologist, experienced in the area of seizure disorders, is only the beginning. If the accused person is a minor, the diagnostician should be someone who is also experienced in and conversant with the diagnosis in that age group. The question of automatisms needs to be established by the use of EEG telemetry, and some would add that it should occur on closed-circuit television, as well. Demonstrations of aggression related to a seizure should be handled by an attempt to induce the seizure and have it on a videotape with accompanying EEG readings. Even if the results are positive, it could still be challenged on the basis that this was not what actually occurred during the commission of the violent act in question. However, it would support the claim that analogous behavior did occur. The individual's history should also indicate past episodes of aggression or violent behavior. For legal purposes, a neurologist or psychiatrist would have to be willing to express an opinion that these factors were related to the seizure disorder, and to be available for answering other legal questions.

Case Example[28]

Seth Grant was one among several individuals in a bar. A patron, whom he did not know, and the tavern owner got into an altercation. When the police arrived, the patron was escorted outside. A hostile crowd of about 40 people were cheering the patron when, suddenly, Seth Grant, heretofore totally uninvolved, leaped into the air and struck an officer twice in the face. Great force was needed to subdue Grant who was described as excited, agitated, and upset. In jail an hour later, he was observed having symptoms of a grand mal seizure.

Grant's medical history revealed a preexistent diagnosis of psychomotor epilepsy for which he was on medication, and also verified that he had had a number of violent attacks of varying severity. A previous attack in which Grant assaulted someone with knife in a hospital had resulted in his being shot in the pelvis and kidney by a police officer. At his current trial, Grant testified that he recalled nothing about the bar episode and had only "woken up" in the hospital 3 days later. His psychiatric expert testified that he had had a psychomotor seizure that "prevented his conscious mind from controlling his actions." There was conflicting testimony about his being "alert and awake" at the time of the arrest and in jail. A question was also raised about the grand mal seizure in jail, as it would not necessarily mean that he had had a psychomotor seizure while at the bar.

The jury was instructed in terms of the Illinois Test for Insanity: that as a result of a mental disease or defect, the defendant would have to lack substantial capacity to either appreciate the criminality of his conduct or conform his conduct to the requirements of the law for him to be found not guilty by reason of insanity. The jury found Grant guilty of aggravated battery and obstructing a police officer, but the court sentenced him only on the former charge. On appeal, it was noted that the insanity question did not distinguish an individual whose behavior was caused by an automatism during which the defendant was not conscious of what he was doing. No instruction had been given the jury involving involuntary conduct, and, on that ground, the case was reversed and remanded with directions for a new trial.

Apart from other issues, the above case raises the interesting legal dilemma of what instructions should be given in such cases.

Cases involving voluntary conduct cause difficulty not only for philosophers and clinicians, but particularly for the legal system with its need to assess culpability based on an individual performing a voluntary act. The Model Penal Code, which produces recommendations by a scholarly group of attorneys and law professors, listed exclusions from the definition of a voluntary act:[29] 1) a reflex or convulsion, 2) a bodily movement during unconsciousness or sleep, 3) conduct during hypnosis or resulting from hypnotic suggestion, or 4) a bodily movement that is not a product of the effort or determination of the actor, either conscious or habitual. This scholarly recommendation stated that a voluntary act should have an element of conscious control over the behavior, but did not attempt to resolve the age-old debate between free will and determinism or how much control. The code is an attempt to exclude, in a crude way, behavior seen as nonvolitional. The rationale on one hand is that a person's sense of autonomy would be undermined if they were held accountable for behavior they could not control. It is also argued that a sense of justice is vitiated in holding such people accountable. The problem arises in a broader sense from many people thinking they cannot control themselves. Hence, as a minimum, there is a requirement for some attendant alteration of consciousness. Of course, because an unconscious person cannot carry out any act, there remains a quandary that gives rise to the doctrine of automatism, implying some (but how much?) limitation of the awareness of their acts.

Other Organic Disturbances

The list of clinical conditions in which automatisms are alleged to occur has been widely expanded from its origins, and now includes possible problems on a genetic, hormonal, or neurochemical level. In fact, the range of these conditions tend to blend in with the dissociative disorder group in which no organic pathology is being asserted. This change increases the legal confusion in that it increases the range of medical experts who are ever willing to testify on opposite sides and render diverse opinions. The possibilities then include seizures, postictal states, and a variety of altered states of consciousness that can either accompany delirium and dementia or exist in their own right. Altered states can also occur from infectious processes, toxins, tumors, head injuries, and various metabolic diseases such as diabetes or Cushing's syndrome.

Questions about hypnotized individuals carrying out criminal acts continue to be argued without a satisfactory resolution. The affirmative argument against liability for these individuals' behavior is that they are subject to, and dependent on, the hypnotizer. Yet ascribing such helplessness to the individual does not square with current knowledge about the nature of hypnotizability, in that some may choose to submit to such procedures and others may be extremely suggestible by nature.

Matters become even more debatable when there are suggestions of automatic states related to somnambulistic (i.e., sleep walking) or hypnagogic states. Somnambulistic states always raise interesting legal questions about the nature of responsibility for behavior. Excerpts from the *The King v. Cogdon* case illustrate fundamental issues about responsibility for criminal behavior in this regard.[30] This unreported case, heard in the Supreme Court of Victoria before Mr. Justice Smith in December 1950, though clear as to its facts and unchallengeable in law, was seen as compelling a reconsideration of some of the basic premises of responsibility for criminal actions.

Case Example

Mrs. Cogdon was charged with the murder of Pat, her only child, a 19-year-old daughter. Pat had for some time been receiving psychiatric treatment for a relatively minor neurotic condition of which, in her psychiatrist's opinion, she had been cured. Despite this, Mrs. Cogdon continued to worry unduly about her. Describing the relationship between Pat and her mother, Mr. Cogdon testified: "I don't think a mother could have thought any more of her daughter. I think she absolutely adored her." On the conscious level, at least, there was no reason to doubt Mrs. Cogdon's deep attachment to her daughter.

To the charge of murdering Pat, Mrs. Cogdon pleaded not guilty. Her story, though somewhat bizarre, was not seriously challenged by the Crown, and led to her acquittal. She told how, on the night before her daughter's death, she had dreamed that their house was full of spiders and that these spiders were crawling all over Pat. In her sleep, Mrs. Cogdon left the bed she shared with her husband, went into Pat's room, and awakened to find herself violently brushing at Pat's face, presumably to remove the spiders. This woke Pat. Mrs. Cogdon told her she was just tucking her in. At the trial, Mrs. Cogdon testified that she had been told and still believed that the occupants of a nearby house bred spiders as a hobby, preparing nests for them behind pictures on their walls. It was these spiders that in her dreams had invaded their home and attacked Pat. Mrs. Cogdon had also had a previous dream in which ghosts sat at the end of her bed and she said to them, "Well, you have come to take Pattie." It did not seem fanciful to accept the psychological explanations of these spiders and ghosts as the projections of Mrs. Cogdon's subconscious hostility toward her daughter, a hostility that was itself rooted in Mrs. Cogdon's own early life and marital relationship.

The morning after the spider dream, Mrs. Cogdon told her doctor about it. He gave her a sedative and, because of the dream and certain previous difficulties she had reported, discussed the possibility of psychiatric treatment. That evening Mrs. Cogdon suggested to her husband that he attend his lodge meeting, and asked Pat to come with her to the cinema. After he had gone, Pat looked through the paper, found no tolerable program, and said that, as she was going out the next evening, she thought she would rather go to bed early. Later, while Pat was having a bath preparatory to retiring, Mrs. Cogdon went into her room, put a hot water bottle in the bed, turned back the bedclothes, and placed a glass of hot milk beside the bed ready for Pat. She then went to bed herself. There was some desultory conversation between them, and just before she put out her light, Pat called to her mother, "Mum, don't be so silly worrying there about the war, it's not on our front door step yet."

Mrs. Cogdon went to sleep. She dreamed that "the war was all around the house," that soldiers were in Pat's room, and that one soldier was on the bed attacking Pat. This was all of the dream she could later recapture. Her first "waking" memory was of running from Pat's room, out of the house to the home of her sister who lived next door. When her sister opened the front door, Mrs. Cogdon fell against her, crying, "I think I've hurt Pattie." In fact Mrs. Cogdon had, in her somnambulistic state, left her bed, fetched an ax from the wood heap, entered Pat's room, and struck her two accurate forceful blows on the head with the blade of the ax, thus killing her.

Mrs. Cogdon's story was supported by the evidence of her physician, a psychiatrist, and a psychologist. The burden of the evidence of all three, which was not contested by the prosecution, was that Mrs. Cogdon had a form of hysteria with an overlay of depression, and that she was of a personality in which such dissociated states as fugues, amnesias, and somnambulistic acts were to be expected. They agreed that she was not psychotic. They hazarded no statement as to her motives, the idea of defense of the daughter being transparently insufficient. However, the psychologist and the psychiatrist concurred in hinting that the emotional motivation lay in an acute conflict situation in Mrs. Cogdon's relations with her parents; that during marital life she suffered very great sexual frustration; and that she overcompensated for her own frustration by overprotection of her daughter. Her exaggerated solicitude for her daughter was a conscious expression of her subconscious emotional hostility to her, and the dream ghosts, spiders, and soldiers were projections of that aggression.

The jury believed Mrs. Cogdon's story and regarded the natural consequences of her acts as being completely rebutted by her account of her mental state at the time of the killing and by the unanimous support given to it by the medical and psychological evidence. She was acquitted. It must be stressed that insanity was not pleaded as a defense—Mrs. Cogdon was acquitted because the act of killing itself was not, in law, regarded as her act at all.

As stated in the case documents, this case "illustrates the impossibility of . . . satisfactorily . . . sever[ing] 'act' from 'intention.' . . . Thus, Mrs. Cogdon's action not being 'voluntary,' no question of criminal liability arose. . . . Mrs. Cogdon escapes basically because of the state of her consciousness; not because she had no conscious intention or rational motive to kill, a state she shares with many convicted murderers. She was "asleep"; had she been "awake" her only defense would have been one of insanity.

But the difference between being asleep and awake is not absolute. Consciousness is not like a light, either off or on; it is a finely graded scale ranging from death to the extreme awareness of the artist. Only instruments such as an EEG can chart certain variations of consciousness between people and in one person at different times. Had Mrs. Cogdon been awake—that is, just a little more conscious, a little more aware of her actions, then her act may have had to be regarded as voluntary. The line is an extremely fine one, as is shown by the fact that in and during her dream Mrs. Cogdon was "aware" of the ax, her daughter, and the soldiers. Not unexpectedly, she could not remember this part of the dream after the event, for often people struggle to repress profoundly disturbing and shocking memory traces. Thus all people dream, but some, for various reasons, remember more than others. Nor would Mrs. Cogdon's position have been legally different even if she could have then recalled all the dream, including the killing. Her exculpation lay not in the state of her memory but in her inability to bring into consciousness her emotional motivations and, consequently, her diminished awareness of the deed.

Hormonal Theories

Another group of cases raising issues of altered biology in connection with a homicide are those related to hormonally altered states at the time of the homicidal act.

Premenstrual syndrome. One recent area of disagreement has centered on the diagnosis of premenstrual syndrome (PMS) and its relationship to violence. This is not an official diagnosis in DSM-IV, and it is listed in an appendix for categories for which there is insufficient information to warrant inclusion as an official diagnosis. Hence, DSM-IV lists it as "Research criteria for premenstrual dysphoric disorder." The argument rages as heavily as the hormones themselves are alleged to rage. Those who argue affirmatively hold that PMS is a hormone deficiency state that renders perpetrators unable to control their actions when these symptoms are present. Some now describe PMS as a mental disorder, but this is contrary to its use as a legal defense.[31] The medical profession continues to have diverse views about whether PMS is a syndrome or an illness.

One analogy drawn is between PMS and the phenomenon described over the centuries as postpartum psychosis and infanticide. Presentations of postpartum psychosis can vary from mild depression to outright delusional states with hallucinations. The occurrence of postpartum symptoms only a few days to months after parturition suggests an etiology based on hormonal alterations, although, again, psychosocial stressors cannot be ignored. However, the argument does not stop with the suggestion of hormone alterations. It is alleged that the behavior from such a physiological disturbance does not fit the pattern of a mental illness, and the acts are more in the nature of automatistic acts. PMS merits further discussion in view of its increasing publicity and in anticipation of its increased future use in legal settings. Medical testimony, as well as critiques by social commentators, will be the deciding factors in its use or abandonment until more definitive court rulings are obtained.

Some feminist critiques have raised questions regarding the disease status of PMS. Their objection to seeing PMS as a specific hormonal imbalance that can be medically managed is that it is an overly simplistic and premature explanation. Such an approach views the problem in terms of a body needing repair rather than someone immersed in a gender-based social system that induces problems. Others challenge that PMS is not a valid clinical entity, and that the causal explanations proffered to account for its syndrome status are insufficient. Those arguing in favor of it being viewed as a disorder are seen as biased in their observations and explanations leading toward a linear, reductionist type of thinking. Questions have also been raised about reports cited in support of establishing a premenstrual syndrome. Many of these reports lacked control subjects; some research suggested no difference between hormonal profiles of females alleged to have PMS and those who do not. Other investigators have confused statistical variation connected with premenstrual changes with the presence of an abnormal state.

Different studies have produced a seemingly endless list of symptoms compatible with almost any diagnosis, or with no diagnosis in particular. One study listed 150 symptoms categorized into five groups: affective, neurovegetative, central nervous system, cognitive, and behavioral disturbances.[32] When any of these occur in the premenstrual period, the supposition is that the symptoms are attributable to the syndrome. In 1961, Dalton studied 156 English women who were incarcerated and who had committed a crime in the previous 28 days.[33] She divided the menstrual cycle into 7 four-day segments and found that 49% of the women were either in the premenstrual phase (4 days before menstruation) or menstruating (the next 4 days) at the time of their crimes. Her conclusion was that hormonal changes (e.g., increased aggression, irritability, labile emotions, lethargy, carelessness) either caused the actions or impaired their ability to avoid detection. However, Horney challenged this interpretation by arguing that committing the criminal acts, and the stress of arrest and imprisonment, could trigger early menstruation.[34] In addition, she pointed out that 155 of the 156 women had been convicted of nonviolent crimes. The safe conclusion is that the symptoms of PMS as an explanation for violent crime is more correlated with publicity than empirical data.

Other considerations with regard to hormonal factors. There is merit in investigating the possibility that some type of hormonal changes occur in relation to an individual's proneness to violence. However, several impediments also exist in documenting relevant hormonal levels and their effect on an individual's actions. Investigations into the connection between hormones and violence often attempt to determine whether higher levels of certain hormones are present in those who exhibit violent behavior. However, the simplicity of such research may conceal many of the medicolegal problems that can arise from too easy causal attributions.

For example, establishing a murderer's hormonal levels at random intervals does not indicate whether the level may actually have been abnormal at the time of the murder. In addition, simply obtaining a hormone level at any one time does not reflect the totality of the individual's endocrine functioning; the complex interactions within the hypothalamic-pituitary-gonadal system must also be considered, such as concentrations of hormones in the brain, low levels of neurotransmitters, different sensitivities at receptor sites, and postreceptor effects.

There is also the confounding influence of alcohol and nonmedical drugs that can alter results of hormonal assays and blood levels of certain sexual hormones. Another possibility is the connection between hormonal levels and diverse, endocrine diseases (e.g., diabetes with hypoglycemic episodes, Cushing's syndrome, hyperthyroidism).

Results from a Swedish study of "normal" 16-year-old adolescents, in which the subjects reported on their verbal and physical aggression in response to what they saw as provocations, indicated a significant association between the aggressive behaviors and plasma testosterone levels.[35] A few years earlier, investigators had found elevated levels of plasma testosterone in 52 rapists and child molesters.[36] The level of testosterone was correlated with the degree of violence and the symptoms self-reported on an inventory. In a later study, some of those same investigators found no significant differences in testosterone levels between a control group and the violent group.[37] Again, a major deficit in such studies is that the level of hormones at the time of the violent act is not available. Although it may be deemed impossible that such levels could be accurately attained, the inference is nevertheless made by advocates that the hormonal level could have been abnormal at the time of the violence.

Critics of any hormone-violence causal relation argue that diverse causes are possible for violence even when altered plasma levels of hormones are found, and that no causal connection can be drawn between elevated hormonal levels and violence. Perhaps this is why authors of many improvised studies using subjects from prison populations have failed to find significant correlations. At a minimum, a baseline level of androgens would have to be established for the participants in these studies. Of those studies that have focused on hormonal levels and violence, at least three have found no connection. One group of investigators found that, when a synthetic form of progesterone or estrogen was administered to sex offenders, it had no noticeable effect on their aggressive behavior.[38] Another group who studied thousands of hostile patients in state hospitals concluded that there was no difference between men and women in such studies.[39] Similarly, researchers in a later study failed to find any differences in androgen levels, particularly testosterone, among murderers, assaulters, and a control group.[40]

Green, in the book *Sexual Science and the Law,* thoroughly reviewed the simplistic thinking that leads to attempts to control serious sexual violence either by way of surgical or hormonal castration.[41] Proponents of such intervention have argued that by blocking the effects of androgen, there should be a blocking of sexual behavior and presumably any connected violence. Unfortunately, the degree of aggression and testosterone levels are poorly correlated. Although results from some European studies on surgical castration have indicated less recidivism in castrated sex offenders compared with those who did not undergo such treatment, the results have been variable, especially if carried out on young males. There would also be much legal and social objection to such procedures in the United States. As a result, studies in the United States have focused on treating sex offenders with medroxyprogesterone acetate (Depo-Provera) and outside the United States with cyproterone acetate (CPA). One difficulty in discussing this work with respect to homicidal violence is that the legal category of sex offenders is extremely heterogenous, and only a small number of offenders have acted in homicidal ways. Hence, if these drugs can reduce homicidal levels of violence in connection with sexual acts is unknown.

Critical analyses could similarly be presented with regard to other hypotheses about hormonal possibilities, such as those involving the hypothalamic-pituitary axis, the thyroid, or the adrenal glands.

Posttraumatic Stress Disorder

Consideration of automatisms possibly related to seizure disorders or altered hormonal states has now been extended to consideration of posttraumatic stress disorder (PTSD) as an exculpating (or at least mitigating) condition with respect to homicidal behavior. The reasoning behind this concept is that some type of traumatic event occurs that alters the physiological, as well as the typical psychological, functioning of an individual (see discussion of abused persons in Chapter 7). A host of symptoms are then said to emerge, such as memory loss, sleep impairment, nightmares, reliving of the traumatic event, intrusive thoughts, exaggerated startle response, decreased emotional responsiveness, feelings of alienation, and dissociative conditions. In the latter state, the individual is portrayed as reliving the event as if he or she were once more present as a participant. Such reasoning was promoted originally for veterans of the Vietnam War who had been in combat, were self-medicating themselves with narcotics or alcohol, and who subsequently committed violent assaults, including homicides. The automatism defense was often raised in this context using this diagnosis. Although the concept of a traumatic neurosis is not new, its use in this form as exculpatory for homicides has been.

Individuals involved in diverse types of traumas may have come from unfortunate social backgrounds. These traumas of developmental origin are used to argue that a homicide occurred during an automatized state because the individual was predisposed to the violence from the childhood traumas. The possible traumas that can be used for legal defense purposes are endless and include the following: past physical alterations that induced a traumatic state; being assaulted; fearing repeated assaults and, hence, having a need to strike out first; and being abused as a child in either a physical, sexual, or emotional manner.

The idea of automatized homicides associated with earlier traumas may be extended to include homicides occurring subsequent to the emergence of multiple personalities or brainwashing events. However, assertions that an automatism defense is equivalent to that provided by "a disease of the mind" are questionable. This branches into quite a different pathway in terms of a legal defense, and for what follows if this defense is successful in court against homicide charges. There would be minimal justification, in the absence of any disease, to engage in a civil commitment process and hospitalize someone for a stress syndrome after such an acquittal.

Hypoglycemic States

Similar complexities beset the assessment of hypotheses about a connection between hypoglycemic states and violent behavior. Studies of this relationship are often not comparable, with some referring to violent behavior, others to states of aggressiveness, and others to antisocial behavior. Some simply report the presence of irritability associated with hypoglycemic episodes. A distinction is also made between the sources of hypoglycemia, such as from physiological variations after an excessive release of insulin on a postprandial basis (also called functional hypoglycemia) in contrast to a state of fasting hypoglycemia, which may be associated with islet cell tumors or chronic alcohol abuse. The only safe conclusion at present about hypoglycemic states is that such states are only one of many other variables operating in aggressive behavior, including personality variables as well as the entire phenomenon of interpersonal reactions present in many social situations. Although a rare case of extreme violence may be connected with hypoglycemia, it is so entwined with other factors that it is difficult to achieve any causal specificity.

Role of Neurotransmitters

Some current hypotheses have focused on serotonergic neurotransmitter processes. Since Asberg et al.'s 1976 study, in which it was found that patients with the lowest level cerebrospinal fluid (CSF) 5-hydroxyindoleacetic acid (5-HIAA) concentrations were most likely to attempt or commit suicide by violent means,[42] there have been subsequent studies. Investigators in one study reported CSF 5-HIAA concentrations as being inversely related to the incidence of overtly aggressive behaviors.[43] Rather than being used to focus on a specific diagnosis, the question of altered serotonin metabolism has entered the picture in attempts to explain violence. Two other groups assessed CSF 5-HIAA levels in men connected with a homicide and men who had attempted a suicide.[44,45] Both groups found that lower levels of CSF 5-HIAA prevailed in those with a history of aggressive behavior as well as suicidal behavior. Maiuro and Eberle studied men who had killed or attempted to kill in a cruel manner, after first excluding those with diagnoses of schizophrenia or major affective disorders, and found that the remainder had a lower level of CSF 5-HIAA.[46] Brown et al. reported that young adults with low levels of CSF 5-HIAA tended to have a childhood history of aggressive conduct disorder that included acts such as lying, stealing, killing a pet animal in a rage, and impulsive fire setting.[47]

Exactly what implications the results from these studies have for homicidal violence are unclear, although stimulating findings continue to be made involving altered serotonin metabolism, as well as altered levels of dopamine and noradrenaline. The basic idea is that something has gone awry with serotonin metabolism, whatever the attached diagnosis might be, and that the serotonergic aberration may represent a state or trait phenomenon. Recently, investigators confirmed that a selective deficiency of the enzyme monoamine oxidase A with a point mutation in the structural gene on the X chromosome existed in a group of five males with borderline mental retardation and impulsive aggression.[48] Given that earlier work had focused on the idea of a serotonin deficiency (also called low serotonin syndrome) in cases of violent behavior, this work raises a question about the possibility of the opposite from the oxidase impairment.

Cerebral Hemisphere Dysfunctions

The increase in research at the micro level looking for genetic aberrations related to neurochemical difficulties on the macro level is fairly recent; however, research on aberrant functioning in the cerebral hemispheres, in which anatomical and physiological factors relevant to violence have been studied, has had a much longer history. This latter type of research has waxed and waned over the past century.

The founder of the school of positivistic criminology, Cesare Lombroso, in the nineteenth century, sought to find signs of degeneracy in criminals. He focused on lateral asymmetries, such as abnormal asymmetries in the face and imbalances in the cerebral hemispheres.[49] In fact, the positivist revolution has been extended from its origins in biology to the current state of biological criminology. Earlier precursors have been related to phrenological thinking in which the assumption was that an abnormal exterior skull reflected an abnormal interior. It was also held that an abnormal anatomy would imply abnormal physiological functioning. The failure to confirm this type of theorizing as time went on led to its abandonment and ridicule. However, the idea that something could be impaired in the cerebral hemispheres of someone who committed a violent act such as murder has never gone away.

Currently, researchers see a biological abnormality as perhaps one variable among many that can produce an individual vulnerable to violent acts. More recent hemispheric research has delineated differential features between the functioning of the left and right hemispheres, with the left operating in the area of sequential information processing on a verbal level, and the right hemisphere functioning on the level of mediating spacial stimuli. In the early 1970s, Flor-Henry questioned whether psychopathy was associated with left hemisphere disturbances.[50] In a subsequent study, Yeudall found 72% of violent criminals had left hemisphere dysfunction compared with 79% of nonviolent criminals, who had a right hemisphere dysfunction.[51] Yeudall's study was subsequently criticized on the basis that the subjects studied were gathered from a criminal population, which would be expected to have a greater loading of individuals with neurological abnormalities, and that the criteria used to diagnose hemispheric dysfunction were not specifically spelled out.[52]

Along this same line, Nachshon and Denno investigated the hypothesis that "delinquent subjects" would show a higher incidence of left-sidedness compared with a control group when measured in terms of hand, eye, and foot preferences.[53] Although delinquent subjects may be a long way from homicidal subjects, one of the six groups Nachshon and Denno studied was classified as very violent. This group showed a significantly higher incidence of left eye preference, interpreted as a left hemisphere dysfunction by the authors. These results did not demonstrate that such a hemispheric asymmetry exists in someone who murders; however, their results and other empirical studies are intriguing because of the paucity of much experimental data dealing with extreme human violence.

Although it would be presumptuous to jump to a conclusion that a statistical association between hemispheric dysfunction and certain kinds of violence establishes any kind of causal relationship, certain questions about the meaning of the statistical association are raised. One possibility is that a right hemisphere dysfunction could impinge on emotionality, which would contribute to impulse control problems. A left-sided hemisphere dysfunction could upset the role and use of language and coping skills in controlling violent impulses. Foresight and anticipation could also thereby be impaired, perhaps as seen in the prevalent diagnosis among male children of attention-deficit hyperactivity disorder. These types of deficits become more ominous as adolescence is approached, and in some people continue their effects into adulthood. Perhaps this all leads back to questions about frontal lobe syndrome, the effects of head injury, early childhood head injuries, an individual's proneness to overreact to alcohol, frontal lobe connections to the anterior-temporal cortex, and hippocampal-amygdala areas connected to some type of central nervous system diathesis for violence. Deficits in these processes tend to alter the way an individual perceives the world and uses techniques to adapt and cope. In that sense, they interfere with the effectiveness of psychological mechanisms and defenses and lead to it being more difficult for controls to be exerted. In a primary preventive sense, it means that, for this subgroup, it is crucial to determine what prenatal, perinatal, and postnatal factors may induce such deficits. In a secondary preventive sense, it means that social and emotional assets can sometimes limit the effect of these disabilities. This is where traditional emphases on ameliorating socioeconomic conditions, resolution of family conflicts, intervention with special schooling and counseling for those with deficits in cognitive functioning, and supportive therapies have been used. However, the consistent uses of these interventions at a high caliber of performance, and over an extended duration of time, has limited their effectiveness in a majority of cases.

In more recent times, biological explanations have turned away from the hemispheres and toward chromosomes. The example of the "supermale" XYY chromosome is instructive. The theory was posited that an extra Y male chromosome suggested hypermaleness; therefore, increased aggression and the expectation of increased violence with those having the extra chromosome seemed as reasonable as Lombroso's ideas 100 years earlier.[54] This explanation was suggested by initial investigations into the connection between chromosomal abnormalities and violence, in which investigators often relied on prison populations and used flawed methodology. The media sensationalized reports of hypermale killers throughout the 1960s and 1970s, particularly after Richard Speck, who murdered eight nurses, was inaccurately described in the media as being an XYY male. Later studies examining XYY males found the results of early studies to be inconsistent. Since then, studies using random populations have failed to confirm the XYY-violence hypothesis.[55] Questions remain as to whether XYY males have a heightened probability of impulsivity that could contribute to violent behavior.

∎ Conclusion

Flaws in most neuropsychological and neuropsychiatric research on violent behavior in themselves make generalizations precarious. Moffitt has done a thorough analysis of these limitations, which can only be highlighted here.[56] In most research involving crime, the lack of an adequate control group is striking. Certainly this is true for studies of extreme degrees of violence, such as homicides. At the other end are clinical reports that, at best, offer excellent insights and hypotheses. In fact, perhaps congruent with positivistic criminology, the more microscopic the examination of an individual murderer, the more difficult it is to generalize beyond what may seem idiosyncratic. Although killing is still a relatively rare event, it does mean that there is often a conflict between seeking in-depth knowledge about why a particular individual behaved in that manner versus knowledge using larger numbers and listing diverse variables.

In empirical studies, which often emphasize methodology and statistical analysis, those included in "violent groups" are almost always males, which parallels their prevalence in any study of crime. However, there is a comparative lack of data for females. A more serious flaw is that there are rarely adequate controls for demographic and environmental data. Some studies do not even give the age, gender, or race of those studied. The range of ages in studies may be enormous. In some communities, race has been eliminated from databases on the premise that collecting such data in itself is an example of racism rather than an attempt to isolate significant variables to remedy the situation. Although socioeconomic status may be given, the impact of this variable on prenatal or perinatal factors is often ignored.

What is inescapable in studies of homicidal violence is that studying the perpetrators is always a retrospective event. Although it would be possible to do some longitudinal prospective studies, these would focus on certain behaviors and traits related to aggression and violent behavior. Such studies have been done, but they would be next to impossible to obtain for a group for potential homicide perpetrators. The limitations of data obtained from someone awaiting trial for a homicide or raising an insanity defense have long been known. Similar limitations exist for studying those in prisons or mental hospitals who have committed homicides.

Where do these quandaries leave us? In one of the most complete models of studying future adult criminality, it was found that biological and environmental variables can predict only 25% of future adult criminality for males and 19% for females.[57] I note that, although statistical significance was attained in the study, it still left 75%–81% of the criminal behaviors unexplained. I question whether, despite the statistical techniques in that study being as good or better than most social science studies, varying degrees of free will and determinism must be acknowledged with respect to criminal actions. It also means that it should be realized that dichotomies between the biological and social factors are passé.

■ References

1. McDougall W: An Introduction to Social Psychology. New York, Barnes & Noble, 1960

2. Bibring E: The development and problems of the theory of the instincts. Int J Psychoanal 22:102–131, 1941

5. Lorenz KZ: On Aggression. New York, Harcourt, Brace & World, 1966

6. Tinbergen N: The Study of Instinct. Oxford, Clarendon Press, 1951

8. Kupfermann I: Genetic determinants of behavior, in Principles of Neural Science, 3rd Edition. Edited by Kandel ER, Schwartz JH, Jessel TM. New York, Elsevier, 1991, pp 1987–1008

9. Pardes H, Kaufmann CA, Pincus HA, et al: Genetics and psychiatry: past discoveries, current dilemmas, and future directions. Am J Psychiatry 146:435–443, 1989

10. Mark VH, Ervin FR: Violence and the Brain. New York, Harper & Row, 1970

12. Pincus JH, Tucker GJ: Behavioral Neurology, 3rd Edition. New York, Oxford University Press, 1985

13. Crichton M: The Terminal Man. New York, Knopf, 1972

14. Delgado-Escueta AV, Mattson RH, King L, et al: The nature of aggression during epileptic seizures. N Engl J Med 305:711–716, 1981

15. Hermann BP, Whitman S: Behavioral and personality correlates of epilepsy: a review, methodologicol critique and conceptual model. Psychol Bull 95:451–497, 1984

16. Monroe RR: Behavioral Disorders. Cambridge, MA, Harvard University Press, 1970

17. Leicester J: Temper tantrums, epilepsy and episodic dyscontrol. Br J Psychiatry 141:262–266, 1982

18. Weiger B, Bear D: An approach to the neurology of aggression. J Psychiatr Res 22:85–89, 1988

19. Tonkonogy JM: Violence and temporal lobe lesion: head CT and MRI data. J Neuropsychiatry Clin Neurosci 3:189–196 1991

20. Whitman S, Hermann B, Black R, et al: Psychopathology and seizure type in children with epilepsy. Psychol Med 12:843–853, 1982

21. Achenbach T, Edelbrock C: Manual for the Child Behavior Checklist and Revised Child Behavior Profile. Burlington, VT, Thomas M Achenbach, 1983

22. Lewis DO, Pincus JH, Shanok SS, et al: Psychomotor epilepsy and violence in a group of incarcerated adolescent boys. Am J Psychiatry 139:882–887, 1982

23. Herman BP, Whitman S: Behavioral and personality correlates of epilepsy: a review, methodological critique and conceptual model. Psychol Bull 95:451–497, 1984

24. Mendez MF, Doss RC, Taylor JL: Interictal violence in epilepsy. J Nerv Ment Dis 181:566–569, 1993

25. Raine A: The Psychopathology of Crime: Criminal Behavior as a Clinical Disorder. New York, Academic Press, 1993

26. Tonkonogy JM: Violence and temporal lesion: head CT and MRI data. Journal of Neuropsychiatry 3:189–196, 1991

27. Gunn J: Medical-legal aspects of epilepsy, in Epilepsy and Psychiatry. Edited by Reynolds EH, Trimble MR. Edinburgh, UK, Churchill, Livingstone, 1981, pp 165–174

28. People v Grant, 46 Ill App 125, 360, NE 2d 809 (1977)

29. Model Penal Code, Section 2.01, American Law Institute, Philadelphia, 1962

30. Morris N: Somnambulistic homicide: ghosts, spiders, and North Koreans. Res Judicate 5:29–32, 1951

31. Severino SK, Moline MJ: Premenstrual Syndrome: A Clinician's Guide (Diagnoses and Treatment of Mental Disorders). New York, Guilford, 1989

32. Moos RH: A typology of menstrual cycle symptoms. Am J Obstet Gynecol 103:390–402, 1969

33. Dalton K: Menstruation and crime. British Hedical Journal 2:1752–1753, 1961

34. Horney J: Menstrual cycles and criminal responsibility. Law and Human Behavior 2:25–36, 1978

35. Olwens D, Mattsson A, Schalling D, et al: Testosterone, aggression, physical and personality dimensions in normal adolescent males. Psychosom Med 42:253–269, 1980

36. Rada RT, Laws DR, Kellner R, et al: Personal testosterone levels in the rapist. Psychosom Med 38:257–268, 1976

37. Rada RT, Kellner R, Stivastava C, et al: Plasma androgens in violent and nonviolent sex offenders. Journal of the American Academy of Psychiatry and the Law 11:149–158, 1983

38. Money J, Daléry J: Sexual disorders: hormonal and drug therapy, in Handbook of Sexology. Edited by Money J, Musaph H. Amsterdam, Elsevier/North Holland, 1977, pp 1303–1310

39. Tardiff K, Sweillam A: Assault, suicide and mental illness. Arch Gen Psychiatry 37:164–169, 1980

40. Bain J, Langevin R, Dickey R, et al: Sex hormones in murderers and assaulters. Behavioral Sciences and the Law 5:95–101, 1987

41. Green R: Sexual Science and the Law. Cambridge, MA, Harvard University Press, 1992

42. Asberg M, Traskman L, Thoren P: 5-HIAA in the cerebrospinal fluid: a suicide predictor? Arch Gen Psychiatry 33:1193–1197, 1976

43. Brown GL, Goodwin FK, Ballenger JC, et al: Aggression in human correlates with cerebrospinal fluid amine metabolites. Psychiatry Res 1:131–139, 1979

44. Lidberg L, Tuck JR, Asberg M, et al: Homicide, suicide and CSF-5-HIAA. Acta Psychiatr Scand 71:230–236, 1985

45. Linnolia M, Virkkunen M, Scheinin M, et al: Low cerebrospinal fluid 5-hydroxyindole-acetic acid concentration differentiates impulsive from nonimpulsive violent behavior. Life Sci 33:2609–2914, 1983

46. Maiuro RD, Eberle JA: New developments in research on aggression: an international report. Violence and Victims 4:3–15, 1989

47. Brown G, Kline W, Goyer P, et al: Relationship of childhood characteristics to cerebrospinal fluid 5-hydroxyindoleacetic acid in aggressive adults, in Proceedings of World Congress of Biological Psychiatry, Vol 7. Edited by Shagass C, Josiassen R, Bridger W, et al. New York, Elsevier, 1985, pp 177–179

48. Brunner HG, Nelen M, Breakefield XO, et al: Abnormal behavior associated with a point mutation in the structural gene for monoamine oxidase A. Science 262:578–580, 1993

49. Gottfredson MR, Hirschi T: A General Theory of Crime. Stanford, CA, Stanford University Press, 1990

50. Flor-Henry P: On certain aspects of the localization of the central systems regulating and determining emotion. Biol Psychiatry 14:677–698, 1979

51. Yeudall LT: A neuropsychological perspective of persistent juvenile delinquency and criminal behavior discussant, in Forensic Psychology and Psychiatry. Edited by Wright F, Bahn C, Reiber RW. New York, Annals of the New York Academy of Sciences, 1980, pp 349–355

52. Hare RD: Psychopathy and laterality of cerebral function. J Abnorm Psychol 88:605–610, 1979

53. Nachshon I, Denno D: Violent behavior and cerebral hemisphere function, in The Causes of Crime: New Biological Approaches. Edited by Mednick SA, Moffitt TE, Stack SA. New York, Cambridge University Press, 1987, pp 185–217

54. Sarbin TR, Miller JE: Demonism revisited: the XYY chromosomal anomaly. Issues in Criminology 5:195–207, 1970

55. Witkin HA, Mednick SA, Schulsinger F, et al: Criminality, aggression and intelligence among XYY and XXY men, in Biosocial Bases of Criminal Behavior. Edited by Mednick SA, Christiansen KO. New York, Gardner Press, 1977, pp 165–188

56. Moffitt TE: The neuropsychology of delinquency: a critical review of theory and research, in Crime and Justice: An Annual Review of Research, Vol 12. Edited by Morris N, Tonry M. Chicago, IL, University of Chicago Press, 1990, pp 99–120

57. Denno DW: Biology and Violence: From Birth to Adulthood. New York, Cambridge University Press, 1990

CHAPTER 3

Schizophrenia, Delusional Disorders, and the Prediction Problem Regarding Homicides

The problem of determining the relationship between homicide and schizophrenia is a subset of the broader problem of the relationship between violence and any type of mental illness. Making valid and reliable predictive statements about such a relationship is an elusive process. Some homicides are bizarre and can only be understood in the context of psychotic thought processes. Schizophrenic individuals or individuals with a blatant delusional system are often thought of as being "crazy," with the media sometimes helping to foster this image. The connotation is that that these people are running loose in the community and likely to be violent. One persistent scientific question, then, is, Why is it so difficult to predict homicidal violence within this group of individuals who may be so disturbed? It is understandable that it is difficult to predict violence occurring in connection with other types of mental disorders, as individuals with those disorders do not act so strikingly bizarre, but it would seem that it should be easier to make predictions in connection with schizo-phrenia.

■ Public Image of Mentally Ill Individuals as Being Crazy

Males and, to an increasing extent, females, who have engaged in various types of killings for which the motive has never been clarified are often simply placed in an amorphous category of "crazy killers." This popular image of mentally ill people as being violent is shaped by the endless stream of novels involving violence and killing, as well as television portrayals that are constructed or based on actual killings. It was easy to see how this image was reinforced during the past century, at least up through the 1950s, when mentally ill patients were involun-tarily committed to mental hospitals, and the public saw them as a group of strange people that needed to be isolated from the rest of the community.

However, one might have thought that, over the last 30 years, as mentally ill patients have gradually been moved into communities and been maintained there with psychotropic medications, the public's increased contact with them might have ameliorated their image prob-lem. In reality, the assumption behind deinstitutionalization that these patients would be effectively treated in the community setting has largely remained unfulfilled, with the result that large numbers of homeless, victimized, mentally ill individuals live on the streets of all major American cities and cannot access needed treatment. Thus dein-stitutionalization may have had the opposite effect on the public; rather than revising their image of mentally ill patients, members of the public, who lack the tools for understanding the plight of these people, have become more frightened from their increased encounters with them. It should be noted that the image of mentally deranged individu-als or "lunatics" being violent evolved in earlier centuries—a good deal earlier than the institution of involuntary hospitalization processes. Hence, it is not likely that the image problem will abate in the near future, either.

Still, the question remains as to whether mentally ill individuals merely carry the image of being crazy people and being more homicidally violent, or whether they actually are. Depending on the answer to this question, several specific implications are presented. One is whether the social policy and legal decisions that have shifted large numbers of mentally ill people into the community have been correct. If it is established that mentally ill individuals do in fact commit an inordinate number of homicidal acts, then community policies, practices for releasing mentally ill individuals into the community, and current civil commitment criteria will need to be reexamined.

An interesting paradox arises when a comparison is made between mentally ill individuals who have committed violent acts and non–mentally ill individuals who have committed sexual offenses. Courts have upheld statutes and legislation related to psychopathic individuals who commit sexual crimes that allow them to be detained long after their criminal sentences have expired.[1] Their extended confinement is justified on the pretext of a civil commitment process based on their alleged dangerousness, even though they have never been diagnosed with a major mental illness and treatment results for this legal category are questionable.

Similar questions may arise on how schizophrenic individuals who commit homicides should be handled by the criminal justice system, even those who reach a state of remission. It may be argued that schizophrenic individuals who commit homicides deserve sentences as long as those currently being imposed on other, non–mentally ill individuals convicted of homicide in the United States or even, in the case of first-degree murder, should be sentenced under the capital punishment statutes now on the books in 36 states. The public's desire for retribution accompanied by assumptions of schizophrenic individuals' potential and continued dangerousness can be powerful influences on those deciding on punishments in terms of a just-deserts model.

Studies of the prevalence of mental illness among homeless individuals have provided widely varying estimates, in part because the definitions of mental illness used are unclear. A further difficulty is that some studies on the prevalence of schizophrenia often exclude "street people" because they are more difficult to reach and include for survey purposes. Nonetheless, the studies that have been conducted seem to indicate that 30%–40% of homeless people may suffer from a major type of mental illness.[2] When bizarre homicidal acts occur in communities, glaring headlines and coverage may focus on this group, with the specious rationalization by civil libertarians that such acts reflect or should reflect community norms of "the right to be crazy." The New York case of Juan Gonzalez illustrates the problem. Juan had initially told the staff at a Manhattan shelter, "I am going to kill. God told me so. Jesus wants me to kill." After being sent to a hospital, he was released in 48 hours, and 48 additional hours later stabbed nine people aboard the Staten Island Ferry, resulting in two deaths. Another case that garnered publicity was that of Jorge Delgado, who clubbed an usher to death at St. Patrick's Cathedral in New York City after running through the church naked.[3] Similar cases, with their dramatization of bizarre homicidal violence, are found in every major American city.

■ Validity of Predicting Violence in Mentally Ill Individuals

Overextension of Psychiatric Expertise

The increasing interdependence of the legal and the mental health systems over time has become a double-edged sword. Psychiatric expertise has been expanded into areas beyond civil commitment and not-guilty-by-reason-of-insanity issues, such as in the areas of diverse competency questions, assessment of sex offenders' responsibility for their acts, assessment of sex offenders for treatment programs, or matters of sentencing and release from penal institutions or mental hospitals. Psychiatrists, and increasingly other mental health workers, are asked to assess individuals' dangerousness as well as diagnose any mental illnesses. The consequences of psychiatrists and others being asked to do more than they were obliged to do or might be capable of, in what many consider to be an overextension of their expertise, has been inevitable. For example, psychiatrists have begun to be held legally accountable for missing predictions of homicidal violence. Perhaps this turn of events was inevitable, given the legal cases in which psychiatrists (and other mental health personnel in similar roles) have been found to have a duty to warn third parties of possible violence from patients. This legal burden was subsequently expanded to the principle of the "duty to protect" others, in which a psychiatrist was to make a prediction of violence so that third parties would not be injured.

The academic problem of prediction must be distinguished from the practical one. Whether psychiatrists, or anyone else, can theoretically make valid predictions about the future occurrence of homicidal violence should be sharply distinguished from the practical situation of not making such a prediction and then subsequently being held legally liable for violating a duty to warn or to protect the victim.[4] The denial of having such predictive talents goes to the issue of attempting to deny legal liability in malpractice cases for erroneous predictions or failure to make such predictions. The latter situation has been amply discussed, subsequent to the initial California case involving Tatiana Tarasoff, who was murdered by her ex-boyfriend several months after she broke off their relationship.[5] The mentally ill boyfriend had revealed his murderous thoughts to a psychologist at a student health service; the psychologist then notified the campus police, urging them to hospitalize the man. The police felt they had no basis to hospitalize him, but it was later held that the psychologist and supervising psychiatrist could be considered liable for not warning Ms. Tarasoff that her life was potentially in danger. The reasoning, after the fact, was that the clinicians should have been able to predict the homicide, at least to the extent that they should warn the people who were enmeshed in the patient's delusional, and violent thoughts.

The validity of making such predictions has been challenged on both legal and clinical grounds. The initial legal attack was a constitutional one, involving the use of the standard of dangerousness in the civil commitment of mentally ill individuals. The validity of a dangerousness standard of prediction was challenged both on substantive and due process grounds; in the latter arena, it was argued that the process of making such predictions could lead to an unreasonable deprivation of liberty.

One by-product of the legal misuse of the prediction of dangerousness standard as the criterion used for civil commitment by courts and legislative enactments from the 1970s onward was the increasing tendency to turn mental hospitals into facilities whose primary purpose was the detention of those who were labeled mentally ill and dangerous rather than the treatment of mentally ill individuals. The result of this change was clearly described by Stone, who referred to those "incarcerated" in the hospital system as a modal mental hospital population comprised of the mentally ill who were thought to be dangerous that evolved as a result of these policies.[6] Thus the hospital populations began to consist primarily of males ages 20–40 years who floated among different mental hospitals, prisons, and the community. Many of these individuals presented the problem of having comorbid diagnoses and serious character disorders, mixed in with episodes of psychosis. Substance abuse and dependence were also often present. Individuals with these combined psychiatric and social disturbances have an increased potential of being violent as well as being more resistant to neuroleptic medication.

Ability to Achieve Only Weak Predictability

The initial theoretical denouement regarding the prediction of dangerousness by clinicians came in an article that used calculations to demonstrate that dangerousness was routinely overpredicted.[7] A basic problem in dealing with predicting homicidal violence is that it is a rare event, with a low base rate (i.e., a low incidence in the population). Because homicide itself is a rare event, there is an accompanying greater margin of error in predicting it. Consider a hypothetical case in which the incidence of killing in a community was 1:1,000, and that there was a test that could predict those incidences with 95% accuracy.[7] (Of course, no predictor test exists that is even close to making such accurate predictions, including those based on the best of any available clinicians' assessments or even actuarial tables.) Then, 100 of every 100,000 people would be killed, and the test would be able to predict 95 of those 100. However, another group of 4,995 people would be identified as potential killers who would not actually kill. To make sure no killer was on the loose, even with the 95% accurate instrument, the 95 plus 4,995 individuals would have to be segregated from the community. This means that 54 harmless people would be detained for every one who was, in fact, dangerous, for the community's safety to be ensured. Most individuals and groups would see this as an unacceptable standard.

By 1984, a "second generation" of predictors who had become less zealous in their predictions, recognizing the limits of accurate prediction, began to emerge.[8] It had been hoped initially, perhaps too optimistically, that violence prediction could be examined from a relative rather than an absolute moral-political position in which decisions to incapacitate people are not necessarily being made solely on clinical grounds.

Predictions of violence are customarily one of two types: clinical appraisals or statistical-actuarial methods. Clinical appraisals rely on the experience and professional expertise of decision makers. Statistical or actuarial appraisals rely on weighting key characteristics that are specified in advance, then using those scores to make a statistical prediction. Statistical techniques generate rules based on analyses of data from prior cases to measure the accuracy of such rules with respect to those prior cases as well as to future cases. To the surprise of many clinicians, the actuarial method comes out ahead as a predictive technique, even over the wisest of clinicians' judgments. One group of investigators reviewed nearly 100 comparative studies in the social science literature on the relative accuracy of clinical and statistical predictions of violence.[9] In every study, the actuarial method equaled or surpassed the clinical method, sometimes by a substantial margin. Those with some grounding in probability theory try to claim that such group statistics cannot apply to single individuals or events. Yet, to say that an individual has unique features not factored into the statistical prediction does not negate the possibility that he or she also has common features that feed into the generation of rules with predictive power.

The implication of the above discussion is that, if a bet were to be made about the best way to make predictions, the money should be placed on a statistical-actuarial approach. Such an approach would appear to have the greatest potential for a study of homicide prediction. Of course, even here the limitations on trying to predict that a schizophrenic individual will commit a homicide in the future overwhelmingly weigh against the predictions' accuracy. More recently, the trend has been to try to make much more limited types of predictions, such as whether someone will be violent in a psychiatric hospital unit, or what the relationship between a patient's admission symptoms and future assaultive behavior while an inpatient will be.[10] Even a recent attempt to achieve the narrow objective of determining which patients brought to an emergency room could have been predicted as being dangerous concluded only that certain state variables were associated with patient dangerousness, such as the immediate expression of hostility, agitation, impulsivity, hallucinations, or mania.[11] Demographic variables (e.g., age, gender, employment status) were not found to be related to patient violence when assessed in clinical settings. Note that these types of narrowly defined studies dealt with individuals already defined as raising some concern about violence by virtue of their being brought to the emergency room of a hospital. This is a long way from making predictions in an open society about a future homicide. It indicates how great a disparity exists between current scientific capability to make predictions and the expectations of predicting violence that have evolved within the legal system and the accountability that has been attached to those predictions.

■ Early Studies of Violence and Mental Illness

Definitional Problems

Articles addressing the relationship between mental illness and violence continue to flow. The original studies abounded in definitional and methodological problems. The term *violence* itself has been subjected to shades of interpretation, and many times a distinction between types and degrees of violence was not made beyond references to bodily contact between people. Some studies that focused on intrafamilial violence included slapping—of a spouse or a child—as an act of violence. Although slapping can be viewed as an act of violence at times, with such a definition it is not surprising that high figures are recorded. One example is the figure of 93% of American parents spanking their children to discipline them.[12] The use of physical force is believed to be widespread in American families involving not only children but spouses and elders.[13] At the opposite end, few of the studies have confined themselves to a homicidal level of violence, even with only one diagnosis in mind, such as schizophrenia. This raises a problem of having to extrapolate from various degrees of assaultive behaviors to homicides.

There are also problems in securing agreement on the definition and criteria used for mental illness. With respect to schizophrenia, past studies have used different criteria than current ones. Unresolved questions remain about what should be regarded as an illness (or disease) and what should be regarded as a disorder. Should studies be confined to acute psychotic episodes for schizophrenic individuals, or should they include a broader definition of anyone who was at one time diagnosed as schizophrenic? There is also the problem of comorbid disorders, such as the "intrusion" of diverse personality disorders into schizophrenia, and how to determine which diagnosis, or whether both diagnoses, operated with respect to a homicide. Unfortunately, for purposes of seeking explanations, a linear type of relationship has often been assumed in many studies, something that rarely exists in reality. Causal attribution is a much more complex state of affairs, but a much more realistic assumption.

Hospital Studies

The unreliability of many studies can be illustrated in early work that addressed the problem of mental illness and violence up to the mid-twentieth century. Authors of those studies usually concluded that mentally ill individuals were less likely to be violent than the general population. However, all of the studies were carried out on hospitalized mental patients, with their previous arrest rates or court conviction records being compared with those of the general population. Because many hospitalized patients during the first half of this century were confined for long periods of time, this placed them in a special category of long institutionlizations, and few valid conclusions could hold up about their violent propensities. The years spent hospitalized often coincided with the years in which the patients' violent behavior would have been at its peak if the patients had been at liberty in a community.

During the mid-twentieth century, especially before the 1955 era when tranquilizer medications were introduced, the presumption could be made that a certain level of violence was going on even while schizophrenic individuals were hospitalized among patients or with staff. In contemporary hospital settings, follow-up comparisons could be made between one inpatient unit that used neuroleptic medications and another that did not, or some individuals who did receive medications and those who refused. Again, this would still be investigating a narrow group of hospitalized patients, relying on diverse criteria for schizophrenia as well as then extrapolating those violent tendencies to "homicidal violence." All of this is considerably removed from a connection between a specific mental illness, such as schizophrenia, and homicides occurring in communities, without even considering the complication of a comorbid illness.

Studies of Nonhospitalized Patients and Follow-Up Approaches

Following early efforts up to mid-century to study hospitalized mentally ill patients and their tendency to act violently, different approaches were tried. One approach was to study a broad range of psychiatric patients, not just those who were hospitalized. Authors of these studies then sought to obtain data to determine the subsequent incidence or prevalence of violent behavior among those patients. The patients could have been once hospitalized but discharged at the time of the study, or they could have been patients living in the community. Many investigators tended to use arrest rates as the defining measure indicative of violence. This approach led to underestimates of violent incidents. A second approach focused on mentally ill individuals who had committed violent criminal acts and attempted to ascertain what psychiatric symptomatology had been present at the time of the occurrence. This approach would lead to questions about diagnoses to be raised because it would be relevant to legal questions, such as insanity sentencing, and so on.

A selective look at the approach investigating subsequent criminal acts of those labeled as psychiatric patients illustrates how early studies led to questionable conclusions that violence or criminal acts were less frequent among mental patients. Because the focus in this approach was on hospitalized patients, a majority of the "nonorganic" cases would have had schizophrenic diagnoses at that time. Authors of a 1922 study followed patients for a period of 10 years after their discharge.[14] In many ways, this was a marvelous piece of research for the time, being done before grants or subsidies were available for such research. Only 12 of the former patients were arrested (1.2%) during the follow-up period, which then led the researchers to an unwarranted conclusion about the low incidence of violence among mentally ill individuals. Subsequent studies continued to focus primarily on arrest rates, also with the conclusion that, because arrest rates were lower following discharge, violence was obviously lower in that population. The methodology of these studies had not changed by 1945, when investigators in one study concluded that being hospitalized contributed to lowered subsequent arrest rates.[15] The sample population of 1,676 in that study had an 18.4% police record before hospitalization and a 5.2% police record after release, with no homicides recorded. Investigators in another study followed 1,638 former psychiatric inpatients for 6–12 years subsequent to their discharge from a psychiatric unit. By 1958, at the conclusion of the study, none of those patients were reported as having committed a homicide or having died by homicide.[16] However, intervening variables were not considered in leading to such results. Thus, by 1970, these earlier studies were being criticized on the basis of their selective relevance, not taking into account the decrease in criminal behavior that can occur with age, and the lack of any control groups.[17]

During the 1960s, a shift in thinking had begun in which former hospitalized patients were thought to be just as likely to engage in violent behavior as those in the general population. With respect to certain crimes, findings began to emerge that these patient groups might even have a higher incidence of violence. Rappaport and Lassen collected data on patients discharged in 1947 and 1957 from all but one state hospital in Maryland and compared their arrest rates with those of the general population based on data from the Federal Bureau of Investigation's *Uniform Crime Reports*. Although they found no indication that male patients had higher rates of murder or negligent manslaughter than did males in the general population, the patients did have higher arrest rates for robbery than did the general population.[18] Female patients were found to have higher arrest rates for aggravated assault than females in the general population, but lower rates for murder and robbery.[19]

At that time, studies were also beginning to become more focused, such as addressing the question of the specificity of diagnoses. However, the contaminating influence of diagnoses comorbid with schizophrenia was still not given primary recognition. In their follow-up study of 1,141 male veterans, 95% of whom carried a schizophrenic diagnosis, Giovannoni and Gurel did find that these veterans' rate of violent behavior as seen in homicide, aggravated assault, and robbery exceeded that of the general population.[20] Such studies began to draw attention to the problem of comorbidity, in that a subgroup of the schizophrenic individuals were noted to have problems with alcohol. By 1978, Sosowsky, reporting arrest rates of 201 California state mental patients compared with the rates of those in their local counties, found that those patients had a higher arrest rate for violent offenses, both before and following their hospitalization, than did the general population.[21]

The Retrospective Approach

Another approach used to study the relationship between serious mental illness and violence has been to use a research strategy that begins with a designated group of individuals who had already committed a criminal offense. Some studied were under arrest or charged with a crime, whereas others had already been convicted of multifarious offenses. Again, only some of the offenses were homicides, so that the investigators tended to group homicides and other assaultive behavior under the heading of "violence." The methodology used in these studies has been varied, including checklists, psychological testing, and descriptive types of diagnoses. Occasionally, some phenomenological or psychodynamic reports have been used, but these were more in the nature of illustrating the subjects' psychopathology rather than lending themselves to obtaining statistically significant results.

An example of this approach was seen in the work of Guze and Cloninger, in which 209 convicted male felons were studied, with a focus on their descriptive diagnoses. An interesting array of diagnoses was present, with sociopathy, alcoholism, and drug dependence being found more frequently in this group than in the general population.[22,23] This confirmed the impression that forensic psychiatric professionals had long held about the presence of personality disorders and substance abuse in a criminal population. However, after 8–9 years of follow-up, they found that those members of the group who had diagnoses of schizophrenia, manic-depressive disease, or organic brain damage did not have a higher incidence of violence than did the general population. A similar 2- to 3-year follow-up of female felons revealed they had higher rates of sociopathy, alcoholism, drug dependence, and hysteria. Yet, the more serious mental illnesses, such as schizophrenia and manic-depressive illness, were not reported in these females. Although the approach of grouping felons together and then diagnostically assessing them is interesting, it does not provide information with respect to whether certain combined diagnoses may have been the predisposing variable in homicidal behaviors.

The selectivity factor for homicide could be pursued by focusing on those arrested or convicted only for homicide, but this has rarely been done in any systematic manner. To implement such a project would require large numbers of individuals who would need to be assessed in terms of multiple variables. A combined group would be composed of those arrested and perhaps taken to mental hospitals or found incompetent to proceed to trial, as well as those who were kept in the criminal justice system. Individuals who were arrested but not tried for homicides should not be conflated with those who were convicted and those who were found not guilty by reason of mental illness for a homicide. Once again, the problem of comorbidity looms as a pervasive problem, especially with the high rates of substance abuse and dependence present in such a cohort. A study involving the Bellevue catchment area in New York City found that, in a group of mental patients, the presence of alcohol and drug dependency doubled those patients' chances of being arrested.[24]

Again, a plaguing question is whether a major mental disorder, such as schizophrenia, or a comorbid condition is making the major contribution to the propensity to violence—homicide or otherwise. Alternatively, it could be factors other than a psychiatric diagnosis.

A partial answer to this question came in Swanson et al.'s study of violence and psychiatric disorder in the community,[25] using the database from the Epidemiologic Catchment Area (ECA) Study. In the ECA study, based on household surveys, mental illness was seen as a modestly significant risk factor for violent behavior. Swanson et al.'s analysis showed that 90% of the individuals with a serious mental disorder (i.e., schizophrenia or major affective disorder), excluding substance abuse, were not violent. However, this estimate was based on the subjects' self-reports. More specifically, because mental disorders are actually rare among the general population, the proportion of violence that may be attributable to mental illness alone was less than 5%.

Two questions with regard to the ECA data can be posed. One is which types of mentally ill people may pose a risk for violence in the community; the second relates to the specificity of what kind of violence. Also important are the precipitants of violence and the context in which it occurs. The contaminating factor is the possibility that substance abuse alone could be the variable that increases a person's relative risk for violent behavior. A high rate of harmful acts within a community might then come from a "loading" of people who have one of the serious mental illnesses but who primarily act only when under the influence of combinations of drugs or alcohol. In Swanson et al.'s study, nearly a third of those with schizophrenia or a schizophreniform disorder met criteria for drug abuse or dependence.

■ Predicting Homicidal Behavior in Schizophrenic Individuals

Before looking at the specifics of homicide and schizophrenia, one caveat must be noted. Questions about violence and schizophrenia often elicit extreme reactions from those who believe that such efforts unnecessarily stigmatize a certain group of mentally ill individuals, such as viewing schizophrenia as a neurological disease might do. It is only with further research that the validity of any connection between schizophrenia and violent behavior can be confirmed or disconfirmed. It is hoped that accumulated evidence will serve to improve treatment and use better preventive measures. A person's dynamics and psychopathology, predisposing factors of a biological and social nature, and current environmental variables all contribute to some final common pathway for a homicide to occur. Too often the complexity of these multifactorial elements is ignored.

Specificity of Studies on Schizophrenic Individuals

One important question is whether anything specific can be said about homicidal violence when only the diagnosis of schizophrenia is considered. Studies give estimates that range from 8% to 45% of individuals with a schizophrenic diagnosis showing tendencies toward violence. Various possibilities can account for such a wide variance in these studies. One is that the diagnostic criteria for schizophrenia have changed and, despite the use of checklists such as those used in the current American Psychiatric Association's *Diagnostic and Statistical Manual of Mental Disorders* type of approach, clinicians may differ even on symptoms for checklist inclusion. The shifting of schizoaffective disorder out of the schizophrenia grouping to "psychotic disorders not elsewhere classified" in DSM-III-R[27] and then back into "schizophrenia and other psychotic disorders" in DSM-IV[27A] may have contributed to some variance in definitions used in the studies. In addition, other types of schizophrenia, such as the disorganized type and especially catatonic variations, may have violent outbursts associated with them that are different from those seen in paranoid schizophrenia. Yet the former varieties of schizophrenia are not investigated for extreme violence nearly to the degree that the paranoid varieties are. However, such people appear fairly routinely in emergency rooms and are held in jails.

Whether an act of homicidal violence can be specifically connected to the signs and symptoms of schizophrenia remains a plaguing question. In a Swedish study of violent acts committed by 74 schizophrenic patients, the investigators found that only 36.5% of those acts could actually be related to an active hallucinatory or delusional state.[28] One further question that then arises is if it is the impaired interpersonal relations of schizophrenic individuals that primarily give rise to their disposition toward a violent act. The low-grade interpretive distortions that impinge on schizophrenic individuals' relationships with others could color events leading to a homicide. Within this framework, the active symptoms and signs may not then always be the sine qua non leading to a homicide. This consideration makes interpretations of the hows and whys of a homicide committed by a schizophrenic person perhaps more complicated to make, but at least potentially closer to the way such events actually unfolded.

Opinions vary widely as to what proportion of those in a criminal justice population have "pure" schizophrenia that is not mixed in with other, comorbid diagnoses. It is prudent to keep in mind that schizophrenic individuals, like those with other major mental disorders, have an increased risk for substance use and abuse.[29] They also have an increased risk for personality disorders.[30] As noted earlier, when a schizophrenic person commits a homicide, the question always arises if the act is attributable primarily to schizophrenia, the person's drug or alcohol disorder, a personality disorder, or to a complex amalgam of all these problems. Alternatively, none of these factors may have been the primary factor leading to the homicide, but instead factors relating to some other basis for the person's behavior may have been operational. Just because these diagnostic problems exist in a person does not mean that they always explain why a killing has occurred. It is intriguing to note that, in studies from Sweden and Denmark to Canada, about half of the homicide offenders with diagnoses of major mental disorders did not have any additional substance abuse diagnoses.[31–33]

Yet another approach has been to differentiate a high-violence group from a low-violence group based on neurological findings, such as impairments in coordination, tandem walking, hopping, stereognosis, and graphesthesia.[34] Just as with other approaches, specific neurological variables need to be assessed in efforts to determine whether people with schizophrenia are more subject to violence than those in other groups. The presence of certain organic findings, if confirmed in schizophrenic individuals, would then raise new questions as to whether these constitute the predisposing diathesis toward homicide.

Another subtle difference that can create discrepancies in study results is which subjects have been studied, and when. For example, one study began with a group of individuals who had committed homicides, but who had already been designated as mentally ill with accompanying diagnoses. In starting with such a group, 57% of the murderers were given a diagnosis of schizophrenia.[35] Using such a skewed sample gives a quite different result than if a general population of murderers were used. Other investigators have focused on specific kinds of murder, such as sexual or serial murders. Even apart from basic methodological principles of adequate sample size and the means of investigation, the incidence of schizophrenia may also vary as a correlate of what type of homicide is being studied.

The role of stalking behavior in those with an unfolding thought disorder also needs to be considered. Many of the studies have focused on such behavior when directed at conspicuous targets, such as political figures or movie or sports celebrities. However, stalking with a homicide potential goes on in the more mundane areas of life as well. Some stalkers are schizophrenic, although certainly not all stalkers are. It seems surprising that the stalkers who approach their targets do not seem to be the ones who commit actual acts of violence.[36] However, psychiatrists are just starting to acquire more knowledge about this subgroup.

Other Delusional Disorders

Diagnoses of delusional disorders raise yet a different set of complications. Since 1980, when borderline personality disorders became an officially recognized diagnosis in DSM-III[37], the potential for violence in those who carry this diagnosis with its micropsychotic episodes is always a possibility. Comorbidity has been stressed as a complicating factor, but here it is not confined to drug and alcohol abuse. Diverse types of personality disorders can make a significant contribution to homicidal behavior in those who also carry a schizophrenic disorder. What type of schizophrenia is being studied, where, and in what setting, may have a significant impact on findings about violence. Volavka and Krakowski reported that results from European studies showed a lower incidence of violence in schizophrenic individuals than the American studies, and an unsystematic observation from China and Japan suggested a lower incidence in those countries of patient violence connected with schizophrenia.[38]

State of Mind When Committing Crime

One controversial issue has been whether violence occurs more frequently in those with a schizophrenic illness during psychotic episodes or when they are free of psychotic states. Differences in schizophrenic individuals' potential for dangerousness among studies may well reflect the variable of when those individuals are seen. If evaluated at an early period when acutely disturbed, the conclusions reached in the assessment may be quite different than if subjects were studied following a period of treatment and hospitalization. The typical example is an acutely paranoid schizophrenic individual who responds quite readily to neuroleptic medication. If the same person is seen only a few weeks later, a very different clinical picture may emerge with respect to an assessment of homicidal dangerousness. The point cannot be emphasized strongly enough that transposing the results of studies done in inpatient settings to the schizophrenic population in communities is highly unreliable.

A classic study was done in 1967 by two famous criminologists, Wolfgang and Ferracuti.[39] In their analysis of the literature dealing with psychiatric aspects of homicide, they did not find that any specific diagnosis was connected to perpetration of a homicide. They then concluded that few murderers were psychotic. Yet, based on current knowledge, questions about their conclusions can be raised. How valid were the diagnostic studies carried out on groups of murderers in the criminal justice system in the 1960s? Current assessment techniques have more specificity in detecting disorders in such individuals. Diagnosis has achieved greater levels of sensitivity and specificity even on a purely descriptive level. Unfortunately, few past or present studies devote the time and resources to reconstruct what the mental state of individuals was at the time of committing the homicides, unless a mental illness defense has been contemplated legally and an expert team of lawyers and psychiatrists have been able to study the case intensively.

One approach to assessing the influence of psychotic symptoms to criminal behavior was that used by Rogers et al.,[40] who differentiated "high-visibility" patients from "low-visibility" patients; the distinction was based on the former patients' displaying behavior such as verbal threats whereas the latter patients did not. The goal was to correlate different psychopathological characteristics in each type of patient. The high-visibility group scored higher on the hostile-suspiciousness factor of the Brief Psychiatric Rating Scale (BPRS), whereas the low-visibility group scored higher on the withdrawal-retardation factor of that scale. Certain symptoms suggested a higher potential for serious violence, such as the presence of delusions, especially well-planned paranoid ones. Violence occurring in a disorganized psychotic state, such as in undifferentiated schizophrenia, was thought to pose less of a threat from its being poorly focused, although its unpredictability could have ramifications. Rogers et al. also found that symptom pictures involving command hallucinations as well as more exotic syndromes such as erotomania or the Capgras syndrome could increase an individual's tendency toward committing homicide. The acutely psychotic individual with thought fragmentation, hallucinations, and misinterpreting would be seen as posing a higher danger.

When investigations are extended beyond the descriptive level to address the subtleties of whether an altered mental state was present at the time of the killing, questions arise about the degree of regression or disorganization that was present, from which one could infer a psychotic state. These are different types of questions using different criteria to address inferential subtleties about a person's mental state and cognitive processes. Few studies, beyond a few intensive legal cases, have carried out the intensive assessments necessary. If such intensive evaluations were done, it would be necessary to distinguish whether differences occurred among the various types of homicides. Distinctions would need to be made among types of killers, such as sexual killers and serial killers. With regard to schizophrenic individuals, distinctions would need to be made among those who exhibited episodic dyscontrol, killed sadistically, dismembered their victims, or murdered children; children who murdered their parents; those who killed their spouses; as well as the impulsive type of killer once referred to as "sudden murderers."[42]

This means that many of the types of murderers discussed in this book would require psychiatric investigation in which the possibility that their mental state was changed at the time of the killings must be entertained. Their system of controls could be seen as faltering at the time because of a psychosis, some variant of schizophrenia, or a schizo-phreniform state. Although the incidence of schizophrenia appears similar in different countries and cross-culturally, the incidence of violence actually varies for individuals given a diagnosis of schizo-phrenia. The type of cross-cultural situation in itself merits a more ex-tended inquiry. Within the designated group of mentally ill murderers, the most frequent single diagnosis given is usually paranoid schizophre-nia. Yet, even with diverse populations, that diagnosis is given in only about 25% of cases. Only in one study did the diagnosis reach 40%.[43]

Legal Issues

A diagnosis of schizophrenia in someone who has committed a homi-cide often raises major legal issues involving an insanity defense. Initial issues of a person's competency to participate in a trial may surface; such a ruling would negate the possibility, at least for a time, of an individual standing trial. These initial issues would include clearly establishing the diagnosis of schizophrenia because an accurate diagno-sis is necessary for any legal or clinical planning. In making this diagnosis, several signs and symptoms and diagnostic tests can be used to confirm or rule out schizophrenia (none of which are addressed here.) In essence, clinical material from the patient is used, as well as whatever extraneous sources are available about that person's behavior and how the homicide took place. This may include information from relatives (e.g., spouse, parent) or friends, as well as medical records from treating physicians or past hospitalizations—psychiatric and other—that would help establish the diagnosis and behavioral patterns. Unless such information is incorporated into an evaluation, later re-search relying on the listed diagnosis is questionable.

A contemporary examination of the individual focusing on his or her current level of functioning is also called for. This involves general impressions of how the person conducts himself or herself, the pattern and content of his or her speech, the type of thought processes and content that have preoccupied him or her, the kinds of moods and affect that have predominated, and his or her style of relating to others and to himself or herself. In addition, a traditional sensorium examina-tion may be useful in some cases to screen out factors such as deficits in orientation to time, place, and person; to determine the ability to abstract and assess cognitive functioning; to assess the capacity for remote and recent memory; and to evaluate the usual material incorporated in mental status examinations involving the capacity to perform different types of calculations, interpret proverbs, and so on. Psychological testing for personality functioning and an intellectual assessment are routine. As a general rule, it is wise to obtain a general physical and possibly a neurological examination if no recent one has been performed. All of these evaluations are used to determine if the primary signs and symptoms of a schizophrenic disorder are present and how they might be related to a homicide. The following case illustrates the unfolding of homicidal violence in a schizophrenic individual.

Case Example

A 40-year-old, single male was charged with the murder of his 70-year-old mother. An interesting phenomenon was that, despite an IQ of 138, based on the Wechsler Adult Intelligence Scale–Revised, the man had worked most of his life at a newsstand in the central part of a major metropolitan area. Over the years, he had become known to the many people who would buy their magazines or newspapers from him. No one suspected his superior intelligence, which was undoubtedly far above that of a great majority of his newsstand patrons, as he always dressed shabbily, was usually friendly in a quiet unassuming way, and kept to himself. Although he did not graduate from high school, he would frequently spend his spare time assembling and disassembling complex stereo and computer equipment, in addition to reading heavily intellectual-type books. He had always lived with both parents until 10 years before the homicide, when his father died; after that he continued to reside with his mother.

In the course of interviewing him, what appeared most striking was his expression of his suffering and anguish resulting from what he felt he had been exposed to over the preceding several years. It had begun when he felt himself becoming fragmented because of experiencing extraneous intrusions into him of some type of electrical current or electrical rays. These not only influenced him, but were experienced as "invading and assaulting" him. He had never been able to understand the source of these intrusions until shortly before he assaulted and killed his mother, when he first began to associate the events as somehow connected with her. Although he had slowly begun to drink more alcohol at the times when his auditory hallucinations increased in intensity, he was not otherwise a drinker. He referred to the electrical influences operating on him as "ghosts" or "spirits" that interfered with his life, and the drinking provided some relief from them.

A crucial transition occurred when he tried to synthesize what was responsible for the events that were happening to him. In contrast to the success he had in unraveling stereos and computers, his efforts failed to unravel the sources of electrical intrusions on himself. The idea emerged that something like ghosts were responsible for putting the strange thoughts in his head or for making him hear the voices directed to him that caused him to become very agitated and hurried in his behavior.

A startling change occurred when he began to experience voices coming out of radios or television sets, even when they were turned off. He would then disassemble the sets, but voices kept coming from the parts. His first thought was that some religious group might be behind the persecution, tormenting him because of his disavowal of religion and leaving of his church years ago. He next began to feel vulnerable to public exposure at the newsstand, because he was so visible there to whatever or whoever was persecuting him. He began to feel uneasy and became extravigilant. At times, he would simply leave the newsstand and walk around the block, particularly when the voices became more pressing. At those times, he experienced electrical currents coming from street lampposts when he walked by them, and he would hurry back to his newsstand.

Riding on buses began to bother him because he heard voices that he connected with the electrical systems used on the bus. As a result, he began to walk rather than use public transportation. When voices shifted to threats against his life, he became acutely agitated. They never said how they were going to kill him, but he became convinced his life was in jeopardy. While at home, he became frightened and began bolting doors and adding extra locks, as well as pushing chairs against the doors at night. In some undefined manner, he began to suspect that his mother was the culprit behind these events.

Thinking that his mother might be planning to kill him to get his money, he changed ownership of his government bonds to revert to the government in event of his death. However, that gave him no relief. A new symptom became obvious when he would look at immobile objects, such as a fist or sharp object (e.g., pen, razor). He would then feel sharp pain when he experienced the fist as hitting him or the razor cutting him. On one occasion, he looked at a nail file and felt it was penetrating his eyes to the point of blinding him. He became unable to distinguish whether events that were reported in the news had special significance for him, such as events involving celebrities or a criminal event such as a local robbery. Personalistic use of phrases began to occur in his auditory hallucinations. A voice would say, "We're going to dehand you," which meant to him that his hand was going to be removed. Rhyming and punning of words occurred, such as hearing the word "devacilate," which he interpreted as referring to a procedure to remove his veins, or "demasculate," which he interpreted as a procedure to remove his organs and nerves.

The culmination of his delusions came on a night when he became fully convinced that if his mother was not one of the main perpetrators of the misery being inflicted on him, she was at least aware of what was going on and was doing nothing to help him. He concluded that his mother was allowing whatever was in store for him to happen, whether it be pain, suffering, punishment, even perhaps death. He had one vivid memory of standing in a doorway between the living and dining rooms, seeing a pinkish white spot on his mother's cheek below her left eye that looked like a "patch of flesh" in her left eye socket, and figuring that her eyeball had come out. "I seemed confused. I didn't know if she was dead or alive, and I thought, 'Oh! Oh! We had an argument and I must have hit her.'" At the same time, he was frightened of angering his mother, because she might ask him to move out of the house. "I was afraid that if I had to leave home, how could I plug up all the electrical outlets or shut off the electricity in other places like I had done at home because they wouldn't allow me to do that."

Although he could not remember more details of the events of that evening, the police reports and the autopsy on the mother indicated that her head had been beaten so severely by the leg of a chair that had been found near her body, that no visible sign of a head being attached to her body remained. He recalled that, once during the night, he had come down from his bedroom and noted that "My mother's head looked like it was dissolved from acid and not pleasant. The bone and everything else looked like it had been dissolved—as though acid had been spilled on it. I knew then that she was dead." At that point, he called the police.

In many ways, this fascinating and ghoulish case emphasizes the importance of clearly establishing a diagnosis and the validity of that diagnosis. Clinical issues must then be considered to inform legal decisions about whether an individual is able to stand trial, and, if so, whether he or she is mentally ill to the degree of meeting the prerequisite insanity standards in that jurisdiction.

In this case example, the defendant did not appear to know that killing his mother was wrong, given the delusional context in which the killing occurred. Once he became convinced that his mother was, in some manner, involved in the life experiences he was having, her life was in serious danger. Unless there had been significant therapeutic intervention, or it was found that these psychotic episodes would come and go, the possibility of a gradually unfolding and expanding psychotic process was present. The defendant's belief that he was involved with the victim in some type of persecutory system put him in the role of logically believing he needed to protect himself. The ideation that the electrical forces from outlets and equipment, as well as from outer space, were causing him difficulty, the form of his physical symptoms, and his belief that he was being attacked at first centered around his home, then expanded to his job site, and finally led him to conclude that his mother was the persecutor. All these thoughts coalesced on the night of the killing. He began to fear that his mother would throw him out of the house and he would not be able to maintain his elaborate defenses to hold the electrical systems in abeyance. It is not unusual with such psychotic episodes that the specific details of a significant act of violence are not remembered. Instead of this not remembering being an attempt on the part of the perpetrator to dissimulate, it is a type of posthomicidal reparation that occurs subsequent to a psychotic fragmentation in which a homicide has occurred.

This type of case may give rise to a multitude of legal issues involving a defendant's competency before coming to trial or the state of his or her mind at the time of the killing. Although the case example does not present unusual clinical difficulty in diagnosis, it is a good one to illustrate related problems. Many encountering the case might expect that it would easily fit into a legal niche of insanity, as is often the case. However, it need not be so, as many variables—legal and political—impinge on insanity dispositions. One argument that might be raised within a traditional framework of legal tests is whether, because of his mental illness operating at the time of the killing, this defendant knew the nature of his violent act. A relevant question is whether he knew he was factually destroying his mother, or whether he perceived her at the time as some robotized object or a computerized source of audio messages directed at him. However, if he knew his act was wrong, did he believe it was a necessary act to eliminate the source of his persecutions?

From a strict prosecutorial position, many of these arguments might be objectionable because, even given that the person was psychotic and delusional, the psychotic framework did not necessarily mean the person was under an immediate fear for his life because of his delusions and hallucinations. As a consequence, the prosecutor's position would be that the extreme solution this defendant took was not proportional to the threat facing him, even accepting his delusional belief. In other words, his being convinced that he was being tormented within a delusional system might only justify an equivalent response in return, which would be something short of a killing. These types of cases could lead into an elaborate discussion of the insanity defense and its vicissitudes, but the point here is simply to illustrate how legal uncertainties can arise even when a schizophrenic person kills someone in the midst of a psychotic episode.

■ References

1. Group for the Advancement of Psychiatry: Psychiatry and Sex Psychopath Legislation: The 30s to the 80s. New York, Group for the Advancement of Psychiatry, 1977

2. Lamb HR: The Homeless Mentally Ill. Washington, DC, American Psychiatric Press, 1984

3. Isaac RJ, Armat VC: Madness in the Streets. New York, Free Press, 1980

4. Felthous AR: Duty to Warn or Protect: Current Status for Psychiatrists. Psychiatric Annals 21:591–597, 1991

5. Tarasoff v Regents of the University of California, 17 Cal 3d 425, 551 P2d 553 (1974)

6. Stone A: Law, Psychiatry and Morality. Washington, DC, American Psychiatric Press, 1984

7. Livermore JM, Malmquist CP, Meehl PE: On the justifications of civil commitment. University of Pennsylvania Law Review 117:75–96, 1968

8. Monahan J: The prediction of violent behavior: toward a second generation of theory and policy. Am J Psychiatry 141:10–15, 1984

9. Dawes RM, Faust D, Meehl PE: Clinical versus actuarial judgment. Science 243:1668–1675, 1989

10. Lowenstein M, Binder RL, McNeil DE: The relationship between admission symptoms and hospital assaults. Hosp Community Psychiatry 41:311–313, 1990

11. Beck JC, White KA, Gage B: Emergency psychiatric assessments of violence. Am J Psychiatry 148:1562–1565, 1991

12. Stark R, McEvoy J III: Middle class violence, in Violence in the Family. Edited by Steinmetz SK, Strauss MA. New York, Harper & Row, 1974

13. Gelles R: Family violence. Annual Review of Sociology 11:347–367, 1985

14. Ashley MC: Outcome of 1000 cases paroled from the Middletown State Homeopathic Hospital. State Hospital Quarterly 8:64–70, 1922

15. Cohen LH, Freeman H: How dangerous to the community are state hospital patients? Connecticut State Medical Journal 9:697–699, 1945

16. Hastings DW: Follow-up results in psychiatric illness. Am J Psychiatry 144:1057–1066, 1958

17. Gulevich GD, Bourne PG: Mental illness and violence, in Violence and the Struggle for Existence. Edited by Daniels DN, Gilula MF, Ochberg FM. Boston, MA, Little, Brown, 1970, pp 309–326

18. Rappaport JE, Lassen G: Dangerousness arrest rate comparison of discharged patients and the general population. Am J Psychiatry 121:776–783, 1965

19. Rappaport JE, Lassen G: The dangerousness of female patients: a comparison of the arrest rates of discharged psychiatric patients and the general population. Am J Psychiatry 123:413–419, 1966

20. Giovannoni JM, Gurel L: Socially disruptive behavior of ex-mental patients. Arch Gen Psychiatry 17:146–153, 1967

21. Sosowsky L: Crime and violence among mental patients reconsidered in view of the new legal relationship between the state and the mentally ill. Am J Psychiatry 135:33–42, 1978

22. Guze S: Criminality and Psychiatric Disorders. New York, Oxford University Press, 1976

23. Cloninger CR, Guze SB: Psychiatric disorder and criminal recidivism. Am J Psychiatry 24:266–269, 1973

24. Zitrin A, Hardesty AS, Burdock ET, et al: Crime and violence among mental patients. Am J Psychiatry 130:144–146, 1976

25. Swanson JW, Holzer CE III, Ganju V, et al: Violence and psychiatric disorder in the community: evidence from the Epidemiological Catchment Area surveys. Hosp Community Psychiatry 41:761–770, 1990

27. American Psychiatric Association: Diagnostic and Statistical Manual of Mental Disorders, 3rd Edition, Revised. Washington, DC, American Psychiatric Association, 1987

27A. American Psychiatric Association: Diagnostic and Statistical Manual of Mental Disorders, 4th Edition. Washington, DC, American Psychiatric Association, 1994

28. Virkkunen M: Observations of violence in schizophrenia. Acta Psychiatr Scand 50:145–151, 1974

29. Mueser KT, Yarnold PR, Levinson DF, et al: Prevalence of substance abuse in schizophrenia: demographic and clinical correlates. Schizophr Bull 16:31–56, 1990

30. Goodwin FK, Jamison KR: Manic Depressive Illness. New York, Oxford University Press, 1990

31. Lindquist P: Criminal homicide in northern Sweden. Int J Law Psychiatry 8:19–37, 1989

32. Gottlieb P, Gabrielsen G, Kramp P: Psychotic homicides in Copenhagen from 1959 to 1983. Acta Psychiatr Scand 76:285–292, 1987

33. Beaudoin MN, Hodgins S: Homicide, schizophrenia and substance abuse or dependency. Can J Psychiatry 38:541–546, 1993

34. Krakowski MI, Convit A, Jaeger J, et al: Neurological impairments in violent schizophrenic inpatients. Am J Psychiatry 146:849–853, 1989

35. McNight CK, Mohr JW, Quinsey RE, et al: Mental illness and homicide. Can J Psychiatry II:91–98, 1966

36. Deetz PE, Matthews DP, Von Duyne C, et al: Threatening and otherwise inappropriate letters to Hollywood celebrities. J Forensic Sci 36:185–209, 1991

37. American Psychiatric Association: Diagnostic and Statistical Manual of Mental Disorders, 3rd Edition. Washington, DC, American Psychiatric Association, 1980

38. Volavka J, Krakowski M: Schizophrenia and violence. Psychol Med 19:559–562, 1989

39. Wolfgang ME, Ferracuti F: The Subculture of Violence. New York, Barnes & Noble, 1967

40. Rogers R, Gillis JR, Turner RE, et al: The clinical presentation of command hallucinations in a forensic population. Am J Psychiatry 147:1034–1037, 1990

42. Blackmun N, Weiss JM, Lambert JW: The sudden murder: three clues to preventive interaction. Arch Gen Psychiatry 8:289–294, 1963

43. Lunde DT: Murder and Madness. Stanford, CA, Stanford Alumni Association, 1975

CHAPTER 4

Borderlines and Homicide

The Quest for Vindication

■ Validity of and Criteria for Diagnosis of Borderline Personality Disorder

When the diagnosis of borderline personality disorder (BPD) is a possibility in someone who has committed a homicide, a pervasive issue that arises is the diagnostic validity of the entity. Although the same question arises with many other diagnoses in terms of a differential diagnosis, it arises in a more cogent form with BPD individuals. The reasons for this are multiple. For the purposes of this chapter, I wish to note that this disorder has been subjected to diverse interpretations, from being viewed as a subtle form of schizophrenia to being conceptualized as a neurotic condition in psychoanalytic theory.[1]

Use of the Diagnostic Interview for Borderline Patients[2] and the American Psychiatric Association's *Diagnostic and Statistical Manual of Mental Disorders* criteria have improved the validity of diagnosing this disorder. However, questions remain as to whether the diagnosis, officially recognized only since 1980 in DSM-III,[3] has yet been adequately conceptualized. The problem is attributed to the mixture of fluctuating symptoms and behaviors listed, which comprises both states and traits. It has been noted that, because only five of the eight criteria listed in DSM-III-R[4] need to be present to make the diagnosis, there are 93 different ways to arrive at the diagnosis.[5]

As recently as the late 1970s, it was argued that BPD was an independent diagnostic entity, although there was no preponderance of evidence to weigh either for or against this hypothesis.[6] Another set of questions have arisen as to whether there is a need for a different formulation of this personality disorder, with suggestions that a revised formulation would see the problem more in terms of levels of a disordered self-organization rather than simply symptoms and behaviors.[7] In addition, a large overlap exists between BPD and other types of personality disorders, which raises questions about the pervasiveness of comorbidity. This is particularly true for diagnoses involving drug and alcohol abuse and the spectrum of impulse disorders. Comorbidity with Axis I affective disorders is often noted.[8] In turn, this has given rise to continuing debate as to whether a group of those with BPD actually reflect a subtype of a mood disorder. Finally, other lines of inquiry suggest the possibility that certain kinds of biological dysfunctions are present more frequently in those with the BPD diagnosis,[9] such as shortened rapid eye movement (REM) latency and sleep continuity disturbances, abnormal dexamethasone-supression test results, and abnormal thyrotropin-releasing hormone test results. Whether these changes are due to comorbid depression is the question.

It has been noted that agreement in diagnosing BPD using different diagnostic instruments hovers at around 50%.[10]

Although questions about the validity and reliability of a BPD diagnosis are still unanswered, they are listed here simply to indicate that questions may be raised when this diagnosis is considered for a homicidal person or group in clinical, legal, or research arenas. They are also mentioned as words of caution before turning to the forensic implications of such a diagnosis and its relationship to homicides.

■ Etiology of Borderline Personality Disorder and Propensity Toward Violence

A key question in creating a theoretical formulation about BPD and violence is to ask what special vulnerability exists in the structure of this type of personality that allows a homicidal type of act to occur. The lack of specificity about the etiology of borderline personality and its functioning is troubling; however, certain formulations and inferences can be made. Most striking in this regard is the significance of the BPD individual's pervasive and enduring hatred, a hatred that persists and guides a person who superficially appears to be socialized and integrated much of the time.

However, multiple theories exist to explain the etiology of BPD.

Early Theories

The nineteenth century ideas about temperament are forerunners of attempts to understand BPD people. The first approach to explaining those people who displayed anger mixed with moodiness was that they had a choleric temperament, which was marked by a quality of irritableness. Later theorists distinguished such a group as having an innate amount of aggression. Over the ensuing decades, other theories attempted to relate the behavior of this group of people to schizophrenia by way of schizoid elements. By 1968, Grinker et al. had delineated four subtypes of BPD individuals, all four of which had the "core syndrome" of acting out of anger.[11] The angry core was seen as the connection to their impulsivity and instability. Liebowitz and Klein used the term "hysteroid dysphoric" to refer to impulsive female patients who were chaotic, moody, unreasonable, tempestuous, and irritable.[12] Extreme forms of behavior in this group were witnessed in violent acts where chaotic impulsivity, wildly oscillating extremes of love and hate, and compulsive promiscuity are played out.

Given BPD individuals' manipulative qualities, a number of variations can occur. One is where third parties are lured into carrying out acts of violence at the individual's promotion. For example, one girl told her boyfriend lurid tales about her father molesting her, stories that were never proven true. The boyfriend was then incited to kill her parents.[13] Diverse types of distortion, lying, and manipulation are played out to various degrees in "doing someone in," up to and including committing a homicide. Sometimes homicides involving such behaviors are behind the duplicity present in business dealings or white-collar crime that has backfired.

Biological Theories

As noted earlier, various hypotheses have been suggested to explain the source of BPD individuals' hatred. Biological theorists have proposed that some intrinsic neurological deficit of brain dysfunction or a genetic predisposition contributes to BPD individuals' problems with impulse control. Biological theorizing looks for something deviant in neuropsychological functioning, perhaps hyperirritability, as a precursor to impulsivity. From there, the generalizations extend to hypotheses such as temporal lobe epileptic variants, with violence as an accompaniment; episodic dyscontrol; panic attacks; dissociative syndromes; premenstrual syndrome with destructive behavioral components; and bipolar II disorder or cyclothymia as possibilities corresponding to different manifestations of the borderline group.

Physiological Theories

Stone used an analogy to a neurophysiological model that has either an exaggerated or prolonged response to explain a BPD individual's impulsivity.[14] The BPD person may react to less intense provocative situations than others because he or she has a lowered threshold for provocation, a more rapid triggering of a response, an exaggerated response, or a response of extended duration. If one or more of these are possibilities can be confirmed, it would not be unexpected to find such people having heightened possibilities for outbursts of violent behavior. Extreme degrees of the personality organization keep the person in a state of action readiness, with a brooding need to act that can last for months or longer.

Such physiological theorizing postulating an inherent instability in the borderline individual is congruent with clinical observations. The implications of such a physiological theory would be congruent with the inherent instability clinically seen in BPD individuals. Based on features such as a brooding sensitivity with a readiness to perceive slights, the "tinderbox" potential of exploding in a burst of rage or to take some calculated act of vengeance, seems logical given the preceding thinking. Added to this proposed neurophysiological propensity toward impulsivity, developmental experiences, such as diverse types of trauma or abuse, may then contribute to this tendency or cause the impulsivity in their own right if they have been severe enough.

The difficulty, of course, is that although this hypothesis of inherent physiological instability seems logical, it has not yet been confirmed. Furthermore, there are no cues to predict when a violent eruption may occur. Indicators are lacking to tell us when love will turn to hate, idealization to devaluation, admiration to contempt, loyalty to a person or group to undermining or deceitful behavior, or devotion to envy or vicious jealousy. Even those in close contact with a borderline individual, and not a joint participant in his or her psychopathology, will make false negative predictions because of the rapidity of the extreme shifts and impulsivity of BPD individuals' actions.

Childhood Theories

Beginning investigations of the precursors of BPD personalities in childhood have not yielded much knowledge beyond the conclusion that there is little agreement on how such a disorder manifests itself in that age group.[15] It is important to distinguish the diagnostic symptoms or traits that become evident during childhood or adolescence from those childhood antecedents that later contribute to someone in adulthood showing BPD characteristics. Most work has involved the latter. Herman et al. distinguished a recurrent theme of childhood trauma as an antecedent,[16] whereas Links emphasized the family's exerting a high degree of hostile control through one or both parents as contributory.[17] Apart from the majority of theories, which propose abuse in childhood as the significant variable, some theories have relied on Mahler's separation-individuation theory.[18] Masterson and Rinsley posited that maternal overinvolvement, with the mother relying on the child to meet her own needs, was an important factor in development of BPD,[19] whereas Adler focused on the maternal figure as an inconsistent regulator of the child's needs and impulse life."[20] Results from one empirical study of 776 adolescents with personality disorders indicated that the joint presence of maternal overinvolvement and maternal inconsistency could predict the emergence of BPD.[21]

Psychoanalytic Theories

Among psychoanalytic theories, Kernberg's explanatory models have many implications for determining a person's proneness to violence.

His original model posited that an individual's aggressive drive emerging in the developmental period between 8 months and 36 months posed a threat to libidinal object ties.[22] The result of this struggle was defensive efforts to keep aggressive and libidinal urges separate in images of the self and other objects. Such efforts give rise to a defensive splitting and other primitive defenses. Adler went beyond postulates of a failed integration of self and object representations attributable to ambivalence in his proposal of a developmental failure in the formation of "soothing-holding introjects" during the separation-individuation phase during the second and third year.[23] The resultant introjects are what can cause harm. The possibility then exists for some future regressive loss of function to the state of recognition memory and reliance on transitional objects. During such regressions, terrifying states of aloneness can occur, with fears and fantasies activated on the level of threats to the annihilation of the self or to parent figures. In terms of the cases discussed in this chapter, such a primitive ego state can be hypothesized as the state possibly present during homicides.

However, other psychoanalytic theorists have seen no need for such proposals, believing that classical theory is sufficient to explain the clinical observations about BPD individuals.[24] The ambivalence of the BPD person is seen as reflecting the anal stage of development, with splitting explained as a displacement of aggression from a loved, caretaking object to preserve the object from a fantasized destruction. Violence would then be seen as a displacement mechanism gone awry.

Pursuing a broader theoretical perspective to the problem of BPD individuals and homicidal violence leads to an examination of the vulnerabilities accompanying a BPD organization. One vulnerable area has always been the tendency to a diffusion of identity. Researchers have delineated an identity cluster, consisting of identity diffusion, empty feelings, and boredom.[25] A personality with chronic interpersonal problems in the areas of intimacy, empathy, and assessment of others' intentions (as well as the person's own intentions) places that person in a higher risk category for acting on his or her aggression. It also produces greater difficulties in his or her love life, which is the context for many acts of violence and homicide between intimates. Not being able to assess accurately one's own intentions becomes a greater problem when there are similar difficulties in assessing others. The potential is then present for acting on misinterpretations and escalating violent behavior. Some of these disturbances appear as hysterical symptoms.[26] On other occasions, there may be symptoms of dissociative disorders.[27] Grizzly types of murders, such as those from multiple stab wounds or the burning of a dwelling with the victims inside, may occur in a depersonalized state.

■ Epidemiology of Violent Behavior in Borderline Personality Disorder Individuals

Epidemiological questions regarding BPD individuals and violent behavior are difficult to answer because of the continued uncertainty about the etiology and pathogenesis of BPD individual's violent behaviors. Intriguing questions, such as the following, have been raised:

- Do BPD individuals exhibit homicidal types of violence more frequently than some other comparative diagnostic group?
- Do they exhibit more homicidal types of violence compared with a control group selected from the general population?
- More specifically, do they more frequently behave in a violent or dangerous manner than those with some other psychiatric diagnosis, such as schizophrenia or antisocial personality disorder?
- Does the dangerousness present in BPD individuals have any specificity connected to it in terms of which kinds of homicidal violence accompany particular aspects of their personality organization?

Answers to unresolved questions about the underlying basis for a borderline personality structure will have a bearing on the assessment of homicidal behavior and may reflect a manifestation of these individuals' instability. Perhaps more sophisticated taxonomic devices will allow confirmation or disconfirmation of whether some of the violence seen in borderline disorders is a manifestation of an affective illness, or whether it reflects a comorbidity situation for those with this diagnosis.

BPD individuals' tendencies to misinterpret comments and behaviors and take umbrage quickly because of their oversensitivity leaves these individuals prone to striking out both verbally and physically, often to an exaggerated degree (e.g., "to teach [those who have offended them] a lesson"). Given the chronic and episodic symptoms and traits of those with a BPD diagnosis, the question could be asked why more of them have not been involved in homicidal behavior. An initial answer is that perhaps many more borderline people are involved in serious violence than has been realized. This lack of recognition may be attributable to several factors. One reason is the absence of an official diagnosis of the disorder before 1980, although BPD was applied to diverse types of patients for decades. Hence, a variety of diagnoses may have been given to people who had engaged in homicidal behavior who would now be diagnosed as having BPD. As noted earlier, many individuals who become entangled in the legal system in diverse ways still do not receive an adequate diagnostic assessment, which minimizes the true incidence of violence in those who carry this diagnosis.

Another reason for the difficulty in assessing to what degree BPD individuals may be involved in violence, and, more specifically, the difficulty in predicting when they may become violent, is that they often present as being "normal." The mass media often refer to "inexplicable killings," supposedly performed by a person heretofore seen as normal. Although "normal" may be used here in the sense of having no previous hospitalizations for mental illness, it suggests the possibility of a borderline personality organization operating. Casual friends and associates, based on their observations of their surface-level behavior, often see BPD individuals as socially involved and not as misfits.

Few longitudinal studies carried out on BPD individuals have included the variable of violence. Investigators in one study followed 62 males who had once been hospitalized at the New York Psychiatric Institute for treatment.[28] Their files were later assessed and found to meet criteria for what we would now diagnose as BPD. There was then a retrospective follow-up over various lengths of time based on when the person had initially been hospitalized. Four of the group were found to have committed murders and 7 to have committed suicide, giving a rate of 20% having been involved in violent acts with fatal consequences. The investigators did not inquire about lesser degrees of violence. Another investigation based on inpatients at the Institute of

Living in Hartford, Connecticut, found that 69% of a BPD cohort had engaged in antisocial acting out (e.g., violence toward property of others, criminal acts, promiscuity, running away, serious substance abuse problems) before hospitalization.[29]

■ Characteristics of Borderline Personality Disorder That Predispose to Violence

Many of the traits associated with the diagnosis of BPD listed in DSM-III-R would seem to carry a predisposition toward violence. The group of cases used herein for illustration fulfill DSM-IV criteria, as well as criteria from the Diagnostic Interview for Borderline Patients.[2] However, confining assessments of dangerousness to descriptive criteria may miss some of the protean manifestations that add to violent propensities, so that some characteristics are missed. Limitations exist from the equal weighting given the nine criteria in the diagnostic manual. However, such limitations do not foreclose discussion of the dangerousness potential inherent in these individuals' behavioral manifestations. In the case examples used in this chapter, the individuals have been the principal participants in criminal litigation, civil litigation, or both, which have been precipitated by their behavior. The intriguing questions are the tendency of other BPD individuals for violent behavior and what cues exist that an individual may be on such a pathway.

Two characteristics of BPD individuals' behavior provide the possible mechanisms for a relationship between BPD and the occurrence of homicidal violence: BPD individuals' unstable moods and impulsivity. In some, these moods are connected to the enduring hatred that many with this diagnosis have, whereas in others it is part of a concomitant depressive picture. The crucial point would be where the person's capacity for accumulated rage intersects with his or her high potential for an impulsive outburst.

Affective Instability

Depressive symptomatology. The difficulties in offering specific hypotheses at this time about violent behavior in BPD individuals can be seen when it is noted that, based on Axis I phenomenology, a prevalence rate of 40%–50% for major affective disorders is found in borderline patients.[30] Some believe the prevalence may be lower.[31] Zanarini et al., in their research, used a lifetime prevalence for the diagnosis; they found that 100% of the those diagnosed with BPD met DSM-III criteria for an affective disorder. Another 84% also met criteria for substance abuse, an area that needs a similar critical assessment.[32]

Depressive symptomatology may raise the risk of BPD individuals' behaving violent. All of the factors that lead to violence in some depressed people can also be present in BPD individuals with a comorbid diagnosis of depression, which increases the risk of violence from the joint effect. In some cases, their provocations elicit retaliatory behaviors in others. In other cases, it is a result of projective identification defenses in which they believe their own anger or rage is being directed against them by another and they take action accordingly. The instability is not confined to suicidal behaviors or gestures. The most striking quality about the depressions of BPD patients is the accompanying instability often connected with their sensitivity to rejections. As Stone stated, "Minor events lead to major upsets; major events that most people take in their stride lead to catastrophe" (p. 304).[33]

Signs and symptoms of a severe depression may emerge on top of a chronic type of characterological depression. This phenomenon of "double depression," which has been widely discussed, may also mask the potential for violent tendencies.[34] On one hand, BPD individuals have a notable lack of resiliency and adaptability. On the other hand, they have a low capacity to tolerate the pain associated with depression, further adding to their homicidal risk.[35] Hypotheses about biological mechanisms operating in more minor self-injurious behaviors in BPD have also been noted and may similarly apply to the occurrence of more serious violence.[36]

Suicidal tendencies.   It is interesting that clinicians are more attuned to the possibility of suicidal than homicidal behavior in connection with BPD. Perhaps this lack of attention to the homicidal behaviors of individuals with this diagnosis exists because, following a homicidal act, these individuals are then shunted into the legal system, where they are less likely to receive clinical appraisal and focused research than are their suicidal counterparts. One long-term follow-up study of those with a BPD diagnosis indicated a suicidal risk of 5%–10%.[37] The suicide rate has been found to be 55 times higher than that of the general United States Caucasian population.[38] Continuing alcohol abuse, chaotic impulsivity, and a history of parental brutality or sexual molestation are cited as the keys to suicide in these individuals.[39]

Perhaps the same variables that contribute to suicidality—such as a sensitivity to rejection and reactions to the threat of loss—operate with regard to the potential for homicidal behavior as well. For example, when BPD individuals' close relationships are disturbed, they try to manipulate the situation to regain control; when the control does not materialize, they become more desperate, leading to feelings of abandonment and rage. A state of increasingly precarious self-regulation may follow, with the potential for impulsive acts.

Self-destructive behavior involving danger to others. Recurrent suicidal attempts or gestures are dangerous states, and they may occur multiple times in BPD individuals. Although these acts do not necessarily involve the risk of direct violence to others, the safety of others can be impinged on because of these individual's poor judgment or impulsivity. Such behavior includes driving at high speeds, various accident-prone behaviors, and suicidal gestures. In one case, the patient engaged in a histrionic ploy of leaving the car running in a closed garage while not in the car. However, this person had forgotten that a child was asleep in the house and that the gas fumes would escape into the child's bedroom from the attached garage. The child died of asphyxiation, and the person was charged with homicide.

Another area that has given rise to debate is whether the traits in antisocial, histrionic, narcissistic, and borderline personalities reflect separate entities or are different manifestations of one underlying personality disorder. In the background is how the BPD patients' capacity for displaying dramatic, self-absorbed performances might also be reflected in these other diagnoses. The features of intense, brooding anger coupled with mood instability may coalesce in a quest for self-vindication. Feeling that they have been used by others, they then search for an occasion to strike back self-righteously. They make rash decisions, resulting in an impulsive act, and sometimes to violence, even homicide. The act may occur in the context of feeling panicked about having been abandoned and needing to confront functioning on one's own. Rupturing such dependency ties elicits destructive rage toward those who they blame for their current state. Although many issues remain unresolved, this sequence of events in which these personality traits lead to violent episodes can be illustrated in actual cases.

Cyclicity of affective states.   One consequence of BPD individuals' affective instability is that they tend to cycle through emotions quickly. For example, one day their mood may be quiet and sad, with some verbalizations of hopelessness, and the next day it may be euphoric. However, relief from their depressed mood seems to be connected to the intensity of their anger and hate, rather than the cycling of emotions per se. If too much anger is abated or their anger is abated too quickly—such as may happen when it is treated with psychotherapy or pharmacotherapy—the depression may intensify. Deprived of one of their typical mechanisms for handling depressive affect—their anger—they may make impulsive decisions, such as signing out of an inpatient unit, stopping psychotherapy, ceasing medications, or making more dramatic gestures. Later, they rationalize their leaving treatment either in terms that it did not help them or feeling that the therapist was not sympathetic enough to their suffering.

Such complaints are similar to those that occur in the context of their relationships with intimates or in their daily social life. Manipulative behavior is a common modus operandi of attempting to cope with minor affective disturbances. What is often missed is the potential on some occasion to go beyond their "affective storms." A succession of people in therapeutic roles, from a variety of mental health fields with different treatment modalities, may have fused the BPD patients' past and present hatred and anger toward others into now focusing on one person or group. However, the ever-ready potential to act out an angry role as a miscarried attempt at self-help remains. BPD individuals, like people with antisocial personality disorders, may begin to "burn out" over time and on long-range follow-up have different personality disorders such as histrionic or avoidant.[40] However, that may not occur with respect to the younger subgroup who verge in and out of the "border" of dangerous behavior and may come from more traumatic developmental backgrounds.

A typical situation arises when there is a seemingly unpredictable outburst of high-risk behavior. The behaviors may fluctuate with such rapidity that a clinician (let alone others who are in contact with the patient) cannot keep ahead of the patient. It is not unusual for BPD individuals to have engaged in a pattern of secret and devious behavior over an extended period of time that is suddenly exposed. In retrospect, when an in-depth clinical history is put together, it is easy to see how subtle patterns of eccentric behaviors have operated in a person. Many times, the history will reveal that person having behaved in unpredictable and unstable ways for some time. In a statistical sense, because dangerous behavior represents only a small number of the deviant behaviors engaged in, there is always the difficult problem of predicting these rare events.

Apart from the obvious—that instability in any setting increases the likelihood of a violent act—the question is whether there is any specificity connected to instability in BPD individuals. On one hand, their excessive adoration and groping for someone to idealize is doomed to disappointment given the nature of humans; however, in these individuals, such disappointment does not remain as a disappointment but goes on to a state of felt betrayal or a need for revenge in the context of unremitting hatred. One person in the midst of a divorce from a BPD partner stated, "I could handle all the upsets, lies, and uncertainties, but I couldn't continue to live with someone I felt hated me so much." The partner was later charged with conspiracy to commit murder when she tried to hire someone to kill her former husband.

Impulsiveness

Two of the criteria listed in DSM-IV under BPD—unstable and intense interpersonal relationships and impulsiveness—when taken jointly carry a high potential for dangerousness. Background subtleties illustrate how a violence potential is reached. The impulsiveness is viewed as a personality trait and not confined simply to an occasional impulsive act, such as in the following case example:

Case Example

A woman in her late 20s was a defendant in a criminal suit as well as a civil lawsuit brought by a female colleague in her former company and their joint male supervisor. Initially, she had seen herself as the favorite of the supervisor, an assessment made on the basis of his bantering with her when alone or when mingling with a group of fellow employees. Although her interpretation was that she was being singled out for this specialness, other employees described the supervisor as a generally gregarious and friendly person.

Things reached a crisis when she realized a new female employee had begun dating the supervisor. She then shifted into devaluing him as "dishonest, worthless, and a person who used people." Previously a good worker who "performed for him," she began to brood about the "betrayal." While at dinner with a friend, she found herself talking "out of control about that no good bastard." Although not a drinker, she became intoxicated and went back to the office about 10:00 P.M., thinking that he might be there and hoping to have a confrontation. Finding him absent, she proceeded to wreak havoc on several offices, including her own. Special effort was taken to destroy personal effects and mementos in the offices of the supervisor and the employee he was dating, along with slashing furniture with a knife. On leaving the scene in her vehicle, in which she was driving at a high rate of speed, she collided with another vehicle in which a person was killed.

Because nothing had been reported stolen from the office, the vandalism indicated another basis for the behavior. Thousands of dollars in damage had been done, and a criminal and civil law suit were initiated. On psychiatric evaluation, the woman expressed gratification that the supervisor had not been present as she had had the conscious thought of killing him that evening, possibly being killed herself, or both. Instead, an innocent driver was killed in the course of a series of impulsive acts.

An interesting parallel existed from the woman's college years when she ran for a sorority office but lost the election to a friend. Her view of the friend abruptly shifted to someone who had betrayed her by entering the race after she had. A few weeks later she misinterpreted a comment made by the former friend at a dinner meeting and shoved a piece of pie in her face.

This woman had a pattern of chronically unstable and intense interpersonal relationships that were ordinarily concealed by her dedication to hard work, physical attractiveness, and her ability to pick up new relationships and abandon old ones. Although such relationships rarely moved beyond a superficial level, they allowed her to adapt superficially while not revealing her hidden vulnerabilities. The impulsivity of her behavior on the night in question was not the first of such behaviors, although other events had usually been concealed and had not involved homicidal intent.

Sometimes the patient's history reveals a heightened propensity to react as described above in response to misguided advice from a friend or professional person. The latter individual may be manipulated into acquiescing or condoning some initial steps on the basis of the patient's pleading behavior about how they have been wronged. In some cases, therapists with unresolved problems of their own in this area may promote the patient's behavior as a way of obtaining a vicarious revenge from their own unresolved conflicts. The rash advice offered may be a nonviolent course of action, such as separating from a marriage, breaking up a dating relationship, filing a lawsuit, quitting a job, moving to another part of the country, and so on. When the patient's decision involves an overt act of responding to an affront— real or exaggerated—and a felt need for revenge, the possibility of some degree of harm to another, including homicide, arises.

Case Example

A case that began in a seemingly innocuous manner quickly escalated. A divorced wife bought a new house. When her former husband learned about it, he brooded about how unjust it was that her life was now much better than his. Over the years he had been treated for depressions combined with impulsive behavior. One night he ventilated about the situation in a group therapy session. The therapist had the participants vote as to whether his anger was justified, and his fellow therapy patients voted that it was. Later that night, during a rainstorm, he drove onto the front lawn at his former wife's new house, leaving deep tire ruts that later required a new lawn be laid. Police were called and a high speed chase ensued, with shots being exchanged between the police and the former husband. The man was wounded and later charged with attempted murder. When seen for an independent psychiatric examination for legal purposes a year later, he was still clinging to his belief that his behavior had been justified, based on the vote in group therapy, and still ruminated about ways to hurt his ex-wife.

Rage and Tantrums

Separating the brooding anger displayed by BPD individuals from a periodic paranoid ideation may be quite difficult. Rage reactions draw on anger as well as paranoid thinking and, once again, the problem of comorbidity arises.

Case Example

After her marriage ended in divorce, a 45-year-old woman began to trail her ex-husband in a detective fashion and amass data on him. This occurred without an expressed desire on her part to reconstitute their marriage. In earlier marriage counseling, their relationship had been described as having unrequited affection and better ended. However, after it did end, the wife brooded about revenge to demonstrate what a "womanizer" he was. Although she could discover only one woman in his new life, she became convinced that he had relationships with several women. Her anger at his "deceit" was intense and unremitting, and did not wax and wane as it had during her earlier depressive states. In time, stalking her ex-husband and his lady friend to restaurants or to their respective apartments did not suffice to calm her.

As a next step, she obtained the woman's name, called her, and introduced herself as the ex-wife. She spoke in a pleasant voice to the woman on the phone and arranged a luncheon with the woman, throughout which her pleasant attitude persisted. After the luncheon, the new lady friend became suspicious of the ex-wife as she saw no purpose in pursuing the relationship. When the husband's lady friend refused subsequent offers to meet after the initial luncheon, the ex-wife's anger grew. The ex-wife then made a series of phone calls to the woman, telling her, as the ex-wife put it, "all the bad things I could think of." Even the woman's decision to hang up the phone without listening each time the ex-wife called, in the hope that the calls would cease, had little effect. Eventually, the woman called the police to report the harassment. At that point, the ex-wife decided to "turn the tables" by reporting her former husband and lady friend as the ones who were harassing her by making nuisance calls with lewd comments. This stalemate then shifted to a step-up in dramatic actions.

The ex-wife went to the president of her former husband's company, whom she knew as a person of strict morality, and told him that, during the last years of their marriage, her husband had been having affairs. This led to the president calling the husband in; the husband denied the ex-wife's allegations and became enraged about her lying. In response, he went to his ex-wife's residence where a shouting match led to objects being thrown, physical pushing, his physically assaulting her, and, eventually, the ex-wife stabbing and killing her ex-husband in what she described as self-defense.

The above case example illustrates the desperate efforts of a BPD person to deal with the recurring depression and rage she felt subsequent to a loss and how the mishandling of the loss resulted in a homicide. The ex-wife's increased risk-taking behaviors and tantrums reflected her attempt to relieve her paranoid brooding and regain control by going on the offensive. Her stalking behavior was similar to that seen in other BPD people whose impulsivity becomes more prominent as their control over it falters. Those who stalk celebrities or political figures often seem to have a background of brooding anger and mood instability, characteristics that carry the potential of danger. Cases in which an individual has depression mixed with rage reactions hold the potential for tragic consequences, such as the "fatal attraction syndrome." The movie, *Fatal Attraction,* has been critiqued from a feminist viewpoint as portraying a certain type of woman as the provocateur in this type of situation.[41] The following clinical case antedated the movie and again illustrates the stalking theme:

Case Example

A young female in her 20s dated a man for more than a year, after which he broke off the relationship. He subsequently began to date another young woman, whom he married 9 months later. A few weeks after returning from their honeymoon, the new husband returned to their apartment to find his wife lying dead on the floor. An autopsy listed 97 stab wounds on her body. After first being a suspect, the husband was cleared and the investigation eventually led to the former girlfriend who, it was determined, had earlier been stalking the apartment. The girlfriend underwent hypnosis and amobarbital interviews, arranged by her legal defense team, through which a fragmented story emerged. Based on that story, an insanity defense was entered. Throughout the pretrial and trial, the woman presented the image of a buoyant, talkative, flirtatious, and denying young woman who seemed dissociated not only from her act of homicide, but from the entire proceedings. The woman was eventually found not guilty by reason of insanity.

The drama did not end there; a subsequent legal case arose out of her desire to marry a fellow inmate while she was confined in a state hospital as mentally ill and dangerous. Although her reality testing seemed intact, her feeling of reality was impaired by her dissociative qualities.

Emptiness, Loneliness, and Fears of Abandonment

Accompanying many of the illustrated behaviors are states of desperation experienced as feelings of emptiness and aloneness. Defensive activities, such as frenzied social and work overcommitments to avoid being alone, are well-known patterns BPD individuals follow to temporize the loneliness. Even for the group of BPD individuals with adequate social skills who mingle with others, there is loneliness and a sensed lack of fulfillment in their relationships. What persists is a quest to blame others for their unhappiness. When disappointments occur in the course of life, their rage accumulates, along with the potential for someone to become the recipient of their stored rage in an actual or symbolically murderous act. These individuals' competence is only an "apparent competence," given their heavy reliance on others. Such reliance makes the possibility of abandonment more threatening.[42] To head off the abandonment fears, these people engage in a variety of threats, manipulations, claimed entitlements, blackmail, and maneuvers, including using children to attain their end. It is when these measures are unsuccessful that the BPD individual escalates his or her behavior into more high-risk behaviors that involve the possibility of violence.

The following is a more extreme example of violence occurring in connection with BPD. This example involved a micropsychotic episode that evolved with paranoid thinking:

Case Example

A recently separated woman, who had been treated for depression by various therapists in the past, became anxious about living alone and feeling a lack of support. She began to wonder whether her phones were bugged or if others had obtained a key to her house from her former husband. Although not sure about these ideas, she changed the locks and initially felt reassured when her young daughter was with her. However, the feeling of security did not continue and she began moving from one hotel to another or staying with relatives or friends. When she had exhausted all of these alternatives, a series of panic attacks occurred. Some of these involved intense fears that she was being followed when driving. Matters were brought to a head one evening when she began speeding on a freeway to escape cars she thought could be classified as either "friendly" or "unfriendly" in an attempt to lose her supposed pursuers.

Feeling her anxiety mounting, she decided to get off the freeway and drive to the first office building she could find. Exiting the freeway, she feared it was too dangerous to park in a lot and, instead, drove her car directly through the front doors of an office building. She then sat in the locked car until she felt reassured that the people surrounding the car would not harm her. Unfortunately, someone who had been near the doors she had driven through later died from injuries sustained by the car's entrance.

Substance abuse problems are another complication in BPD individuals' effort to combat loneliness. However, substance abuse also raises the potential for violence. For those who are not self-supporting, chemical dependency may lead to illegal behaviors, such as involvement in prostitution or selling drugs. Others begin the use of such substances during work hours, thus jeopardizing successful past employment; threats to their job performance or security then affect their vulnerable status. Some use drugs to satisfy their need for sensation seeking or to engage in high-risk activities. Whatever the basis, substance abuse heightens the possibility of violent activities in BPD people. The following case example illustrates the destructive combination of abandonment fears with substance use:

Case Example

A well-groomed and stylishly dressed 32-year-old man sought help for recurrent depressed states. He had undergone several earlier attempts to treat his depression, varying from psychoanalysis to chemotherapy. Although he had always had a succession of women in his life, he needed constant reassurances that they would remain loyal to him. Eventually, he would begin nagging them about their activities and possible faithlessness to him. The tempo of these verbal exchanges would increase, and the confrontations between the man and his girlfriend would become accusatory. The man's spying on these women in their places of employment, casually dropping by too often, or standing in nearby office buildings to see who they would leave with at lunch or at the end of the day, would eventually precipitate crises. The outcome for the man was a rage reaction; he would explode with accusations and often become physically abusive. In some cases, his behavior would end the relationship, whereas in others it led to efforts at being reunited, seeking counseling for co-dependency, and other helpful interventions.

In the context of breaking up a relationship, or before a new relationship began, this man would be assailed by feelings of being alone in the world with no one close to him, and then begin to visit prostitutes. Action-oriented behaviors, such as high-speed drives at 100 miles per hour, were another part of his pattern. These might involve drag racing against anonymous others. Some of these ventures would be carried out under the influence of drugs or alcohol, and the man would eventually end up "thawing out." He once entered treatment for chemical dependency and was told by a counselor that he was addicted to one of the medications a previous psychiatrist had given him but now refused to prescribe by phone. The man continued to obtain the drug by visiting various physicians' offices.

This man eventually became entangled with the law on several occasions, such as being charged with attempted murder when he got into a fight, resulting in the victim lapsing into a coma for days with a skull fracture and subdural hematoma, but surviving. There also was a civil lawsuit for harassment resulting from his appearing at a woman's place of employment so frequently that his behavior was noticed by fellow employees and her supervisor. On another occasion, he filed an ethics complaint against the psychiatrist he felt had made him dependent on the medication and who he later blamed for his difficulties.

Endless legal involvements often loom in these types of situations, based on events such as hit-and-run accidents, fights or quarrels with people BPD individuals feel have slighted them, and assaults on friends or lovers.

Disturbed Sense of Reality

Another characteristic that may emerge in those with a BPD organization is a disturbance in their sense or feeling of reality. This is different than their reality testing being impaired, such as in a psychotic organization, where differentiation from others is difficult. BPD individuals are usually capable of distinguishing their inner life from the world of external events, apart from during any micropsychotic episodes that may be experienced. However, their confused social reality creates difficulties. It leads people and organizations with whom they deal to misjudge their actual social capabilities based on external behaviors. What goes for social poise may be a thin veneer for lurking misinterpretations.

Splitting as a defense. To further understand BPD individuals' proneness to violence, the theoretical construct of splitting as a defense is often introduced. It is well known that BPD individuals oscillate in their assessments of others between idealizing the others as good and devaluing them. The shift to badness raises the potential for their seeing another as a persecutor. Diverse primitive defenses related to the splitting are projective identification, omnipotence, omnipotent control, primitive idealization, and devaluation and denial.[43] These defenses induce an unevenness in personal relationships that contributes to impulsive behavior. The individuals shift from manipulativeness and arrogance to helplessness and seeking to blame others for their predicaments. In the midst of poorly regulated anxiety, depressive states and rage emerge, with the possibility of acting on the murderous rage.

Superego functioning also makes its contribution to the imbalance between the punitive aspects of some wrongful act or fantasy of an individual and the idealized notion of how he or she should perform. The result is the lack of a stable, internalized system of morality.[44] On one hand, guilt and depression emerge; on the other, there is manipulation and exploitation. What this reflects is splitting into the extreme of the all-good or all-bad representations of the self and others. Rather than being realistic ideals, the ideals are driven by power, domination, and perfectionism. One reason for the lack of integration is the intensity of aggression influencing self and object representations. Attempts to bring together the extreme degrees of love and hate toward the self and others initiates confusion, anxiety, and depression. The theory is that conflict over aggression in childhood during the oral and anal stages is later projected, leaving them prone to attribute a paranoid imagery to parental figures later in their life who are then seen as dangerous. These confused internal images later leave the BPD person vulnerable when disagreements arise and tend to make them more likely to act on their hatreds.

Disconnected quality of behavior. Another contributing variable to violent behavior—the smoldering resentments and enduring hatred—may seem incongruent with the theory that BPD individuals frequently vacillate between opposites. In line with this characteristic, these individuals often do not seek just a vindication or victory, but sometimes a total annihilation of a selected target who becomes a hated object and once again is seen as responsible for their unhappy plight. Such targets may be chosen from anyone and anything connected to an event or time in the individual's past or present life. Although tantrums and rage reactions occur, such "ventilating" at best only leads to a temporary alleviation of BPD individuals' turmoil. Distorted memories persist and contribute to future blowups as fantasy stirs up needs for future reenactments. If there is no current provocation, past ones will serve. Perhaps some past wrongs to justify their acts need to be embellished or even invented. Such confusion may help explain the *pseudologia fantastica* seen in BPD individuals.[45]

What results is a disconnectedness in behavior from long-term memory. Assessments about probabilities of behavior are decoupled from the overall assessment functions that customarily operate in people. Unmodulated responses occur abruptly and may not directly be in response to a present situation. An unpredictable and exaggerated response, to the point of violence, corresponds to this type of instability. Hence, the minor slights or rejections become monumental. Competition that emerges in some areas of a BPD individual's life (e.g., those involving appearance, work, social life) are perceived not just as competition but as threats to his or her life, prompting the individual to rise to the level of needing to destroy someone.

Such an overlearned memory maintains old grudges and misinterprets them in their present environment. The "sore spots" persist and later trigger stereotyped maladaptive responses. Maltreated or abused children or adolescents may not only overreact to those in authority or those of the opposite sex, but as they develop may remain prone to misinterpret overtures, gestures, or words. They remain ripe for making accusations about another, taking umbrage, or perhaps attacking others outright—if not physically, at least verbally or in some devious way. In a longitudinal follow-up of 206 former BPD inpatients, an analysis of variance found parental brutality as the factor most likely to predict a worse than average outcome.[33] Poor outcomes were noted in those who had been jailed following behaviors based on impulsivity, flaunting the law, or had developed counteraggressivity from parental cruelty.

Clinical descriptions of dissociated states with dramatic alterations in personality have been present since the nineteenth century. Such splitting as part of a borderline syndrome helps explain how some homicidal-level acts can occur. The hallmark is the fluctuating emotional state of BPD patients, with their accumulated and slowly subsiding rage. Situations go awry if there is too rapid an attempt to dissipate their hate, such as may happen in the course of some treatment processes, or in therapeutic relationships that tap their profound ambivalence. Disruptions of attachments in daily life provide another explosive possibility. When they experience such a lack of homeostasis, a dissociative episode may intervene that allows them to flee into an altered personality who then permits violence.

In an altered state, diverse types of destruction may occur: suicide attempts or gestures, head banging, wrist slashing, object throwing, attacking of others, or a homicidal-level attack. An abrupt shift into a blatant, smiling, *la belle indifférence* may subsequently appear. One perpetrator of a homicide, undiscovered at the time, joined mourners in expressing his deepest regrets about the death of a loved one. Others manifest "attacks" at sites connected with the deceased, such as funerals or ceremonies, in which their external signs of grief may be conspicuously striking. In one case, a person later indicted for a homicide attended the victim's funeral. Mourners were impressed by the depth of grief they witnessed in him. An interesting twist in these type of situations occurred when a woman reported to the chair of a company selection committee that, when she was a co-worker, she had once carried on an affair with the leading candidate for a senior position. Sometime later after the man had committed suicide, the woman sent condolences to his wife, along with offers of friendship, although the woman and the wife had never met. Such vicarious killings by way of "killing his chances" are rarely uncovered publicly.

■ Legal Considerations:
Personal Responsibility and
Borderline Personality Disorder

Given the traits and behaviors of individuals with the BPD diagnosis, a recurring problem that arises, often in legal or ethical contexts, is the question of their responsibility for their behavior. This question is more challenging for this group than for those with any other diagnosis. Although a psychiatrist becomes aware of the dynamics and interactional systems that reveal shifting patterns between the victim and the victimizer or the oppressed and the oppressor, issues involving appraisals of responsibility do not usually arise in clinics, and addressing such questions is usually discouraged.

Responsibility questions are not confined to the criminal area, as civil actions may be later instituted against perpetrators of homicides for wrongful death actions. Alternatively, these individuals and the attorneys hired to represent them may raise issues about the limitations of responsibility for their behavior, often in the context of BPD individuals seeing themselves as being the wronged party. Also, these patients' life orientation may be a litigious one where they have initiated suits. Problems arise when they become the aggressor because of their propensity to react or to exact revenge. In some cases, their previous physicians or lawyers become potential victims, sometimes on a homicidal level.

In the criminal area, the issue of responsibility may arise through some variation of an insanity defense, diminished responsibility approaches, or allegations that sexual or physical abuse is responsible for their behavior. The area is a quagmire of confused efforts to handle legal issues, given the lack of conceptual clarity in psychiatric thinking about which types of personalities are to be seen as responsible for their behavior. Some argue that such questions should be dealt with outside the province of medicine or psychiatry. However, it is difficult to bypass the issues because, at least implicitly, the questions touch on psychiatric preconceptions about behavior on many levels. A key issue is how and to what degree BPD individuals' capacities to exercise choice and to make decisions are affected by their personality functioning.

Analogous quandaries arise in the frequently encountered area of alcoholic individuals who become involved in legal difficulties associated with their propensity to become intoxicated and act in destructive ways. Although the emphasis in treatment programs dealing with alcoholism is that such people have a disease and may or may not be in control of themselves, exercising choices such as entering treatment programs and giving up drinking are implicit in the programs' approaches. Some are particularly critical of the viewpoint that alcoholic individuals lack free will and should not be viewed as responsible for their behavior.[46]

Similar questions arise with regard to comorbid disorders that may be present in BPD individuals. Allegations of behavior occurring in trancelike states, fits, or fugues or through multiple personalities may be raised. For example, recently efforts have been made to extend the boundaries of nonresponsibility to include violent acts ascribed to premenstrual syndrome or battered woman's syndrome if they are seen as part of the syndrome of borderline personalities. The reasoning is that the perpetrator has developed such a physiological vulnerability or has been living in such a state of fear from past assaultive behavior that he or she lacks the capacity to make choices about behavior, such as when assaulting someone or committing a homicide. A similar position has been argued in the case of BPD individuals who endured physical or sexual abuse as children when they commit violent acts. The conclusion urged may be that the person should not be seen as currently responsible for his or her actions because of the impact of past traumatic occurrences. The problem is that such a position is unsupported by empirical data about the long-term consequences of abusive home environments in connection with adult violence.[47] Some also stress the genetic antecedents in those prone to violence.[48]

These exculpatory issues are troublesome because of the increased frequency with which they are raised in connection with the BPD diagnosis. The question is the degree to which such behavior reflects some type of cognitive dysfunction, even given that the choice to commit violence is a troubled one. Can these individuals control their behavior to a degree similar to others who have certain personality traits and experience life stresses? Why does a particular BPD person commit a homicide whereas others with the same diagnosis do not? Specifically, could they have done otherwise but simply chose not to?

Without becoming lost in an endless philosophical debate as to whether someone who ought to behave in a certain way can do so, the clinical inferences of this situation can be examined. It is logical to distinguish the overall group of BPD cases from the subgroup of those individuals with this diagnosis who have had a major psychotic or micropsychotic episode imposed on their borderline state at the time of homicide. Even these psychotic cases raise issues related to the perpetrator's responsibility that are not easily resolvable and are often contested in court. However, there are clinically distinguishable signs and symptoms when a BPD individual has experienced a psychotic episode. If it were to be argued that all impulsive behavior occurring in BPD individuals occurs on a psychotic basis, which is an unproven assumption, it would shift the entire level of discussion away from just BPD individuals to all psychotic people. This raises broader issues such as whether or not most BPD cases, if not personality disorders, are to be viewed as psychotic whenever individuals with that diagnosis behave in a violent manner. Such a circular argument is likely to confuse matters further.

It would not be clinically sound to classify as psychotic every eruptive and violent act of a BPD individual. The person who destroyed the offices of her colleagues was quite willing to see herself as lacking control over her behavior. People who act from motives of spite, malice, hatred, envy, revenge, and so on are subsequently quite eager to see their behaviors as being explained, and therefore excused, because certain emotions were predominant or seemed overwhelming at the time. Assessments become more difficult when BPD individuals appear to be experiencing micropsychotic episodes. Believing they are in danger, such as being pursued on a highway leading to efforts to escape, even at the cost of driving a car into the entrance of a building and killing someone, are more complicated. In such cases, a psychotic diagnosis might be added. Yet, in most cases, the thread of commonality in the behavior seems to be unmet power needs that are masked and rationalized by a stated helplessness and lack of control.

An ultimate issue operating in such cases is whether impulsive behavior occurring in a borderline personality should be seen as reflecting an incapacity to exercise choice. Or does such behavior rather reflect a person who wishes and chooses to behave in that manner from other motives? Is a person with BPD so incapacitated that he or she could act in no other way at the time of the violent act? This would mean that the capacity to choose was impaired to such a degree that self-restraint was an impossibility. Such a line of reasoning should presumably hold not only for a particular act, such as homicide, but also for other diverse and scheming behaviors. To argue otherwise would imply that a qualitative difference exists in such personalities that they are held responsible only for some impulsive acts but not others, and confusion would reign from trying to decipher which is which.

The question of personal responsibility should be extended beyond the legal setting. If confined to legal situations, such reasoning would lead to a position that a valid argument for nonresponsibility can be made only when an impulsive or scheming act occur that leads to a charge in a courtroom. A BPD individual's responsibility should also be questioned in connection with other types of provocative behaviors as, for example, when a BPD individual feels a powerful desire to "do someone in" by verbal gossip or slander, rather than to restrain himself or herself. Are they unwittingly in such a predetermined ego state that, in one of their emotional storms, their outburst cannot be controlled any more than a homicidal act? Similar questions operate for minor outbursts such as throwing objects at people, shoving a piece of pie in someone's face, or the little acts of lying, deception, and exaggeration that occur as part of BPD individuals' daily functioning.

Conversely, if each of these types of behavior is seen as one of a series of choices the person is making, with diverse motives and gratifications operating, the consequences accruing from the behavior would be interpreted quite differently. The behavior is then less readily tolerated or acceptable. Instead, it may be seen as "typical" of certain people by those who know them well and who learn to tread carefully around them. Such "adaptation" by associates should not be confused with exculpation based on the view that the person could not control his or her actions.

Serious consequences may follow, depending on which view of borderline behavior is taken. If BPD individuals are seen as "out of control," what follows is a perspective that they are "sick" and not to be assessed as blameworthy. Perhaps, like other sick people, they deserve pity. Such an assessment of illness may allow a host of "fringe benefits" to accrue to them, such as referrals for treatment, disability payments, participation in support groups, collection of awards in civil litigation actions, as well as permission to continue acting periodically in the manner they have, since their uncontrollable illness may reassert itself in the future.

A contrary view takes a position that BPD individuals are responsible for their actions. From this position, they are no longer seen as having permission to behave in the ways they have in the past or be classified as nonculpable. The "sick" role of attributing their behavior to past adverse influences, either from genetic endowment, childhood experiences, or unfortunate encounters in adulthood, is not seen as an acceptable excuse for their actions. These people would then be expected to assess their future behavior by calculating their anticipated pleasure against the painful consequences of continuing to play the odds of living in their flamboyant and provocative style.

Clinicians are aware of the need some patients have to increase the tempo of their behaviors when they are not being successful in achieving sought-after goals. For BPD individuals, the resultant behaviors are tantrums, rages, and attacks. Halleck has commented that it is important not to assess responsibility in terms of whether the behavioral outcome seems rational or irrational.[49] The difficulty is that treating professionals often make moral judgments and then seek to buttress their moral conclusions clinically by using the BPD diagnosis as the basis for saying someone lacked the capacity to control homicidal acts. At a minimum, a conceptual framework is needed when responsibility is tied in with a clinical goal of helping someone function differently in the future. Although this would not exculpate one from errant behavior in a legal sense, it would at least keep psychiatrists from becoming trapped in assessments, rightly or wrongly, where patients and attorneys maneuver them into playing the role of moralist without their realizing it.

■ References

1. Knight R: Borderline states. Bull Menninger Clin 17:1–12, 1953
2. Gunderson JG, Kolb JE, Austin V: The Diagnostic Interview for Borderline Patients. Am J Psychiatry 138:896–903, 1981
3. American Psychiatric Association: Diagnostic and Statistical Manual of Mental Disorders, 3rd Edition. Washington, DC, American Psychiatric Association, 1980
4. American Psychiatric Association: Diagnostic and Statistical Manual of Mental Disorders, 3rd Edition, Revised. Washington, DC, American Psychiatric Association, 1987
5. Clarkin JF, Kernberg OF: Developmental factors in borderline personality disorder and borderline personality organization, in Borderline Personality Disorder. Edited by Paris J. Washington DC, American Psychiatric Press, 1993, pp 161–184
6. Berelowitz M, Tarnopolsky A: The validity of borderline personality disorder: an updated review of recent research, in Personality Disorder Reviewed. Edited by Tyrer P, Stein G. London, Gas Kell, 1993, pp 90–112
7. Kohut H: The Restoration of the Self. New York, International Universities Press, 1977

8. Pope GH, Jonas JM, Hudson JI, et al: The validity of DSM-III border-line personality personlity disorder. Arch Gen Psychiatry 40:23–30, 1983

9. Kaplan HI, Sadock BJ: Personality disorders, in Synopsis of Psychiatry/Behavioral Sciences/Clinical Psychiatry. Baltimore, MD, Williams & Wilkins, 1991, pp 525–542

10. Kavoussi RJ, Coccaro EF, Klar HM, et al: Structured interviews for borderline personality disorder. Am J Psychiatry 174:1522–1525, 1990

11. Grinker RR, Werble B, Dyre RC: The Borderline Syndrome. New York, Basic Books, 1968

12. Liebowitz MR, Klein DF: Hysteroid dysphoria. Psychiatr Clin North Am 2:555–575, 1979

13. Olsen J: Cold Kill. New York, Atheneum, 1987

14. Stone MH: Towards a psychobiological theory of borderline personality disorder. Dissociation 1:2–15, 1988

15. Greenman DA, Gunderson JG, Dane M, et al: An examination of the borderline diagnosis in children. Am J Psychiatry 143:998–1003, 1986

16. Herman JL, Perry JC, van der Kolk BA: Childhood trauma in borderline personality disorder. Am J Psychiatry 146:490–495, 1989

17. Links PS: Family environment and family psychopathology in the etiology of borderline personality disorder, in Borderline Personality Disorder: Clinical and Empirical Perspectives. Edited by Clarkin JF, Marziali E, Monroe-Blum H. New York, Guilford, 1992

18. Mahler M, Pine F, Bergman A: The Psychological Growth of the Human Infant. New York, Basic Books, 1975

19. Masterson JF, Rinsley DB: The borderline syndrome: the role of the mother in the genesis and psychic structure of the borderline personality. Int J Psychoanal 56:163–177, 1975

20. Adler G: Borderline Psychopathology and Its Treatment. New York, Jason Aronson, 1985

21. Bezirganians, Cohen P, Brook JS: The impact of mother-child interaction on the development of borderline personality disorder. Am J Psychiatry 150:1836–1842, 1993

22. Kernberg OF: Borderline Conditions and Pathological Narcissism. New York, Jason Aronson, 1975

23. Adler G: How useful is the borderline concept? Psychoanalytic Inquiry 8:353–372, 1988

24. Abend SM, Porder MS, Willick MS: Borderline Patients: Psychoanalytic Perspectives. New York, International Universities Press, 1983

25. Hurt SW, Clarkin JF: Borderline personality disorder: prototypic typology and the development of treatment manuals. Psychiatric Annuals 20:13–18, 1990

26. Fahy TA: The diagnosis of multiple personality disorders. Br J Psychiatry 153:597–606, 1988

27. Putnam FW: Diagnosis and Treatment of Multiple Personality Disorder. New York, Guilford, 1989

28. Stone MH, Stone DK, Hart SW: Natural history of borderline patients treated by intensive hospitalization. Psychiatr Clin North Am 10:185–206, 1987

29. Andrulonis PA, Vogul NG: Comparison of borderline personality subcategories to schizophrenic and affective disorders. Br J Psychiatry 144:358–363, 1984

30. Akiskal H: Subaffective disorders: dysthymic, cyclothymic, and bipolar II disorders in the "borderline" realm. Psychiatr Clin North Am 4:25–46, 1981

31. Kroll J: Borderline Conditions. New York, WW Norton, 1988

32. Zanarini MD, Gunderson JG: Axis I phenomenology of borderline personality disorder. Compr Psychiatry 30:149–156, 1989

33. Stone MH: Long-term outcome in personality disorders. Br J Psychiatry 162:299–313, 1993

34. Keller MB, Shapiro RW: "Double depression": superimposition of acute depressive episodes on chronic depressive disorders. Am J Psychiatry 139:438–442, 1982

35. Maltsberger JR, Lovett CG: Suicide in borderline personality disorder, in Handbook of Borderline Disorders. Edited by Silver D, Rosenbluth M. Madison, CT, International Universities Press, 1992, pp 335–338

36. Russ MF: Self-injurious behavior in patients with borderline personality disorder. Journal of Personality Disorders 6:64–81, 1992

37. Plakun EM: Prediction of outcome in borderline personality disorder. Journal of Personality Disorders 5:93–101, 1991

38. Stone MH: Borderline personality disorder, in Abnormalities of Personality: Within and Beyond the Realm of Treatment. New York, WW Norton, 1993, pp 215–257

39. Stone MH: The Fate of Borderline Patients. New York, Guilford, 1990

40. McGlashan TH: The Chestnut Lodge follow-up study, III: long-term outcome of borderline patients. Arch Gen Psychiatry 43:20–30, 1986

41. Greenberg HR: Fatal attraction: bring the lady a bug. Academy Forum 33:14–15, 1989

42. Linehan MM: Behavior therapy, dialectics, and the treatment of borderline personality disorder, in Handbook of Borderline Disorders. Edited by Silver D, Rosenbluth M. Madison, CT. International Universities Press, 1992, pp 415–434

43. Perry JC, Herman JL: Trauma and defense in the etiology of borderline personality disorder, in Borderline Personality Disorder. Edited by Paris J. Washington, DC, American Psychiatric Press, 1993, pp 123–140

44. Kernberg OF: The psychotherapeutic treatment of borderline patients, in Borderline Personality Disorder. Edited by Paris J. Washington, DC, American Psychiatric Press, 1993, pp 261–284

45. Snyder S: Pseudologia fantastica in the borderline patient. Am J Psychiatry 143:1287–1289, 1986

46. Fingarette H: Heavy Drinking: The Myth of Alcoholism as a Disease. Berkeley, CA, University of California Press, 1988

47. Widom CS: Does violence beget violence? Psychol Bull 106:3–28, 1989

48. DiLalla LF, Gottesman II: Biological and genetic contributors to violence—Widom's untold tale. Psychol Bull 109:125–129, 1991

49. Halleck SL: The concept of responsibility in psychotherapy. Am J Psychotherapy 36:292–303, 1982

CHAPTER 5

Dependent Personality Disorders and Killing

A seeming paradox exists regarding individuals who have dependent personality disorder (DPD): how can a person who seems so meek, gentle, and desirous of pleasing others commit such a horrendous act as killing another human being? When considered overtly, the two essential features of DPD individuals' personalities—the pervasiveness of their dependency needs and their submissiveness—would not seem to predispose them toward violence, either against others or against themselves. What follows is a discussion of those aspects of the dependent personalities that, under the right circumstances, can lead to a violent eruption.

■ From Childhood to Adulthood: Roots of Dependency

Although some argue that the personality traits consistent with DPD emerge only in young adulthood, the more pervasive psychiatric view is that the behaviors actually emerge much earlier and are noticeable in childhood by those who have contact with these individuals.[1]

Once a person with DPD reaches adulthood, the roots for the pattern of emotional attachments he or she will develop have been laid. Powerful effects from the time when the person was more fragile and perhaps literally could not survive alone remain. The remnants of these cognitive processes persist into adulthood and lie ready to spring to the ascendancy in complex relationships. Not only do these people feel they cannot survive without the person with whom they have chosen to have a relationship, but they feel insignificant to others in their own right. Their behavior conveys that, only through the person they have selected for such a special attachment role, can they survive and have a meaningful sense of self.

In adulthood, some DPD individuals present a facade of independence. In fact, there are those who have been able to achieve success in a particular vocation, as long as their dependency was not disturbed. Others have handled their unresolved conflicts through the role of caring for others with similar dependency problems. In the jargon of the popularized mental health idiom, these people are considered to be "codependent," meaning that their identity has become based on their taking care of other people or assuming responsibility for them. This behavior pattern conceals their own dependency conflicts. In many ways, however, this description oversimplifies the nature of dependency conflicts; it is based on an extension of the disease concept of addiction to more pervasive personality disturbances and character phenomena.[2]

■ Predisposing Factors

Let us now turn to some of the factors that can lead to acts of homicidal proportions by DPD individuals. Their prominent needs to be cared for and nurtured are obviously not unique to them, and, to a casual observer, their lives often seem outwardly successful and uneventful. However, their difficulties arise when they feel their need to be loved is not being met and in how they react to that feeling. Many of the characteristics discussed below overlap and in reality cannot be separated; they are separated here only for the sake of discussion.

Inability to Free Self From Dependency

A core conflict in DPD individuals is their belief that their well-being is necessarily contingent on others—often a particular person or institution. The absence of or betrayal by that person first engenders feelings of helplessness mixed with frustration. The frustration and anxiety occur in the context of a fragile security system that is easily upset. As a corollary, they experience an affective state in which they feel they are not in charge of their life and lack an autonomous existence. With minimal coping devices to handle the specter of threatened losses, their self-esteem system remains under threat. When the devices to reinstate such a relationship do not succeed, depression or the use of addictive substances to palliate the anxiety and loneliness are often seen. As has been shown in social psychology and cognitive psychology, more benefits accrue to those who are able to exercise more choices in their life and are not constrained by feeling compelled to carry out certain behavior to maintain their security.[3] Attempted breakups almost always meet with initial decisions to return to the relationship, although, at least on one level, the relationship is perceived as painful and destructive.

Similarly, it is possible that the partner may be caught up in a reciprocal pattern on a different level. Then, power plays between the partners emerge in a desperate quest for a sense of power over the other in an effort to avoid the deep abyss of feeling alone and powerless. In the course of such relationships, the illusion is perpetrated that their relationship is deep, meaningful, and caring. On occasion, brief insights occur that not only do they not particularly care for each other, but they desperately wish they could be free of the entanglements and destructive aspects of the relationship.

Case Example

A 35-year-old white male had become attached to a woman from whom he felt he could not separate. Their relationship was volatile, destructive, and a source of pain for both of them, although he felt that his was the more painful role. He had met his partner when he was a patient in a chemical dependency treatment unit. The woman had also previously been treated for chemical dependency, but at the time of their meeting was working as a counselor on the unit. They were immediately attracted to each other. Shortly thereafter, they arranged to see each other clandestinely, both on and off the unit, and soon became sexually involved. Following his discharge from the unit, their relationship continued. They both began to use drugs again, although she was able to keep her usage to a minimum level.

Once removed from the institutional setting, the relationship began to show difficulties. The woman was demanding and controlling, and the man began to resent the demands she made on him. Rather than confronting her with her manipulative and extractive behavior, he conformed his behavior to her demands based on his fear that he might lose her. In time, her flirtatiousness and flamboyance in the presence of other men began to upset him. Although she seemed more mature than he and to have more worldly experience, she reminded him of girls he had known in his adolescence. Both individuals were of superior intelligence; he had pursued a doctorate degree for a time, and she had received superior marks in college before dropping out after 2 years because she became bored.

After 9 months, she told him she would be leaving in 2 days for a week's vacation to think over their relationship. She did not tell him where she was going, and her relatives would not disclose her whereabouts. When she did not return in 3 weeks, he obtained the phone number of her residence in a different city from her former place of employment. When he called one night at 11:30 P.M., a man answered the phone; from the noise in the background, it was obvious that a party was being held at her home. He immediately hung up, but called again the next morning. She answered and informed him she did not wish to see him anymore and that he should not call. Contrary to her wishes, he began calling often, sending letters, and eventually announced that he was coming to see her. When he arrived, he found she had moved without leaving a forwarding address. He began to drink heavily, go on binges, and engage in high-risk activities such as driving at excessive speeds and becoming intoxicated to the point of unconsciousness. In desperation, he readmitted himself, heavy with nostalgia, to the unit where they had originally met. He remained preoccupied with her rejection, fantasized about her with other men, and dwelled on the humiliation of his experience with her. At that point, he decided he would find out where she was through her parents.

He left the treatment unit, and stopped in a liquor store to buy a fifth of liquor on the way to her parents' home. He entered through a basement window, went to the kitchen and waited for them to come home. When her father came into the kitchen, they shared a cup of coffee; the father then said he would take him back to the hospital. They talked about the past, which aroused the man's nostalgia, with the twist that he recalled only the good times. When the mother came downstairs and saw him, became agitated, and insisted they leave for the hospital immediately.

In response, the man announced that he would not leave until he got their daughter's phone number or address. They tried to convince him that she did not wish to see him and that he should return to the treatment unit. He grabbed a kitchen knife and held it up to their dog, with the ultimatum that the dog would die if they refused to give him their daughter's address or phone number. When the father threw hot coffee in his face, he reacted by plunging a knife into the father's chest and killing him. In attempting to intervene, the mother was also stabbed and killed.

In the above case example, all the elements of pathological dependency were present, coupled with other signs of character pathology. Mixed elements, including sadomasochistic traits, were seen in both parties, although only one committed an act of homicidal violence. This case example illustrates how the victim of such violence need not be the primary person in the relationship but could be third parties or in some cases innocent victims unbeknown to either of the principals. In this particular case, the man, in his cringing inadequacy and inability to leave a relationship that was doomed and painful, progressed along a path of personal disaster that eventually involved others. He felt incapable of living without the person who had become the recipient of his deep and untapered attachments. He had never developed the ability to accept emotionally that one can survive various losses, build new relationships, and somehow, in time, survive for the better. Instead, he perceived an internalized, pervasive threat that survival was not possible without this other person, no matter what the price. This further illustrates the power of such attachments—much like a child who cannot thrive or live without the presence of the parenting object.

Similar types of killings can also be ascribed to the "Othello syndrome." Two ill-matched people with obvious incompatibilities feel a profound need for each other, but cannot break off their relationship even though they sense danger. On one hand, a supposedly gentle and guarded young girl abandons her father to go with the Moor; on the other hand, the Moor, in late maturity, has always avoided such entanglements and believes he is risking his career by engaging in one now. Distrust and jealousy are fostered by his alter ego, Iago.[4] The young girl, Desdemona, needs to establish her power by defending Cassio, Iago's rival for Othello's trust, and exploits her seductiveness. She senses danger, yet cannot leave the situation and would not even if she could. When Othello falsely believes she is irretrievably lost to Cassio, he cannot bear her loss or tolerate his jealousy and kills her, attempts to kill his evil spirit, Iago, and finally commits suicide.

Inability to Deal With Conflicts

Some DPD individuals use psychoactive substances to quell their fears of abandonment. However, for those who do not resort to substance use, being without the significant other creates a feeling of emptiness and of being at the mercy of one's own feelings of fear, smallness, and insignificance. To conquer the feelings engendered by this state of helplessness and total inadequacy, some of the most brutal acts can occur in the form of a homicidal restitution.

Case Example

A man had been involved for 12 years in what seemed to be a good marriage, based on public observations that he adored his wife. Yet, behind the scenes, he held two jobs to meet their many financial and social demands. In time, loans also had to be taken out, which led to accumulated debt. Meanwhile, his wife engaged in the flamboyant lifestyle that she desired, with or without him. When she began to come home at 1:00 A.M. or 2:00 A.M., his need for denial of what this might mean was maintained by accepting her reasons that she had simply been having a good time with friends.

Up to this point, this would simply have been one more marriage in trouble, but there would be no hints of the potential for a homicide.

The interesting phenomenon in such cases is why, at a certain point, the defenses break down. Sometimes, the final common pathway leading to their breakdown can be uncovered, but in other cases it remains a mystery.

Case Example *(continued)*

Eventually, the husband could no longer deny his suspicions about the veracity of his wife's version of what she was doing when out. A predisposing factor was the prolonged attempt to keep up their expensive lifestyle without relief. Playing into the situation was the wife's expectation that things would continue in this vein indefinitely.

When she failed to return home by the early hours one morning, he drove to bars and night spots they had once gone to together or she had gone to alone in the past. At one of them, a bartender told him he had seen a woman who fit his wife's description leave with another man. The husband waited at home for her return, at which time he asked where she had been. She gave the customary answer of being out with friends. For the first time, he confronted her with his belief that she had been out with another man. She responded, "So what if I was? At least, I can have some fun with him and not be worried all the time like you are." Within the space of a few seconds, he took a gun from a drawer and fired several shots at his wife, killing her.

At the time of his subsequent psychiatric evaluation after the killing, he was filled with remorse, and sobbingly told how much he missed his wife and what a wonderful person and wife she had been. He offered no explanation for what he had done, and had trouble accepting the fact he was the person who had committed such a violent act. He did not recall firing the shots, and could only remember taking the gun from the drawer.

At the time of the homicide, feeling abused and victimized, this man's repression and denial, which usually operated, had temporarily broken down, allowing his hatred and aggression to emerge through his defenses. After the homicide, however, he returned to his customary behavior as a subservient and loyal person. The problem was that, in this brief out-of-character interval, a homicide had been committed.

The weakness in the psychological defenses DPD individuals operate with over their lifetime is seen in their inability to deal with conflicts that have often existed over many years. The postponement of dealing with the conflicts has allowed them to continue their seemingly well-adjusted lifestyle. Even apart from a homicide occurring, what they live through is a high price to pay for the inability to deal with the way their conflicts intrude on their life. In the above case example, the man's image of servicing his wife to keep her happy, with minimal self-gratification apart from securing erratic dependency gratification, was overwhelmed when he could not reconcile his wife's impinging disloyalty, dishonesty, and lack of appreciation for his dedication and suffering with the new evidence of her disloyalty. In many of these cases, after the homicidal act, the old pattern of defenses is reconstituted, coupled with the re-idealization of the partner and their relationship. Except for the death of their partner, these individuals revert to the prehomicide status quo, with the difference that they often spend many years institutionalized.

A serious dilemma posed by individuals with a dependent personality disorder is that they never know when their maladaptive defenses may fail; nor can this breakdown point be gauged much better by mental health professionals. Their self-esteem is so contingent on pleasing others and waiting on them that they do not wish to face the anxiety and discomfort of confronting the difficult dilemmas that exist, which makes therapeutic efforts tenuous.

When disputes between lovers arise, desperate attempts are made to continue the relationship at any price. In the last case, the price would have been for the man to accept that his wife was exploiting him, a price that would be intolerably high for the little affection that he received from her. Consequently, the issue of whether he was capable of leaving the relationship was raised. In the past, he had handled being victimized by the exploitative behavior of his wife by placing himself in a position of needing to deny his anger and resentment and to keep portraying himself as an individual constantly working against odds to make others happy, particularly the woman he loved. Although victimization served to distance himself from his mounting aggression and anger toward his wife, it simultaneously allowed him to maintain his self-image as a peace-loving person without murderous desires. His anger would be projected onto others to maintain this image.

Desire to Keep Relationship at All Costs

In cases where a joint murder-suicide occurs, the DPD individual may have been motivated not only by the wish to destroy the person who disappointed him or her, but also by a fantasy of the two (or more) of them being together in some other type of existence, paradisiacal or not. Based on interviews with DPD individuals who have survived suicide attempts subsequent to committing a murder, it does appear that their wish to be restored to perfect bliss with the person they had overidealized was one of their driving motives to the homicide-suicide attempt.

Deep Ambivalence

A question arises as to why a DPD person cannot simply act more rationally and give up the past relationship and look for a new one. Given that the relationship has had a good deal of pain attached to it, this would seem a logical step. Such a solution would also be parsimonious if available. Any person involved in an intense relationship is disappointed when his or her expectations are not fulfilled. Resentment and anger are inevitably experienced. However, it is the presence of deep and unresolved ambivalence that prevents a DPD person from objectively examining his or her shortcomings in search for the answer to why a relationship with a friend, employer, lover, spouse, or other is not going well. Only when the ambivalence is not too prominent can the anger be expressed and the processes of detachment begin. However, when anger or hate surface in a relationship between a person with DPD and his or her partner, it is more difficult for that person to step back than it is for others. The lack of sufficient distancing keeps the intensity of his or her ambivalence at a high level.

Placing Blame for Unhappiness on Others

DPD individuals find others to be at fault if they do not respond in the manner they demand; they hold the inculcated view that others ("need satisfiers") exist for the purpose of meeting their needs when the occasion arises. The potential for more violent behavior becomes higher when DPD individuals shift their thinking to believe that others are not only at fault, but must pay a price for disappointing them, even to the degree of needing punishment. In some cases, their internal conflict progresses to a debate about whether suicide, homicide, or a homicide-suicide finale is the needed course of action.

When a DPD individual attacks others—physically or verbally—the implication is that others are responsible. Impulsive acts of rage and anger to manipulate others are especially possible for these individuals when comorbid states of histrionic or borderline personality disorders are present. Wanting desperately for others to take over and alleviate their pain makes their frustration with accompanying anger inevitable.

The persistent illusion is that others can solve their problems and, by their not doing so, they are responsible for the DPD individuals' misery. The typical situations that raise these conflicts to homicidal levels are seen in marriages that are coming apart, love relationships threatening to end, betrayal in business or personal relationships, prolonged divorce negotiations where attorneys or judges may be blamed as well as former partners, custody disputes, or divorce settlements where one party seems to get an unfavorable distribution.

How does the frustration and resentment finally rise to a homicidal level in these settings? Conversely, why do not more people commit homicides in such emotional dilemmas? A beginning answer is that DPD individuals attack others in ways that are to some degree the equivalent of homicide far more frequently than is appreciated—sometimes the attacks are physical, but, more typically, are verbal or through social manipulations that incur the wrath and indignation of the others. Lawsuits are one device for attacking someone else and securing the support of others—that is, those that one pays to help them, such as attorneys or experts. In turn, such attacks may lead the party being attacked to respond by counterattacks or countersuits.

In some of these situations, the anger is displaced onto mental health workers, attorneys, or judges. For example, in one homicide case, through 3 years of futile divorce negotiations, the husband consistently blamed his wife's attorneys for the difficulties. He eventually shot the attorney, thereby continuing to deny that it was his wife who had been the one who first moved for a divorce and who had hired the attorney.

Consider the reflections of a man who had killed his wife and daughter sometime after his wife told him she was leaving him. He had come to realize that his pleading efforts to avoid her leaving him had failed. Two years after the homicides he reflected,

> I can't understand why I did it. In fact, I still sometimes doubt it was me who did it. I'm not someone who kills people. It's like she's still with me. Why did she have to try and leave? She treated me badly. I was embarrassed by her a lot . . . yet we had such wonderful times together. I keep thinking over the good things we did and of what our future would have been like. How can I stop thinking of her? I still dream about her and wake up thinking of her.

This pattern of DPD individuals attacking others, based on their own unhappiness and frustration, is not uncommon. The attacks reveal their ambivalence because, in one way, they reflect distorted relationships that have become altered if not lost. It is important to note that, more than serving as a means of revenge, the attacks on others through formalized mechanisms, such as lawsuits, dragged on for years on appeals, are another way of prolonging relationships. It is a matter of prolonging the relationship one way or another, and if it needs to be done via legal entanglements, it keeps the respective parties involved and avoids a total separation. In that manner, the self-recriminations can also more easily be directed against others. After such situations have ended, a suicide or homicide becomes more likely. Attacks on a more conspicuous level are DPD individuals' attempts to alleviate their own distress in a more easily understood manner.

Need for Immediate Response

The relationship problems experienced by DPD individuals are multiplied by their inability to tolerate periods of waiting or ambiguity. Their demands for an immediate solution to their relationship problems or to be restored to a sense of homeostasis by the presence or efforts of others alternate with the threat that they will become immobilized by the onset of depression, if this has not already occurred.

Depression and Denial

As noted, DPD individuals may experience occasional depressive epi-sodes when their feelings of helplessness are prominent; however, for most of their lives, they are not seen as clinically depressed by others or by themselves. Their reactions are rather of the situational variety with depressed affect.

Because individuals with DPD assume subservient roles in some part of their personal lives, they often function at a much lower level than they are capable of, both in terms of their personality attributes and intellectual capacities. Hence they may be underachievers in some major areas, even though they are talented. They often lack of a sense that they are important and worthwhile in their own right or that they can exert a significant influence on how others behave toward them. Many live lives of quiet desperation, simply hoping not to have their structured dependency disrupted. They often feel frightened, if not terrified, at the possibility of losing their support system within their family network. This corresponds to their belief that they have little influence over having their basic needs met in relationships with oth-ers. Blatant denial may serve to keep them functioning until a massive disruption looms.

Anxiety and Obsessional Symptoms

When the dependency techniques are not working, DPD individuals often display related behaviors that reflect anxiety disturbances and obsessionality. One sequence of obsessional behavior may involve their having difficulty in making a decision, seeking advice from others about the decision, but, then, after making the decision, recapitulating it and seeking reassurance from diverse sources that the decision was the right one. Other anxiety-ridden characteristics include their being uncomfortable when alone and trying diverse ways to avoid being alone, or their engaging in maneuvers to extract support from others. These behaviors surely reflect an individual in a state of conflict, but they do not serve as predictors of a homicide.

Comorbid Disorders

The high incidence of a dual diagnosis can complicate efforts to understand DPD. Comorbid disorders may include substance dependence or abuse, major depressions, or diverse anxiety disorders. Also, overlap with other personality disorders (e.g., histrionic, schizotypal, narcissistic, avoidant personality) is often found.

Another variation is that they may develop actual physical pain or disability with somatization processes. Chronic fatigue syndrome, a diagnosis with many vagaries, may fit many of these people.[5] In one case, after months of largely staying in bed for 24 hours a day, an individual emerged with his old-style zest and energy. This unfortunately led him into confrontations and eventually into what he believed was a justified homicide against someone who had earlier wronged him.

The significance of drug and alcohol abuse can also be gauged in the context of such dependent personality problems. The chemicals can help maintain, for a period of time, an illusion of being attached and not alone.

■ Behavior Patterns Within Dependent Personalities That Can Lead to Violence

In examining the DPD individual's more covert behavior patterns, just how some of these behaviors can lead to a violent act become clearer. These individuals' dependence on others, coupled with their fear of being alone, sets the stage for them to experience major anxiety episodes coupled with fears of abandonment. On one level, they engage in defensive maneuvers to ward off the possibility of being alone. Ingratiating behavior with others, or attempts to "bribe" others into continuing relationships, are typical ploys characteristic of their lifetime patterns of tenuous adjustment. Their fears are not confined solely to losing love when a relationship is severed; instead, their work efficiency and their entire capacity to continue functioning are compromised when a dependent relationship is threatened or not working smoothly. DPD individuals go to great lengths to prevent a rupture of relationships, be they love relationships in a romantic sense or relationships meeting some other need (e.g., general affection, acceptance, attention, praise). Unfortunately, their sensitivity to an anticipated rupture of relationships is often so high, and their fear of loss so great, that they begin to take defensive and anticipatory measures early, which then become expansive and exaggerated.

In general, many of these people form attachments in what they believe at the time are love relationships. At first, the relationship seems to promise meaning and new significance in their lives. It is believed these new relationships will be the "cure" for their loneliness and their sense of being lost or of not connecting with meaningful relationships. In such a situation, all the hallmark characteristics, if not the addictive qualities, of a dependent state are seen. In a broad sense, DPD individuals' distorted attachments and love relationships may seem so commonplace that it is easy for observers to miss some ominous potentials.

Once they are involved in this kind of relationship, it is almost impossible for them to extricate themselves because they fear a return of their deep loneliness. This loneliness is not perceived as being transient but rather as something overwhelming to them, even to the point where they feel they will not be able to survive if the relationship ends. The thought of this significant relationship ending induces a high level of anxiety, or even panic states, in which they are devastated, helpless, and hopeless.

In their precarious state of trying to assure themselves that their dependency needs will not be left perpetually unmet, a regressive shift may occur wherein they begin to sense that their situation cannot continue as it has been. The realization can emerge slowly or precipitously. The experience appears to be one in which they sense either that the emotional protection of a relationship could be lost or that the approbation received from a key relationship will no longer be forthcoming. Further, their submission or dedicated service, if not obeisance, no longer works. Even credible achievements in an objective sense do not suffice to reassure them, because this reassurance emanates overwhelmingly from others' praise. At its worst, this slavish dependence on others for a sense of self-esteem has built-in limits of having to live in an atmosphere of avoiding conflicts or competitiveness. Pushed to an extreme, masochistic personality traits may become part of the picture in that this avoiding confrontation and seeking ways to submit to others allows others to gain the ascendancy.

Individuals with DPD do not feel capable of carrying out separations that might otherwise occur at this stage. Their symbiosis negates that degree of freedom. They need to remain attached despite how punishing and painful the relationship has become and regardless of the strivings they feel to become more free and autonomous. At that point, some may also resort either periodically or regularly to using drugs or alcohol.

When a relationship shows signs of breaking up, DPD individuals first try diverse ways to prolong a relationship. They may engage in desperate measures or pleading to entice the other person to stay involved.

Or they might withdraw from the situation in an attempt to gain some distance from the other person involved in the relationship; by so doing they hope that they can expand their repertoire to include new ways of gaining reassurance. However, the odds are that, in time, they will fall back on their more traditional patterns of ingratiating and placating others or, as a variation, doing tasks or "dirty work" others will not do with the hope and expectation that a sense of tranquility and jaded confidence will return from their extra efforts. When they then shift back into their pleading or possibly threatening maneuvers, it is an indication that their renewed efforts are not working. They are now approaching a danger point for possible violence.

Defects in Ego Functioning

Often DPD individuals are seen as being inadequate people because of their conveyance of helplessness; however, that explanation is too simplistic for understanding how something as complex as a homicide can occur in their personal lives. Individuals with many of the other personality disorders also have types of inadequacies that may contribute to a final common path toward a homicidal act. However, those in the DPD group have certain characteristics in their sense of self that accompany the defect. Their problem with self-esteem has been operational throughout their development and into adulthood, and become the antecedent vulnerability that leads them to an ultimate homicidal act. A certain combination of circumstances elicits the final state of helplessness.

Many defects in basic ego functions are present, which is what leaves DPD individuals vulnerable to spiraling into a homicidal state and thwarts them from acting on the basis of their sensed needs. Their dependence, with the inability to step out of such destructive relationships, reveals a limited perspective and narrow focus to their existence. Although some refer to this as an impairment in reality testing, it is not on the level of psychotic thinking. Rather, it is a prominent awareness of the limitations existing in the degrees of freedom they have in their lives. For those who also have some borderline personality features, impulsive acts and exercise of poor judgment start to appear. They begin to portray themselves as not having control over themselves or misinterpret therapeutic help. They have a sense of being caught in the grips of powerful forces with which they cannot deal. Even more ominous is a situation in which a person is not aware of the degree to which he or she is distorting the assessment of the person with whom he or she is involved. They feel unable to delay, reflect, and wait for resolution of painful situations because they do not wish to endure the pain, anxiety, and loneliness.

In time, a correlative amount of aggression will accumulate within them and induce a state of discomfort. Yet, they are unable to express their excess anger openly because, by so doing, they would risk being further pushed into the precarious state of being abandoned. The situation of having to choose between expressing anger, with the accompanying threat of possible further loss of support, versus doing nothing and feeling helpless to continue living one's daily life cannot persist indefinitely. As noted, a person so conflicted may shift into a depressive episode with a full emergence of a major depressive disorder and increased suicidal possibilities.

Another possibility is that their anger and rage will lead to more impulsive behaviors. The latter may occur in attempts to coerce rescue efforts or to punish others, especially the one they see as being the source of their pain. They may begin to dwell on how to hurt the other person on an equivalent level to what they feel. A form of pseudocontrol results over their unresolved aggression. Rather than turning in new directions, which would imply a resiliency in seeking new sources of gratification, the dependent individual is fixated on one or a few limited devices. Hostile feelings, ambivalence, and thoughts of revenge predominate with regressive efforts to gain security, as in the following case example:

Case Example

A middle-aged man's wife of 25 years left him a note saying she was leaving him and moving to another part of the country. Following her departure, the man began to spend evenings with his widowed mother in a residence for the elderly. While there he would read the newspaper much like he had every night with his wife. After several months, his behavior switched into another level, with him dwelling on why she should be entitled to go off and lead a happy life while he suffered. Eventually, he tracked her down, stalked her, and killed her in the midst of an argument.

■ Homicide in Context of Marital Relationship

One of the first people to study the depth psychodynamics of homicide committed in a marital relationship was Bruno Cormier.[6] His investigations were not confined to those homicides that were labeled as a product of a mental illness or motivated by material gain. Cormier sought to get away from focusing on the individual's reactions either at the time of apprehension for a murder or at the time of trial, when the more immediate or early consequences of a homicidal act become prominent. At trial, a contemporary emotional state (e.g., jealousy, infidelity, adultery, alcoholism, marital violence) often becomes the focus of inquiry as one of the usual precipitants of a killing. What Cormier wanted to do was explore how a homicide could occur in the ordinary context of ongoing love relationships in which friends and acquaintances of both parties had not seen them as being much different than anyone else. To pursue this project, he followed a group of men 2–8 years after they had been convicted of killing either their wife or a woman with whom they were involved in a committed relationship. The key to each of these men was a pervasive pattern of unresolved dependency conflicts. Similar formulations could be offered about women caught in these dependency predicaments.

In studying his cohort of men, Cormier observed that, irrespective of their social class, a strong tie existed between the partners in all of these relationships. Each partner realized that they needed each other for help in solving their mutual problems. Mixed with the good times were disruptions based on occasional distrust, jealousy, or need to retaliate for a hurt. Yet, despite a heightening of the difficulties to the point of overt aggression against the partner, even to the point of threats to kill, no long-term separation between the partners occurred. However, at some point, one of the partners' attachment for the other began to weaken. Perhaps the emotional cost of the relationship had finally taken its toll.

Parting at that point would seem logical and, with time, an imperative, but it often does not occur. The inability to start the processes of loosening the dependency tie and facing reality is a crucial variable if a possible catastrophic ending is to be avoided. At a certain point in the natural history of these "normal" homicides, one party begins to realize that, although he or she cannot seem to separate from the partner, he or she cannot go on indefinitely in the pattern that exists either. Both partners are trapped with each other as if by fate. In some cases, it is revealed that one or both partners had begun to have preoccupations that killing might be the solution. Eventually, at a point of intense emotion, when continuing the relationship is inconceivable but separating also seems impossible, a homicide occurs.

■ Perpetrator's Reactions Following Homicide

Perpetrators' reactions to having killed someone can vary in cases where they have unresolved separations. Although some may then attempt and succeed in committing suicide, those who survive such an attempt continued to be preoccupied with death for many years. Some have a sense of loss, like an amputation of a part of their self. At times, this can give rise to transient periods of relief in that they are denying the finality of what has occurred. Yet, denial that anything has happened cannot persist very long. Many of these individuals follow a pattern of first blaming the lover almost exclusively for all the problems before the act of killing occurs, but after the killing see themselves as the only guilty one and entirely at fault. In the great majority of these cases, their guilt is upheld in the legal system, even though they may not be convicted of first-degree murder.

Another change in their perspective following the homicide is that, rather than seeing that there was no solution to their problems, as they did before the homicide, they are now able to appraise the diverse possibilities that were present and why these were not considered. When a DPD individual reaches that junction, a course of genuine remorse and sorrow can begin. The completion of that course can be accomplished only when they have accepted the reality of the loss, after which the processes of painful detachment can finally occur.

Dissociation

Following a homicide, those with DPD may experience a state of depersonalization and derealization as a means of dealing with their attendant anxiety. Some describe themselves as having observed the act or of being numb to any feeling at the time of carrying out a homicide. The crux of a homicidal situation is that the DPD person has put up defenses to the degree that he or she is not capable of experiencing his or her performance of the act, but rather views it as if witnessing someone else doing the deed. The DSM-IV[7] diagnoses of depersonalization disorder or dissociative trance disorder will undoubtedly become quite popular in the legal arena with such cases.

■ Therapeutic Concerns

When caught in a relationship from which they are powerless to extricate themselves, DPD individuals may seek counsel from others about what to do. Those giving advice may direct them to be more self-assertive, carry out other commonsense acts to make them feel better, or simply express their aggression. Unfortunately, expression of their aggression does not assuage the conflicts related to their dependencies. It may actually make matters worse by heightening a sense of failure and guilt when, having followed the advice of others, they do not begin behaving in an "improved" manner. For example, one man had been a member of therapy group where materials on learned helplessness were read. The hope was that, by understanding helpless states, the group members could begin to resolve them. This individual, however, when released from the hospital on a pass, killed his lover. He later expressed thoughts that he was a poor learner.

It is instructive to reflect on cases of misdirected therapeutic efforts where the dependency needs of these people are capitalized on and even accentuated by therapists in the hope that the catharsis will be therapeutic. Some therapists who have pursued this approach have at times promoted vengeful acts, such as the filing of lawsuits, in the belief that these acts will reflect autonomy and promote independence. Therapies that encourage the direct expression of aggression are based on the idea that patients will then not feel as helpless or used by others. What is missed in these approaches is whether the person has enough ego strength to contain and direct their aggression without violence. In these miscarried therapies, the repair of a damaged personality has only been postponed, and it may take much suffering before the person realizes that nothing has been solved within their own personality by simply mobilizing anger in this manner.

■ Conclusion

Inquiry into the background and developmental factors leading to a dependent type personality is always relevant. Some factors allow a partial understanding, but still leave mental health professionals largely unable to prevent the violent outcome that fortunately occurs only in a few of these silent, suffering personalities. In essence, they remain in situations based on their self-image of serving others, and with guilt over too much assertiveness or aggression. Ordinarily, their guilt is tempered through the punishment they receive from others. In the final outcome, the homicide appears to be carried out via an ego-splitting mechanism. One part of the person carries out certain acts that are partially dissociated from totally conscious control and rational functioning. In some of these cases, the defenses may be loosened by alcohol or drugs. In others, it is the background of stress over years of unresolved conflict that prevails.

These individuals routinely use a great deal of denial and repression, but the weakness of these defenses is that they permit these individuals to remain distanced with their deeper feelings of anger. At a certain point, the potential for a homicide is reached. Dissociation that allows a homicidal act is one possibility. The direct breakthrough of all the hate and anger, from which they later attempt to dissociate, is what has occurred, irrespective if later there is some amnesia for parts of the violence from its inconsistency with their self-image.

■ References

1. American Psychiatric Association: Diagnostic and Statistical Manual of Mental Disorders, 3rd Edition, Revised. Washington, DC, American Psychiatric Association, 1987

2. Hauken J: A critical analysis of the co-dependency construct. Psychiatry 53:396–406, 1990

3. Bandura A: Social Foundations of Thought and Action: A Social Cognitive Theory. Englewood Cliffs, NJ, Prentice-Hall, 1986

4. Wangh M: The tragedy of Iago. Psychoanalytic Quarterly 19:202–212, 1950

5. Bock GR, Whelan J (eds):Chronic Fatigue Syndrome: Ciba Foundation Symposium 173. New York, Wiley, 1993

6. Cormier BM: Psychodynamics of homicide committed in a marital relationship. Corrective Psychiatry and Journal of Social Therapy 8:114–118, 1982

7. American Psychiatric Association: Diagnostic and Statistical Manual of Mental Disorders, 4th Edition. Washington, DC, American Psychiatric Association, 1994

CHAPTER 6

Narcissism and Homicide

To understand, beyond a purely descriptive level, how individuals who have narcissistic personality disorder (NPD) can become engaged in violent behavior, some type of theoretical perspective to comprehend narcissistic personality functioning is needed. In reflecting on the diagnostic criteria for NPD, the potential for things to go awry in these individuals becomes clearer. More generally, there is the question of what role a narcissistic core may play in several personality disorders and whether narcissistic injuries are one key to unraveling why some of these individuals become homicidal. What is always intriguing is how so many individuals with narcissistic personalities are quite successful in their lives, be it in artistic endeavors, academia, or business pursuits, and what contributes to other individuals spiraling into endless problems in their interpersonal relationships. Some of those in the latter group are candidates for a culmination in a serious act of violence. It is only in retrospect that the reasons for such violent acts can be suggested.

■ Characteristics of Narcissistic Personality Disorder

Interrelated Feelings of Grandiosity and Unworthiness

Under the DSM-IV criteria for NPD, one hallmark of the disorder is a pervasive pattern of grandiosity, in fantasy or behavior.[1] Individuals with NPD feel the need to exaggerate their accomplishments and talents, and expect that they should be singled out as someone special— even in the absence of corresponding achievements. Even for those whose talents merit applause, whatever is forthcoming rarely is sufficient for their needs. Correlated with this is their difficulty in assessing their actual talents or contributions over the long run. The stage is then set for progressive disagreements and conflicts with others.

Another situation that may occur is when a person with NPD is unable to come to terms with a situation in which someone else may be more unique or accomplished than he or she is in a competitive area. These individuals begin to view the person who is thwarting their own advancement as the chief interferer with the fulfillment of their narcissistic wishes; in this sense, this outside object (the other person) is seen as a flaw in a reality that is already distorted.

Closely allied to the feeling of self-importance is a feeling of unworthiness. In a superficial sense, this may seem paradoxical. However, an examination of these individuals' feelings of worthlessness and inferiority eventually uncovers a core of diminished self-esteem. The result is that even the genuine achievements that accompany their talents often leave them plagued with a sense that they are fraudulent. As a consequence, any legitimate pleasure that should result from their accomplishments is compromised. Instead, they remain preoccupied with how well they are doing and their need to be thought of highly by others.

NPD individuals' need for attention, affection, and admiration seems boundless, and when these are not forthcoming on a regular basis, they resort to manipulative behaviors in an effort to extract the necessary positive feedback, no matter what the price of such behaviors might be. The lack of feedback can range from a lack of compliments to the many disappointments that routinely occur in life. Slights, such as a tone of criticism by another person or not being placed in a position of special importance in some interpersonal relationship or at work, can become sources of brooding. Rage, shame, guilt, and humiliation emerge subsequent to these perceived slights, although they may be hidden under an attempted exterior of indifference.

In the course of seeking relief for this pain, individuals with NPD can become exploitative by using others to aggrandize themselves. They may even become involved in criminal activity—even violent behavior—to accomplish their goals of reestablishing a sense of regained power. For example, they may engage in fraud and embezzlement to enhance their self-esteem and restore their sense of undiminished power. Alternatively, they may initiate schemes to destroy some other person, often one whom they see standing in their way of gaining even greater glory. These dynamics have been witnessed in the collapse of various prestigious investment banks in which individuals' quest for power played out over large stakes merged into criminal activities, despite their already glamorous and successful lives.[2] The same dynamics operate with more minor and petty offenses, reflected in personal violence as a way of bolstering sagging self-esteem. Despite what they achieve through these offensive behaviors—whether they be legal or illegal—NPD individuals still have a constant and pervasive sense of feeling deprived and burdened by seemingly insatiable inner needs, which continues to attack their esteem.

One unstable solution to fulfilling those needs is to merge into idealized or strong authority figures and seek narcissistic sustenance by such a connection. However, merging neither contributes to a person's sense of cohesion of the self nor lessens a person's sense of fragmentation and depletion. To the extent that self-cohesion suffers from these attempts to merge, efforts are directed at ways to regain a sense of narcissistic tranquility.

No matter how these individuals may fail in attempts to bolster their self-esteem, their expectation persists that they are special and therefore entitled to something more than others. Their self-esteem is then maintained by their being an "exception" to the others, one to whom others owe the fulfillment of their expectations and fantasies. If such expectations falter or do not come through, progressively desperate attempts may be made to change the situation. This is the background that can give rise to more desperate antisocial trends in some, even to the point of homicidal violence.

Lack of Insight

Given their exquisite alertness to how others treat them, there might be an expectation that individuals with NPD would be sensitive to the emotional needs of others. Surprisingly, their characteristic self-centeredness makes it difficult for them to have the empathy necessary to recognize the emotional needs or states of others, or even to gauge how others are reacting to them. Their empathic impairment is related, in turn, to their sense of entitlement, manifested in their periodic grandiosity that makes them impervious to realizing, or wanting to realize, how others may react to them. The result is a lack of insight about many of their own feelings.

Blaming Others

The phenomenon of blaming others is an interesting question that can only be answered based on an understanding of diverse types of human developmental processes. At a certain stage in their development, children begin to make attributions that others are at fault for their pain or discomfort. Blaming is seen as occurring early in infancy by way of projecting inner pain to some outside source. It has been theorized that blaming begins much earlier than the more developed model of not blaming others and taking responsibility for one's own discomfort. The latter would require a more developed sense of reality testing along with self-appraisal.[3] Blaming others does not get beyond the level of disavowing and attributing to others part of oneself.

For the NPD individual, blaming becomes a pervasive part of their personality functioning beyond the function it serves in others. Blaming becomes allied with these individuals' other narcissistic components in their need to attribute fault to others.

Experiencing Depressive Symptomatology

The predisposing characteristics of grandiosity and low self-esteem, with their accompanying vulnerabilities, create problems in NPD individuals similar to the diatheses in those with borderline personality disorder. Both types of people are known to be particularly vulnerable to depressive episodes. The narcissistic-based type of depression seems more acutely related to fluctuations in self-esteem in contrast to the fragmentation and regressive types of depression witnessed in borderline individuals. In a sizable number, if not the majority, of individuals with NPD, the depression is often not experienced in a full clinical sense, but rather as a brief situational reaction. Such reactions may be attributable to the functioning of those personality traits striving to ward off a major depression.

If these individuals begin to believe that fate has turned against them, but manage to avoid entering a major depression, they may slip into the role of being a victim. However, the victim role does not persist as long, nor is it as pervasive as in those who have a borderline personality disorder. Resorting to manipulation and exploitation devices allows them to maneuver around the sense of weakness and powerlessness that goes with extended victimization.

Some narcissistic individuals are quite adept at using the victim role to set themselves apart from those who do not portray themselves as victims. By so doing, they gain sympathy from others and allow themselves to feel temporarily superior. Also, by portraying themselves as the ones who have been deprived and misused, they reverse roles with those who may have victimized them in the past. In fact, at times a narcissistic person may switch from being the exploiter to being the one who is exploited when the former role fails to gain him or her success in a narcissistic battle. However, if they stay in the role of a victim too long, or become unable to manipulate their way out of continuing disappointments, they may experience a major depressive episode. This sense of despair emerges when they have failed in their power game and have depleted all their manipulative resources. In this more desperate state, the potential for some violent solution arises.

Paranoid Behavior

It is not appreciated how often pathological degrees of narcissism may leave an individual vulnerable to paranoid disturbances. Such an ominous turn can be related to a sense of misplaced trust in which these individuals feel they have been betrayed, or when brief insights emerge about their own integrity and questions arise about what they stand for.[4] In the latter case, their feeling of being adrift induces an uneasiness within them, accompanied by increasing confusion and hypervigilance. Some take the final regressive step into a persecutory system with delusional ideas, which allows their grandiosity to survive, but at a great sacrifice.

■ Narcissistic Rage

A narcissistic type of homicidal act arises within the matrix of an archaic type of narcissism, referred to as the phenomenon of *narcissistic rage*. As noted, narcissistic individuals may develop an indifferent or cool exterior as an initial response to threats to their self-esteem. However, when their composure gives way, it is striking to see the intensity of their anger and need for revenge.

Theoretically, narcissistic rage involves themes of grandiosity and power; psychodynamically, it involves archaic and omnipotent object representations that have become internalized within the person's psychic functioning. Within this explanatory framework, narcissistic individuals commit acts of homicidal aggression with an absolute conviction that they are necessary to prevent themselves from regressing into infantile states of helplessness if not psychosis.

Narcissistic rage encompasses a broad spectrum of clinical experiences. It is not confined simply to an act of homicidal proportions, but is best visualized on a continuum. Many trivial occurrences of rage occur in states of annoyance or irritation or when someone is aloof or does not reciprocate expressions of warmth to cover his or her rage potential. At the other end of the continuum, narcissistic rage encompasses serious outbursts, such as the furor expressed in a violent attack carried out far beyond what is necessary to achieve a killing (e.g., continuing to beat an already dead body).

In diagnostic terms, narcissistic rage reactions can also be seen in catatonic-type reactions or paranoid delusional systems, as well as in depressive episodes connected with a depletion of self-esteem. Hence, they are not confined to certain types of personality disorders. Narcissistic rage encompasses areas of aggression, anger, and destructiveness in general.

Using the concept of narcissistic rage based on a sense of self-righteousness, Horowitz illustrated how the narcissistic individual's reaction to these assaults can lead to violent actions.[5] Self-righteous rage is a state of mind that arises most frequently during narcissistically vulnerable stages of development. As such, it is more prevalent in those who have experienced pathological twists in their narcissistic development. It is also seen as an emotion that develops in the context of other affective components, such as becoming integrally entwined in a cycle of rage and anxiety. The narcissistic individual, underneath a facade of control, is often left with a chronic sense of embitterment. A withdrawal into a type of apathetic dullness may slowly take place. If seen at that point in clinical settings, a descriptive diagnosis of some type of major affective disorder is often given and some type of antidepressant medication instituted to alleviate some of these symptoms. In a longitudinal and historical sense, this type of depression is coming at the end-stage of these developmental antecedents.

When some narcissistic individuals reach this state of threatened depression, they may attempt to flee into the opposite emotional state. Analogous to manic behavior, the opposite state does not portend less risky behavior. For example, instead of exploding in self-righteous rage, they may pump themselves into a state of buoyancy and seem on top of things. Their sense of entitlement may increase. Instead of experiencing shame, rage, and anxiety, they may experience a sense of excitement or creativity in different areas of their life. Rather than acting out chronic embitterment, their behavior may shift toward heightened social participation in an effort to obtain attention or praise.

Underlying these threatened states is the potential for reaction of self-righteous rage to be triggered. The trigger may occur as a reaction to a real slight by another or to an unintended slight, the seriousness of which is exaggerated by narcissistic individuals' extreme sensitivity and tendency to overinterpret rejections or disappointments. Alternatively, the trigger can be when the narcissistic individual perceives people or organizations as not living up to his or her expectations, following which the narcissistic individual classifies them as behaving badly toward him or her or even others. Such individuals then develop a sense of self-righteous morality or take up causes to reform others, both of which reactions only thinly conceal their own power-seeking needs. For example, they may seek positions of authority or leadership to give them the opportunity to "correct" others. On a psychological level, what they are seeking to do is to rectify their feared depletion of self-esteem or inner resources before it is too late. In some way they sense that the situation is becoming dangerous.

Developmental Factors Seen in Rage States

Diverse explanations exist for the emergence of rage states. Rage states were once simply viewed as an individual's expression of increased aggressivity, presumably temperamental or genetic in origin. Early learning theory models used a frustration-aggression model in which rage was seen as an exaggerated response to frustration.[6] In terms of explanations of how some people with NPD can become homicidal, it is unfortunate that DSM-IV excluded a criterion that DSM-III-R had. That criterion referred to such a person reacting to criticism with rage, shame, or humiliation, and it was excluded on grounds of a lack of specificity. Other explanations shifted to view the breakthrough of rage as more connected with a breakdown of the ego defenses that ordinarily serve to control aggression.[7] The episodic dyscontrol syndromes were one psychological explanation used to show the varying degrees of aggressive breakthroughs that could occur. Later, a neurophysiological model to explain rage reactions was introduced independent of theorizing about NPD in which the breakthroughs of rage were seen in terms of failed neural substrates of inhibition.[8] The possibility of such a vulnerability in NPD and BPD cannot be discounted in all cases.

More contemporary psychodynamic theorists began to introduce concepts of disturbances in narcissistic equilibrium as an explanation for why rage reactions occur in narcissistic personalities. Kohut, Kernberg, Jacobson, and Mahler stressed instabilities of self and object representations.[9-12] Developmental theorists added in the component of antecedent factors from earlier periods of strain or traumatized experiences when a child sought certain parental responses. Kohut saw narcissistic rage as related to not having one's needs met in the context of the person's grandiosity. In contrast to the child who learned to have control over his or her destructive types of assertiveness, the child on a path of narcissistic development was the one who had trouble separating from key figures. In reaction to the failure of significant authority figures to be consistent in setting limits on the narcissistic child's demands, that child would develop expectations that his or her imperious needs should be gratified on demand. When those demands were not met by others, he or she would experience humiliation and as a result enter a state of being hurt or wounded. This experience of great humiliation could then lead to a more extreme state of narcissistic mortification. In situations of excessive indulgence or traumatization, the child is set up to maintain a set of beliefs that he or she can actually manipulate control of a situation, despite quite the opposite being true. It should be noted that Kernberg did not view the aggression in narcissistic people as arising soley from others inducing frustration but rather having intrapsychic origins. A deep envy was part of the clinical picture of wanting to destroy someone.

This misbelief that one can control all situations could also be interpreted as a type of cognitive distortion. Children caught in such a dilemma begin to feel that their well-being is contingent on maintaining their sense of personal omnipotence and control. To react otherwise would allow old anxieties, aroused when their wishes were not met, to reappear. As a result, they may attempt various types of distorted self-assurance. If a parental figure is not empathic to the child's demands, this sets the stage for a further development of rage reactions. By forcing a child to face the reality that he or she is not actually omnipotent, given the child's need for control, the child is then set up to experience humiliation. The imposed need for the child to accept his or her dependence on others for maintenance of self-esteem leaves that child in a precarious balance. Groping for security, but hating dependency, the child is induced into a traumatized vulnerability in which he or she feels a mixture of shame and weakness from seeking attachments.

Children who are so conflicted may then develop the potential for experiencing anxiety states and possibly rage reactions. Some children react by becoming withdrawn and apathetic, seeming to develop the descriptive characteristics of a depressed child. Others begin to develop the nucleus for diverse expressions of pathological narcissistic development. Adult psychopathology always looms as a potential consequence of the vulnerability in their deficient self-esteem system. When they encounter similar stressful situations in which their control is weakened, the potential for rage reactions with accompanying violence occurs. Depressive episodes, panic attacks, somatization disorders, and depersonalized states are what cloak the violent potential.

By the time they reach adulthood, the unrealistic attitudes and expectations that others will be at their service has become ensconced. Maturity in years does not bring an acceptance about the unreality of their expectations. Although at times their family may gratify them, they are left feeling vulnerable, weak, or a failure. The sense of failure to themselves and their loved ones intermingles with assertions of grandiose claims and expectations about their prospects and ambitions. For the lucky ones, good relationships may have developed despite their vulnerabilities and may have altered their life course so that they become able to develop better coping skills in adulthood. Because some narcissistic individuals have genuine talents, they may have experienced situations that were genuinely rewarding despite the fact that they were out of their manipulation or control. Yet others become entangled in a type of pathological development that leads to their perceiving others as either all good or all bad. Their corresponding self-image begins to alternate between being either worthwhile or worthless. At that stage, they have the tendency to externalize and view their own bad attributes as existing in the world of others. This externalization in turn allows them to rationalize using others, sometimes leading to aggressive, if not sadistic, behavior. If a rage eruption threatens or a violent act occurs, it is seen as at least partially justified on the basis of their having projected a sense of badness onto others.

Self Psychology Perspective on the Development of Rage

To understand the role of narcissistic rage, I turn to clinical contributions from self psychology and ego functioning, especially with regard to how one's sense of the cohesion of the self emerges. Also important are the process of idealization in personal development and a child's history of relationships with parental figures, especially as related to power relationships. Some parents relate to a child in an empathic manner to an extended degree so that a narcissistic merger occurs between them. Part of the personality of the child is then viewed as part of the parent's own; at other times, the parents may respond to the child as having a sense of self independent of them. Within this simplified framework, all degrees and varieties are possible.

In the realm of thwarted narcissistic development, consideration needs to be given to such factors as the impact of unmet ambitions on individuals' personality functioning, reactions to those who thwart them, wishes to dominate that cannot be fulfilled, desires to be outstanding and the center of attention, and yearnings to merge with powerful figures with whom they can identify. To the extent that a person does not have a sense of ego fulfillment in one or more of these areas, that person is left vulnerable when occasions arise that require mechanisms to deal with new disappointments. The individual's striving for a total justification and triumph over another who is perceived as having damaged his or her self-esteem sets the stage for an eruption of rage.

In the course of their lives, most people experience and then move on from traumas or insults to the ego, a process that requires periods of transition and new adaptations. These traumas or insults most likely reactivate emotional experiences from key earlier periods when the self was being formed, and the individual builds on his or her previous reactions to similar situations. The individual's current reaction involves not his or her self-esteem but also involves others with whom he or she is involved in a relationship.

In addition, it is clear that a particular environmental concatenation plays an equal role in developing those tendencies along with a damaged sense of self. A sense of the person's vulnerability can be assessed by how he or she has handled major changes in the past (e.g., the demands of moving from one geographic area to another, separation and divorce, deaths, entering military service, changing jobs, dealing with sudden financial reverses, not getting a promotion). Such experiences provide in vivo tests for an individual's specific weaknesses and strengths in terms of his or her sense of self, and allow a tentative model to be formed that illustrates vulnerabilities or sources of security that exists in the person's narcissistic realm and that may be manifested in fluctuations in his or her self-esteem. A parallel development is that, throughout life, an individual's self-representation changes over time.

In summary, extensive changes in the self are required to deal with certain kinds of developmental transitions from early childhood onward, as well as in the various changes in the self required in adulthood. The danger in responding to situations calling for change is that, if earlier types of self-representation have remained conflicted or faulty, the rebuilding process from the new situation can be difficult. The person's vulnerability lies in his or her preexisting type of psychopathology, which is reactivated in the contemporary context. Particularly striking are earlier conflicts involving individuation that have not been resolved.

How a Narcissistic Rage Can Lead to Homicidal Behavior

What specifically leads to a homicidal act in the context of narcissistic rage? How is it to be classified in terms of clinical knowledge and dynamic factors for an individual?

Narcissistic components are present more frequently in homicides than is usually believed. For example, many of the killings that are encompassed under the clinical heading of rage reaction or the legal heading of temporary insanity have been perpetrated by someone with narcissistic disturbances. A more detailed clinical scrutiny would see these killings as situations in which a narcissistic injury or injuries have occurred, and in which the killer saw a need to right what was perceived as a wrong perpetrated on him or her. Though the act might have seemed to be precipitous, most likely it had, in fact, been developing over an extended period of time, with the killer brooding and fantasizing over the need to do something to rectify the situation, even though his or her thoughts might not actually have reached homicidal proportions. As noted earlier, the intrusion of paranoid ideation can further confuse the situation and miss the correct diagnosis of the individual's motivations. All factors may then finally converge toward a homicidal act to resolve the person's long-standing sense of injury.

The clinical connection is ultimately between the act of violent aggression that occurs and the antecedent narcissistic vulnerability. It is in this context that legal complexities are added when concepts such as premeditation or intentionality are raised in courtrooms in attempts to assess responsibility for these killings.

Several variables lead to a final common pathway for an individual to exhibit rage reactions of homicidal proportions. The key seems to be an experience of some type of threat to one's vulnerable self that becomes magnified far beyond the objective nature of the threat. When the person perceives himself or herself as being under threat, or having the potential for becoming victimized, someone in the external world is customarily singled out as the hostile aggressor. The aggressor might actually be a person or a situation that develops because of the narcissistic individual's sensitivity to innocuous comments, slights, or non-achievement. In response to the perceived aggression, the narcissistic individual experiences not simply fear but eventually rage if the situation is not righted.

The rage may also be felt within the context of a role reversal, in which the narcissistic individual's sense of badness is externalized; therefore, when the evil is seen as coming from the external world, an attack on the bad object seems much more justifiable. In the event this externalization fails, a painful inner state of emptiness and depression looms. The person with an extreme narcissistic vulnerability lacks the capacity to assess the situation accurately and correctly assign blame for his or her pain. Something in the cognitive processes of assessing information realistically about others and oneself is deficient. Even if assessments are temporarily accurate, there is the problem that the assessments do not remain stable over time. This difficulty in processing information to assign blame is the crucial weakness. Instead, their ego deficiencies set them up to attack someone impulsively in a burst of self-righteous rage. Feeling humiliated, weak, and put on by others, their interpretation falls back on needing to attribute blame for someone having deliberately done things to them. They are left vulnerable to react with miscarried attempts to remedy a chronically devalued sense of self.

Feelings of shame and the need for revenge. When narcissistically vulnerable individuals are put in extreme positions where their self-esteem is severely threatened, they seem to respond in two ways: via a shame mechanism that leads to withdrawal and hiding, or via an outburst of rage that leads to some type of aggressive action. In this sense, shame and rage are classified as manifestations of a disturbance in narcissistic equilibrium. Some portray these individuals as being caught in a vicious repetitive cycle, with increased anger leading to guilt, guilt leading to submissive types of behavior, submission leading to reactive aggression, aggression leading to more guilt, and so on. The failure to individuate from those with whom one has close attachments, as seen in the following case example, is frequently found:

Case Example

A 19-year-old male, who had once been a fine student, repeatedly landed himself in difficulties because of his drinking and marijuana use. During his high school years, countless people became involved with him in an effort to "get him back on track." Clinics, in-patient hospital units, and counseling were all tried. In the year following graduation from high school, he became insistent about his need to get away from home and his overcontrolling parents. However, after a period had passed without his taking any action, others became indifferent to his complaints. Instead of remaining sympathetic they would simply tell him, "You're 19 years old. Go ahead and leave." His forays of leaving always resulted in excuses to return and a failed sense of being able to separate.

An attempt to get the young man involved in therapy ended when insurance coverage for the therapy expired. Eventually a major argument occurred between him and his parents, who now began to tell him he was no longer welcome to stay at home. After having words with his father, the two physically fought. At one point the son struggled loose and took a brief walk. Feeling shame and humiliation at his having hit his father, but more generally for having failed his parents over several years, he returned home, went to his room, and got a gun. Pausing outside the room his parents were in, he heard them agreeing he would have to leave. He felt further ostracized and into the room and shot them both.

The following is another case in which perceived slights and humiliation lead to a homicidal outcome:

Case Example

A man did not receive a promotion in his job that he thought he deserved. Being a dedicated employee, he had long assumed that hard work and dedication, such as spending far more hours in the office than required, would lead to a promotion. What he was not registering was his lack of interpersonal relationships with many of his colleagues. The applicant who did receive the promotion came from another division, but had once worked under him.

The first affront to his narcissistic tranquility came when he did not get a salary increase. He rationalized this as occurring on the basis of a faltering economy. The next year he neither received a salary increase nor a bonus, and had more difficulty assimilating these affronts. At that time he sought an explanation from his supervisor but received only vague answers. For several weeks he brooded that the supervisor was the person thwarting him and responsible for his depleted sense of self. This thought originated not from a sense of paranoid delusional thinking but rather in the context of his needing to find the person primarily responsible for dealing him the injury. He ignored the results of evaluations of his work performance and personality done by different people over many years. At this stage, as later revealed by his wife, his behavior began to change and he began to have outbursts of rage toward her and their son over minor transgressions or failures on their part to do things just the way he wanted them done, such as his wife being late for meeting him or his son not achieving top grades in school. He was reacting with violent anger to minor frustrations caused by people who were important narcissistically to him but who were failing him in little ways when his ego needed major infusions of support.

He also began treating others at work unduly harshly, as a result of the narcissistic injury his failure to gain recognition caused him. He rationalized his behavior toward his wife and son on the basis that they were better off for his being consistent in his anger to them and that being too tolerant was not good for his son. On occasion, he would drink to excess and hit them but then blame it on the alcohol. He eventually found that his behavior at home created family difficulties but did not alleviate the narcissistic hurt from his employer. At that time, he began to develop anxiety-related and depressive symptoms of sleeplessness, periods of agitation, and increased hypochondriacal concern about excess flatulence and pressure in the sternum.

He was unaware of the increase in his sarcastic rage.

Eventually, his lack of empathy following these rageful out-bursts, outbursts that he rationalized as being justified by his being morally right, led his wife to leave him.

Finally, his conflict led to action. He constructed a bomb, wrapped it in a brown paper bag as if it had been mailed, and gave it to a secretary to deliver to his supervisor. When the secretary became suspicious, the package was checked by experts and found to contain an explosive that could detonate. It led to the man being investigated and criminally charged with attempted murder after which he received psychiatric intervention.

Narcissistic rage often exhibits the person's underlying need for revenge. In doing clinical assessments of those who have already acted on the basis of murderous rage, it becomes clear that they were not able to move beyond the wrong that was done to them and the need they felt to induce hurt or retaliation. In its more extreme manifestations, the need for revenge arises in the context that an individual has suffered a persistent and unresolved narcissistic injury. Dedicated efforts to right the wrong now begin. It is this sense of righting a wrong that distinguishes narcissistic individuals' behavior from others' simple expressions of aggression. The trigger that stimulates this type of narcissistic rage can be quite minor in someone narcissistically vulnerable to begin with, such as an episode of ridicule, teasing, or contempt or something experienced as a "defeat." Children who have been passive recipients of shameful or sadistic treatment (treatment that is sometimes overt, such as physical or sexual abuse, but more often covert, such as being shamed) by others are left with unresolved desires to gain control so they never again have to experience helplessness. Some interpret the eventual reactions of these victims as representing the mechanism of identifying with the aggressor.

Whatever the specific experiences, they leave such individuals in a state of readiness to react when they feel they are once again being placed in a shamed position. They are ready to take action to inflict on others the type of narcissistic injury they are afraid will again be imposed on them. The shame imposed on them leaves them later vulnerable to become enraged over the shame and become homicidal.

It is in this context that some have viewed the experience of childhood physical or sexual abuse as the *sine qua non* for these individuals to try to avenge themselves later in life when they perceive themselves in a situation of being used. An example would be the "battered women syndrome" in which an adult woman has been physically abused in the context of a relationship. If that woman later murders the lover who abused her, the legal defense of duress or self-defense may be used, even though the mate might not have been attacking the woman at the time he was killed. The woman's state at the time of the killing would correspond to that of an ongoing narcissistic injury.

Acting on the need for revenge.   Although everyone reacts to narcissistic injuries with feelings of embarrassment or anger, narcissistically vulnerable individuals react primarily with an intense shame. Apart from the painful aspects of feeling shame, a violent eruption requires one additional step: the hope that, by destroying someone, they will now gain a sense of mastery over an environment that has not been conducive to their self-esteem. They are caught in the contingencies of needing the unconditional availability of approval and admiration from others, or those with whom, on a psychological level, they have become fused. Within this matrix of narcissistic vulnerability, some of the most violent homicidal behavior with a lack of empathy is exhibited.

Experiences of being hurt and wounded can accumulate from multiple occurrences. Narcissistically vulnerable individuals then begin to think that it is not right that only they should be made to suffer. Their thinking takes on magical qualities to the degree that they believe that only when others are removed can their life regain its narcissistic buoyancy. Their constricted thinking is evident in their believing that they cannot attain a sense of security or tranquility until they have either harmed or destroyed a particular individual who has thwarted, disagreed with, or overtly taken opposition to them.

These individuals' need to blot out some seeming offense against them, coupled with the fury from the felt lack of control over the person or object who they think has offended them, is the final step toward a homicide. That is why the events that have occurred to them—often minor slights or events that occurred years earlier—are reacted to with such a disproportionate degree of severity. At its extreme, a preoccupation with revenge may lurk for years. An unceasing compulsion to square accounts with someone after some presumed or actual offense can also arise anew years later. In one case, a man who believed he was sentenced unjustly by a judge began to write anonymous threatening letters to the judge 15 years after the trial. The result of a brooding need for revenge can be not only a "clean" act of killing, such as a shooting, but often a brutal killing, such as a prolonged beating, an incident in which a chemical (e.g., acid) is poured on someone's face, dismemberment, or multiple wounds.

Themes of revenge in response to narcissistic injury abound in literary works. *The Count of Monte Cristo* and *Moby Dick* are two classic examples. Kohut referred to *Michael Kohlhaas,* a well-known work in Germanic countries, written by the great dramatist Heinrich von Kleist (1777–1810), to illustrate what he believed was a separate line of narcissistic development.[14] The insatiable search for revenge subsequent to a narcissistic injury in *Michael Kolhaas* has been interpreted differently by Hamilton, who believed it could be traced to unresolved oral conflicts giving rise to a primitive rage that is acted out.[15] von Kleist actually ended his own life by a suicide. The story of Kohlhaas, briefly retold below, well illustrates the dynamics that can lead to narcissistic types of killing.[16]

> Kohlhaas was a horse dealer and small land owner in sixteenth century Germany. Those who knew him saw him as an honest but at the same time terrifying man. Until age 30 years, he was a model citizen, but a sense of injustice turned him into a robber and murderer. The event that led to his subsequent transformation was a grievous and entirely unprovoked humiliation that he received at the hands of the servants of a nobleman in his community. From the various machinations of these servants, Kohlhaas lost his property; his efforts to redress the matter legally via petitions went unanswered because the petitions were intercepted by relatives of the culprits who had wronged him and who held key positions at the Court of Saxony. Hence, the prince remained oblivious of the wrongs that were being done to Kohlhaas.
>
> These events led Kohlhaas to become a rebel against his sovereign. He assembled a gang and began to burn and pillage villages, in

the course of which inhabitants were robbed and killed. Martin Luther issued an appeal for him to come to his senses, pointing out that the injustice had been done by subordinates and the sovereign had no part in it. He responded to Luther, who then intervened with the sovereign for Kohlhaas to have a safe passage to get a hearing before a competent tribunal. Luther also asked for a pardon for his rebellion. A hearing was held, but court intrigues continued. In the end, the tribunal granted Kohlhaas full compensation for the losses he had suffered for his property, and punished his enemies. This is when an ordinary story would end. However, the court also felt justice would be served only by Kohlhaas being punished for his crimes and ordered that he be executed. Kohlhaas willingly and joyfully accepted his punishment because he had achieved satisfaction for the injustices done to him.

The case described on the previous pages is often held up as an example of the perfect blending of legal and moral justice for a law-breaker.

Dissociating from the act of violence.   There is always the potential for violent acts not being integrated with the remainder of the personality. Aggression is then expressed within the framework of some primitive personality reactions and misperceptions of reality. The primary deficit of an exaggerated assessment of reality plays a key role in an ultimate homicide. This is not the same as saying that reality testing has pervasively broken down in the sense of a psychotic reaction. Rather, it is that these individuals are prone to react with shame, having experienced reversals or disappointments as narcissistic blows to a degree that they have little resilience left. A state of readiness to respond with an outburst of rage toward those people who are in close relationship to them or a displacement to more distant figures are possibilities. Those people they attack are seen as having thwarted or offended them, rather than being seen simply as independent individuals for whom there may be differences in their purposes or behavior. In a developmental sense, the adult with this type of archaic personality structure has a cognitive set that remains isolated from the rest of the personality. From a different perspective, expressions of narcissistic rage can be seen as enslaving the ego and allowing the individual to function only as the tool and rationalizer of a deep hurt that has never healed.

When a homicide is perpetrated by a person with NPD, others are often surprised by the lack of remorse in the perpetrator. Part of the explanation is that the victim has not been viewed by the perpetrator as a human being with his or her own needs and feelings. Rather, the victim is simply viewed as having been a drain on the perpetrator's life or a persistent source of his or her own suffering. As such, there is no empathy with the person destroyed. The need has been to eliminate the source that was impinging on the perpetrator's failed need for control. The individual had hoped to restore his or her grandiosity and avoid further limitations. However, the reality of a homicidal act has intervened. Although some, such as Kohlhaas, may feel that the psychological victory was worth the price, not all do so. For most, their victory is celebrated by a long period of incarceration either in a prison or hospital facility.

The lack of remorse often experienced by NPD individuals is illustrated in the following case example:

Case Example

A young woman was told by her boyfriend that he no longer wished to continue their relationship. She asked him to continue contact through phone calls. In a few weeks he told her he no longer even wanted to do this because the relationship had become uncomfortable for him to maintain. However, she continued to call him at home at various hours of the night and at his office in the daytime, but he never responded to these calls. He felt that the relationship was over, and began to pursue a new social life with a sense of relief. At the time he could not verbalize why he felt such relief, beyond noting that he was enjoying a new social life. In the course of time, he began to date several other women, occasionally frequenting places with them that he had gone with the former girlfriend. After several months, on the pretext of needing to see him about some serious matter, the former girlfriend arrived at his apartment. At a time when his back was turned, she fired several shots into his back, killing him. She expressed little subsequent emotion, but instead displayed an apathetic type of depression with no remorse and minimal anxiety.

■ The Psychodynamics of Narcissistic Killing

In examining in more detail these types of killings, the operation of homicidal aggression rooted in the matrix of an archaic type of narcissism becomes clear. Threats and blows to this narcissism can give vent to one or more acts related to the rage engendered. In this context, it would be erroneous to assume that the homicidal behavior always occurs in the form of wild or "out of control" outbursts. It may take the form of orderly and organized activities to secure revenge, in which the homicidal act is carried out with an absolute conviction about its righteousness. In fact, acts of retaliation may have been held under control for some time by way of an enduring sense of hatred that functions as a homeostatic adaptation.[17] In some cases, a person may feel shame and withdraw in response to being humiliated, with these initial reactions setting the stage for a later overt enactment of rage. What persists is the need for revenge, to right a hurt that may have been simmering for some time. For some it simmers and remains dormant and later becomes activated by some precipitant. In other cases, it consumes an individual over a lifetime with a compulsive intensity that gives no surcease.

It is important to analyze the dynamics to determine what finally elicits a homicidal level of violence in these narcissistic personalities. An initial question is to assess whatever external precipitants may have left residues that have not dissipated over time within a particular person. More immediate events that have been operating, such as provocative acts or words, shaming techniques used once too often, ridicule, or lording it over the person are a few possibilities. The level of sensitivity within a rage-prone personality also needs appraisal. Such approaches usually lead to the uncovering of shame-based reactivities within the person, which leave a person particularly ready to strike back or to ward off anticipated attacks from others. Given such background factors, it should also be noted that some type of plan or devious course of action, may be set in motion in which on one hand there is a planned component, but on the other hand an obliviousness of the risks one is taking and what the ultimate consequences can be to the perpetrator.

The dedication to a course of action is similar to that witnessed in individuals with a borderline personality disorder or even a delusional disorder. The former diagnosis is sometimes only distinguished with great difficulty and fine distinctions. The latter diagnosis has the hallmarks of a belief not subject to reality factors, even though the semblance of logic is present. With NPD, there is often the sway of a powerful need for righting a perceived wrong. It is not an exaggeration to say that to eliminate a sense of hopeless mortification, the person is sometimes willing to pay the price of destroying themselves. This is similar to the psychology of fanaticism that can be enlisted for any cause. Besides righting what is experienced as a wrong inflicted on the self, shame is to be eliminated from having tolerated such past behavior toward oneself. In that sense, the imperfections of the self gnaw at the person, which elicits a secondary rage. The sense that the individual cannot control his or her environment, nor his or her life, is to now be righted. Diminished self-esteem is to be cured by a desperate effort to gain control.

■ References

1. American Psychiatric Association: Diagnostic and Statistical Manual of Mental Disorders, 4th Edition. Washington, DC, American Psychiatric Association, 1994

2. Stewart JB: Den of Thieves. New York, Simon & Schuster, 1991

3. Gabbard GO: Psychodynamic Psychiatry in Clincal Practice: The DSM-IV Edition. Washington, DC, American Psychiatric Press, 1994, p 45

4. Garfield D, Havens L: Paranoid phenomena and pathological narcissism. Am J Psychother 45:160–172, 1991

5. Horowitz MJ: Formulation of states of mind in psychotherapy. Am J Psychother 42:514–520, 1988

6. Berkowitz L: The frustration-aggression hypothesis: an examination and reformulation. Psychol Bull 106:59–73, 1989

7. Lewis M: The development of anger and rage, in Rage, Power, and Aggression. Edited by Glick RA, Roose SP. New Haven, CT, Yale University Press, 1993, pp 148–168

8. Monroe RR: Episodic Behavioral Disorders. Cambridge, MA, Harvard University Press, 1970

9. Kohut H: The Restoration of the Self. New York, International Universities Press, 1977

10. Kernberg O: Borderline Conditions and Pathological Narcissism. New York, Jason Aronson, 1975

11. Jacobson E: The Self and the Object World. New York, International Universities Press, 1964

12. Mahler MS: On Human Symbiosis and the Vicissitudes of Individuation. New York, International Universities Press, 1968

13. Kernberg OF: The psychopathology of hatred, in Rage, Power, and Aggression. Edited by Glick RA, Roose SP. New Haven, CT, Yale University Press, 1993, pp 61–79

14. Kohut H: Thoughts on narcissism and narcissistic rage. Psychoanal Study Child 27:360–400, 1972

15. Hamilton JW: Implications for current concepts of narcissism in Heinrich von Kleist's "Michael Kohlhaas." International Review of Psychoanalysis 8:81–84, 1981

16. von Kleist H (1808): Michael Kohlhaas. Edited by Geary J. Oxford, UK, Oxford University Press, 1967

17. Galdston R: The longest pleasure: a psychoanalytic study of hatred. Int J Psychoanal 68:371–378, 1987

CHAPTER 7

Masochism and Homicide

The Ultimate Enslavement

The combination of victimology, battered partners, and masochism with the subject of homicide may at first seem an unlikely one. Yet, when taken together, the first three phenomena represent a prime mixture from which a homicide may eventuate, the complexities of which may never be resolved. These issues are often raised in courtrooms in cases where spouses or lovers have become enmeshed in distorted processes of intimate relationships.

■ Victimology and Homicide

Defining the Victims of Homicides

Apart from one obvious answer—that, by definition, the victim of a homicide is whomever is killed, more subtle answers are uncovered when the events leading to and following a homicide are examined. For example, there are also those indirectly affected by the killings— children, parents, siblings, friends, lovers, and so on—who must cope and deal with an event that will have a major, ongoing impact on their lives.

Victimology is a theme running through many cases of individuals who perpetrate some type of homicidal act. Indeed, an approach could be taken that views all homicides solely from the perspective of the perpetrator being the victim. Such a perspective would be particularly useful with various types of personality disorder diagnoses. Yet questions can then be raised about who, in fact, is to be labeled the perpetrator-victim in such interactional situations. Among those who should be considered as victims are those people whose disrupted lives and relationships may have led to the homicide. Another approach could be to view all perpetrators as being victims. Perpetrators' victim role is that they will customarily spend decades incarcerated in a prison or a security hospital if they are not executed. The issue pertains to their lack of understanding the diverse ways they have unconsciously pursued such a sacrificial ending throughout their life. In the end, there is only a dead victim and multiple other living victims.

Epidemiological view. There are two key questions to answer in terms of victims: Who, in a certain group, is susceptible to being the victim of potential act of homicide? and What makes them susceptible to such a lethal outcome? An epidemiological approach would be one way to try to detect a group of those most vulnerable. Such an approach reveals homicide perpetrators and victims clustered with a few key variables. In Chapter 1, I note that one group of those most likely to be involved overall in homicides are predominantly young males, especially young black males in large urban centers or in impoverished inner cities. Other groups would be women caught up in painful emotional entanglements, elderly women, or children. Yet, greater specificity is needed in each grouping, such as why young males perpetrate these killings more frequently in certain areas of the country, or what are the psychological and social variables operating in the lives of these women. Questions are raised about whether an increased number of women in the workforce, with a resulting increased exposure to dangerous situations and people, increases their homicidal risk. (However, caution must be taken to ensure that this hypothesis does not lead to the oversimplified assumption that a person's increased chance of being a victim of homicidal violence can simply be correlated with his or her increased exposure.) These types of questions are geared toward examining what is involved in the early stages leading to homicidal violence, even when the parties involved are not registering the potential situations they are living in.

Legal view: only one victim.   In the current era of victimology, discussions about the nature and sources of victimology are easily confused. Distinctions need to be made for heuristic purposes as to how the word *victimology* is being used in discussions about killings. From a legal perspective, the focus is on the person killed as the victim. Efforts are then directed at finding the person who can be charged with the act so that blame can be assessed. Blameworthiness is the key concept within the traditional confines of criminal law. An effort would then be made either to punish the perpetrator in a retributory manner or to punish him or her as a deterrence to others from performing such an act. Although punishment might also be justified from the perspective that it might deter the same individual from again performing such an act, this emphasis may be passé, given the long-term consequences of a conviction whereby the person is removed from society for an extended period. In some situations, incarceration of someone who has killed another may be predicated on the need to incapacitate them because they are viewed as, or assessed to be, dangerous and therefore must be confined. In the not too distant past, the possibilities of rehabilitation were frequently cited for incarcerated criminals, but this goal now seems sadly antiquated for those who commit homicide, given the current mores and emphasis in the American criminal justice system and the way legislatures either create public opinion or react to it. In discussions about the diverse purposes of criminal law and homicide, whatever ideas about victimology surface exert a covert influence in terms of assessing responsibility for acts and degrees of punishment.

The difficulty with a narrow legal assessment of who is seen as a victim and what is to be done to the killer-victimizer is that it bypasses the major part of the criminological and clinical work that has been produced about victimology. Sociological approaches have zeroed in on the relationship between the victim and the killer, focusing on a host of demographic variables about each, such as their ages, socioeconomic status, family structures, and personal histories of violence, among other characteristics. Clinical approaches have inquired into prehomicidal behavior that may have existed and interactions between the perpetrator and others that may have led to a homicide. A psychiatric approach would also address clinical issues involving diagnosis and the intrapsychic and interpersonal dynamics associated with a particular killing.

The Process of Becoming a Victim

Homicidology, like suicidology, involves a reconstruction of events after the fact. As more knowledge is gained, more indicators become available about what may have been premonitory signals. However, current knowledge is focused on the early stages and the natural course of events leading to homicide.

Perception of self as victim.   When studied retrospectively, it is clear that many later victims did not perceive themselves as victims at all in the early stages of events leading to a violent outcome, even though they were caught up in a potentially explosive situation. Their own predisposing personality conflicts and reliance on denial and avoidance may have prevented such awareness. An equal contributor could be traditional or cultural values that were operative in reinforcing their defenses against awareness of being in this role. These victims may have seen themselves as being in a situation no different from that of many other people around them or what they had witnessed as part of their earlier life. The masochistic tendency to attribute responsibility to themselves for what was occurring is often the most difficult part of their conflicts, for it blinded them from perceiving themselves as entitled to a less conflict-ridden life and a more worthwhile existence.

One pattern often seen is that future victims continually return to crisis situations, the same relationships, and the same milieu in which they have previously have been harmed or injured. A prime example is those who are involved in "battered" marital or love relationships. Unfortunately, the recent emphasis of avoiding any imputation of blaming the victim who is assaulted or killed has led to limited efforts to understand the stages and processes that can result in harm, if not doom. This is not to say that crisis intervention, which extricates a person from a highly volatile or dangerous situation, may not be required, but that, for purposes of understanding as well as future prevention, it is necessary to grasp the patterns of complexities that exist in such relationships.

A transitional change occurs when individuals begin to sense they might conceivably be a candidate for some future violent act, even to the point of wondering if they might be killed. To understand this process in an individual means a shift from an epidemiological approach of statistical possibilities to the psychological factors operating in a particular individual who is a participant in such processes. One of the major difficulties in assessing the process is that the role of victim is present in many different individuals and under such diverse conditions. In addition, the term *victim* is now so widely utilized that it is unfortunately used to ward off any critical analysis in which attempts to understand the victim are made to seem tantamount to blaming the victim. Hence, discussions of the concept become confused. In the past, the opposite situation existed, with roles of victims being ignored or tolerated by a society that simply viewed victims as living out their life destiny in this manner.

The question why some people experience extreme forms of violence, even to the degree where their life has been threatened, yet do little in response, has been debated at length. There will continue to be explanations offered that vary from the "culturally trapped" version to the "masochistically bent" model. The question why some individuals continue to remain in a victim role is a very complex one, and sometimes misguided efforts by "rescuers" to extricate them only increase the potential for their being either a victim or perpetrator of homicidal violence. At the borderline between theories of social psychology, which view victimization as acceptance of a role, and psychiatric theories is the realization that the attitude and acceptance of being a victim is not primarily a conscious choice. More likely, it is the result of a confluence of a set of beliefs and attitudes conveyed to certain individuals about what expectations they are entitled to in the world. It also involves ideas they have about their capability of using their initiative and not necessarily seeing themselves as responsible for those who treat them in a poor manner.

In addition, there is often a lack of viable options existing in the social world of some of these people. At the time, it may seem like an easier choice simply to adapt to a role one is in than to risk the consequences of protest or resistance. Such an adaptation is especially easier for younger people. However, all too frequently, it is easier to see oneself as the victim of a system that is "doing one in" than to take the difficult course of protesting and groping one's way out. In a critical analysis of victims, situations must be distinguished between one extreme in which one person sees all his or her unhappiness and misery as something unjust for which others are responsible and the other extreme in which it is all accepted as his or her due.

When a person reaches a stage in which the transition into being a victim of extreme acts of violence has occurred, prying the person from that role is quite difficult. The need to feel in control of what happens in one's life can lead to desperate measures to avoid the alternative state of helplessness. More extreme traits of a given personality disorder then emerge and defenses become mobilized. The experiential state of seeming helpless, without any way out of a dilemma, can give rise to contemplating desperate measures. For example, people with a patho-logical dependency may easily have their feelings of being abandoned aroused in the matrix of hopeless entanglements in love relationships that are seen as having no apparent exit except by a major act or declaration. What they do not comprehend is the degree of their destructive rage and hatred at the object they are dependent on.[1] The situation is a coercive demand to be cared for and to remain in a relationship, but a time bomb if the entitlements that go with one's being used are no longer operating or are threatened.

Reacting to one's sensed helplessness. Those caught in the victim role have several choices as to how they can react to their role. The majority of these individuals, with or without therapeutic intervention, somehow confront their life situations and initiate actions for change; they do not see the possible solutions to their dilemmas as being fixed in some deterministic manner. This means they cast off their victim role with its accompanying rationalizations and confront the situation they previously viewed as having no way out of other than to rid themselves of their tormentor in some final solution. Only a small minority of individuals actually come to an endpoint where they see no solution for their dilemma except through an act of killing. The Menendez case in California is a classic example of this, in which two brothers killed their parents, claiming earlier childhood sexual molestation by the father.[2] (The increasing popularity of such defenses in courtrooms where antecedent abuse is claimed as a justification for a homicide, with the added basis of fear that the perpetrator's own life is in jeopardy, merits discussion in its own right.)

The decision that the individual makes is then added to the many variables operative in determining the final outcome of the situation. Typical initial options are reporting the behavior to police, a social agency, or center for victims. Even when these types of intervention are successful, at least in terms of removing the person from the victimizing situation, the potential for danger can rise even further because the person is ultimately disappointed by this result; often it would be their hope that only the abuse, and not the relationship, would end.

One variation is where one or both parties in the relationship seek therapeutic intervention. Here, too, more variables—in terms of the quality of the intervention and its aftermath—are added into the equation leading toward a final outcome. Although almost all providers refer to their programs as therapy, vast differences exist between them. Some advocate working around a high-risk relationship without trying to terminate it versus the approach of strengthening a person's adaptive techniques in the short run but with an ultimate goal of terminating a relationship. Practical questions abound: How far should therapeutic interventions go to make a person uncomfortable with a role they are in? Might such interventions add to the stress a person is already experiencing and thereby indirectly lead to violence by such efforts?

Perhaps more than in any other field, the distinctions among therapeutic intervention, advocacy, and actually taking over the decision-making functions for a victim become blurred. The consequence of disrupting existing relationships through therapeutic intervention usually affects several people, especially if legal action against some type of earlier violence is brought as a consequence of the therapy. There is also the added stress on the participants of their having to deal with official agencies or court systems, with the attendant lack of privacy and perhaps publicity.

The process of going public with one's plight as a victim of violence or abuse (e.g., reporting abuse to the authorities, publicly separating from the accused perpetrator) in itself may carry the label of being a "loser." Mutiple factors operate to entrap people in abusive relationships, such as the degree of commitment to the relationship (e.g., presence of children), poor-quality alternatives to leaving, and the nature of their interdependence.[3] Even if a person is an innocent victim, this label raises connotations of being viewed as someone not in charge of his or her life, as someone who is unable to personally deal with his or her life situation. A connotation of incompetency may be why a male may find it difficult to admit to being in a victimized status. The situation is complicated further when the victim is urged by a counselor or someone they have consulted to go public; other than the major social consequences to the individual of such an action, there is also the individual's accompanying realization that he or she did not initiate the action but was simply carrying out someone else's (e.g., the counselor's) plan, which realization in effect maintains the person in a helpless position.

Currently, a great effort is made to avoid blaming the victim for his or her predicament. Yet, such an effort alone cannot negate the subsequent fallout from the helplessness experienced by the victim. This is even more acute for the adult victim of serious violence than for a child or elderly victim of abuse. The reason is that a child or elderly person is viewed differently than is an adult involved in a relationship with his or her peer (i.e., another adult). The quality of shame in being a potential victimizer-murderer, as well as a potential victim-murderee, leaves both sides periodically wanting to expunge this part of their life and start over. Yet, their past leaves them vulnerable to extortion to conceal the situations. The extortion can be literal in some cases and psychological in others. By keeping past outbreaks of violence private, the person is hoping, or betting, it will not result in a homicide. (Based on statistics, the probability of such a violent outcome between partners is small.) In many situations, however, this privacy is only relative. Often, individuals being victimized informally share their dilemma with friends or neighbors. Then, given the number of individuals who are involved in any type of professional or educational role, in which case they would be required by mandated-reporting legislation to report violence, it is very difficult to keep such family situations private. These mandates apply not only to legal minors, but also to those who are interpreted as being in a "vulnerable adult" status. There are also duty-to-warn statutes or case law that states that potential victims of any violence are to be given notice, presumably so they can act to protect themselves from possible danger. Such legislation and legal cases put the burden on professionals to carry out such official and public reporting.

Sociological view on becoming a victim.   Some emphasize that an individual is simply trapped in a social system that produces victims and will continue to do so. Hence, unless there are societal changes in the underpinnings of this system of victims, violence can be expected. A frequent example is that of women caught up in a patriarchal family system with partners who view them as their property to use or abuse as they wish. The victims of such abuse are viewed as having little chance of altering the situation since they are seen as fighting a cultural system. A less drastic view is that such individuals are burdened by trying to function in such a system. However, the system is not seen as monolithic but rather a system in the process of change. More radically opposed views do not necessarily see institutionally fixed mores being as controlling as they once were. Although the significance of personality characteristics is denied by some in favor of a cultural determinism, these characteristics operate even if one concedes that cultural factors exert a great influence.

■ The Abused Person and Homicide

Increasingly, cases in which one who was once abused strikes out against his or her abuser are being seen in the courts, with the syndrome known as "the battered spouse syndrome" and its variants being raised as a legal defense. Only the dramatic cases of this phenomenon, such as a wife cutting off the penis of her husband after he has beaten her or children killing parents after being abused by them, receive constant media coverage; however, more mundane versions of these cases are played out daily in courtrooms across America. Because of the increasing use of this syndrome as a defense for homicide, this type of homicidal behavior needs to be examined from a legal perspective—that is, whether it is justified in cases where someone has been so victimized, and what responsibility that person has for those actions—but also from a clinical perspective—that is, trying to understand such homicidal behavior. From the latter perspective, it must be recognized that diagnostic categories never arise in a scientific vacuum; this principle applies both to battered spouse syndrome, which may be a subtype of posttraumatic stress disorder (PTSD), and for other diagnoses that involve patterns of self-defeating or masochistic behaviors.

Using social theory on victimology, coupled with psychiatric knowledge of personality disorders, a broader consideration of the complex and controversial issues surrounding a battered spouse killing his or her partner can be obtained. Although some of these cases involve male perpetrators, the issues are most often raised when a female commits a homicide. In this section, I focus the discussion on situations in which a woman has killed a male partner whom she alleges has physically abused her in the past. I will not look at the vagaries of verbal abuse that could allegedly lead to sufficient provocation to kill a partner, although such cases are also arising in the context of a claim for killing in self-defense.

Who Are Battered Women?
An Interpersonal Perspective

Descriptions of the interpersonal lives of battered women are different from many of the stereotypes provided. A false stereotype is that the battered woman is a passive person who does not fight back. In fact, most battered women have fought back at some time. This fact in itself is subject to different interpretations. One view is that their fighting back is an effort to bolster their sagging self-esteem. Another is that these women learn to express their anger and hostile feelings by striking back.

In one study of 400 battered women, 92% of the women thought the batterer could kill them, but 54% also thought they could kill the batterer.[4] Such data indicate the magnitude of the risk for a potential homicide within such a population. In addition, 87% of those women stated that they thought they would be likely to die during a battering incident. Threats of suicide were present in 48% of the batterers and in 36% of the women. None of the women perpetrated a killing, although most of them had fantasized the batterer's death in the course of their relationship. In some cases, this admission of having fantasized about the killing is raised to challenge the woman's self-defense strategy by claiming that the killing had been premeditated.

Browne calculated that 12% of homicides in the United States are committed by women, and that most of them are committed by battered women who allege they have killed in self-defense.[5] Several points merit discussion here. The first is that these cases arise from a variety of background situations; often the only common thread among them is the womens' claims of being battered having led them to the homicide to protect their life. In some cases, there is a background of physical beatings administered by the male in the relationship, with several earlier and unsuccessful attempts by the female partner to extricate herself from the situation. At the other extreme is a man who strikes a woman during a heated quarrel, which culminates in her striking back and killing him. In yet other cases the killing occurs hours or days following an argument. Sometimes the homicide is planned far ahead of time, being seen as "the only way out," and in others, the homicide may be unplanned, but may occur because the weapon (e.g., kitchen knife, gun) is conveniently available. In still other premeditated situations, a third person is hired to do the killing. The presence or absence of children may be another significant variable, both in terms of their immediate presence at the time of the killing or in terms of the woman claiming that she killed the abuser for the children's sake as well.

A three-phase cycle of violence was proposed by Walker.[4] It is based on a tension-reduction learning model that operates in intimate relationships. In this framework, violence between intimates is seen as always progressing toward a more serious level. Respites may occur from such events when one of the parties commences legal action or attempts clinical interventions. Walker's first phase is one of the building up of tension in which a woman attempts to exert some control over her life by trying to give the man what he wants in view of threats that he will beat her. Next, inevitably, is the period when the control no longer works and battering incidents begin to occur. The hypothesis is that the psychological release of tension in the relationship functions as a reinforcer of the cycle. The third phase is one of loving contrition, or simply no tension, which also serves as a reinforcer to the pattern and contributes to maintaining the relationship.

Walker's theory is based on the paradigm of a learned helplessness model. The woman is exposed to repeated random and inescapable aversive stimuli. Eventually the woman loses confidence in her ability to predict whether she can control the violence by her own behavior. She adapts to the situation through using cognitive distortions such as minimalization, denial, and splitting of the mind from the body during painful times. Such mechanisms have also been viewed as survival techniques.[6] Those who use therapeutic attempts to interpret this behavior as random, and to focus on the good side of the male, are viewed as misinformed and using misguided therapeutic efforts.

Psychiatric Considerations

The reasoning supporting the battered spouse syndrome is that a woman who has been battered is experiencing PTSD associated with the psychological impact of abuse. The procedure at trial is first to introduce expert testimony that the battered spouse syndrome exists in the case at hand. It is then elaborated as a version of PTSD if a formal diagnosis is needed. Such an approach can raise questions about the validity and reliability of PTSD in general, and more specifically about its use in battered spouse syndrome cases. These issues are then relevant to clinical discussions and to the context of the implications for these allegations in a courtroom. An important point to be underscored is that the PTSD diagnosis is not used for purposes of introducing an insanity defense nor even for a diminished responsibility defense. Rather, the diagnosis of PTSD and its subsidiary diagnosis for a battered woman are presented as an explanation and justification for the act in an exculpatory sense. The woman in question is usually portrayed as a woman who was terrified because of the past physical assaults perpetrated on her. Her emotional state is described as the normal response of a terrified human being to the abnormal and dangerous environment to which she has been exposed. There also seems to be a presumption that the only significant diagnosis found in a battered woman in such a situation who commits a homicide is PTSD, or at least the only one seen as legally necessary.

An opposing view would argue that the validity of the battered woman's syndrome is based on inadequate research and theoretical inconsistencies. Because a key legal issue in trials using the battered spouse syndrome defense is the standard of self-defense, a crucial criterion is deciding what is meant by being "in imminent danger of serious bodily harm or death." How continuous must a state of believing that one is in imminent danger be? If the atmosphere is more or less continuous, the advocates would argue that it does not matter whether the beating was recently or days ago. In response to the question why the woman did not shoot just to wound or maim, the reply is given that such action would not resolve the woman's ongoing fear of bodily harm or death once the man had recuperated. Therefore, it is argued that the woman had to kill the man to be relieved of the fear that he would kill her in the future.

A common finding among the diverse contexts in which a battered spouse syndrome is used is that there has often been either minimal or no psychological evaluation of the parties before the killing, testifying either to the illness or competency of the involved parties. Attempts at marriage counseling would not be included within the realm of psychological evaluation, as there is usually no preexisting assessment with respect to diagnosis or personality functioning. This lack of a competent psychological appraisal may actually be seen as a boon by the legal defense team because they would not want anything introduced that could pertain to the possibility of some abnormal mental state existing in the perpetrator that would detract from the issue of a justifiable homicide; the woman's actions, seen as the actions of a victim having a battered spouse syndrome, are subsumed under a self-defense argument. If such an approach is used, clinical insight into the parties is bypassed entirely. Any past counseling that has been attempted is used not to focus on diagnostic insights into the parties, but solely on whether a battered spouse syndrome was present before the event took place and updating the validity or usefulness of this evaluation to the present case. If the homicidal act has already occurred, the consideration is whether the background provides sufficient evidence of victimization to argue for a defensible homicide.

There are those who, in supporting a battered woman defense to homicide, see it as essential that a therapist become the victim's advocate and wholeheartedly accept the victim's position in contrast to adopting a neutral or value-free stance. This lack of neutrality is in opposition to traditional psychotherapeutic approaches and family therapy, and it blurs the distinctions between advocacy and clinical assessment.

Sociological Viewpoint

A feminist perspective on problems of intergender violence provides a further insight to understand this defense when such killings occur. Wife abuse is generally seen as a reflection of power differences existing between the genders. Physical violence is viewed as the most efficient means of social control to maintain dominance over women.[7] From this perspective, it would seem unnecessary to use other theoretical frameworks to explain extreme violence between partners. A family systems approach, commonly used by those who work with families, for example, would be interpreted as ignoring the crucial significance of gender as the key variable. For similar reasons, questions about the possible presence of psychiatric disorders in either party would be viewed as perhaps interesting but largely irrelevant.

The question of why a battered woman would kill her partner remains intriguing in its own right. The usual answer given is more of a sociological one, based on a position that men have been socialized into believing they have a right to control women and therefore see it as permissible to use violence on women. The result is that there are battered women. This basic position may be generalized to see violence against women as the core of violence in the world. Such a gender-based psychology, or perhaps sociology, arose in the late 1960s in opposition to psychological theories of male and female behaviors as innate and biologically based;[8] these theories were seen as biased, both in their empiricist approaches and how hypotheses were formulated and tested. Although this sociological focus was originally used in sex discrimination cases, it was eventually extended to oppression of women. Women who were subjects of violence were viewed as victims of coercion.

Comparisons have been made between the situation of battered women and that of a hostage who is kept under the control of a captor. Social institutions of marriage and the related patriarchal family structure are viewed as conducive to a form of captivity that permits and sanctions the use of force to control women. Rather than viewing the family as a safe haven from violence and intrusion from outside forces, it is seen as a cloak for violence that can occur within it. Operating within this framework, traditional views are seen as inhibiting professionals from looking inside families to see how the system of dominance and abuse can operate. When a killing does occur within such a family milieu, it is used to confirm the view that a marriage always has the potential of ending in violence. As a corollary, advocacy is seen as necessary to reveal the state of marriage as it actually exists. Advocacy is also seen as a necessary step to make such domination public knowledge. The situation of a woman standing trial for murder of her partner is viewed as a paradigmatic political situation through which an activist approach can reveal what actually had transpired in a marriage under the veil of family secrecy.

Legal Considerations

To transpose such a sociological view of the relationship between the genders into the legal setting once a homicide has occurred requires a change in how the standard of self-defense is interpreted. Whereas self-defense has customarily been predicated on demonstrating facts that a person had a reasonable perception of some imminent danger, some jurisdictions have allowed redefinitions so that the standard used shifts to how an "objective reasonable woman" or a "subjective reasonable battered woman's perceptions" can be applied to these situations. The need is to portray the woman who kills as living in a state of perpetually fearing for her own life. Underlying this shift is the position that the danger of great bodily harm or death is always imminent for a battered woman.

Another legal difficulty is the context in which the eventual homicide occurred. In one study of women who had killed a man, 86% were

202 ■ HOMICIDE: A PSYCHIATRIC PERSPECTIVE

in an active, intimate relationship with the man at the time of the murder.[9] In most typical cases, the battered spouse syndrome defense is raised where homicidal violence occurred in the midst of a struggle. However, this defense becomes more problematic when some time has elapsed between a past violent episode and the homicide. Those people who advocate the syndrome as being exculpatory of homicide are not troubled by these difficult cases. They view the timing of when the act occurs as a relatively insignificant variable. This is because the act is perceived as almost inevitable, barring some unforeseen event or major intervention measures by someone. Such a problem is handled by arguing that a reasonable woman perceives a need to defend herself with a weapon against a man who uses his body to dominate and injure her.

Another difficulty emerges when a woman kills a mate who has been asleep, was lounging in a chair, had his back turned, or was in a state of stupification from drug or alcohol use at the time of the killing. In one case, in which a woman was raped by two acquaintances who then threatened to return and repeat the act, it was argued as reasonable for her to perceive she was still in a state of imminent danger when she shot one of the rapists hours later.[10] A guilty verdict was then handed down because she was not considered to have been in imminent danger at the time. Subsequently, an appellate court accepted the application of imminent to her situation in the sense that imminent did not mean immediate; at a retrial, the woman was acquitted on grounds of self-defense.

The question of the admissibility of expert testimony supporting self-defense in the context of a battered spouse situation has been pursued vigorously since the Ibn-Tamas case in 1979.[11] In that case, the court ruled that the knowledge provided by an expert on such situations was beyond the knowledge of the average juror, and it was more probative than prejudicial to allow such testimony. The expert witness was then seen as providing background data to help the jury make its crucial determination of whether the woman actually and reasonably believed her life was in danger when she killed her husband. Some appellate courts have held such testimony admissible whereas others have rejected it.[12] The U. S. Supreme Court has not ruled on the matter.

Implications of the Battered Spouse Syndrome

There are many implications from homicide trials in which experts testify that a woman who kills her partner under these circumstances was justified in her actions.

Implications on society's image of women. How a female should be viewed and how well the criminal justice system functions are issues that have emerged. One view of women is that they are helpless creatures who cannot deal with force as it is used by physically larger and more muscular males. Although this is undoubtedly true for some women, just as when a smaller man has to confront a physically larger and more powerful male, an extension of the principle to other areas of the criminal law would imply a regression to a primitive societal state in which the weak and helpless either need a more physically powerful champion to protect them or routinely need to carry a weapon to equalize the situation so that they can survive. The image conveyed is that of the caveman giving protection to his woman at the price of the woman's autonomy. In battered spouse syndrome defense cases, defense lawyers use people and experts to testify about a woman's helpless state that was induced by her being subjected to continual battering. Although the old stereotype of the woman actually enjoying the abuse has largely been dispelled, the argument is that now another stereotype is being reinforced—that of the passive female victim in contrast to a person capable of taking charge of his or her own life and, if necessary, testifying to the state of the ongoing and actual troubled relationship with a partner.[13]

A general question, but one the jury must decide in trials, is which image of a battered woman is to be believed: that of a brainwashed, frightened victim or that of a woman who has done what any reasonable woman would do in killing her oppressor after reaching a certain endpoint. The former image is actually a clinical portrayal of a woman with many features of a personality disorder; the latter is a sociological image of a woman existing in an oppressive and male-dominated culture who decides it is time to stop the beatings to avoid living in fear. The inference is that, because society has not created a different milieu in which she can live with a partner, she must take matters into her own hands. From this confused image, a jury may be led to a manslaughter verdict or even an insanity verdict. However, advocates of the battered spouse syndrome defense want the verdict to be not guilty, based on the premise that the woman dealt rationally with a situation that required her to take self-defensive actions and not because she acted insanely. Furthermore, it is desirable to avoid the administrative complications (e.g., psychological treatment, medications, forced hospitalization) that follow a not-guilty-by-reason-of-insanity verdict.

Validity of battered woman syndrome defense for all battered women. There is also confusion when assessing the impact of battering on an individual woman who has subsequently killed the significant partner in her life. A persistent question is why all women in such predicaments do not kill. The battered spouse syndrome has been formulated as a theory about women in general who have been battered.[14] However, the difficulty with it is that it does not explain the psychological idiosyncrasies of different personality styles and defenses among individual women. Matters are forced into an either-or categorization based on whether sufficient characteristics of a battered woman syndrome are present for any given woman. The result, as it is for allegations of PTSD in legal settings, is to make sure all the usual descriptive symptoms are listed.

More troubling psychiatrically is the seeming compartmentalization of large numbers of women who have killed a spouse or lover into the same diagnostic format as though there are no differences in their personalities, motives, or diagnoses. It is an approach that seems to take a constrictive view rather one that encompasses diverse possibilities operating with different diagnostic possibilities, such as when a male commits a homicide. It raises a question as to whether women are ever seen as killing a partner for some reason other than being victimized. Analogous questions arise when women who have been convicted of homicide and imprisoned are subsequently released by a governor's pardon. A mixture of diverse motives for killing might well be present in such cases, varying from battered women responding in desperation to their plight to pecuniary motives or delusional possibilities.

■ Self-Defeating Personalities and Killing: Myth or Reality

Personality disorders have never been free from some type of pejorative connotation; however, the debate regarding establishing a diagnosis of self-defeating personality disorder has been a particularly grueling and vicious one. Often the personality disorders are based on sociological theory. For example, some posit that certain groupings of behaviors and attitudes that they see as congruent with being primarily an adaptive response to a coercive environment are mislabeled as personality disorders. With regard to self-defeating personality disorder, supporters of this view would see these type of behaviors as adaptive to a milieu in which misogyny is seen as an endemic condition in a society, and obedient behavior is a reflection of a traditional female role. Thus, they hypothesize, the seemingly adaptive nature of a female who exhibits self-defeating behavior is so prevalent that it is not recognized as a result of abuse. Specific criticisms of this diagnosis from a sociological perspective are as follows:

1. The diagnosis is gender-biased and will be misapplied to women.
2. A normative behavior in women will be subject to misinterpretation.
3. The criteria reflect adaptation to victimization.
4. There is an assumption that a person can choose to be removed from victimized situations.
5. The diagnosis will be misused in courts.[15]

From a clinical standpoint, the diagnosis of self-defeating personality disorder has been criticized because it relies excessively on subjective criteria and lacks standardized instruments. Such criticisms could be raised about many diagnoses, especially in the personality disorder categories in which there is a lack of consensus on even how to assess personality diagnoses.[16] The criteria for these diagnoses resonate with clinicians when it is a specific personality disorder they are familiar with and that may have relevance in homicidal situations. Although this approach may have some validity, the question remains that when a diagnosis such as self-defeating personality disorder relies on the clinician's assessment of subjective components (e.g., assessment of the patient's internal motivational patterns), whether it can meet the criteria for an acceptably valid diagnosis. When comorbidity is present with this diagnosis, there can be considerable overlap with avoidant, dependent, and obsessive-compulsive categories. However, some believe the diagnosis is distinguishable from these other types of disorders.[17]

In essence, critics of the diagnosis of self-defeating personality disorder believe that the tools currently available for its assessment and diagnosis, as well as that of other personality disorders, do not equip clinicians to differentiate between someone who has a persistently disordered personality from someone who is reacting to an adverse social milieu. If that critique is accurate, the focus should logically be on the more pervasive presence of abuse as a societal and legal problem rather than on delineating specific traits within a group of people. Hence, it would be concluded that clinicians who look for intrapsychic motivation in self-defeating behaviors confuse a result for a cause. However, this argument seems inconsistent in some respects. When a male assaults his female companion, his actions are not seen as solely the societal response of someone who is blindly caught up in exhibiting his male prowess. If a homicide results from such assaults, the psychiatric diagnosis of the perpetrator becomes of great interest. In fact, 80%–90% of those who assault their wives may have personality disorders.[18]

The concern of diverse groups was that self-defeating personality disorder could impinge on the validity of the battered spouse syndrome as a grouping under PTSD, given that masochistic personality was considered to be a legitimate diagnosis. In this argument, self-defeating personality disorder was attacked as a diagnosis that had no empirical basis and lacked any scientific validity.[19] In contrast, these groups argued that there were sufficient scientific criteria for battered spouse syndrome to be included under PTSD.[20] Lurking throughout the arguments was the thread that diagnostic formulations regarding masochistic personalities were more appropriate for those who had a primary and underlying disturbance that sometimes led them to kill their lovers rather than for those reacting under the primary influence of a PTSD brought about by being the victim of continual assaults.

Features of Self-Defeating Personalities

The descriptive features proposed for self-defeating personality disorder pointed to a pervasive pattern of self-defeating behaviors beginning in early adulthood and that were manifested in diverse contexts. The description "masochistic personality disorder" had been abandoned to avoid historic implications from older psychoanalytic views that connected female sexuality with masochism or from the belief that people derived pleasure from suffering.[21] Self-defeating individuals were seen as avoiding or undermining pleasurable experiences and being drawn to situations or relationships in which they would suffer, yet structuring matters in such a way as to prevent others from helping them. As included in the DSM-III-R appendix, eight diagnostic criteria were given for this disorder, five of which were needed to make the diagnosis (listed in Table 7–1).[22] If the criteria are viewed behaviorally, they suggest an individual predisposed to becoming involved in situations where the probability of self-destructive or violent behavior is increased. Those who have worked in the criminal justice system, or in forensic settings, will be immediately impressed with how many of these characteristics fit males in a court population, who make up at least 90% of criminal cases.

Note the caveat in which the diagnosis is not to be used if the self-defeating behaviors occur only in response to, or in anticipation of, being physically, sexually, or psychologically abused. Similarly, if the person is depressed and shows such behavior, the diagnosis does not apply. The key is to distinguish whether the self-defeating behavior is a persistent pattern that is not limited to situations of actual or anticipated abuse. For example, a person with many past destructive behaviors might only recently have become a physically abused victim.

As might be expected, self-defeating behaviors are commonly seen in diverse personality disorders, such as borderline personality disorder, dependent personality disorder, obsessive-compulsive personality disorder, and avoidant personality disorder, as well as becoming entwined in some dysthymic and major depressive episodes. If the diagnosis of self-defeating personality disorder were to be used, it would have a good deal of comorbidity.

Although not part of the criteria listed, some propose that individuals exposed to physical, sexual, or psychological abuse as a child, or being reared in a family where there was spousal abuse, predisposes them to having a self-defeating personality disorder. This is similar to what has been argued by some as the predisposing factor for development of borderline personality disorder. Not everyone would agree that events in childhood are causally related to the emergence of a

Table 7–1. DSM-III-R criteria for self-defeating personality disorder

A. A pervasive pattern of self-defeating behavior, beginning by early adulthood and present in a variety of contexts. The person may often avoid or undermine pleasurable experiences, be drawn to situations or relationships in which he or she will suffer, and prevent others from helping him or her, as indicated by at least five of the following:

1. Chooses people and situations that lead to disappointment, failure, or mistreatment, even when better options are clearly available.

2. Rejects or renders ineffective the attempts of others to help him or her.

3. Following positive personal events (e.g., new achievement), responds with depression, guilt, or a behavior that produces pain (e.g., an accident).

4. Incites angry or rejecting responses from others and then feels hurt, defeated, or humiliated (e.g., makes fun of spouse in public, provoking an angry retort, then feels devastated).

5. Rejects opportunities for pleasure, or is reluctant to acknowledge enjoying himself or herself (despite having adequate social skills and the capacity for pleasure).

6. Fails to accomplish tasks crucial to his or her personal objectives despite demonstrated ability to do so (e.g., helps fellow students write papers, but is unable to write his or her own).

7. Is uninterested in or rejects people who consistently treat him or her well (e.g., is unattracted to caring sexual partners).

8. Engages in excessive self-sacrifice that is unsolicited by the intended recipients of the sacrifice.

B. The behaviors in A do not occur exclusively in response to, or in anticipation of, being physically, sexually, or psychologically abused.

C. The behaviors in A do not occur only when the person is depressed.

Source. Reprinted with permission from American Psychiatric Association: *Diagnostic and Statistical Manual of Mental Disorders,* 3rd Edition, Revised. Washington, DC, American Psychiatric Association, 1987. Copyright 1987 American Psychiatric Association.

self-defeating personality disorder in adulthood. In Walker's study of 400 cases of self-identified battered women, she did not find support for such a causative relationship; instead, she interpreted the relationship between these factors as simply one of coexistence.[4] The behavior of the women was not seen as self-defeating in nature, but rather as their effort to protect themselves as best they could. Walker felt interpretations of behavior patterns as self-defeating was based on two contradictory assumptions: that the behavior patterns were part of an inherent self-destructive pattern but were identified also as part of the criteria for diagnosing that self-destructive condition.

It is paradoxical that, because a woman is more likely to be the victim of a homicide at the time she attempts to terminate a self-defeating relationship, it would appear that her chances of surviving are better if she simply remains in such a relationship. Thus it could be argued that a battered woman who tried to adapt to a relationship was only trying to survive. Yet, it could also be argued that her staying in the relationship perpetuated her self-defeating pattern of behavior. In fact, the initial separation period is also likely to be the time when the potential for violence is maximized against not only the woman but also the man (perpetrated by the woman). A question is whether the price of freedom for an individual is that of increasing the risk of violence and possible homicide.

Tentative Conclusions Regarding Self-Defeating Personality Disorder

Some tentative conclusions can be offered from this continuing controversy about the diagnostic validity of self-defeating personality disorder in connection with homicide. One approach would be to view the self-defeating behaviors as part of a comorbid picture of different personality disturbances, especially dependent personality disorder and borderline personality disorder. In addition, self-defeating behaviors can be part of the clinical picture of depressions not evolving in response to an actual or anticipated physical abuse. Impulsive, angry, acting-out behaviors would then be viewed as part of a repertory of responses accompanying an existing depression. In a study using the Structured Clinical Interview for DSM-III-R[23] and the Personality

Disorder examination, Skodal et al. found that self-defeating personality disorder overlaps substantially with the borderline personality and dependent personality disorders and concluded that the diagnosis seemed redundant.[25] What was then left was that self-defeating behaviors are simply present in many diagnoses.

A quite different approach is to interpret self-defeating types of behavior as part of PTSD, in which the response is expected given the distressful situation a person has been in. Yet, many fundamental issues remain unresolved about PTSD because this category was created primarily for individuals who were reacting to major disasters, military combat, or criminal assaults.[26] Epidemiological surveys continue to use these given diagnostic criteria and to find a high prevalence of this type of PTSD in communities. It is not clear how PTSD relates as the immediate response to any given trauma and how the pervasive responses of anxiety and depression to stress should be distinguished from PTSD. Not only are there many subclinical variants of PTSD, but the course and duration of PTSD vary a good deal as well. A homicide victim or perpetrator of a homicide may often be assessed with this diagnosis.

■ Understanding Masochism and Homicide From a Psychodynamic Perspective

Acknowledging the controversy surrounding even the validity of the diagnosis of a masochistic character does not negate its heuristic value for raising explanatory hypotheses when a homicidal act has occurred. If the theoretical framework being used in explanations is made clear, and the inferential processes specified, psychiatrists would not be confined to viewing the immediate behavior as being simply reactive, but could inquire into the intrapersonal conflicts as well as the interactional and social factors. Searching for an explanatory model in homicides requires one to focus on an individual who has already committed the act. Just as with murder mysteries, the psychiatrist must operate after the fact to reconstruct the events, but here the detective work is not to find the murderers, but to explain the way the perpetrator's mind operated.

In formulating explanations of a perpetrator's masochistic behavior, it must be noted that masochism is not used here in the restrictive sense of erotogenic or sexual masochism. These types of masochism involve various sexual acts in which pain is sought out as pleasurable. Although some of these practices can lead to a death, it is usually by a mischance rather than a calculated act of homicide when such a result occurs. These acts should be distinguished from the group in which killing accompanying some type of sexual acts is the primary goal. The majority of masochistic acts that lead to an eventual homicide are more subtle. Their nature only becomes clearer when a detailed clinical assessment can be carried out and corroborated by outside information. This group comprises the far larger grouping of masochistic behaviors in which characterological or "moral" masochism are operative.

Early Psychodynamic Theories

Explanations of masochistic tendencies leading to violence have been offered in diverse theories and in a growing body of literature. Various schools of thought exist and, to complicate matters further, within each school theories have shifted over time. Freud's thinking on this topic was a classic example of changing theoretical viewpoints. Freud ultimately came to view masochism as the struggle between the ego representing the life instinct against another basic instinctual source—the famous death instinct; the instinctual nature of the struggle was often played out in the context of oedipal conflicts and defenses. Masochism was seen as deriving from the superego, with a defensive submission to the father as a defense against castration. That is what led Freud to label such traits as passive and feminine. Suffering and seeking punishment by overt or covert means became the masochist's goal. True masochists were seen as those who never missed a chance to turn the other cheek when they had a chance to receive a blow.[29]

Many questions remain unresolved within one or another psychodynamic viewpoints. In early theories, the preoedipal period was not focused on much; instead, questions about the role of early ego development, superego precursors, processes of separation, narcissism, attempts to resolve conflicts over submission and suffering, and protective ego roles as contributors to masochistic patterns arose. Many of the leading figures in psychoanalysis in the 1930s and 1940s wrote about these issues within and without the classic Freudian framework.[30]

Succeeding generations have continued to grapple with the problem. In the following discussion, I do not review all of the fluctuating theoretical positions and shifts, but rather take the approach of extracting something from the theories that is relevant to homicides. The question is how these individuals with a diathesis toward self-defeating interpersonal relationships, whatever the cause, might eventually end up behaving in a homicidal manner.

A Synthesized Psychodynamic Theory on Masochism and Homicide

Many complexities within the individual ego and interpersonal life operate in masochistic individuals to predispose them to an ultimate homicidal act. These complexities involve a recurring set of behaviors in which some variety of self-defeating behavior, often of an unconscious nature, eventually sets the stage for a violent response. It is not the person's eventual, overt act that offers the key to his or her motivation, but a pattern of characterological traits that have led that person into humiliating or punitive relationships with other people.

One common feature found in masochistic killers is that they have often submitted to positions or tasks that are emotionally painful in their daily life; these might or might not be overt acts of abuse. Rather, the essential component is one of the person's being trapped in an abject, submissive, or exploited position. The progression from being humiliated or punished to becoming the perpetrator of such actions is so subtle that only those who have known the person quite well throughout their lifetime could sense these patterns and their enduring quality.

Three components are key to understanding the transition from being the masochistic object of aggression to the perpetrator of such aggression—suppressed aggression, narcissistic tendencies, and depression. If one begins from the position that the vulnerability of a person with a masochistic personality structure to commit a homicide lies partly in the difficulties they have in dealing with their aggression, and then several things begin to fall into place. Narcissistic aspects in masochistic phenomena play an integral part in the development of homicidal tendencies. Kernberg argued that an understanding of the narcissistic aspects of masochism as related to these individuals' hatreds and the psychopathology of aggression is just as important as focusing on sadistic tendencies and wishes.[31] In the background, there is the proneness to depression. A confluence of these tendencies seems to operate in the cases that result in homicide. Some people become depressed when they realize their hatred is mounting and they cannot control others around them. They sense that any expression of their overt anger or even sadistic tendencies and wishes would elicit guilt over such acts of wrongdoing. One pattern found repeatedly in homicide cases has been that the person initially attempted to counter these tendencies or undo some aggressive acts. In intimate relationships, the perpetrator may attempt to undo the aggressive acts by engaging in exaggerated acts of niceness or being submissive.

Problems emerge from a feeling of psychological coerciveness that is present in these self-defeating relationships. Masochistic individuals use diverse maneuvers to induce guilt in those on whom they are dependent, especially when they feel that their needs continuously remain unmet or they have provoked rejection. Whereas one outcome may be a depression in response to a sense of defeat, another may be mobilized anger. These individuals' harsh self-assessment may be turned on those they consider responsible for their plight and the source of their unhappiness. Eventually, alternations between angry outbursts and unconsciously putting themselves into situations where they are maltreated reflect the beginning of a breakdown in their ego controls, as well as attempts to deal with the unremitting and overcritical demands of their superego. Hence, it is not inconsistent to see sadistic ("murderous") attacks on people who have played key roles in their lives.

These attacks reflect the individuals' attempt to maintain their emotional well-being by shifting the demonstrations of humiliating behavior in an effort to regain control over their own life. It signifies that on some level they are developing an awareness that techniques of control by suffering are not working. In the meantime, these individuals are eventually moving toward a state of desperation in which they conclude that it is time for them to do something about their predicament of being treated badly by someone else. These are not the same dynamics operating as when they seek external praise and admiration based on their narcissistic needs. It rather reflects a thwarted sense of closeness and being taken care of that they sense is not going to be restored despite the pain and suffering they have endured.

The ascension of these self-defeating and sadistic tendencies lowers these individuals' threshold for a state of action, which leaves them at risk for a primitive and destructive striking out. Homicide then becomes a possibility, although other impulsive acts or a continual return to self-abasing behavior are more likely. Some people become assaultive, whereas others fall back on suicidal gestures or self-mutilations. Attempts to distinguish rage attacks occurring in these individuals from those seen in borderline personality disorder individuals may become more of an academic exercise because the dynamic psychopathology overlaps. Pathetic attempts to regain control over others through self-abasement may be a last effort to thwart the full expression of their hatred.

The experience of narcissistic mortification induces a frightening loss of control in these individuals. Both their inner and outer worlds seem beyond control. The threat of loss of control reveals such a degree of weakness in these individuals that it can be taken as a token of an imminent collapse or annihilation. The dual needs of regaining control over others and over oneself coexist. Denial or repression may transiently serve to contain the sense of being overwhelmed and helpless. Yet, accompanying the state of paralysis from the mortification is that of feeling utterly humiliated from their grandiose self being overwhelmed. Eventually, seeking the source of such a blow, or projecting the terror and misery experienced onto an external object, allows their rage to become more focused on an "enemy." When this object becomes focused on at the same time as these individuals sense an annihilation or even a psychotic decompensation, that is the crucial period for a homicidal act. Some type of victory is needed to triumph over an impending sense of devastation. Although suicide is one solution, a better solution may seem to be to destroy their oppressor. At this point, their superego functioning has moved from a position of restraint or guilty control to that of joining in a destructive act that has the quality of righteous assertion.

Another variety of masochistic enslavement that can manifest itself in a homicide is seen with the problems connected to a delusional (paranoid) disorder, especially of the erotomanic type. Such cases (discussed in Chapter 3) reflect acts based on delusions; for example, when one holds the distorted belief that someone is keeping one's beloved from one and then concludes that such an interferer must be eliminated. The victim need not be the person who is the object of the delusional belief, since he or she can be the person seen as doing the interfering. However, if such individuals believe the person who supposedly loves them has altered his or her love for them, the change may frequently be attributed to someone else malignantly operating on the beloved object. Their twisted altruistic reasoning takes the form that it is better for their former loved one to die than to be unable to reciprocate their love.

Stalking Patterns

In some stalking cases, the masochistic individual has held the fantasized belief that some other person has been attracted to him or her for years, although that belief may have waxed and waned over the years; they act only after some mischance has pushed them into it. Celebrities or other well-known community figures are often the recipients of such special attention. They may have been stalked over time, but this may be revealed only after some threatening or homicidal act. Unsigned letters may be sent to those being stalked in which hostility is interwoven with allusions to the mutual destiny of the letter writer and the addressee. Letters may refer to the writer's suffering and torment, with accusations of how his or her heart is being torn apart or life ruined unless given some acknowledgment that his or her feelings are being reciprocated. The John Hinckley case, involving the actress Jodie Foster, would appear to fit into this category. Many of these people's lives have been uneventful and they have often lived in relative isolation, not becoming conspicuous until some public act brings them into the public eye. Sometimes their persistence and forced attentions give rise to complexities and embarrassments for families and places of employment, which are fortuitously better than an outcome of homicide.

A more subtle, and, consequently, more difficult situation to detect is related to self-defeating patterns in a love relationship that is not reciprocal or in which one partner wishes to withdraw. Here we are not usually dealing with delusions per se, but rather the dynamics of sadomasochistic features in people who continue to be attracted to those who flatly reject them. When these situations emerge abruptly, in contrast to within the context of long-standing and conflicted relationships, there is also the possibility of a manic episode intervening. The individual seems to abandon his or her past commitments and norms and neglect many other aspects of his or her ongoing life to pursue someone who may be only mildly interested in or even indifferent to the individual. Narcissistic aspects are operative in the individual's self-absorption with this one person. To suffer the pains and disappointments of such a pursuit seems to enhance the pride of the sufferer.

The more common situation is where a love relationship once existed but the feelings of one of the parties have changed, as in the following case example:

Case Example

A 30-year-old man lived with his lady friend for 6 years. Together they had a 5-year-old child; the woman's older child from a previous relationship also lived with them. After 6 years, the woman informed her partner that she no longer wanted to continue the relationship. His first reaction of denial slowly gave way to one of incredulity that her feelings could have changed. However, acquaintances felt the woman had become bored with him over the preceding 2 years. He refused to leave the apartment. A year later, she obtained a court order to put him out of the apartment. Despite this, he periodically reappeared, which eventually led to contempt of court charges. When a new man moved in with the woman, the tempo of the original boyfriend's behavior increased, and the potential for violence became magnified. One night, after having stalked the apartment for some time, the man burst into the apartment during a party and shot his former partner, her new male friend, and both children.

What explanation can be offered for such killings? Often they are simply referred to as revenge killings, yet this seems an insufficient explanation. One reason for this is that the person often has not resolved his or her continued idealization of the previous love object. In addition, to a point, such individuals endure the suffering of being excluded and rejected. In the above case, the man suffered for the sake of the woman who had rejected him and become indifferent to him for a whole year.

In some cases, the rejecting person is more sadistic in their rejecting behavior. During the period of rejection, the man in the above case example would talk about his anguish to anyone who would listen, including various therapists. At times, his depression and suicidal ideation were discussed. His continued idealization of the woman contained elements of distortion in seeing her as being more financially successful than she actually was. He believed that through her he would share in her idealized attributes and attainments, and his beliefs interfered with his ability to loosen his attachment to her. When he saw that his grandiosity was not going to continue to be realized through her, and no one else was to be considered as having value for him, he resorted to a final destructive act. Suicide subsequent to homicide is always possible in these cases. This man did not commit suicide, but simply went to a nearby restaurant he often frequented and drank coffee while awaiting his arrest. However, it could be said that serving the three consecutive terms for murder to which he was sentenced was a suicide equivalent. In dynamic terms, this man's grandiose self would not let him literally destroy himself.

Malignant Masochism

Committing a homicide in some cases might be just a more final and climactic failure reflecting diverse areas of difficulties in the person's life. A final self-destructive act could unconsciously reflect the ultimate in self-denial. These individuals might be bound up in conflicts for years over controlling others and being controlled. The external trappings give them the appearance of being controlled and manipulated by a spouse, lover, employer, or other person. Yet, as noted above, victimization is one more method of control by way of a distorted display of aggression. A perplexing dynamic in such submissiveness is the individuals' need to induce guilt in those who maltreat them. In the long run, attempts to do this are usually unsuccessful. The mechanism appears related to the self-righteousness present in masochistic individuals' control system. The mission is to change the other party—much like a person wishes to point out the mistakes of those who were once presumed supportive of them.

Asch referred to the extreme end of such self-destructiveness as *malignant masochism* because of the intensity of the self-destructive components with prominent hostility.[32] In these people, even more than in other self-defeating individuals, gaining control over others becomes the primary mission in life. The battle commences at a young age, and may acquire sophistication as part of a set of character defenses throughout development to adulthood. The pattern of achieving success by being a failure or thwarting others is commonly seen. Sometimes the battle over control is fought within, as witnessed in periods of drug or alcohol abuse. These individuals often stress their ability to control their usage of substances simply through will power. Similar variations can be played out through bulimic or anorexic behavior patterns. Externalization of the conflict to their environments is done through skillfully provoking or manipulating others into seemingly maltreating them or inciting others to carry out such acts. In one case, subsequent to the homicide, the perpetrator's employment record revealed that this individual had instigated investigations of a series of grievance complaints at several jobs against several people. Matters had dragged on for several years without resolution by committees that, in retrospect, appeared simply to dismiss the complaints. However, the very nature of these entanglements became a source of pride for this person as they allowed a demonstration of suffering because of the frustrated attempts to make others accept guilt over their predicaments to become evident.

Even in legal cases where there is a trial or settlement in these individuals' favor, or some grievance judgment is made against another party, they experience only short-term relief. This may be because the other party has not been seen as experiencing sufficient suffering, but only anger and resentment. The complainant continues to feel that something unjust has been done to him or her that needs to be righted.

The pleasure in controlling, at whatever price, leads to repetitive role enactments with similar themes in diverse settings. Those who attempt to treat these individuals, by whatever therapeutic modality, also witness the similarity in repeated therapeutic failures. Lurking in the reenactments is always the threat of retaliation against them. When depressive components are also present, there is the combination of courting punishment from within and without.

In the context of these backgrounds, a homicide may occur in response to an internal conflict, with superego functioning insufficiently ameliorative, and based on failed needs to externalize and punish others. On one hand, there is the need to appease a punitive and overcontrolling source from within that ultimately knows no surcease. At the same time, there is the need to find some culprit in the external world and attack and punish this person. The final scenario is a striking out, in what is often portrayed as a variation of self-defense, provocation in a fight, or attempt to overcome a thwarted grievance. Both by descriptive symptoms and signs, and by psychodynamic formulations, there is often a diagnostic overlap. In other cases, there is the feeling of failure if a key person, seen as the culprit who is somehow responsible for their unhappiness, has gained distance from the entanglement. Such a removal must then be punished. In the following case example, the balance in the relationship tipped so that the person who was initially enslaved by her insecurities became less conflicted and wanted to extricate herself. Such a transition left the partner feeling confused and betrayed. In this stalemate, a rage reaction led to a homicide.

Case Example

A young couple in their 20s had lived together for 2 years. At the time they met, she was insecure and wanted to be rescued from her parental home. In the beginning of the relationship, he saw himself as the victim of her unfounded jealousies and haranguing about women with whom he worked. Although these accusations never totally ended, a shift occurred when she no longer needed him to meet many of her needs. His discomfort mounted when he felt he had progressively less to offer her and sensed her reduced needs for him. Because his role of maintaining her esteem had become less important in the relationship, he resorted to other forms of self-sacrificing, such as her routinely driving their car to work while he rode a bus. Anger at being her "puppet" emerged. His attempts to induce guilt in her for his sufferings, which attempts had formerly led to reconciliatory moves, became less effective.

When she announced she was going to move back with her parents, he became physically violent for the first time. Feeling progressively helpless to control her, he initiated arguments and would not relent. Public scenes occurred, with one or both of them walking away from the other. After an argument, he would drink to excess, something he had not previously done. His justification was that the arguments allowed him to drink. He was experiencing two areas of failure: not being in control of the current situation and a failure of what he had expected to be a long-term relationship that would lead to marriage.

The police had been called to their home on two occasions for domestic disputes when neighbors heard her screaming during assaultive episodes. On a third occasion the police did not arrive in time; the woman had already died from intracranial hemorrhaging. The man had now achieved the ultimate in punishment and in subjugating himself. It is problematic whether a freedom from internalized controls that induced him to act out his murderous rage succeeded in his need to continue to think that she was the one who needed rescuing. His unresolved needs to obey internal edicts to provoke and subjugate others remain untouched and continued to be played out in a location par excellence for reenacting such dramas—a state prison. Only at the price of relinquishing his sense of self could he maintain the belief that he had no role in his own fate.

■ References

1. Coen SJ: The Misuse of Persons: Analyzing Pathological Dependency. Hillsdale, NJ, Analytic Press, 1992

2. Dunne D: Menendez justice. Vanity Fair 57:108–118, 159–166, 1994

3. Rusbult CE, Martz JM: Remaining in an abusive relationship: an investment model analysis of nonvoluntary dependence. Personality and Social Psychology Bulletin 32:558–571, 1995

4. Walker LEA: The Battered Woman Syndrome. New York, Springer, 1984

5. Browne A: When Battered Women Kill. New York, Free Press, 1987

6. Walker LEA: Psychology and violence against women. Am Psychol 44:695–702, 1989

7. Yllo K, Borgad M (eds): Feminist Perspectives on Wife Abuse. Beverly Hills, CA, Sage, 1988

8. Maccoby EE, Jacklin CN: The Psychology of Differences. Palo Alto, CA, Stanford University Press, 1974

9. Mann CR: Getting even: women who kill in domestic encounters. Justice Quarterly 5:33–51, 1988

10. Bochnak E (ed): Women's Self-Defense Cases. Charlottesville, VA, Michie Company Law Publishers, 1981

11. Ibn-Tamas v United States, 407 A2d 626, Washington, DC, 1979

12. Gillespie C: Justifiable Homicide. Columbus, OH, Ohio State University Press, 1989

13. Schneider EM: Describing and changing: women's self-defense work and the problem of expert testimony on battering. Women's Rights Law Reporter 9:195–222, 1986

14. Crocker PL: The meaning of equality for battered women who kill men in self-defense. Harv Women's Law Journal 8:121–151, 1985

15. Firester SJ: Self-defeating personality disorder: a review of data and recommendations for DSM-IV. Journal of Personality Disorders 5:194–209, 1991

16. Zimmerman M: Diagnosing personality disorders. Arch Gen Psychiatry 51:225–245, 1994

17. Nurnberg HG, Siegel O, Prince R, et al: Axis II comorbidity of self-defeating personality disorder. Journal of Personality Disorders 7:10–21, 1993

18. Hart SD, Dutton DG, Newlove T: The prevalence of personality disorder among wife assaulters. Journal of Personality Disorders 7:329–341, 1993

19. Walker LEA: Terrifying Love: Why Battered Women Kill and How Society Responds. New York, Harper & Row, 1989

20. Comments: a critique and proposed solution to the adverse examination and problem raised by battered woman syndrome testimony in State v Hennum. Minnesota Law Review 74:1023–1061, 1990

21. Widiger TA: The self-defeating personality disorder. Journal of Personality Disorders 1:157–159, 1987

22. American Psychiatric Association: Diagnostic and Statistical Manual of Mental Disorders, 3rd Edition, Revised. Washington, DC, American Psychiatric Association, 1987

23. Spitzer RL, Williams JBW, Gibbon M, et al: Structured Clinical Interview for DSM-III-R: User's Guide. Washington, DC, American Psychiatric Press, 1992

25. Skodal AE, Oldham JM, Gallaher PE, et al: Validity of self-defeating personality disorder. Am J Psychiatry 151:560–567, 1994

26. Davidson JRT, Fou B: Posttraumatic Stress Disorder: DSM-IV and Beyond. Washington, DC, American Psychiatric Press, 1992

29. Freud S: The economic problem of masochism (1924), in Standard Edition of the Complete Psychological Works of Sigmund Freud, Vol 19. Translated and edited by Strachey J. London, Hogarth Press, 1961, pp 155–170

30. Grossman W: Notes on masochism: discussion of the history and development of a psychoanalytic concept. Psychoanal Q 55:379–413, 1986

31. Kernberg OF: The psychopathology of hatred, in Rage, Power and Aggression. Edited by Glick RA, Roose SP. New Haven, Yale University Press, 1993, pp 61–79

32. Asch SS: The analytic concepts of masochism, in Masochism: Current Psychoanalytic Perspectives. Edited by Glick RA, Meyers DI. Hillsdale, NJ, Analytic Press, 1988, pp 93–115

CHAPTER 8

The Depressed Person and Homicidal Behavior

U nraveling the web of events and motivations leading to someone with a depressive disorder committing a homicide presents
a major challenge. An interesting paradox exists in people's perception
of depression and acts leading to a death: whereas suicide is automatically assumed to be related to a depressive disorder, the same relationship is not assumed to be a given when homicide and depressive
disorders are considered, even in the view of psychiatrists. It is typically
assumed that there is no persuasive argument for such a relationship.
These responses occur particularly among those who have not assessed
depressed people who have actually engaged in serious acts of violence
other than attempted suicide. In this chapter, I appraise the problem of
homicide and depression and offer a specific hypothesis about homicides and psychotic depressive states.

A two-pronged approach is necessary to understanding the relationship that may exist between depressions and homicidal behavior:
one prong relies on epidemiological data and the other on clinical data
based on direct contact with the perpetrators of homicides. Both
approaches contribute to psychiatrists' knowledge about homicides,
although they use different knowledge bases with their respective

limitations. Recently published, outstanding texts dealing with depression have not contained any discussion about the problem of homicide.[1,2] Similar omissions of discussions about depression and violence occur in review articles, although a few refer to violent episodes in manic patients.[3] Rosenbaum and Bennett examined 17 randomly selected psychiatric textbooks and found that 11 did not mention homicide at all, and only 2 mentioned homicide as having a possible connection to depression.[4] Yet the problem of suicide is routinely discussed in psychiatric textbooks, even though almost as many homicides as suicides occur annually in the United States—about 26,000 homicides to 29,000 suicides. Furthermore, the risk of death by homicide in the United States is about two-thirds that of death by suicide.[5]

■ Linking Depression and Homicide: The Need for Diagnostic Specificity

The possibility of a relationship between some type of depression and homicidal violence is simply a variant of the same question that can be raised for different diagnoses. Findings must initially be predicated on the validity and reliability of a diagnostic nomenclature, as well as the sensitivity and specificity of the diagnostic system and the diagnostic instruments used.

One vexing problem in accurately diagnosing depression in homicidal individuals is that often a person is given a depressive diagnosis only after they have committed a homicidal act. The diversity of types of depressions raises questions as to whether such homicides should be viewed as having any connection with the depressed state at all, or whether more diagnostic specificity should be required.

Different Types of Depressive Diagnoses

People who engage in homicidal behaviors often carry different affective diagnoses. Some have the diagnostic characteristics of dysthymia, whereas others appear to be experiencing a major depressive episode, and still others exhibit homicidal violence in the course of an acute manic episode. Even though these different hypotheses can be proposed to explain the relationship between homicide and each type of mood disorder, it is essential that a sufficient explanatory framework be developed to guide clinical approaches, whether those approaches are based on a descriptive, nosological approach or a psychodynamic framework.

Even if individuals with a mood disorder are assumed to be a homogenous group, the problem of dual or multiple diagnoses among those individuals exists. There is a high rate of overlap between individuals with a depressive diagnosis and other comorbid disorders, particularly substance abuse or dependence or some types of personality disorders. For example, a large number of those with borderline personality disorders often act impulsively and also carry depressive diagnoses. Such comorbidity not only leaves academic questions unanswered, but promotes confusion in trying to resolve legal issues. A question arises as to whether the majority of those who are depressed and commit a homicidal act carry a predisposing personality diathesis, whereas a "purer" sample of depressed individuals would not be as statistically likely to commit a homicide but instead might commit suicide. These queries mean that, when relying on epidemiological data, the element of diagnostic uncertainty must be kept in mind because the diagnoses may be taken as a given without reference to the degrees of uncertainty and comorbidity that exist.

Neurotic Depression Versus Endogenous Depression

Epidemiological perspectives suggest that a certain type of depressed individual may be most prone to engage in homicidal behavior and be in a high-risk group. This raises questions about predisposing factors for the vulnerability. In the quest for specificity, clinical indicators suggest that a person with increased risk be in the midst of a psychotic depression or be caught in a depression that is progressing in severity into such a state. However, scholarly discussions pay minimal attention to this subtype of mood disorder.

The topic is usually discussed in the context of *endogenous depressions,* a term that emphasizes vegetative signs and symptoms such as psychomotor retardation, sleep disturbances, weight loss, difficulty in concentrating, and anhedonia, and perhaps alludes to a different quality of mood disturbance. Originally, a distinction was made between endogenous depressions and *neurotic* or *reactive depressions,* a distinction made based on the severity of the depression.[6] However, it was found that a major environmental event could be found in the background of those with severe depressions just as readily as for those with less severe states of depression. Further, the term *neurotic,* originally identified with reactive types of depression, was seen as pass, and no longer a valid appellation. In cases of homicides, precipitating factors seem to operate equally in both those depressions once cast as endogenous as well as those called reactive.

The debate on the validity of the endogenous-neurotic distinction has shifted to indices involving prognosis and outcome, response to treatment, and biochemical studies. Complicating matters are studies whose results contradict what was once thought to be well-validated outcome results in which endogenous depressions were supposedly associated with a poorer prognosis and higher morbidity than neurotic depressions. In their study, Keller et al. found a high degree of chronicity across all types of depression, despite modern treatments, with 12% of the sample patient population they studied not recovering during a 5-year period.[7] A relevant question then becomes what the potential is for homicide in the group with unremitting depression.

Significance of Delusions and Hallucinations

In discussing a group of depressed individuals with homicidal potential, the presence of delusions and hallucinations is significant, in addition to the standard signs and symptoms of depression listed in DSM-IV.[8] Some simply refer to this as a delusional major depression because it appears that the hallucinations are less frequent than the delusions. This subtype reflects a recent widening of the scope of depression from earlier classifications; in the past, individuals with these symptoms were often given a schizophrenic or schizoaffective diagnosis. The classification of patients with mood-incongruent psychotic, affective illnesses is important.[9] They would appear to possess the characteristics of a group of depressed individuals with a higher homicidal potential.

A paradigm shift has occurred on how to view psychotic symptoms in depressed people. By the time of DSM-III,[10] the process had been reversed from diagnosing affective illness by way of excluding schizophrenia to diagnosing schizophrenia after the exclusion of an affective illness. The result was a category of mood-incongruent psychotic disorder. A labored attempt was made to give schizoaffective disorder its own criteria, consisting of conditions that did not meet the criteria either for schizophrenia or a mood disorder. At one time, patients with this diagnosis were viewed as presenting with both a schizophrenic and mood disorder, whereas at another time the criteria consisted of psychotic symptoms without mood symptoms. Schizoaffective disorder was accurately described in DSM-III-R as one of the most confusing and controversial concepts in psychiatric nosology. In DSM-IV, schizoaffective disorder is described as an uninterrupted period of illness during which a major depressive, manic, or mixed episode concurrent with symptoms that meet criterion A for schizophrenia is present. A great variety of temporal combinations is then possible in terms of the prominence of different symptoms. When the question is the diathesis toward homicidal behavior, the concept of a psychotic major depression seems more parsimonious.

It is not unusual to think of psychotic behavior when a bipolar disorder with a manic episode is diagnosed. Results from one study indicated that manic patients may be more likely to show psychotic symptoms than patients with depression.[11] In another series of 68 manic patients, it was found that 47% had delusions, hallucinations, or both.[12] These delusions are usually grandiose, but they may also have a paranoid component. Although the paranoid delusions may be an early symptom of mania, it is often difficult to assess the delusional quality of assertions when they are made in an expanded mood. Hallucinations also often have a grandiose theme, and the diagnosis can be particularly difficult to delineate from paranoid conditions if the hallucinations fuse with grandiose themes. In this context, voices may be suggesting or commanding violent acts. If the homicide victim is an intimate, there is a tendency to attribute the motivation for the homicide to jealousy.

Two approaches predominate in descriptive attempts to diagnose psychotic depressions. One stresses the presence of delusions and hallucinations; the second assesses the severity of the depression dimensionally by rating symptom severity. The key seems to be the pattern of hallucinations and delusions specifically related to guilt or hypochondriacal concerns, which clinicians tend to underestimate as patterns of psychotic thinking.

Estimations of the frequency of psychotic depression vary because of the lack of strict criteria, as well as its failure to be recognized as a distinct syndrome. The qualifier "with psychotic features" is added in DSM-IV, indicating a thought disorder with delusions or hallucinations. Thus psychotic depression is not conceptualized as a separate entity although, as noted above, Schatzberg and Rothschild have noted the uniqueness of psychotic depression versus nonpsychotic depression based on computerized literature searches in which the biology, family transmission, course, outcome, and treatment in the two groups were compared.[13] The distinction is important from the evidence indicating violence is partly associated with delusions in the mentally ill.[14] In practice, different definitions may be used to diagnose psychotic depressions, along with varying levels of scrutiny of psychiatric symptoms. As a result, estimates of its prevalence vary from 16% to 54%.[15] If the hypothesis being put forward has validity—that homicides perpetrated by depressed people primarily come from the psychotic subgroup—then classification and proper use of the concept is crucial to understanding and predicting homicidal phenomena. There is also the possibility of a poorer treatment response in this subgroup to standard antidepressant treatment, which increases the likelihood of homicidal behavior over time.

A variety of symptoms may be present in a psychotic depression that may in the future have predictive implications for homicidal behavior. Some delusions in psychotically depressed individuals have a paranoid quality with ideas of reference, suspiciousness, and persecutory themes. Others have a guilt-ridden quality of being sinful or a nihilistic component. Somatic delusions are a third variety of delusions whose significance is often missed by considering people who have them as being merely hypochondriacal. Over half of psychotically depressed people experience more than one kind of delusion.[16] Auditory and visual hallucinations occur with equal frequency, and even tactile and olfactory hallucinations, customarily thought to be more associated with organic pathology, can be present.[17]

Other symptoms in psychotically depressed individuals are severe psychomotor agitation or depression, prolongation of the depression, ruminating qualities, and a failure to respond to treatment, all of which carry the risk of an unpredictable and explosive outcome. There is also the possibility of dissociative states occurring in individuals with or without a history of early abuse or trauma. Psychotic symptoms may be experienced during these states, and a homicide can occur during depersonalized states with later partial amnesia. Assessment is complicated in such cases and, if organicity is ruled out, the question of malingering frequently arises.

■ Epidemiological Questions and Directions for Research

Until recently, there was a seeming dichotomy in perceptions of mentally ill individuals in comparison to the general population: public and politicians perceived mentally disturbed people as more violent, whereas researchers in the social and behavioral sciences did not detect significant differences in those people from control groups. Advocacy groups for those with mental disorders supported the findings of the latter group. Such advocacy occurred outside the realm of scientific discourse. However, the resultant confusion has had an impact on social policies, in legislation, and in courtrooms.

The epidemiological approach does not focus on the specifics of how any particular depressed individual committed a homicide, nor does it seek to elicit specifics about the final common pathway eventuating in homicide. The pathogenesis of such behavior is bypassed, not because it is insignificant, but rather because the epidemiological line of inquiry is interested in answering a different type of question. However, the presupposition of an epidemiological approach is that the diagnoses leading to a homicide do have validity; lacking validity, the conclusions of that approach become suspect.

Given a valid diagnosis, the search for a significant relationship can go in one of two directions. In the first approach, a group of depressed people are selected who have been given some type of depressive diagnoses; they are then tracked for any subsequent incidence of homicidal-like behavior. The "homicidal-like" phrase should not pose a serious problem because, by definition, it means behavior that could easily have resulted in a homicide, even if a legal homicide did not actually result. Hence, many acts that would be classified as aggravated assaults, such as shooting someone but not killing them because a vital organ was just barely missed, would be included. Limiting the group to only those who successfully completed a homicide would result in a literal and tighter subject group. Although such a definition would lend more specificity to the search, the constrictiveness would bypass many behaviors in perpetrators among depressed individuals that are behavioral equivalents to completing a homicide.

A more troubling problem is how to define a perpetrator as being depressed. Even assuming diagnostic validity, should the depressed group be confined to those with a major depression, or should it also include those with a bipolar disorder? Should the group be broadened further to include those with a dysthymic disorder as well? What about those in a state of mourning who engage in such behavior? One solution would be to classify each subgroup under the general heading of being depressed until a large enough sample were obtained. The traditional approach of relying on hospitalized patients, in contrast to those attending outpatient clinics or attempting to use a random community sample, poses methodological problems. Studies of homicidal-type behavior in this model are likely to focus on hospital populations and only occasionally include some clinic groups.

In the second approach, the search begins with a group that has already been classified as homicidally violent in that populations from jails or correctional facilities are chosen. The search would then retroactively examine the incidence of depression among those individuals in an attempt to assess their clinical state at the time of the homicide (similar to determining a person's mental state at the time an offense was committed). One practical problem encountered in formulating such a framework is the difficulty in obtaining an adequate sample of depressed individuals who have engaged in such an extreme of violent behavior. In the United States, only a small number of those accused or even convicted of a homicide are psychiatrically examined in contrast to the situation present in many European countries where the majority of such a group are examined.[18]

Monahan pointed out three types of studies in which the relationship between having some type of mental disorder and violent behavior has been assessed in hospitalized mental patients.[19] From these three types of studies, an analogy can be made to the specific case of some type of depressive disorder and homicidal violence. One type of study focused on the retrospective analysis of data for acts that occurred before the person was hospitalized. A second type tabulated violent behaviors that occurred while the person was in a hospital setting. A third type used follow-up studies that tracked the incidence of violence after a person was released from a hospital. When like kinds of studies are grouped together, the following statistics are found: results from 11 prehospitalization studies indicated that a prevalence of 10%–40% (median, 15%) committed acts of violence shortly before hospitalization; results from 12 hospital studies also indicated that a prevalence of 10%–40% (median, 25%) committed acts of violence while on the hospital ward; and the results of the most recent posthospitalization studies (although there are studies dating back to the 1920s) indicated that 25%–30% of male patients had a violent episode within 1 year after discharge.[20] However, all these studies lacked diagnostic specificity.

By use of the empirical approach, the first step is to find those who have already committed a violent act, and the second step is to determine the incidence of some preexisting type of mental disorder. If mental disorders do contribute to violent behavior, then the supposition is that the prevalence of mental disorders should be higher in this population than in a control group. One traditional method used with this approach is to study the incidence of mental disorders in incarcerated individuals; studies using this approach have found that the rate of incidence varied between 5% and 16%, depending on whether a referred or random sample was used. (Of course, violent people exist who have not been institutionalized but, when it comes to homicidal violence, only the few who have not been apprehended are at large in communities.)

Teplin used data from the California Department of Corrections to compare estimates of the prevalence of mental disorders among a group of prison inmates in California, a group of Chicago jailees, and the general population (using data from the National Institute of Mental Health's Epidemiological Catchment Area [ECA] Study[21]).[22]

One finding from that study was that schizophrenia was 3 times more prevalent in the prison and jail populations, and major depression was 3–4 times more prevalent than in the general population. The prevalence of bipolar disorder was 7–14 times higher in prison and jail populations than in the general population. A confounding variable in such an approach is that mentally disturbed individuals are more easily apprehended or give themselves up more readily than "normal" criminals. Yet they also may be more easily diverted to hospitals, even in cases of homicide, and particularly if they have a history of mental disorder. Another limitation that also needs to be kept in mind is whether the diagnosis was actually manifest at the time of the homicide in contrast to such a diagnosis occurring earlier in the life history of a person.

The advantage of mandatory psychiatric examinations for all individuals accused of a homicide was seen in some Scandinavian studies. One dealt with 64 individuals in northern Sweden who committed a homicide between 1970 and 1981.[23] Thirty-four (53%) were diagnosed as having a major mental disorder, and 38% of that 53% also had substance abuse problems. An interesting additional factor was that 85% of the 64 perpetrators were intoxicated at the time of the homicide. In a Copenhagen study conducted over 25 years that focused on just homicide offenders, it was found that 20% of the men and 44% of the women were diagnosed as being psychotic.[24] The presence of psychosis increased the risk of homicide for the men by a factor of 6 and for the women by a factor of 16. In this psychotic group, 41% of the men and 13% of the women had substance abuse problems, and 89% of the psychotic men and 21% of the psychotic women were intoxicated at the time of the homicide.

Limitations of the Studies

Even considering the general question of the relationship between mental disorders and violence, these studies do not provide any answers with respect to the specific diagnosis of depression. Almost all lacked comparative data for the rates of violence among a nonhospitalized control group. The prime defect in all of the studies was that they focused on patients—either in the period shortly before they became patients or after their release. At whatever time period these mentally disordered individuals were studied, they all carried the hallmark of a group selected on some basis for hospitalization.

Almost no research has focused on the possible connection between violence and mentally ill individuals who are outpatients in either public or private settings. In addition, most studies come from public hospital settings and none from private hospital wards. For the follow-up of released hospitalized patients, there is an additional bias because, to be released from public institutions, these patients would have to be judged as not being dangerous—otherwise, they would not have been released. Such a basis for release is especially germane, given the current legal situation of civil commitment being predicated on a standard of dangerousness as well as the possible legal consequences for mental health professionals who release patients who later commit a violent act. Finally, for violence that occurs during or after a hospitalization, it is not possible to detect what relationship may exist between the violence and a mental disturbance present before any hospitalization occurred. It is thus possible that some variables predisposing mentally ill individuals to violence may have been operating independently of the mental disturbance.

These strictures hold for mental disorders in general. There is still a need to gather specific data on the prevalence of violence among individuals who are not in treatment or have not been institutionalized but who may be depressed. One study attempted to reach these non-treated populations by using a database pool of 10,000 subjects from adult households in Baltimore, Maryland; Durham, North Carolina; and Los Angeles, California, that were part of the ECA Study.[25] The study authors used the Diagnostic Interview Schedule (DIS)[26] to assess these individuals; included were five questions dealing with violence; four of these were actually criteria applicable to the diagnosis of antisocial personality disorder, and the fifth related to the diagnoses of alcohol abuse or alcohol dependence. The authors described this test as a "blunt" instrument, in the sense that the answers were based on self-reports by the subjects, and there was some overlap in the questions themselves. For those whose assessment allowed some type of DSM-III diagnosis, the rate of violence was five times higher than for those who did not merit a mental disorder diagnosis. Even more specific for the depression and homicide question was the finding that the prevalence rates for violence among those who received a diagnosis of a major mental disorder (i.e., schizophrenia, major depression, bipolar disorder) was similar. Most striking was the finding that the rate of violence for individuals meeting diagnostic criteria on the DIS for alcohol abuse or dependence and drug abuse or dependence was 12 and 16 times greater, respectively, than the rate for those who had no diagnosis of a mental disturbance. These violent types were mainly young males from the lower class with a substance abuse problem and a diagnosis of a major mental disorder.

The lack of diagnostic specificity plagues epidemiological approaches. The few sound studies that exist do not go beyond breakdowns into major mental disorders and substance use diagnoses.

In another study in which the authors used the DIS to assess 495 Canadian male penitentiary inmates, it was found that 35% of those who had at least one homicide conviction had been diagnosed with a major mental disorder in their lifetime compared with only 21% of those who had no homicide conviction. Again, the comorbidity problem blurs these findings, as 83% of the mentally disordered group also had a history of alcohol abuse or dependence and 64% had drug abuse or dependence.

Congruent with the ECA data were findings from a study seeking the relationship between symptoms and the occurrence of certain life events, in which the Psychiatric Epidemiology Interview was used.[28] In that study, a group of 400 people from an particular area of New York City who had never been in a mental hospital or sought help from a mental health professional were compared with a sample of mental hospital patients from that same area.[29] Many variables were controlled, including the homicide rate of the census tract where the subjects lived. The initial finding was that the patient group was two to three times more violent than the never-treated sample. However, the researchers then did a further analysis in terms of current symptoms. When the factor of current psychotic symptoms was controlled, no difference emerged between the two groups. In other words, the difference in rates of violence appeared to be attributable to the presence of active psychotic symptoms. If the patient group was not experiencing active psychotic symptoms, their violence rate was not much different than the control group from their home community; conversely, when either group was manifesting psychotic symptoms, the risk of violence increased. The inference for the depression-violence question is that, in assessing depressed individuals for their tendency toward violence, whether or not they are experiencing a psychotic major depression is an important factor to be considered. It would also imply the importance of recognizing psychotic depression as a distinct syndrome, as Schatzberg and Rothschild did on the basis of statistically significant differences between psychotic and nonpsychotic major depressions.[13]

Significance of the Studies

At the minimum, the data suggest the significance of a psychotic major depression in one's tendency toward violence. It is more likely that such individuals will behave in that manner than someone who lacks such a diagnosis. If a comorbid condition of drug or alcohol abuse is also present, the risk for violence becomes magnified. It might be added that certain types of personality disturbances, such as borderline personality disorder, which have not been studied in the context of epidemiological studies on violence, may also magnify the risk of violence, just as alcohol or drugs do.

What the data from epidemiological approaches do not imply is that, because someone once had a psychotic episode, he or she is at a perpetually increased risk. Instead, the increased risk of violence is linked with recurring psychotic episodes. It is significant that the overwhelming number of people with mental disturbances are not violent and, more specifically, even those who are psychotically depressed do not usually commit a violent act, let alone a rare event such as a homicide. At best, this is a statistically significant finding that is interesting and that leads researchers in a different direction than many earlier impressions that suggested no significant difference existed between mentally disturbed individuals and a control population. Most violent and homicidal behavior would still be related to other significant variables (e.g., age, gender, socioeconomic level). However, being in a psychotic state should presumably be considered as a variable as well.

■ The Murder-Suicide Phenomenon

Researchers who have tried to distinguish a psychotically depressed from a neurotically depressed group on the basis of suicide attempts or suicidal ideation have obtained diverse findings. In cases of murder followed by suicide involving couples, Rosenbaum found that 75% of the perpetrators were depressed compared with a group who had simply committed a murder and then attempted suicide.[30] But, the assessments of depression were based on the perpetrators' self-report and the observations of a journalist; furthermore, Rosenbaum did not attempt to assess the type of depression. Although the murder-suicide combination is a relatively rare phenomenon in the United States, with a rate of only 6.22 per 100,000, it does shed some light on the vulnerability of psychotically depressed individuals.[31]

Coid found the percentage of homicides involving a suicide in the United States to be only 4%, whereas in Denmark it was 42%.[32] However, the rate of murder-suicide tends to remain similar, perhaps because of a similar prevalence of mental illness in different countries. The principle seems to be that the higher the rate of homicide in a country, the lower the proportion of murder-suicides. However, in Northern Ireland, with its continued civil strife, the inverse relationship was found between homicide and suicide.[33] In West's 1960s study in England and Wales, only 1 in 3 murders was followed by a suicide by the murderer, and only 1 in 100 suicides was coupled with a previous murder.[34] This is reminiscent of old observations about the relationship between aggression and depression in which depression was seen as aggression turned inward.[35]

■ Psychodynamic Hypotheses About Homicides in Depressed States

How the manifestations of a psychotic major depression affect a person's thinking has great relevance in determining the relationship between depression and violence. A psychotic disturbance in thinking is not the only psychopathological hallmark of a severe depression, but it is one significant variable. It is also highly relevant to legal questions that may arise in connection with psychotic depressions. Many outcomes other than homicidal behavior are possible for psychotically depressed individuals, depending on many chance variables (e.g., the type of treatment they receive). However, for these perpetrators and their victims, some hypotheses about the psychotically depressed mind in action can be offered.

The hypothesis is that, when a depressed person commits a homicide, the act is likely to be connected specifically with the presence of psychotic thinking; more specifically, it is most likely a response fostered by a thinking disturbance. One way this shows up is in a dissolution of how affects are processed by the person. In time, a secondary problem emerges about the modulation of the person's actions. Before committing a homicide, the thinking of a psychotically depressed person is dominated by feelings of dejection, guilt, and worthlessness. What is deceiving is how easy it is for even experienced clinicians to miss the transition into a homicidal state. The difficulty appears related to assessing when a person moves from a state of sadness, which can be empathized with as a response to disappointment, into a state of delusionality. Another confusing factor is the psychotically depressed individual's tendency to brood over some supposed wrong, which confuses the problem with paranoid conditions. Yet, no overall fragmentation is present to confirm the paranoid state, and the thought disorder is focused on his or her own shortcomings more than those of others. When the psychotically depressed person progressively withdraws into a state of brooding about his or her shortcomings, a crucial transition has taken place. Too dramatic an interruption of this preoccupied state can mobilize homicidal behaviors.

Case Example

A 40-year-old male had stopped excessive consumption of alcohol 5 years previously when treated for a major depressive episode. Subsequently, he took pride in his changed life pattern and set high goals for himself. Three years later, economic conditions led to the failure of his company. When his efforts to find a new job led to only part-time employment, he became reimmersed in his old pattern of becoming absorbed in his failings. As often happens in cases of suicide when they are viewed retrospectively, his statements and references to his wanting to die and blaming others for his misery were not taken seriously.

One day, during an argument with his daughter, he struck the girl and, becoming angry at himself, put a fist through a window, thereafter leaving blood splattered around the house. When his wife returned home, she called the police but then left the house out of fear for her safety.

Meanwhile, the man had contemplated committing suicide by putting a gun to his head several times, but each time was unable to pull the trigger. His broodings were abruptly interrupted by bright lights shining through the windows and loud speakers with the police telling him to come out. He was instantly galvanized into action with energy he had not experienced in months and began a shoot-out with the police. The exchange of gunfire went on for several hours, resulting in one deputy being killed. Eventually, a sharpshooter's bullet wounded him so that he could not shoot.

During his psychiatric assessment, the man indicated that he had intended to keep shooting to the point where officers would break into the house, gunfire would be exchanged, and he would be killed. Instead, he was charged with murder.

When a psychotically depressed person's anger is mobilized, it allows him or her to externalize the self-hatred that normally immobilizes him or her. It is not uncommon for a severely depressed person to engage in behavior that is challenging or provocative to the police or those in some governmental agency (e.g., pointing a weapon at them, taking a hostage) to elicit a specific response. In some cases, the perpetrator may kill his or her entire family in this manner and then attempt suicide. This is a phenomenon known as *familicide;* it is not uncommon for perpetrators in a large number of these cases to have a psychotic depression before the killings.[36]

One of the striking features seen in retrospect when a depressed or bipolar individual has engaged in homicidal behavior is that those close to that person have sensed a prolonged mood of dejection or irritability in him or her that their attempts at reassurance have failed to alter. Such efforts may have in fact elicited anger, which can be understood as the person resisting efforts to shift his or her delusional beliefs. In contrast, individuals with nonpsychotic depressive disorders may actually seek out reassurance. When deep-seated guilt in the psychotically depressed person progresses to a delusional level, a violent or suffering fate is expected, if not courted. Given a delusional basis of assessing themselves as worthless, whatever adverse outcome that occurs seems just. To take one's own life is also fitting, but some cannot do that for diverse reasons, which then leads to violence on a broader scale. These individuals may expect such a cataclysmic fate or even structure its happening. Patients with agitated features seem most prone to anticipate a disaster. If by chance they are seen by a mental health professional at that time, they articulate their sense of looming disaster in terms of a deserved punishment. If the punishment is not forthcoming, they do not experience relief. The psychotic depressions manifested by signs and symptoms of psychomotor retardation can go to the extreme level of the person being almost immobile, with accompanying vegetative signs; however, when their anger becomes more available for action, it is likely that they will respond not only with suicidal but also with homicidal behavior. At this point, their withdrawal into despair has lifted enough for them to destroy others or themselves.

Emergence of Delusional Thinking

I have referred to delusions as one of the central features in a psychotic depression, along with certain types of hallucinations, which can include command hallucinations for destructive acts. Because the delusions are infrequently elaborated in clinical reports on depression, it may be one reason why the diagnosis of psychotic depression involving homicidal cases is underreported. It has been noted that some clinicians are reluctant to recognize psychotic forms of depression.[37] Goodwin and Jamison noted that, although only about 20% of psychotically depressed patients report having had hallucinations, when they become manic, at least 50% of them report hallucinations.[1] Whether they take action on these beliefs depends on multiple variables, such as the severity, fluctuating nature, and specific content of the hallucinations. Five dimensional aspects of delusions may also contribute to whether action is taken: conviction, extension, bizarreness, disorganization, and pressure.[38] When there is a preoccupation with an intrusive belief, the possibility that the person will act to relieve the situation is increased.[39]

The delusional system of psychotically depressed individuals may reflect their poor self-esteem. However, problems with self-esteem are present in diverse disorders. The difference with those in a psychotic depression appears to lie in the prominence of the degree of hopelessness. If they believe themselves to be beyond the pale of ever being redeemable and accepted as worthwhile, it is not inconsistent for them to engage in murderous behavior; in fact, such action is actually seen as congruent with their internalized image of badness. Paranoid twists can be added when they come to believe that others see them as they do. Perhaps they feel all concerned need to die. The theme of punishing others as equivalent to punishing themselves emerges as a measure of meting out justice for all.

In the 1960s, a series of articles were written that described the "sudden murder" as a single, isolated, and unexpected episode of violent behavior.[40–42] The murders were seen as serving no purpose in the sense of personal gain or profit. Thirteen male murderers so classified were compared with 13 habitual criminals and 13 sex offenders; almost every diagnosis but psychotic depression was considered for the murderers, despite the fact that they described experiencing an incubation period characterized by feeling increased pressures to conform, an increased need to blame others, and progressive isolation. The relationship of these men with their mother was described as ambivalent, with an underlying hostility; they also reported having a hostile, distant father. Strong dependency needs with suppressed anger dominated their development. In that era of DSM-I,[43] psychotic depression was rarely diagnosed, with the preconception toward schizophrenia or passive-aggressive personality diagnoses, although, in retrospect, many of those so diagnosed appear to have been severely depressed.

Brooding fantasies that others have betrayed or abandoned them become mirrored in the enormity of these individuals' delusional beliefs, such as their seeming responsible for the misery of others or the miserable state of the world. To have been the cause of such ongoing misery in others, without a seeming explanation except their own badness, puts them in a mental state comparable to that of a murderer. If they kill someone else or commit suicide, they may experience a sense of relief.

The exaggerated degree of hostile thinking in a deluded person carries the potential for action because the unresolved internalized anger and hate leaves the person in a precarious state. Whereas paranoid individuals are more likely to turn on the environment initially, psychotic depressive individuals struggle to the point at which they are convinced that destroying those around them is an option. This often lends an air of calculation to their actions. Their resulting action may be an attack on intimates, a major act of violence at their place of employment, or a dramatic outburst in a public setting that puzzles those who lack knowledge about the perpetrator's inner anguish. Turning their hate against others in a regressed state reveals their degree of ambivalence and hate. The hate may be turned on those they blame for their failure to achieve or reach some pinnacle of happiness or success. The breaking point may come when they experience an increasing amount of unrelieved guilt in connection with the hate they feel toward loved ones or those on whom they are dependent. In some cases, when a person is betrayed in a love relationship, the third party is murdered, which allows the perpetrator's denial system to maintain that it was not his or her loved one who was responsible for the pain and suffering he or she had been experiencing.

Catathymic States

These explosive outbursts of homicidal violence suggest the idea of catathymia that Wertham publicized, but which was actually introduced earlier by the German psychiatrist, Maier, and perhaps even earlier by Kraepelin.[44-46] Wertham described the state in which a person begins to believe that a violent act is the only solution to relieving his or her state of chronic emotional tension. An antecedent of prolonged conflict finally gives way to an act of violence, following which a sense of relief is experienced. Wertham later viewed catathymic crises as connected with delusional thinking and the presence of a psychotic state.[47]

More recent work has discussed a chronic form of catathymic violence in which an incubation period of depression is the most common affect before a violent act.[48] The incubation period may last for days or months with an accompanying disturbance in formal thinking as part of an obsessional brooding about murder or suicide. In addition to the chronic form, the authors noted an acute catathymic state in which a person experiences a brief incubation period, lasting perhaps only minutes, followed by a sense of overwhelming affect, a sudden inexplicable murder, and perhaps a subsequent amnesia.[49]

More recent authors have viewed catathymic homicides as occurring within a borderline or psychotic personality organization.[50] Homicidal violence is then conceptualized as being perpetrated within the psychopathology of attachment and object relationship theory. The central defense is seen as projective identification, through which the perpetrator attributes increasingly malevolent characteristics to another person who may then become the victim. Though the theory is illustrated by way of erotomania and borderline personalities, the rupture of attachments is often one of the key factors operating in the psychopathology of the severely depressed person. Such a person may be struggling to maintain attachments by delusional formation about his or her worthlessness until the person is overwhelmed by anger and rage.

Final Pathways to Homicide

When there is an effort to punish others as well as to be punished, the delusion has come full circle. The incubation period may be the period in which the psychotically depressed and delusional individual awaits a fateful punishment; when it does not occur, things seem confused and intolerable. A prolonged stalemate may lead to provocative behavior, and eventually to desperate measures to "end it all." In one case, a psychotically depressed man performed a truly heroic act, expecting to die because of it. No one who witnessed his behavior was aware that he viewed this act as an opportunity to end his misery after months of suspenseful waiting for that end to come. Similar beliefs that the end is near and that everything is doomed—nihilistic delusions—are often the background for some do-or-die event. States of agitation in depressed individuals or excitement in manic individuals indicate the switch from the state of inaction they have been enduring for a prolonged period of time to a state of action.

Mass homicidal violence may be witnessed when people in states of severe depression join cults or movements. Although being indoctrinated in a cult may help a person put his or her depression on hold or alleviate its extreme symptoms, such indoctrination is also likely to leave the person with alterations in integrative functions of identity, memory, or consciousness.[51] In such a dissociated state, those in a group setting are more vulnerable to carrying out acts of suicide or homicide. It is possible that the Rev. James Jones and 990 of his followers, who committed mass suicide in Guyana, were in this category. The final suicidal-homicidal behavior of members of the religious cult, the Branch Davidians, who died in a conflagration following a standoff with the ATF and FBI in Waco, Texas in 1993, may have had similar themes. The posited dependence on others of the severely depressed person is congruent with sociological formulations about why certain people become more obedient and conforming than others. It is encompassed under social impact theory, in which people are seen as becoming more vulnerable depending on the forces that impinge on them in terms of strength, immediacy, or in the number of social influences.[52] The attraction of the depressed person to strong authority figures as a way out of their dilemma is congruent with current knowledge about social impact theory as well as how severely depressed people grope for relief. This accounts for why some people would follow a leader to the point of suicide, homicide, or other self-destructive actions. The political implications of such behavior are significant.

It is in the midst of extreme forms of delusional self-abasement in psychotic depressions that dissociative states occur. These emerge by way of psychotically depressed individuals' distancing themselves from reality in addition to experiencing a severe degree of guilt. To live for any length of time with such a burden lends a sense of unreality as well as otherworldliness. One individual who murdered his wife and children, but failed in a suicide attempt, said that he felt he was already dead before carrying out the homicides and attempting suicide. Performing the acts did not seem to matter. Preceding the homicide, psychotically depressed individuals may have a sense that things are changing in some undefinable way. Another possibility is that these individuals experience Capgras phenomena, in which they believe others that they know seem altered and they experience the delusion that the people in their life are doubles. If their thinking takes a turn that someone is exploiting them by these phenomena, the potential for violence is increased.

The phenomenon of depersonalization or derealization interferes with adequate reality testing. Through these distancing processes, the possibility of homicidal behavior is heightened. Vegetative signs and symptoms that accompany a psychotic depression contribute to states of dissociation by virtue of the actual physical changes that occur. Somatic delusions that take the form of bodily wasting, brains rotting, bowels filled with cement, and so on can accompany physical changes. Another phenomenon noted in some cases has been the temporary loss of hearing that occurs preceding and during the actual perpetration of a homicide in a psychotically depressed person (C. M. Malmquist and P. E. Meehl, unpublished manuscript, July 1988). Again, if these changes are interpreted by the person as meaning that he or she is already dead, then the inhibition against carrying out an act of killing is nullified. It is a matter of ultimate nihilism in which someone already dead kills because nothing matters anymore.

■ Future Research Problems

Greater Specificity in Linking Depression and Homicidal Behavior

There is a lack of specificity in attempting to determine whether there is any relationship between depression and homicidal behavior. Is there any specific, predisposing factor in a depressed person's background, that helps to predict whether that person will become homicidal? Hypotheses can only be offered based on retrospective examinations of individuals who have committed homicides.

It is possible that a depressed person's vulnerability to become homicidal rests in the same factors that make him or her prone to a psychotic depression. Although this does not answer why some become homicidal, it does suggest an explanation for why such an outcome occurs. In addition to a biological predisposition, there are often events that have precipitated a psychotic state. Some events may be related to disappointments, losses, or disillusionments. What to others might be an adverse event is experienced by individuals prone to a psychotic depression as overwhelming. The intensity and depth of their responses go to an extreme, and they exhibit a striking lack of resilience to shift into another mode of thinking. The question is why. Perhaps their brooding and obsessional quality leads them to see others as not "coming through" in meeting their needs. Whereas their high levels of drive and ambition may have kept a psychotic regression at bay or fended off extreme biological mood swings, it is difficult to do this repeatedly over a prolonged period of time.

The mental state of some—that they have already committed a homicide—is significant. It reveals not only self-punitive processes, such as the guilt of a murderer before the act, but the dangerous affective state accompanying such distorted thinking. In turn, such a state attenuates the person's internal signals telling him or her to operate in a contrary way. One research methodology would be to use this clinical insight in either a retrospective or follow-up examination of individuals diagnosed as psychotically depressed to confirm if such a sign portends homicidal violence. If so, it would have preventive significance for clinicians working with such individuals who have not yet committed a violent act. Further regression in their affective state brings these individuals to a homicidal state in which distinction between the murderer and the murdered has lost its meaning. This would also correlate with a theoretical position that the special vulnerability of psychotically depressed individuals toward homicidal behavior lies in their cognitive dysfunctioning.[53] Whether the cognitive dysfunctioning antedates the onset of the depression, as Beck would have it,[54] need not be present to explain how a homicide can occur in some cases.

Extreme forms of denial and distortion of reality testing operate in these individuals. Delusional thinking predicated on denial may be elusive to detect. If a homicide occurs, several people will testify that the person acted normally in their view. Perhaps one of the keys in the progression of psychotic depression to the level of homicide is not only a weakening in the perpetrators' general reality assessment, but the beginning of misinterpreting interactions. As an accompaniment, they possess fewer devices to deal with the hostility because of their tendency to brood about their own deficiencies and worthlessness. Clini-

246 ■   HOMICIDE: A PSYCHIATRIC PERSPECTIVE

cal research about transition states into the seeming worthlessness of everything around them would be quite valuable. If paranoid projections occur, a further element of unpredictability is raised. On one hand, their focusing on an external enemy may forestall the ultimate need to destroy themselves and others; on the other hand, it may mobilize them to a homicidal act.

Factors Triggering the Decision to Act

In many cases, the reasons why some psychotic depressive individuals commit homicides whereas others simply stay depressed for long periods of time or else commit suicide are impossible to differentiate. From clinical observations, it appears that psychotically depressed people detest themselves to an inordinate degree and hold cognitive distortions about themselves and others. On an operational level, it is not surprising that, given their degree of hatred, some of these people can kill others as well as themselves. Yet, psychiatrists' ability to predict homicide is as limited as it is for predicting suicide.

Although individuals who have engaged in murderous behavior have often castigated themselves to an extraordinary degree, they have not directed this behavior at others to the same degree. This disproportionateness between their self-hatred and their expressed hatred toward others remains unexplained. Whereas such delusions that are based on self-hatred might explain this degree of self-condemning as well as self-punitive behavior, they do not explain homicidal behavior. The killing of a loved one could be understood in part by saying that the perpetrator's identity had become so fused with an intimate that killing the intimate and himself or herself is simply one integral act. The common example of this would be when a mother kills her infant and perhaps herself in the midst of a postpartum psychotic depression. In these cases, the mother talks about her love sparing the infant from having to live in a terrible world. A psychobiological fusion has destroyed herself, or a recent part of herself, based on a delusional conviction. Yet, most homicides in a psychotically depressed group are not infanticides.

What emerges in the larger group of homicides committed by psychotically depressed individuals is the prominence of blaming others. Disappointments in the actual world, or disillusionments in terms of their internalized goals, are not merely experienced as one event among several, but viewed with a sense of finality. The author of one study in which five murderers were assessed, with four of them being psychotic, found that the murder was triggered by a sequence of events, beginning with a blow to the perpetrators' pride, which then tapped into their enormous self-hatred and eventually led to desperate measures—committing the murder—to shore up an unstable pride system.[55] The perpetrators had reached a state in which nothing could be regained or righted anymore. This state is similar to unrequited grief that is perceived as having no endpoint; the person's ability to begin the painful process of grieving is either temporarily stymied or was deficient from the beginning.

A crucial part of the transition to the homicidal state is the emergence of the idea that somebody must pay for one's suffering. This is different from the situation of a suicide, in which only survivors suffer and bear guilt. In some cases, "the world" must pay, which seems to be the mechanism operating in mass killings of loved ones or others. This outcome seems to take place after a prolonged period of regression into a deep and unremittingly depressed state. The validation of delusions in a severely depressed person and whether they are the key variable to homicidal decisions is often viewed skeptically by psychiatrists, and certainly some involved in the legal process. This in itself merits discussion. Self-derogatory thoughts in seriously depressed people meet the criteria of a fixed belief that is objectively false. To hold to a belief about oneself that is so negative, in the absence of strong, contrary evidence, does not seem any less delusional than a belief that one is being poisoned or the grandiose idea that one may be some special person. A depressed person's somatic delusion that his or her body is rotting is somehow more readily accepted as delusional than a psychological belief about the self that he or she is so worthless as to be beyond redemption. These dilemmas are illustrated in the following case.[56]

Case Example

A 30-year-old man who showed symptoms of a major depression brooded about suicide for months. His usual pattern of a high level of work performance had fallen off. In an attempt to lessen his depressed state, he had an affair outside his marriage, which only compounded his guilt. After months of ambivalent procrastinating about his state, and in the midst of watching the television movie "Barabbas," in which a guilt-ridden man seeks redemption and sets Rome on fire, an act of multiple homicide occurred.

Near the end of the movie, he shot his wife, who was sitting on a couch opposite him, in the forehead and then ran around the house spilling gasoline and setting the house on fire. After all four of his children burned to death, he proceeded to tie a gun with a string attached to the trigger to a stove in the garage. He then shot himself at a distance of 8 feet. That bullet went through the right side of the sternum. He then stepped to the right and shot himself a second time in an attempt to have the bullet enter near his heart. The second bullet ricocheted around his rib cage and exited. He then slipped a rope around his neck and wrists and hung himself with his wrists extended through the loops on an inverted U iron clothes pole. Some teenagers who were attracted by the fire discovered him, and he survived. The jury found him guilty of second-degree murder despite expert testimony regarding his insanity defense.

Resistance to Accepting Delusionality in Depressed People

There are reasons why it is difficult to accept the reality of psychotic thinking in severely depressed people. Even the seriously depressed person does not appear that different from others in contrast to those with some other types of psychosis. If others view such a person as psychotic, it raises implications for others, including clinicians themselves, who must deal with such disturbed states. Second, a tenuous link exists between verbalizations made by psychotically depressed individuals and the degree to which it is believed that their words parallel their actual internalized mental states. Pleas for help, which clinicians hear endlessly, from delusional people have a side effect of increasing clinicians' skepticism about the validity of self-abasement claims. The result blurs the distinction between legitimate cases of those who are severely depressed and the "worried well." Demanding, complaining, or provocative aspects complicate matters further as they convey that the person is complaining about someone other than himself or herself.

However, even if these self-condemnatory accusations are taken at face value, a third difficulty involves a problem of semantic interpretation. A person's self-assessment often lies somewhere between the realm of fact and his or her value system. If the statements are seen as more reflective of the value system, and not a factual state, then the statements tend to be discredited. If the clinician can determine where such statements can be referenced and checked against facts, there is a greater tendency to accept them as delusional. For example, the statement made by someone that he or she is at fault for a tornado that has caused damage and some deaths is likely to sensitize the clinician to the possibility of a delusion, whereas a person who simply states, "I'm a worthless person" may not.

The problem of different normative values raises other issues. If people with strong moral beliefs about a matter violate these beliefs, it is difficult to say that a subsequent guilt-ridden attitude is delusional. For example, someone who believes that engaging in homosexual behavior is morally wrong but who then acts in that manner and begins to brood and condemn himself or herself would not automatically be classified as delusional. What is needed is an appraisal of the severity of the self-condemnation, its persistence, and its amenability to change. The confusion resides in value statements where an objective reality is elusive in an effort to infer that reality testing has become significantly impaired.

This leads to a related difficulty. Even if the value system of an individual can be explained, at least in philosophical terms, it is still difficult to attain a sense of agreement on objective matters. This holds not only among clinicians, but for individual citizens called on to make judgments about guilt in a public forum such as a jury, which involves the truth status of a person's self-appraisal and subsequent responsibility for behavior in a criminal court.

Civil Liability of Issues

A different type of problem is increasing in our litigious society. Although the clinician may find it difficult enough to diagnose psychotic depressions, and the condition does tend to be underdiagnosed, there are increasing practical implications for failure to make such diagnoses. Clinical and research limitations may not catch up to demands for accountability by relatives in distressed states or relatives of innocent victims. Civil lawsuits involving medical liability in connection with acts of violence are increasing. These arise not only when such a diagnosis is missed, but when its severity is misgauged. Jury awards may be horrendous, even in commonplace clinical situations, for example, a $5.8 million jury verdict awarded in the case of a man who told the police he was depressed and suicidal subsequent to breaking up with his girlfriend. He was involuntarily committed to a state hospital for 5 days, then discharged on the belief that he could no longer be kept hospitalized. Two weeks after being released for outpatient treatment, he entered a house with a .357 magnum and shot three people; one was killed and two others wounded, following which he committed suicide. The claim of the plaintiffs was based on a failure to diagnose a major depression with its implications for violent conduct.[57]

■ References

1. Goodwin FK, Jamison KR: Manic-Depressive Illness. New York, Oxford University Press, 1990

2. Paykel ES: Handbook of Affective Disorders, 2nd Edition. New York, Guilford, 1992

3. Tardiff K: The current state of psychiatry in the treatment of violent patients. Am J Psychiatry 149:493–499, 1992

4. Rosenbaum M, Bennett B: Homicide and depression. Am J Psychiatry 143:367–370, 1986

5. Reiss AJ Jr, Roth JA: Understanding and Preventing Violence. Washington, DC, National Academy Press, 1993

6. Grove SM, Andreasen NC: Concepts, diagnosis and classification, in Handbook of Affective Disorders, 2nd Edition. Edited by Paykel ES. New York, Guilford, 1992, pp 25–42

7. Keller MD, Lavori PW, Mueller TI, et al: Time to recovery, chronicity, and levels of psychopathology in major depression: a 5-year prospective follow-up of 431 subjects. Arch Gen Psychiatry 49:809–816, 1992

8. American Psychiatric Association: Diagnostic and Statistical Manual of Mental Disorders, 4th Edition. Washington, DC, American Psychiatric Association, 1994

9. Kendler KS: Mood-incongruent psychotic affective illness. Arch Gen Psychiatry 48:362–369, 1991

10. American Psychiatric Association: Diagnostic and Statistical Manual of Mental Disorders, 3rd Edition. Washington, DC, American Psychiatric Association, 1980

11. Black DW, Nasrallah A: Hallucinations and delusions in 1715 patients with unipolar and bipolar affective disorders. Psychopathology 22:28–34, 1989

12. Silverstone T, Hunt N: Symptoms and assessment of mania, in Handbook of Affective Disorders, 2nd Edition. Edited by Paykel ES. New York, Guilford, 1992, pp 15–24

13. Schatzberg AF, Rothschild AJ: Psychotic (delusional) major depression: should it be included as a distinct syndrome in DSM-IV? Am J Psychiatry 149:733–745, 1992

14. Taylor PJ, Mullen P, Wessely S: Psychosis, violence and crime, in Forensic Psychiatry: Clinical, Ethical and Legal Issues. Edited by Gunn J, Taylor PJ. Oxford, UK, Heinemann, 1991, pp 329–372

15. Dubovsky SL, Thomas M: Psychotic depression: advances in conceptualization and treatment. Hosp Community Psychiatry 43:1189–1190, 1992

16. Lyukouras E, Christodoulou GN, Malliaras D: Type and content of delusions in unipolar psychotic depression. J Affective Disord 9:249–252, 1987

17. Coryell W, Zimmerman M: Demographic, historical, and symptomatic features of the nonmanic psychoses. J Nerv Ment Dis 174:585–592, 1986

18. Hodgins S: The criminality of mentally disordered persons, in Mental Disorder and Crime. Edited by Hodgins S. Newbury Park, CA, Sage, 1993, pp 3–21

19. Monahan J: Mental disorder and violent behavior. Am Psychol 47:511–521, 1992

20. Klassen D, O'Connor W: Assessing the risk of violence in released mental patients: a cross-validation study. J Consult Clin Psychol 1:75–81, 1990

22. Teplin L: The prevalence of severe mental disorder among male urban jail detainees: comparison with the epidemiological catchment area program. Am J Public Health 80:663–669, 1990

23. Lindqvist P: Criminal homicide in Northern Sweden 1970–1981: alcohol intoxication, alcohol abuse and mental disease. Int J Law Psychiatry 8:19–37, 1986

24. Gottlieb P, Gabrielson G, Kramp P: Psychotic homicides in Copenhagen from 1959 to 1988. Acta Psychiatr Scand 76:285–292, 1987

25. Swanson J, Holzer C, Ganju V, et al: Violence and psychiatric disorder in the community: evidence from the epidemiological catchment area surveys. Hosp Community Psychiatry 41:760–770, 1990

26. Robins LN, Helzer JE, Croughan J, et al: National Institute of Mental Health Diagnostic Interview Schedule: its history, characteristics, and validity. Arch Gen Psychiatry 38:381–389, 1981

28. Dohrenwend BP, Shrout P. Egri G, et al: Measures of nonspecific psychological distress and other dimensions of psychopathology in the general population. Arch Gen Psychiatry 37:1229–1236, 1980

29. Link B, Cullen F, Andrew H: The violent and illegal behavior of mental patients reconsidered. Am Soc Rev 57:275–292, 1992

30. Rosenbaum M: The role of depression in couples involved in murder-suicide and homicide. Am J Psychiatry 147:1036–1039, 1968

31. Palmer S, Humphrey J: Criminal homicide followed by offender's suicide. Suicide Life Threat Behav 10:106–118, 1980

32. Coid J: The epidemiology of abnormal homicide and murder followed by suicide. Psychol Med 13:855–860, 1983

33. Curran PJ, Finlay RJ, McGarry PJ: Trends in suicide in Northern Ireland. Psychological Medicine 5:98–102, 1988

34. West DJ: Murder Followed by Suicide. Cambridge, MA, Harvard University Press, 1966

35. Kendell RD: Relationship between aggression and depression. Arch Gen Psychiatry 22:308–318, 1970

36. Malmquist CP: Psychiatric aspects of familicide. Bull Am Acad Psychiatry Law 8:298–304, 1981

37. Akiskal HS, Puzantian VR: Psychotic forms of depression and mania. Psychiatr Clin North Am 2:419–439, 1979

38. Kendler KS, Glazer SM, Morgenstern H: Dimensions of delusional experience. Am J Psychiatry 140:466–469, 1983

39. Woodis G: Depression and crime. British Journal of Delinquency 8:85–93, 1957

40. Lamberti J, Blackman N, Weiss J: The sudden murderer: a preliminary report. Journal of Social Therapy 4:2, 1958

41. Weiss J, Lamberti J, Blackman N: The sudden murderer: a comparative analysis. Arch Gen Psychiatry 2:669–678, 1960

42. Blackman N, Weiss J, Lamberti J: The sudden murderer; III: clues to preventive interaction. Arch Gen Psychiatry 8:289–294, 1963

43. American Psychiatric Association: Diagnostic and Statistical Manual: Mental Disorders. Washington, DC, American Psychiatric Association, 1952

44. Wertham F: The catathymic crisis. Archives of Neurology and Psychiatry 37:974–978, 1937

45. Hinsie LE, Campbell RJ: Psychiatric Dictionary, 3rd Edition. New York, Oxford University Press, 1960, p 111

46. Kraepelin E: Lectures on Clinical Psychiatry, 3rd English Edition. Edited by Johnstone T. New York, W Wood, 1913

47. Wertham F: The Sign for Cain. New York, Macmillan, 1966

48. Revitch E, Schlesinger L: Psychopathology of Homicide. Springfield, IL, Charles C Thomas, 1981

50. Meloy JR: Violent Attachments. Northvale, NJ, Jason Aronson, 1992

51. West LJ: Persuasive techniques in contemporary cults, in Cults and New Religious Movements. Edited by Galanter M. Washington, DC, American Psychiatric Press, 1989

52. Jackson JM: Social impact theory, in Theories of Group Behavior. Edited by Goethals GR, Mullen B. New York, Springer-Verlag, 1987, pp 111–124

53. Perris C: Towards an integrating theory of depression focusing on the concept of vulnerability. Integrative Psychiatry 5:27–32, 1987

54. Beck AT: Cognitive Therapy and the Emotional Disorders. New York, International Universities Press, 1976

55. Ruotolo A: Dynamics of sudden murder. Am J Psychoanal 29:162–176, 1968

56. Malmquist CP, Meehl PE: Barabbas: a study in guilt-ridden homicide. International Review of Psychoanalysis 5:149–164, 1987

57. Psychiatry: Medical Malpractice 8:49–50, 1992

CHAPTER 9

Juveniles and Homicide

One way to view the problem of homicides committed by juveniles is to see it as paradigmatic for the wider problem of serious forms of juvenile violence. The justification for such a paradigm comes from the realization that, when using quasi-legalistic classifications, such as those that are applied in the juvenile justice system, an enormous overlap exists in the behaviors of the perpetrators of homicidal types of violence. Cases of attempted murder and the endless cases of aggravated assaults committed by juveniles are separated by a thin line, especially when the violence occurs in group settings. For example, an act of juvenile vandalism in which a baseball bat is swung, hitting another youth in the back of the head, may in one case result in a death whereas in another case only a brief state of unconsciousness. However, the legal consequences for juveniles in such circumstances are far greater than for adults. The consequences can vary from probation in a juvenile justice system without any criminal sanctions on one hand to certification to an adult criminal court, with all of the vagaries inherent in that process,[1] and a later conviction for first-degree murder. In this chapter, these types of cases are discussed in the context of some of the psychiatric aspects of juvenile violence that can result in a homicide.

The behavioral examples do not in themselves make the problem of juvenile homicide per se seem any different than homicides in other age groups. Many of the same types of psychological and social factors that feed into homicidal proneness in an adult population operate in juveniles. However, in assessing problems of juvenile psychopathology, there is the added dimension that these juveniles are not fully formed biological organisms, at least to some degree, and do not have psychological attributes that are solidified in terms of an ultimate character structure. Another dimension to the problem is that adults do not like to think of children being able to commit the same types of homicidal acts as adults. Such a revelation makes the subject of juvenile homicides one of great fascination for the public and the media, who never seem to tire of confessional stories involving adolescents. In all of these cases, the element of a horrific fascination permeates the description of extreme violence perpetrated by an adolescent.

It is important to keep in mind that juveniles who commit homicides do not form a homogeneous group anymore than do those who commit specific delinquent acts.[2] Although it is sufficiently difficult to classify homicides legally, it is even more difficult to classify them by psychopathological states, especially when perpetrated by adolescents.

With these caveats in mind, I examine various kinds of homicides perpetrated by juveniles. One possibility is that homicide is an individual act in which certain types of psychopathology may be detected and an attendant diagnosis given that partially explains it. Sometimes the act is a homicide perpetrated against one family member, or it may be an act of familicide perpetrated against an entire family. In yet other situations, the act erupts in the context of a violent confrontation between two juveniles in which one is seriously injured and the other may be murdered. Another alternative is homicide perpetrated by juveniles in groups or gangs. These occur in the context of group dynamics operating on the basis of challenge, provocation, and the need to defend one's turf or ego. Whatever the setting, gunshot wounds had become the second leading cause of death among teenagers by the 1980s.[3]

The problem of juvenile violence itself has been subject to a great deal of controversy. Such violence occupies an enormous amount of time and effort in agencies that deal with juveniles and the juvenile justice system. Unfortunately, most explanations for juvenile violence lack sufficient specificity to confirm what has transpired when a homicide results. Discussions must rely to a good extent on hypotheses or inferences from clinical material and the social context.

■ Epidemiology of Homicides Committed by Juveniles

The variety of homicidal violence encountered in adolescents is almost legion. The following cases illustrate typical varieties of cases that are processed through juvenile court systems in United States cities:

- A 16-year-old boy used an ax to kill his entire family.
- A 15-year-old boy raped a young woman in her 20s then panicked and, from fear of discovery, decided that he should kill her.
- An adolescent male robbed a delicatessen. When the store clerk seemed to challenge him, he shot and killed the clerk, and ran from the store without taking anything.
- An adolescent girl was lured into prostitution. She later assisted her pimp in holding down another girl so that the pimp could cut her throat as a way of disciplining her for running away. The girl died from her throat injuries.
- Two adolescents physically pummeled a 35-year-old male homosexual in an episode of gay bashing and then bragged about it in school to their peer group. The parents found it difficult to take the act seriously because they felt "gays were only getting what was coming to them."
- One night while drinking beer, a group of six adolescents stated their intention to find someone on the streets, whomever it might be, and beat them up. One of the men they beat died. The juveniles and their lawyers made a plea to remain in the juvenile system, rather than being certified to adult criminal court, on the basis that the juveniles had no intention of killing anyone and there had been no premeditation as they simply went out for "kicks" and to "live it up."
- A 17-year-old girl and her girlfriend would periodically go on forays or rob people for jewelry or clothes. One night, a young

woman was spotted wearing an expensive leather jacket. When she refused to give it up, they shoved her to the ground and shot her.
• Two rival gangs challenged each other, resulting in drive-by shootings and some of the members being killed.

The subject of violent crime among juveniles in the United States is such an emotionally laden topic that it is difficult to discuss it objectively, even for professionals. Juvenile violence rises and falls parallel to whatever variations are occurring in the area of adult homicidal violence. Two facts must be recognized: violence in the United States is higher than in other Western countries, and serious juvenile violence follows the same patterns as those witnessed in adult violence.

A disproportionate amount of crime exists among juvenile males, particularly those ages 18–25 years; it also occurs more frequently in juveniles ages 16–17 years compared with younger adolescents. Yet the statistics do not indicate any significant bulge in terms of homicidal violence for juveniles that has not been paralleled by similar increases occurring in adult violent offenses during the same time period. In the past, the rates for extreme acts of juvenile violence simply followed the rates for violence in adults. However, in the past few years, as will be discussed, the rates have been changing. For example, in 1986, adolescents under age 18 years constituted 27.7% of the United States population, but only 4.1% of all juveniles arrested were charged with violent crimes.[4] When there was a more noticeable increase in overall juvenile violence, it was more likely to be related to an increase in the number of juveniles in the population at that time, which then becomes reflected in the overall number of homicides committed by juveniles. A similar phenomenon has been observed with adolescent suicides, in that the dramatic increase in suicides between 1956 and 1976 among those ages 15–24 years reflected the proportions of that age group in the United States population during that period. Hence, whereas the data for 1990 indicate that 30,906 people died by suicide, with 4,869 of these in the 15–24 age group, this was third behind the numbers in the 25–34 and 35–44 age groups. One reason for this was the large number of adolescents and young adults in the population compared with other groups. However, Holinger pointed out that that rate of suicide in the 15–24 year age group was the lowest of any age group with the exception of the 5–14 year age group.[5]

In the United States, homicides comprise about 80% of the number of suicides (see Chapter 1). Holinger's 1990 data also reveal a difference between suicides and homicides in the adolescent and young adult groups. In the 15- to 24-year-old group, the rate of death by homicide is higher than for suicide; in fact, this age group has the highest homicide rate of any group in the United States.

Data from the Center for Disease Control's National Center for Health Statistics reveal that nearly half of the 26,513 homicide victims in the United States were from the group between 15–34 years.[6] In that age group, homicide had become the second leading cause of death for males. From 1985 to 1991 the annual crude homicide rate had increased 25%, but the rate for persons ages 15–34 years increased by 50%. From 1963 through 1985 the annual homicide rates for 15- to 19-year-old males were one-third to one-half the rates for the next higher 5-year age groups (20–24; 25–29; 30–34). However, by 1985–1991, the annual rates for males 15–19 years increased 154%, surpassing the rate increase in the next three age groups (which increased by 76%, 32%, 16%, respectively). During the 1985–1991 period, age-specific arrest rates for murder and nonnegligent manslaughter increased 127% for 15- to 19-year-old males, again higher than the next three age groups.

These types of changes in the annual homicide rates for 15- to 19-year-old males from 1985 to 1991 reflect a dramatic shift from the earlier period of 1963–1984. Firearm-related homicides accounted for 88% of all homicides in the 15- to 19-year-old male group in 1991 and 97% of the rate increase from 1985 to 1991. Although attaining causal specificity is difficult, it can at least be hypothesized that the increased recruitment of juveniles into the drug market and the diffusion of guns to young people were significant variables. Although part of this pattern is related to gang violence in major metropolitan areas, the phenomenon of gangs in major metropolitan areas is not new in American society. Yet, it must also be kept in mind that juvenile gang homicides increased from less than 2% of all homicides in 1987 to almost 5% of all homicides in 1993; in 1987, 317 people were killed in juvenile gang homicides and in 1993, 1,147 were victims of .juvenile gangs.[7]

However, caution must be exercised in interpreting these figures because the figures may be skewed by various factors. For example, some of cases figured into the statistics may be cases in which multiple juveniles acting in a group perpetrated one homicide. The result is that they would have all been legally charged on some level with a homicide as a group offense. In fact, more group killings of this type are committed by juveniles and youths than adults. At the time of a murder, public fury often increases demands for an arrest, resulting in some overcharging. The charges made at the time of the arrest may subsequently be lowered in the course of plea bargaining and delays in the case, a favorite legal defensive maneuver. Ultimately, some of the charges may be completely dismissed.

Figures from the Office of Juvenile Justice and Delinquency Prevention have indicated that, in 1990, an estimated 3,200 individuals under age 18 years were arrested for murder and nonnegligent manslaughter, a figure representing 14% of all arrests for those types of crimes. The data showed 39% of those 3,200 were white; 59%, black; and 1%, from other racial or ethnic backgrounds. Males accounted for 95% of those arrested for these offenses. The 3,200 figure represented a 60% increase from the 1981 figure.[8]

Nature of Crimes Committed by Juveniles

Some researchers argue that violent offenses ascribed to juveniles might not actually involve the occurrence of significant physical harm to a victim during the commission of the offenses. For example, results from one study from Columbus, Ohio involving 811 juveniles with at least one violent crime in their records revealed that 72% of those juveniles did not threaten or inflict significant physical harm during the commission of the violent offenses.[9] Authors of another study from 1981 in which a cohort of 50,000 youths were followed from birth into adulthood found that only 22 of this group later committed two or more aggravated offenses in which physical harm was inflicted or even threatened.[10]

However, the significant variable may not be whether or not physical harm occurred but rather the occurrence of violent crime itself. It does appear that serious violence occurring at a young age is a premonitory sign of later violence. Hamparian et al. have shown a continuity between violence committed by a juvenile with violence committed by an adult.[11] Although there is a paucity of adequate data about violent crimes and criminal careers, in one study of a London cohort it was found that the majority of juvenile violent offenders went on to commit adult nonviolent offenses. In that study, the authors did not find that the majority of adult violent offenders had been previously convicted of violence as a juvenile.[12]

Weapons and Juvenile Crime

Pertinent to this discussion is the question of whether juveniles usually use weapons in committing violent offenses. In one early study, Wolfgang et al. followed all the boys born in Philadelphia in 1945 and then those living in the city between their 10th and 18th birthday; they found that of the 9,934 offenses known to police, weapons were involved in only 263.[13] In a 1970s study in New York City, weapons were found to be involved in only 17% of violent juvenile offenses.[14] However, data taken from victim crime surveys have indicated that the use of weapons was higher, with juvenile offenders using weapons in 27% of the offenses, although guns were used in less than 5% of the cases.[15] The current significance of firearms connected to murders in the adolescent age group is striking. In 1990, gunshots caused one in four deaths in the adolescent age group. In 1990, 4,200 teenagers were killed by bullets, compared with 2,500 deaths only 5 years earlier.[16] Almost half of the black males ages 15–19 years who died in the United States in 1989 were murdered, usually with a gun.[17] In 1989, homicide victims ages 10–19 years numbered 2,771, with 80% being shot with guns and 10% stabbed. This was noted to be a 140% increase from 1979 figures for black males in that age group.[18] The major victims of juvenile violence are other juvenile peers, except for the victims of purse snatchings. It is startling to compare homicide rates for young males in the United States with those in other countries (this is done in Figure 9–1).

On the perpetrator end, 17% of all individuals arrested for violent crimes in 1991 were younger than age 18 years.[19] Much of these results are attributed to the increase in gun carrying among youths. National data have revealed that, among high school students, the monthly prevalence of weapon carrying in 1990 was 20%, with the highest incidence found among black and Hispanic males (39% and 41%, respectively).[20] However, little is known about the variables responsible for this increase. One study of two public junior high schools in Washington, D.C., found that, although knife carrying was associated with aggressiveness, it was not related to serious delinquency; however, gun carrying did appear to be a component of highly aggressive delinquency and not just a purely defensive behavior.[21] In Seattle, a survey of half of the public high schools indicated that 34% of the students reported having easy access to handguns, with the highest prevalence reported by black male students at 59%.[22]

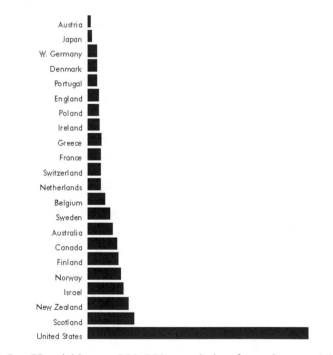

Figure 9-1. Homicides per 100,000 population for males ages 15–24 years, 1986–1987.
Source: Adler F, Mueller GOW, Laufer WS. *Criminology*. New York, McGraw-Hill, 1991, p. 234.

■ Personality Disorders in Juveniles Committing Homicidal Types of Violence

One of the more controversial topics at present is the relationship of personality disturbances that have their origin in childhood and adolescence to later adult disturbances. These early diagnoses are important with respect to homicides among juveniles because, whatever later diagnoses are attached to those who commit a murder, the possible developmental relationship of the two diagnoses to a homicidal outcome must be examined.

Cautions About Applying Personality Disorder Diagnoses to Children

In DSM-IV,[23] children are not recognized as having distinct personality disorders. The result is an assumption that disorders in the development of their personalities are contained within the grouping of "Attention-Deficit and Disruptive Behavior Disorders," which includes attention-deficit hyperactivity disorder (both specific types and not otherwise specified), conduct disorder, oppositional defiant disorder, and disruptive behavior disorders not otherwise specified. The reasoning of those who believe personality disorders should not be diagnosed in children is that the thrust of development, and its fluctuations, are such that children's patterns or traits are not yet stable and may later shift. The position is that such factors make it difficult to diagnose personality disorders in childhood and that, therefore, it is more desirable to use other diagnoses.

Another objection to labeling children with personality disorder diagnoses is the social stigma attached to the diagnoses as well as the tendency that, once a diagnosis is applied to a child, that child will have that diagnosis in perpetuity. The hope remains that intrapsychic alignments or the forces of development will resolve whatever is promoting certain kinds of antisocial behavior. If developmental phenomena are such that evolving patterns do not tend to overcome the types of chronic distortions in development that are occurring in the child's personality, then one of the childhood diagnostic categories is supposed to function as an interval diagnosis. Subsequently, those personality traits still persisting once a child reaches age 18 years can be given the corresponding adult personality disorder diagnosis. If they do not persist, then not having labeled the person with the diagnosis in childhood is seen as having achieved a desirable outcome.

Juvenile Behavior Correlating With Borderline and Antisocial Personality Disorders

An initial line of inquiry is whether some predictive trends can be seen in childhood behavior patterns that are relevant later to homicidal types of violence in adolescence. Part of the answer to this inquiry lies with future clinical work and research; through these, greater validity in terms of correlating various childhood diagnoses with those found in adulthood may be attained. A congruency between childhood symptoms and adult symptoms, or greater clinical ability to trace the unfolding symptoms and states or traits corresponding to adult personality disorders, would also allow a better prediction of future diagnoses. For example, persistent shyness in childhood or adolescence may correspond to a diagnosis of avoidant personality disorder in adults, oppositional-defiant disorder may correlate with several personality disorders, and certain developmental disturbances may correspond to schizotypal personality disorders. In turn, the various manifestations of conduct disorder could be viewed as reflecting some type of personality disorder cluster that eventually will end up in the borderline, narcissistic, or antisocial personality disorder grouping.

Antisocial behavior.   Currently, the criteria for the diagnosis of antisocial personality disorder require that a conduct disorder must be present before age 15 years and that antisocial personality disorder cannot be diagnosed until age 18 years. However, it is likely that, in the future, these restrictions will be removed and antisocial personality disorder, as well as borderline personality disorder, will be diagnosed during adolescence. The reason is that more astute diagnoses and research should reveal manifestations of these disturbances as persistent over time and their salient features or forerunners as emerging quite early in personality development. Kernberg has stated her belief that a diagnosis of antisocial personality disorder should be made from age

15 years on when there is a lack of guilt and remorse and at least four of the following patterns:

- An inability to sustain consistent work behavior or the equivalent behavior if the person is a student
- Failure to conform to social norms of lawful behavior
- Irritability and aggressiveness as indicated by repeated physical fights or assaults
- Failure to honor financial obligations
- Failure to plan ahead or impulsivity
- Lack of regard for the truth
- Recklessness with regard to personal safety or the safety of others
- Lack of remorse or feeling justified in having hurt, mistreated or stolen from another[24]

If the diagnoses of antisocial personality and borderline personality disorder were allowed in adolescents, they would be quite frequently found in individuals who commit a homicide. Apart from a few blatantly psychotic juveniles, most homicidal acts by juveniles occur in a group for whom an earlier diagnosis of conduct disorder in childhood could be made. As adolescence continues, these individuals' behaviors appear to be some precursor of either a borderline personality disorder or an antisocial personality disorder. Occasionally, a juvenile with more striking paranoid symptoms seems to be expressing this type of thinking in the context of a fragmented type of borderline disorder organization or schizophreniform behaviors.

Unfortunately, the younger child who presents symptoms of some variation of a disruptive disorder is simply fitting into a descriptive appellation that includes behaviors that can vary from homicidal violence to stealing, truancy, absenting from home, and arson. To make matters more nebulous, four main groupings of conduct disorder are listed in DSM-IV:

1. Aggression to people and animals
2. Destruction of property
3. Deceitfulness or theft
4. Serious violation of rules

Whether these categories will achieve any greater validity or reliability then earlier classifications of group type, solitary aggressive type, or undifferentiated type, is problematic.[25] In one 4-year follow-up study, Cantwell and Baker found that the diagnosis of conduct disorder was not a stable one and that, after 4 years, many of the initial diagnoses of conduct disorder had been changed to other diagnoses.[26] These diagnoses may have changed to milder diagnoses, such as adjustment reaction, whereas in other cases the behaviors may have progressed to a more prominent type of antisocial behavior, similar to adult personality disturbances. However, in addition to the disruptive disorders, some type of mood disorder may have surfaced that could be related to aggressive or violent behaviors.[27] Some have suggested that a neurological central nervous system dysfunction, along with learning disabilities, could contribute to an individual's tendency toward aggressiveness. These are all seen as factors potentially predisposing one to impulsivity or violent behavior.

There has been some work indicating that biochemical measures may present another dimension in assessments of aggressivity, measures that would overlap with various diagnoses along a neuropsychiatric continuum. One group found a correlation between low levels of 5-hydroxyindoleacetic acid in the cerebrospinal fluid and the severity of physical aggression in a 2-year follow-up of children and adolescents.[28] Another group, who assessed central serotonergic function in aggressive and nonaggressive boys with attention-deficit hyperactivity disorder by way of prolactin response to fenfluramine challenge, found that the aggressive group had a significantly higher response.[29] This would correlate with suggestions that serotonergic sensitivity in those with borderline personality disorders contributes to their fear and anger and, hence, their impulsive-aggressive behavior.[30]

Borderline behavior. The role of borderline behavior in adolescents who are involved in homicides is a recurring issue. Some of their instability can give rise, just as in adults, to impulsive outbursts connected with rage reactions. Until recently, it had been customary to diagnose adolescents who appeared to be showing the onset of borderline personality traits as having an identity disorder; now, the trend seems to be to extend thinking about borderline personalities to younger ages. Rapoport and Ismond advocated that children and adolescents be diagnosed with borderline personality disorder, provided that the criteria for that disorder were met and the nature of the disturbance was pervasive, persistent, and not limited to a developmental stage.[31] Children develop a sense of identity at quite young ages, but those who appear headed for a fragmented development are plagued by problems in this regard. In these troubled adolescents, lower levels of defensive operations begin with identity diffusion, which is seen as part of a personality disorder disturbance. Borderline defense mechanisms in the form of denial, projection, primitive idealization, splitting, devaluation, and omnipotent control then appear. The relationship of the juvenile to reality becomes more tenuous, though the capacity to test reality is preserved.

In some of these juveniles, a much more severe type of disorganization may occur that appears to be similar to a psychotic breakdown. A fragmented and bizarre sense of identity emerges in which the individual begins to have a severe constriction in personality functioning and to deanimate animate relations, so that he or she begins to react to people as though they are robotized or simply objects. Animation of inanimate or nonhuman objects is also seen in the way these juveniles react to a toy as though it had some lifelike qualities or to a pet animal as though it were someone that could communicate with them on their own level. These behaviors appear to be last-ditch efforts to stem the occurrence of overwhelming anxiety or depression; by then there is a loss of the capacity to test as well as relate to reality. In some homicides, these areas of psychopathological development are reflected in the juvenile perpetrator's numbing response to the dead victim as though he or she were an inanimate object.

In discussing psychotic behavior in juveniles, Kernberg cited the following case example of murderous behavior:[24]

Case Example

Maria, a 15-year-old girl, displayed borderline behavior. She tried to kill her parents by cooking stews and muffins mixed with rat poison; she also set fires outside their bedroom. Maria referred to her parents, who had come from Latin America, as "minority Wasps." Except for one friend, she felt no one could be counted on. Her parents, who supposedly had ignored her sensitivity by the way they ate and talked, disgusted her. Furthermore, she felt that she could never forgive her parents for not controlling an older brother who had physically abused her.

When adolescents with a borderline personality are examined after the commission of some kind of homicidal act, their personal history usually reveals that certain developmental landmarks have not been attained. Characteristically seen are a history of unresolved massive separation anxieties on entering school or going away to a camp; a lack of consistent internalized standards in terms of what is acceptable or not acceptable behavior; a history of impulsive acts, occurring with a sense of accompanying unpredictability; and difficulty in modulating the expression of affects in diverse types of situations. By the time adolescence arrives, they are further confronted with the increased confusion that goes along with their developing sexuality and its expression. The problems that can result from the interaction of borderline personality characteristics and developing sexuality are seen in the following case example:

Case Example

An adolescent male had been in treatment at a residential treatment center for a year. While there, a girl of his own age had promised to have sex with him one night if he came to her room. However, after arriving at her room, he found that she had changed her mind, with the result that he began to utter a string of profanities at her along the line of "bitch," "slut," and so on. This tirade prompted a female staff member to come to the girl's room to inquire about the commotion. When she asked the youth to refrain from such language, he swung his fist at her, knocking her to the floor, and then kicked her in the head. After being restrained by other staff members, he was asked about the incident. He stated, "She had an attitude problem. She had no right to step in because it was between this other girl and me." He had no sense of the inappropriateness of his behavior in assaulting the staff member; instead, a determined self-righteousness about his behavior prevailed. Thus, this youth's lack of empathy for others— whether staff or members of his peer group—was able to be documented before his committing a homicide a year later.

The relationship of juveniles with borderline personality qualities to their peer group alternates between feeling intimidated and coerced by them on one level and a need to control and dominate them on another level. These juveniles are able to idealize certain adults or older peers, but are also liable to devaluate and turn on them at anytime. In this context of ambiguity and uncertainty, some type of homicidal behavior can occur. Most striking is these juveniles' inability to see the role their provocative behavior plays in assaultive behaviors, which may lead to a homicide as well as their inability to accept responsibility for their own actions.

In a psychodynamic sense, the separation-individuation process, along with other developmental components, has become derailed in these juveniles. What occurs instead are attempts at grandiosity intermixed with identity diffusion. Although sufficient explanations are lacking, it appears that the behaviors are a defense against an overwhelming anxiety of feeling alone and abandoned, much as occurs in adults with borderline personality disorder. If narcissistic components are dominant in the disorder, these behaviors appear to be an effort to overcome a sense of worthlessness and shame by conveying an arrogance and devaluating others. In this vulnerable state, provocations are more likely to elicit reactions that can lead to physical violence, if not homicide, when controls are impaired.

A deformity in these juveniles' superego development prohibits the proper modulation of actions. Instead, what emerges are manifestations of extreme ambivalence as well as outright hatred, expressed within their peer group or family. Pervasive types of splitting mechanisms are observed in which groups and people are split into the customary good guys or bad guys. Shifts in the splitting within the group and between certain individuals further contribute to the potential for a violent outburst. When others become puzzled or confused by the results of these changes going on within a juvenile, misinterpretations of the juvenile's behavior are likely, which may lead to confrontations. This is particularly so because of the sense of grandiosity and entitlement present in these adolescents, who try either to control others totally or to look for someone to subsume their identity under and become an obedient follower. Hence, causes or groups that these youths can join, including the gangs seen in major metropolitan areas, appeal to them.

Difficulties in Diagnosing Juvenile Violent Behaviors

Several difficulties exist in relying on diagnostic groupings such as disruptive behavior disorders to assess homicidality. Although a retrospective diagnostic assessment of juveniles after a homicide may often find a loading from within the disruptive grouping, this extreme degree of violent outcome would be overpredicted by a wide margin. There is the old question of antisocial personality disorders in adults being preceded by some type of conduct disorder historically in childhood, but predicting this outcome from childhood would be quite unreliable. Some study authors have found that conduct disorders predict later criminal behavior.[32] However, others have indicated that only about one-third of conduct disturbances persist into the adult period.[33] The answer to which children will persist and progress in their disruptive behavior remains elusive. Although the possibility exists for a variety of antisocial behaviors (e.g., delinquent acts, criminality of diverse forms, illicit drug use) to evolve, perhaps the most that can be said is that aggressive behavior of some kind is the variable that antedates criminal behavior in 75% of the adult cases.[34]

As noted above, according to criteria listed in DSM-IV, evidence of a full-fledged conduct disorder before the age of 15 years is necessary for the diagnosis of an antisocial personality disorder, which means that a pervasive pattern of disregarding and violating the rights of others must have begun in childhood and early adolescence and continue into adulthood. Hence, the personality disorder is seen as an unfolding over the years. Note that the DSM-IV criteria for conduct disorder are not actually symptoms but signs. The theoretical basis for this is that the assessment of conduct disorders is grounded in signs, although the behaviors can actually be present with diverse diagnoses. This is similar to the approach of listing behavioral criteria for diagnosing a conduct disorder that can also be present with diverse diagnoses. Hence, a 16-year-old who grabs a hammer in anger and attacks another person by beating his head and killing him would meet the overt criteria of a conduct disorder, now diagnosed as an antisocial personality disorder if some of the other criteria were met.

The limitation to the current approach is that it does not indicate the other possible diagnoses. For example, some type of depressive disorder or predisposing neuropsychiatric impairment that makes such impulsive acts more likely might be present. Nor can the possibility of psychotic ideation in which reality testing has been impaired be automatically dismissed. Another explanation could be that there is a fragmentation of the personality in which the victim attacked has been devalued from a previously idealized state. The process is one in which criminological or legal classifications have slipped into psychiatric descriptions, and diverse violent and disturbed adolescents then get classified as "antisocial."

In assessing adolescents who have engaged in murderous behavior, the question as to the significance of the perpetrator's facade of indifference or callousness, which is so often present, is raised. In many of these adolescents, an underdeveloped system of controls and, for some, an outright distortion in their thinking is present. It is easier for them to adapt to the world in which they live, particularly if it is a peer group of adolescents or a gang, by putting on a facade of being tough or macho. However, the facade cannot conceal a type of hypersensitivity or the outright distortion or misinterpretation of others' actions or their intentions. Whether this is ex post facto rationalization is a key question.

The following case example illustrates this type of mixed sensitivity and vulnerability:

Case Example

A gang attempted to burglarize a home. In an effort to conceal their identity so the home owner could not see them, they threw a blanket over him after they knocked him to the floor. The owner's struggle to get up elicited a rage reaction on the part of one of the juveniles, who proceeded to jump on top of the blanketed figure and pummel him, first with his fists and then with a lamp he grabbed. The owner eventually died. The youth later explained his behavior by saying that the owner should not have struggled in the way he did because he should have realized the gang member's purpose in throwing a blanket over him was simply to protect themselves from being identified. This youth's putting the blame for the owner's death on the owner indicated a type of egocentric thinking in which events were explained in terms of the perpetrator being provoked by the nonconforming acquiescence of the person being burglarized, who, the perpetrator felt, should have been empathetic with the gang's burglaring.

Extreme forms of antisocial behavior always carry the potential to culminate in acts of homicidal violence. The question then raised is why these behaviors occur and result in a homicide. From a sociological viewpoint, there is the suggestion that a certain group of adolescents behave in antisocial ways as a primary way of relating to others in society. It could then be predicted that, for some of them, progressive types of violent acts, including homicide, will occur. Thus the behavior is seen primarily as a cultural or environmental expression of these adolescents' antisocialness. A contrasting approach seeks some underlying basis to the antisocial behavior. Diagnostic categories are sought that it is hoped can be specific enough to explain the behavior. Some explanatory models also seek to go beyond descriptive levels by adding in developmental deviations.

■ Schizophrenic Disorders

Some juveniles who commit homicide carry the diagnostic signs and symptoms of schizophrenia. Although comprising a small number, these juveniles should not be overlooked because of the clinical and legal ramifications that accompany the diagnosis. On the other hand, it would be erroneous to limit the discussion of all possible psychotic conditions in juveniles to those occurring in conjunction with schizophrenia. It is unfortunate that the criteria used for diagnosing schizophrenia in juveniles vary among studies, which raises questions about the studies' validity and comparability; as a consequence, data on the incidence of this disorder in juvenile offenders will vary as well. For example, in one study of 14 cases of adolescents condemned to death, several were diagnosed as having a psychotic disorder before their incarceration.[35] Benedek and Cornell, in their study of 72 adolescents who had committed a homicide, found only 5 (7%) of the cohort were psychotic at the time of the commission of the homicide.[36] Labelle et al. studied 14 adolescent murderers, but attributed a psychotic diagnosis to none of them.[37] Several decades ago, the psychiatrist Loretta Bender wrote about "pseudopsychopathic schizophrenia" in which children were identified who she believed were psychotic in childhood, but by adolescence had become antisocial and engaged in violent behavior to a homicidal extent.[38]

Certainly it is difficult to ignore clinical evidence that some adolescents have an operational delusional system that can induce them to take action on that basis. Similarly, an adolescent reporting hallucinations could respond to hallucinatory commands. Lewis et al. evaluated children who had committed a murder and found that, based on interpretations of their history, a significant number had previously experienced psychotic symptoms (e.g., hallucinations, illogical thought processes).[39] The most common symptoms associated with these adolescents' violent acts were paranoid ideation and misperceptions. Perhaps the description of episodic dyscontrol syndromes most closely fits these behaviors in which the psychosis becomes more rampant or ego controls over violence are lessened to the degree that a homicide occurs. The following case example illustrates a case of patricide occurring in the context of delusional and hallucinatory symptoms in an adolescent with earlier schizoid traits:

Case Example

A 15-year-old male who had murdered his father faced certification for trial as an adult. At age 8 years, he had been sent to a child guidance clinic for reclusive behavior displayed in his avoiding peer activities. He progressed through school as a loner, having the occasional solo friendship, although these never seemed to last. Within his family of four siblings, he seemed different than the others in terms of his preferring to be alone. Things progressed satisfactorily in the academic world until he began to miss school a good deal during eighth and ninth grades without providing a sufficient explanation. Another referral was made to a clinic but, on review of the case file subsequent to killing his father, it was noted that he had only talked about superficial things and not about any deeper feelings or confused thoughts.

On the night of the homicide, the youth had been up all night debating within himself whether the pain and suffering he had been experiencing over the past several months was somehow attributable to his father's influence. The content of his obsessional brooding was that his father had treated him differently than the other children by holding out abnormally high expectations for him. During the course of a restless night marked by no sleep and endless pacing, he decided to do something to end his misery. It appears that hallucinations were prominent in terms of his hearing repeated commands to "get it over." In response to this, he took one of his father's hunting guns and posted himself at the exit of the garage where he knew that, sometime that morning, his father would exit on the way to work. As his father pulled out of the driveway, the youth leveled a shotgun blast at his father's head, killing him.

■ Depressed Adolescents and Homicide

Antisocial behavior, including homicidal violence, occurs more frequently in depressed adolescents than is indicated by official statistics. Although depression is routinely associated with suicidal acts, it also contributes to antisocial behavior, and may contribute to homicidal behavior just as frequently as it does to suicidal behavior. Much of the discussion involving adult depressions and homicide (see Chapter 8) is relevant to adolescents and to some younger children as well.

What appears to occur is a sense of helplessness and doom that progresses to an affective state of needing to resolve a crisis rather than staying in a painful state of hopelessness. One option is suicide, but, in what seems a paradoxical solution, homicide appears to offer more hope for alleviating the situation because it will salvage the potential perpetrator's own life. It is by way of this misplaced type of aggression, perhaps as an act of desperation, that a homicide takes place. In some cases where a suicide or violent act has been considered, an act of arson is carried out instead, which is then disowned by the perpetrator, even though the evidence incriminating the perpetrator is overwhelming. As in most of these types of ultimate quests for relief, the act is usually directed toward a loved one, which is seen as an expression of the intense ambivalence that is present in severely depressed people. It should not be forgotten that depression in adolescents, like that in adults, can be of psychotic proportions and affect their behavior through distorted thinking and delusions of hopelessness.

In a study conducted through a juvenile court system over several years with an overall population of 6,500 alleged delinquents, there were 213 motions to certify certain juveniles to adult court. The alleged crimes were mainly those of extreme violence, such as a homicide or an aggravated sexual assault, although a few were included on the basis of two or three prior felony arrests.[40] By use of criteria from the Minnesota Multiphasic Personality Inventory,[41] the Beck Depression Inventory,[42] and DSM-III (for a major depressive episode),[43] 44 of those 213 were diagnosed as being depressed. It is helpful to look at some of the dynamic factors operating in the group, in addition to what seemed to be a predisposition from several first-degree family members having problems with alcoholism and/or antisocial behavior.

The various ego defenses used in this group of adolescents did not appear to have been working even before the violent episode because the adolescents had not been able to contain their various emotions and impulses related to aggression. Questions remain as to why this group's depressive tendencies were expressed in such violent acts rather than through the emergence of some other course of psychopathological development. Although commission of a homicide by an adolescent is not seen as "normal" behavior, a question arises as to when certain signs of impending action should be assessed as clinically significant, such as an adolescent beginning to tell peers that he or she is thinking of killing someone. Related questions are when such signs should be considered indicative of a major mental disorder, and how to determine in the course of an assessment whether the individual's defenses will be able to contain the hinted-at aggression.

Many of the 44 juvenile males in the above-noted study had adopted hypermasculine roles but were inhibited in their capacity for any extended gratification through intimate relationships. They resisted close relationships and attempted to conceal their dependency needs. They displayed similarities to those juveniles whose dependency needs are met through gang participation, except for the fact that, in most of the cases, the homicides did not occur in the setting of gang violence. For some of the youths, there was a strong identification with an aloof or absent father, which left them lonely and angry. When these youths began a progressive withdrawal into their inner world, their behavior initially appeared as a denial of anxiety or agitation. Attempts at forced gaiety would occur in the context of drugs or alcohol use for some. In retrospect, a good deal of sadomasochistic behavior with low self-esteem was present in these adolescents, manifested in their provoking others or damaging their own image or status. In some cases, an unwitting shootout with the police occurred with suggestive suicidal overtones. These events were not consciously thought of as suicide attempts by the adolescents; instead, they simply described it as deciding to continue shooting until no longer capable of doing so or until they were dead.

Although guilt operated in these adolescents, it was often misattributed by professionals to some overt misdeed. Rarely did they connect the guilt as leading to provocative actions that, in turn, led to a cycle of attack and retaliation. In some cases, the cycle got out of hand and led to violence. One interpretation was that the adolescents' capitulation to violence, such as in a group assaulting a victim, was a final act of despair to relieve a depressed state. These adolescents were frequently described by court personnel as being "callous" because they did not seem upset after committing a homicide. This was especially noticeable when they declared that they felt better than they had before committing the homicide. The dynamics of inner relief related to the violent act, which temporarily displaced the depression, was often missed in assessments.

Another model for interpreting this callousness was to interpret their calmness as a sense of relief they seemed to experience after abandoning efforts to change their life. To give up by participating in an act of violence meant that they could bypass demands to measure up to exaggerated expectations through an inflated ego ideal. Such giving up often seemed incongruous to those later involved in evaluating these cases, let alone the public. That an adolescent would feel a homicide had been committed, but that everyone should now simply put it aside so they could get on with their lives, often evoked strong countertransference feelings in those who had to deal with them. These adolescents had minimal insight into the unreality of their desire to have the event simply put aside or forgotten. Because their depression was (even temporarily) alleviated, it was their belief that there was no need to dwell on the past. As one of them stated, "What's done is done.

Let's get on with life." Such verbalizations in a juvenile court system often resulted in their being labeled as psychopathic and promoted their certification to adult criminal court for trial.

Although in some cases the adolescents had experienced excessive physical punishment to the point of physical abuse, in a number of cases an opposite phenomenon was observed. Distinguishing actual abuse from contrived became problematic in many cases once there had been a homicide. In these cases, the youths described being in a state of morbid physical fear of a parental figure. Yet, by their own description, no beatings had occurred. One boy, later charged with murdering several members of his family, made recurrent statements involving his past fears that his father would beat him. Not until a detailed psychiatric inquiry was made did it become clear that no such beatings had ever occurred. A similar distortion occurred involving a girl regarding alleged sexual abuse. Inquiry regarding episodes she described revealed that they had occurred 10 years earlier, when she was age 5 years, and had only involved her getting into bed to cuddle between her parents, something she remembered as being exciting.

These descriptions were not conscious dissimulations by the juveniles because they did not lie about the events. Rather, they were asserted as being factual events that had occurred, even though they had not. Clinicians evaluating adolescents must consider the phenomenon of false memory syndrome as a possible explanation for their assertions, especially if the adolescents had previous contact with therapists or evaluators who started the therapy or interview with assumptions about abuse. In some cases, the adolescents engaged in exaggerated hysterical behavior to portray themselves as being victimized, behavior that was related to repressed components in their personalities. In others, the distortion was related to their anger at realizing how dependent they were, with that realization giving rise to hatred. The anger was then projected onto parental figures, who were seen as persecutors. Often juveniles would use their familiarity (either personal or peer knowledge or knowledge gained through the media) with other abuse cases to provide legal justification for their actions in response to alleged abusive behavior. Another possibility encountered is continuation of a type of conflict that had commenced with the onset of puberty, a stage at which integrations and object choices were necessary but had not been accomplished. The naive quality in some of the adolescents' exaggerations, often at a time when there was a flight into involvement with a peer group, suggested conspicuous struggles about autonomy. At the same time, someone else would be blamed for their states of anxiety and depression.

Retrospective evaluation of the 44 youths indicated activated sado-masochistic trends. The victims of the homicide were either loved ones or coincidental victims (i.e., those on the receiving end of displaced and projected aggression) who happened to be available on the right occasion at the right time. Even if the victims were unknown to the perpetrator, they were often on the receiving end because of the perpetrator's distorted process of thinking and a failure of his or her defenses to contain the aggression. Intriguing questions arise about the dynamics of youths who, involved in even less favorable circumstances and possessing similar vulnerabilities, did not succumb to a homicide. Specificity in explaining why some do and others do not commit homicide is still lacking.

In some situations involving depressed juveniles, a potential for homicidal behavior is reached inadvertently. Prime situations for homicides are muggings, robberies, and encounters related to addictive drug use or distribution, among other situations. The following two case examples illustrate how easily certain of these situations can eventuate in a homicide:

Case Examples

A smaller boy with chronically low self-esteem and depression was baited by a physically stronger boy, which led to a confrontation in a parking lot. At one point, the stronger boy was pulling the smaller one by his hair to a place where the stronger boy wanted to continue beating him. The smaller boy eventually pulled out a knife and, with a single stab to the heart of the bigger youth, ended the fight.

An adolescent boy would handle his depressed states by drinking. While drinking quite heavily he would often become aware of a desire to fight someone. He would often frequent bars or areas near bars in his search for a fight. One night he selected a victim who was more intoxicated than he. They went into an alley, where only one blow was needed to end the actual fight. However, the youth then had an urge to keep beating the unconscious victim and proceeded to do so, including jumping on his head.

Neither of these cases started with a conscious wish to perpetrate a homicide, although presumably the adolescent in the second case eventually came to that point after the fight had begun.

What about the depressed adolescent who becomes aware of a conscious desire to kill someone? One relevant question would be to inquire into the impairment of his or her ability to perceive reality and react correctly. Although this desire to kill may not reflect psychotic thinking to the degree of being prompted by a delusional system in which a supposed persecutor must be eliminated, it could signify a distortion in thinking to a degree that the potential perpetrator cannot assess his or her need to complete the act or appreciate the meaning or consequences of the act. The person usually does not entertain the possibility of his or her own destruction or death.

Depressed adolescents entertaining thoughts about homicide may have some factors in common with suicidal adolescents. One similarity is their belief that the state of despair they are in will continue without relief. A corollary belief is that the act of homicide will relieve their anxiety and tension. Some type of event representing a personal failure with a resultant loss of self-esteem in retrospect can often be identified as precipitating the homicidal act. Although such stressors seem to function to precipitate suicide in those with substance abuse problems, they also operate in depressed, homicidal adolescents. In the following case example, a girl's failures to separate from a close attachment to her mother, and involvement in high-risk activities, led to being an accessory to murder:

Case Example

An adolescent girl had run away from home several times, during which times she would work as a prostitute. She would then return home to her mother, who had strict religious beliefs and would emphasize the sinfulness and guilt associated with the girl's actions. After one failed attempt at remaining separated from her mother, the girl once again planned to return home. Shortly before she was meant to return home, she joined a pimp and another girl in "punishing" a third girl who was trying to escape. The "punishment" was for the girl to have her throat slit (this case was noted earlier). Following this event, there was no need for the girl to either return home or stay in the life she had been leading, for her participating in the homicide had put her fate into the hands of others. She had fought against dependence on her mother, but could not deal with the hostility that accompanied such dependency. She recalled past fears that she would lose control and kill her mother.

Just as in a suicide, depressed adolescents feel trapped in a conflict from which they cannot extricate themselves by decisions of their own. In many cases, the transformation of a state of helpless passivity into one of taking charge of themselves becomes clear retrospectively.

A variation on this theme is the Götterdämmerung finale. This is the stage when the adolescent becomes convinced that nothing matters. In the suicidal state, this finale is reached when an individual's ideation is turned into a belief that the world would be better off without him or her; in a homicidal state, this point is reached when the potential perpetrator comes to believe that nothing has gone right and the time has come to externalize the hopelessness within him or her. Homicidal individuals in this state are inhibited in their ability to think about the misery and suffering that will result for many other people from their act or to feel guilt. At that point, even before the act has occurred, the question about who is to die or who has already been killed is merely theoretical because the decision to kill has been made. The perpetrator experiences a sense of relief or calmness, given that the act is viewed as inevitable. Within this type of thinking, a homicide-suicide attempt may occur when the anxiety resulting from the realization that they are going to kill breaks through, which leads to a suicide attempt.

In those adolescents whose homicidal efforts have somehow been aborted or called off, it is not infrequent for them later to minimize what happened. It may be laughed off as "just a joke." These types of revelations require astute clinical judgment because, at the time of revealing these thoughts, the patient's homicidal impulse may be transiently gone. Yet these individuals still retain a sense of control from knowing that they can always put the plan into action if need be; this realization gives them a sense of power that allows them to view their future as being less bleak than it was before. Their sense of comfort is thus based on the power to effect a homicide when needed, and not on any resolution to any of their conflicts. Unless the clinician can tap into this type of thinking, the difficulty is that these individuals may externally look quite intact and "talk a good game."

The practical problems that emerge when the clinician becomes privy to such internal thought processes are enormous, especially the problems in obtaining the treatment such adolescents need. Their fear of involvement in another relationship that may make them dependent, which is what they see themselves as having conquered, provides a tenuous basis for maintaining a treatment relationship. It is easy to join the adolescent in seeking to blame others as the source of their difficulties, especially because an adverse environment often does exist around them. This mutuality between a clinician and adolescent is a treacherous alliance that carries a homicidal risk.

One of the primary goals in treating these juveniles is to allow them to appreciate cognitive ways to gain control over their impulses, other than through the specious and grandiose ways in which they have been operating or by simply blaming others. The potential to regress and test out whether they are still in control always looms. The pressure from many sources will, unfortunately, be to bypass or ignore the more subtle aspects of their personalities that contribute to homicide, leading to the conviction that homicide or suicide is the answer. The adolescent, and many others involved, may push to forget the past or minimize it. Efforts are often made to persuade the clinician that the homicide, or homicidal thoughts, were just a temporary aberration and should be forgotten. Such efforts at persuasion by the juvenile need close scrutiny.

■ Substance Abuse Disorders

Just as with adults, the use of psychoactive substances can be an important variable in connection with homicides committed by juveniles. Whether the abuse is a primary diagnosis or secondary to some other primary diagnosis, psychiatric morbidity is the problem with these dual diagnosis cases. When dealing with delinquent adolescents, some of whom are becoming more overtly violent as they age, one can see alcohol or drug abuse and intoxication patterns that began at quite an early age. Depending on the particular time and culture, different types of drugs begin to be used. Although many clinics report that it is very difficult to control drug usage if another psychiatric diagnosis is seen as primary and gets treated, other clinics report the opposite; that is, that, if the underlying condition is not treated, the drug and alcohol use continues. In reality both conditions need treatment.

Because substances may be used in attempts to deal with all manner of psychiatric problems, or their use may be heavily peer influenced, it is difficult to dissect conclusively the diverse interacting factors leading to the substance use. The only remedy is to obtain a specifically detailed history and clinical examination of the individual in question. Even then, a separation of diagnoses may be difficult. Two complications may ensue in the treatment of dually diagnosed juveniles. One is the orientation and treatment philosophy of some drug treatment centers for juveniles, which view the use of any medications as unacceptable. This prevents the use of appropriate and controlled medication to treat psychiatric disorders other than substance use or dependence. The second is the viewpoint of drug abuse as the primary, if not sole, problem that has to be dealt with; this approach thereby may ignore other disorders within an individual personality or conflicts within the family.

■ Neuropsychiatric Contributions

One of the more persistent, if not missed areas, in assessing violence in juveniles is the impact of neuropsychiatric deviations. This type of perspective originated some time ago in terms of what were called the sequelae of prenatal and natal birth insults. Subsequent phenomena may be detected as well, such as various types of illnesses, injuries, exposures to toxins, or accidents that could have had an adverse impact on the developing central nervous system of a child.

Frequently, adolescents with a tendency toward violent behavior may have a history of episodes of dizziness or blackouts, sometimes exacerbated by the use of alcohol or drugs. An earlier diagnosis of attention-deficit hyperactivity disorder with concentration problems may complicate matters further. Neurological evaluations often come back with a lack of specific findings, except for reports of various "soft signs" (e.g., poor coordination, spotty performances on memory tests, difficulty in fine motor coordination). The results from electroencephalographic tests are often of the "diffuse generalized abnormality" type, which leaves a lack of a satisfactory explanation. There may also be a correlation with underarousal in the central or autonomic nervous systems. In one study, such measurements at age 15 years were seen as related to a status of criminality at age 24 years.[44] This could be genetically determined or caused by some developmental injuries. Related to this are questions about the possibility or significance of complex partial seizures (discussed in Chapter 2). Such considerations may infiltrate into the realm of possible neuropsychiatric disabilities. Two difficulties accompany these types of questionable findings: one rejects these findings on the basis that their lack of specificity does not allow one to draw any inferences from them; the other accepts these combinations of suggested neurological findings as having had an impact on the child in terms of ultimately making him or her more unstable and causing impulse control problems, which could accentuate his or her difficulties.

Related to the neuropsychiatric findings are the large number of juveniles displaying antisocial behaviors who have a low intelligence level. Although most are not severely retarded, many of them are in the borderline or mildly retarded group, just as their adult counterparts are. There is also a large number in this group who have manifested early learning disabilities that perhaps are related to some of the suggestive neurological findings noted.

The combination of all these factors—neuropsychiatric, intelligence level, and learning problems—in conjunction with the less privileged socioeconomic backgrounds many of these youths come from, places them in a high-vulnerability group for antisocial behavior. It is not an unwarranted inference to see that some of their impulsivity, difficulty in reasoning, and exercise of poor judgment over their behavior in many spheres are related to these antecedent disabilities. It is also well known that children with language and reading disorders have much more difficulty expressing their wants and needs as well as dealing with their feelings. From this perspective, they are much more likely to become impulsive and restless and act out their feelings rather than develop ego controls and patience to deal with frustrating situations. As such, these factors, in a summative way, contribute to the possibility of a homicidal adolescent.

■ Dissociative Phenomena

The diagnostic category of dissociative disorders is often overlooked in adolescents, although theirs might be expected to be a prime age group for the manifestations of various types of dissociative phenomena. Some adolescents who have committed a homicide may simply have lapsed into a brief dissociative state, whereas a small number of these adolescents may actually fit the criteria for the controversial diagnosis of a multiple personality disorder. In many respects, the diagnosis is overused and overdramatized. Whether multiple personality disorder is a valid scientific entity, a figment of distorted imagination, or an iatrogenic state is not yet known despite ardent advocates for all positions.[45]

Variations on these possibilities may appear to be present, especially for those who have been severely traumatized in their early years, which makes them prone to reenact violence in variations of dissociated states. This is not to decide the issue of whether such a diagnosis in itself contributes to exculpation if a homicide is committed. It is rather to illustrate that complex questions can be raised about responsibility when this diagnostic category—one that is closely related to borderline personality disorder phenomena—is thought to be applicable to the perpetrator.

■ Role of Childhood Abuse

It is impossible to discuss any of the diagnoses that involve the extremes of juvenile violence without considering the hypothesis of the impact of parental or adult physical and sexual abuse on a child. This is not a new hypothesis. In the early 1960s, Curtis wrote that abused and neglected children are tomorrow's murderers and perpetrators of violence.[46] From that point on, different clinical reports and research efforts have produced a mixture of impressions and conflicting findings. The question is whether such maltreatment leads to serious violence, such as homicidal behavior, in adolescence and beyond. However, because the issue often arises with retrospective assertions after an act of violence, specifics about the impact of abuse are needed. Widom, in a large sample involving physical and sexual abuse cases, found that, overall, children who were abused and neglected had higher rates of adult criminality than did a control group, as measured by arrests for violent offenses.[47] However, in another study, that same author did not find that abused or neglected children had higher rates of arrest for violent crimes as juveniles compared with control subjects, although females did appear to be at increased risk of arrest for violent crimes as adolescents.[48] The conclusion was that empirical evidence for a "cycle of violence" could not be confirmed in terms of those who were abused recycling the abuse themselves.

However, there is research to support a link between the long-term consequences of physical abuse and adolescent aggression, if not homicidal violence. Results from some studies have indicated that adolescents with violent aggressive behaviors that are displayed outside their families have a higher incidence of having experienced physical abuse than the general population.[49] Other studies do not confirm this.[50] A second research methodology has focused on adolescent boys in residential treatment facilities; these youths have shown a higher rate of past physical abuse compared with less violent or nonviolent male control groups. A third approach has focused on children receiving treatment for emotional problems. It was found that those who had been physically abused showed more aggressive behavior than a nonabused group.[51]

It must be remembered that the majority of abused and neglected children do not become delinquent or criminal, let alone engage in violent behavior. Mones, a defense lawyer who has defended 100 cases of parricide in court, argued that, although even the most severely abused children do not necessarily kill their parents, in the cases where such homicides do occur, the children had all been abused.[52] Yet, of the estimated 2 million cases of child abuse per year, and approximately 26,000 homicides in the United States, only 300 involve murders of parents by children. To a psychiatrist, the most intriguing questions remain unresolved: What allows the homicides to take place when they do? Why do they not occur in the great majority of these abused adolescents? The question remains, given conflicting research data, whether there is a significant subgroup who are abused and then end up more prone than others to violence or repeating abusive behavior. Although no one would advocate the abusive treatment of children, whether this is actually the most significant variable that contributes to the increased incidence of severe violence in adolescence or whether it is it one significant variable among many for those who kill remains to be seen. Again, more specificity is needed as to why a subgroup behaves in a homicidal manner. Inconsistencies in the results of studies can be attributed to diverse study designs, reliance on reports of abuse, and use of arrests as a measure of violence.[53]

Lewis proposed a hypothesis to explain why maltreatment in the form of abuse or neglect may exacerbate preexisting psychobiological vulnerabilities.[54] Lewis viewed abusive behavior as leading to impulsivity and irritability, although whether as states or traits is not clear. In turn, this engenders hypervigilance, paranoia, diminished judgment capacity, and verbal incompetence. All of these consequences serve to curtail the recognition of pain in oneself and others. There is also the related question of innate temperamental differences.

Although there is no specific finding (with the exception of the Lesch-Nyhan disease due to an inborn error of metabolism from an enzymatic defect of hypoxanthine guanine phosphoribosyltransferase manifesting itself in mental retardation and behavioral abnormalities including violence) that any genetic abnormality predisposes one toward violent behavior, there is the position that certain types of inherited characteristics affect the way an individual adapts. Adaptations then interplay with the type of stressors in one's environment. Biological components are often hypothesized, such as testosterone contributing toward vulnerabilities toward violence, which would fit the observation of more males being predisposed to homicidal behavior.

Perhaps the reflections of a biologist best sums up the current evolutionary state:[55]

We may all be going through a kind of childhood in the evolution of our kind of animal. Having just arrived, down from the trees and admiring our thumbs, having only begun to master the one gift that distinguishes us from all other creatures, it should perhaps not be surprising that we fumble so much. We have not yet begun to grow up. What we call contemporary culture may turn out, years hence, to have been a very early stage of primitive thought on the way to human maturity. What seems to us to be the accident-proneness of state-craft, the lethal folly of nation-states, and the dismaying emptiness of the time ahead may be merely the equivalent of early juvenile delinquency. . . . If we can stay alive, my guess is that we will someday amaze ourselves by what we can become as a species. Looked at as larvae, even as juveniles, for all our folly, we are a splendid, promising form of life and I am on their side.

■ References

1. Fingerhut LA, Kleinman JC: International and interstate comparison of homicide among young males. JAMA 263:3292–3295, 1990

2. Malmquist CP: Juveniles in adult courts: unresolved ambivalence. Adolesc Psychiatry 7:444–456, 1992

3. Arbuthnot J, Gordon DA, Jurkovic GJ: Personality, in Handbook of Juvenile Delinquency. Edited by Quay HC. New York, Wiley, 1987, pp 139–183

4. Flanagan TJ, Jamieson K: Sourcebook of Criminal Justice Statistics 1987. Washington, DC, U. S. Department of Justice, 1987

5. Holinger PC, Offer D: Adolescent Suicide. New York, Guilford, 1993

6. Centers for Disease Control and Prevention: Homicides among 15–19-year-old males—United States, 1963–1991. MMWR 43, 1994

7. Bureau of Justice Statistics Clearinghouse: Ten Important Facts About Homicide—Homicide Statistics Information Package. Bureau of Justice Statistics Clearinghouse: National Criminal Justice, 1995, pp 148–462

8. Snyder HN: Arrests of youth, 1990. Office of Juvenile Justice Department Programs Update on Statistics. Washington, DC, U.S. Department of Justice, 1992

9. Miller JG: Last One Over the Wall: The Massachusetts Experiment in Closing Reform Schools. Columbus, OH, Ohio State University Press, 1991

10. Hamparian D: Youth in Adult Courts: An Introduction in Major Issues in Juvenile Justice Information Training: Readings in Public Policy. Columbus, OH, Academy for Contemporary Problems, 1981

11. Hamparian DM, Davis JM, Jacobson JM, et al: The Young Criminal Years of the Violent Few. Washington, DC, National Institute for Juvenile Justice and Delinquency, 1985

12. Farrington DP: Childhood Aggression and Adult Violence, in The Development and Treatment of Childhood Aggression. Edited by Pepler DJ, Rubin KH. Hillsdale, NJ, Lawrence Erlbaum, 1991, pp 33–61

13. Wolfgang M, Figlio R, Sellin T: Delinquency in a Birth Cohort. Chicago, IL, University of Chicago Press, 1972

14. Strasburg P: Violent Delinquents. New York, Monarch, 1978

15. McDermott MJ, Hindelang MJ (eds): Analysis of National Crime Victimization Survey Data to Study Serious Delinquent Behavior in Juvenile Criminal Behavior in the United States: Trends and Patterns. Albany, NY, Criminal Justice Research Center, 1981

16. Rutherford A: Crime, law enforcement and penology, in Britannica Book of the Year. Chicago, IL, Britannica Book of the Year, 1994, pp 116–120

17. National Center for Health Statistics: Vital Statistics of the United States, 1989, Vol 2: Mortality, Part A. Hyattsville, MD, National Center for Health Statistics, 1992

18. Fingerhut MA, Kleinman JC, Godfrey E, et al: Firearm mortality among children, youth, and young adults 1–34 years of age, trends and current status: United States, 1979–88. Monthly Vital Statistical Report 39 (suppl):1–15, 1991

19. Federal Bureau of Investigation: Crime in the United States, 1991. Washington, DC, U. S. Department of Justice, 1992

20. Centers for Disease Control: Weapon-carrying among high school students: United States, 1990. MMWR 40:651–681, 1991

21. Webster DW, Gainer PS, Champion HR: Weapon carrying among inner-city junior high school students: defensive behavior versus aggressive delinquency. Am J Public Health 83:1604–1608, 1993

22. Callahan CM, Rivara FP: Urban high school youth and handguns. JAMA 267:3038–3042, 1992

23. American Psychiatric Association: Diagnostic and Statistical Manual of Mental Disorders, 4th Edition. Washington, DC, American Psychiatric Association, 1994

24. Kernberg PF: Personality disorders, in Textbook of Child and Adolescent Psychiatry. Edited by Weiner JM. Washington, DC, American Psychiatric Press, 1991, pp 515–533

25. Malmquist CP: Conduct disorder: conceptual and diagnostic issues, in Textbook of Child and Adolescent Psychiatry. Edited by Weiner JM. Washington, DC, American Psychiatric Press, 1991, pp 279–287

26. Cantwell CP, Baker L: Issues in the classification of child and adolescent psychopathology. J Am Acad Child Adolesc Psychiatry 27:521–533, 1988

27. Ben-Amos B: Depression and conduct disorders in children and adolescents: a review of the literature. Bull Menninger Clin 56:188–208, 1992

28. Kruesi MJP, Hibbs ED, Zahn TP, et al: A 2-year prospective follow-up study of children and adolescents with disruptive behavior disorders. Arch Gen Psychiatry 49:429–435, 1992

29. Halperin JM, Sharma V, Siever LJ, et al: Serotonergic function in aggressive and nonaggressive boys with attention deficit hyperactivity disorder. Am J Psychiatry 151:243–248, 1994

30. Hollander E, Stein DJ, DeCaria CM, et al: Serotonergic sensitivity in borderline personality disorder: preliminary findings. Am J Psychiatry 151:277–280, 1994

31. Rapoport JL, Ismond DR: DSM-III Training Guide for Diagnosis of Childhood Disorders. New York, Brunner/Mazel, 1990

32. Mannuzza S, Gittelman-Klein R, Konig PH, et al: Hyperactive boys almost grown up, criminality and its relationship to psychiatric status. Arch Gen Psychiatry 46:1073–1079, 1989

33. Rutter M: Pathways from childhood to adult life. J Child Psychol Psychiatry 30:23–25, 1989

34. Loeber R, Stouthamer-Loeber M: Prediction, in Handbook of Juvenile Delinquency. Edited by Quay HC. New York, Wiley, 1987, pp 325–382

35. Lewis DO, Pincus JH, Bard B, et al: Neuropsychiatric, psychoeducational, and family characteristics of 14 juveniles condemned to death in the United States. Am J Psychiatry 145:569–593, 1988

36. Benedek EP, Cornell DG: Juvenile Homicide. Washington, DC, American Psychiatric Press, 1989

37. LaBelle A, Bradford JM, Bourget D, et al: Adolescent murders. Can J Psychiatry 36:583–587, 1991

38. Bender L: The concept of pseudopsychopathic schizophrenia in adolescents. Am J Orthopsychiatry 29:491–509, 1959

39. Lewis DO, Moy E, Jackson L, et al: Biosocial characteristics of children who later murder: a prospective study. Am J Psychiatry 142:1161–1167, 1985

40. Malmquist CP: Depression and extreme violence in adolescence, in Thinking Clearly About Psychology, Vol 2: Personality and Psychopathology. Edited by Grove WM, Cicchetti D. Minneapolis, MN, University of Minnesota Press, 1991, pp 378–401

41. Hathaway SR, McKinley JC: Minnesota Multiphasic Personality Disorder, Revised. Minneapolis, MN, University of Minnesota, 1970

42. Beck AT: Depression Inventory. Philadelphia Center for Cognitive Therapy, 1978

43. American Psychiatric Association: Diagnostic and Statistical Manual of Mental Disorders, 3rd Edition. Washington, DC, American Psychiatric Association, 1980

44. Raine A, Venables PH, Williams M: Relationships between central and autonomic measures of arousal at age 15 years and criminality at age 24 years. Arch Gen Psychiatry 47:1003–1007, 1990

45. Cot, I: Current perspectives on multiple personality disorder. Hosp Community Psychiatry 45:827–829, 1994

46. Curtis CG: Violence breeds violence—perhaps? Am J Psychiatry 120:386–387, 1963

47. Widom CS: The cycle of violence. Science 244:160–166, 1989

48. Widom CS: Childhood victimization and adolescent problem behaviors, in Adolescent Problem Behaviors. Edited by Ketterlinus R, Lamb ME. New York, Lawrence Erlbaum, 1994, pp 127–164

49. Vissing YM, Straus MA, Gelles RJ, et al: Verbal aggression by parents and psychosocial problems of children. Child Abuse and Neglect 15:223–238, 1991

50. Fagan J, Hansen K, Jang M: Profiles of chronically violent delinquents: empirical test of an integrated theory, in Evaluating Juvenile Justice. Edited by Kleugel J. Beverly Hills, CA, Sage, 1993, pp 91–119

51. Malinosky-Rummell R, Hansen DJ: Long-term consequences of childhood physical abuse. Psychol Bull 114:68–79, 1993

52. Mones P: When a Child Kills: Abused Children Who Kill Their Parents. New York, Pocket Books, 1991

53. National Academy of Sciences: Understanding Child Abuse and Neglect. Washington, DC, National Academy Press, 1993

54. Lewis DO: From abuse to violence: psychophysiological consequences of maltreatment. J Am Acad Child Adolesc Psychiatry 31:383–391, 1992

55. Thomas L: The Fragile Species. New York, Robert Stewart/Scribners, 1992

CHAPTER 10

Sexual Killing

The topic of sexual killings is a generic one that includes many other types of homicides. Some of the victims of these killings are children whereas others are adults. Some victims are chosen on a heterosexual basis, some on a homosexual basis; yet a third group of sexual killings involves bisexual perpetrators who select different types of victims over time. In addition, some investigators believe that serial killers (discussed in Chapter 1) are all a variant of sexual killers; however, this is debatable. It is more accurate to say that only some serial murderers are sexual murderers and only some sexual murderers are serial murderers.

Complicating matters further is by what standards a killing is interpreted as being sexualized. Such an interpretation goes beyond seeing the acts in a purely descriptive sense because it involves interpreting behaviors as sexualized, even when a killing did not involve overtly sexual acts. Perhaps the biggest source of confusion and error occurring in the literature is drawing inferences about sexual offenders in general and then applying the deductions to the subgroup of those who are sexual killers. Sexual offenders themselves comprise a heterogeneous group, including rapists, pedophiles, exhibitionists, and voyeurs, to name a few. The great majority of these individuals do not kill and do not even physically assault others. It is unfortunate that most studies have not differentiated sexual from nonsexual killings, and, more specifically, have not differentiated various types of sexual killers.

■ Taxonomy of Sexual Killings

Sexual killings may be classified in different ways. A working breakdown could use the following:

1. Rape killings
2. Sexual lust (or sadistic) killings
3. Killings after a sexual act to destroy evidence

This taxonomic breakdown has the advantage of allowing diverse types of psychiatric or criminological theorizing to be applied to each of these categories, as well as applying individual psychiatric diagnoses in a descriptive or psychodynamic sense. It further allows developmental antecedents in the individual to be looked at as well, something that is quite important in theorizing about the significant variables that may be present and contribute to such an outcome. The individual's various significant or traumatic experiences, including his or her socioeconomic background, can be encompassed by this classification.

Rape Killings

Rape killings are those in which a sexual act, and not the killing per se, is seen as the primary motive for the act; simply put, in the course of the rape, a homicide occurs. However, it must be noted that, in practice, this seemingly neat distinction often breaks down. The following are examples of this type of killing:

- In the middle of a rape, the victim resists, and the perpetrator attacks the victim or strikes him or her.
- In the middle of a sodomous assault on a child, the child attempts to escape, the perpetrator strikes the child, and the child is killed.
- In one real case, a serial killer killed three women on three different occasions and a woman and her two children on an-

other occasion; all these deaths occurred by strangulation. Over a period of years, the perpetrator had developed a preference for having sexual intercourse while the female victim was being strangled; in most cases, he would release the woman from the strangulating hold before she expired, with the release ideally to occur simultaneously with ejaculation. In the cases of the homicides, the ejaculation did not occur early enough and the women died of asphyxiation. Two of the women he killed were prostitutes. A third woman was one he had met in a bar and subsequently stayed with at her apartment for a few days while en route across the country to a different city. The fourth was a woman he had been living with for several months; he stated that he had killed her children after killing her to allow him extra time to leave the area without being discovered (this would be an example of the third type of killing listed above). His later thinking was that the killings were simply accidental; he was unable to appreciate his compulsive need to have his sexual partners helpless and near death as a condition for his completing the sexual act. In fact, it was his masturbation fantasies involving necrophilic acts that revealed this connection.

Lust Killings

Sexual lust or sadistic killers are sometimes seen as the true sexual killers. In contrast with the first group, in which there is a fusion of sexuality and aggression that sometimes directly, but often inadvertently, leads to a homicide, in lust killings the primary goal is to kill the victim as part of a ritualized attack. Although the killing sequence may include an act of sexual intercourse, this is not necessarily the case, and other types of sexual acts may be part of the killing. The primary motivation for the perpetrator is the enactment of some type of fantasy that has preoccupied him or her for some time. The nature of the fantasy may have changed over time.

It is unknown how many individuals in society walk around with such sadistic sexual fantasies but never enact the fantasies in the actual world. The clinical speculation is that it might be very high compared with those who actually do carry out some type of act. The primary question to be asked is, What factors must be operative to allow a subgroup of individuals to breakthrough and act out this fantasy? Presumably, some alteration in ego controls must occur. From a clinical standpoint, it is most likely a series of factors that contribute to such a weakening of control; for example, often months or years of inner conflict, turmoil, and debate are present before commencing such behavior. In this context, themes of power, dominance, and subjugation of a victim are the key; when acts of mutilation or mayhem occur, they have been part of the prevailing fantasy. Rarely has such an act occurred in isolation without such a fantasized enactment.

Killings to Destroy Evidence

The third category of sexual killings are not strictly defined as sexual killings. In these cases, there has been some kind of sexual act, and the victim, or observers, as illustrated in the case above where the women's children were killed, are murdered to prevent discovery. But for the sexual act itself, these would not be classified as sexual murders in a taxonomic schema.

■ Descriptive Models of Sexual Killings

General Considerations Based on State of Victim

From these introductory points, it becomes clearer that it is often difficult to determine what should be classified as a sexual murder. As noted, some investigators believe that most serial killers are de facto sexual murderers. However, a killing in the context of a quarrel between lovers, or a spousal killing, would not be classified as a sexual killing. Similarly, retaliatory types of killing in which there is a sense of betrayal would not be viewed as sexual murders, but rather as crimes of passion. Therefore, the key question is, What are the essential hallmarks, even in a descriptive sense, for an act to be labeled a sexual killing?

Simple evidence of an act of sexual intercourse or anal or vaginal penetration having occurred in the context of a homicide does not in itself mean a sexual murder has occurred, except perhaps in the very broadest sense. Rather, what seems to be the defining descriptive characteristic is evidence of a more bizarre or brutal aspect of a killing that accompanied a sexual attack. The boundaries remain vague, but some more obvious cases would be the following:

- A dead body being left in a sexually suggestive pose
- Objects having been inserted in body cavities (e.g., the anus, vagina)
- Mutilation of parts of the body, if not outright dismemberment
- The manner in which the body was clothed or covered or left uncovered
- Suggestive evidence of sadistic or masochistic practices that were carried out (e.g., use of restraints, attempts at asphyxiation, evidence of dehumanizing treatment of the victim)

These are suggestive descriptive aspects from the external examination of the bodies of the victims and examination at the scene of the crime, independent of any knowledge about the perpetrator.

The Federal Bureau of Investigation Study

Investigative leads on the perpetrator make up another line of investigation into sexual killings. In a research volume on sexual homicides written by a nursing professor and two supervisory agents of the Federal Bureau of Investigation (FBI), Ressler et al. studied 36 convicted and incarcerated sexual murderers.[1] It should be noted that the data on these perpetrators were not all complete, but that the majority of these men did at least agree to participate in the study. To date, this has probably been the largest group of sexual killers to be interviewed for research purposes; subsequently, Ressler et al.'s research has been extensively summarized by others. All of the perpetrators were men and came from different geographical areas. Twenty-nine of the group had attacked multiple victims and 7, only 1 victim, for a total of 118 victims. Nine victims survived; these cases were handled as attempted murder cases. The perpetrators were suspects in more cases than those recorded, but were never brought to trial for these other cases. Official records were used as well as interviews with the offenders; thus the data primarily reflect the recall of the perpetrators.

The offenders gave multiple reasons for participation. Some who admitted the offense stated it gave them an opportunity to contribute to an increased understanding about them. Those who denied guilt saw it as an opportunity to illustrate why they could not have committed the crime. Others saw it as an opportunity to "teach" the police how the crimes were committed and their motivations. These types of conscious reasons undoubtedly concealed a diverse set of motives, but they are interesting in their own right.

A law enforcement orientation to sexual murders, as in the FBI study, has its strengths and weaknesses. The emphasis is on a classification system based on an analysis of the crime scene. As such, it is what a good detective does when confronted with a murder, such as focusing on attention to details at the scene of the crime for purposes of apprehending the guilty party. Details about the position of the victim, the condition of the body, use of a weapon, and so on are basic to such an approach. This type of primary operational mission has the worthwhile goal of promoting the capture of sexual murderers at large, and secondarily preventing other attacks from recurring. What it lacks is a type of in-depth psychiatric explanation and understanding of the murderers themselves, although it may provide suggestions about their developmental history. At best, such an operational approach can only suggest certain psychological and social variables that were also present in the sexual murderer's profile.

Ressler et al. did propose a motivational model involving certain critical personal traits, as well as cognitive mapping and processing, which they believed interacted with each other to produce patterned responses. Their extensive data on this overall group of murderers give the best set of descriptive items about a group of sexual murderers that is available.

The FBI study began with a focus on the perpetrators' early life attachments or their early bonding patterns, which offered a blueprint of how they began to perceive life as existing outside their family setting. The social bonding process that occurs in individuals who commit sexual murders is seen as either failing to occur adequately or being quite narrow and selective in its outcome. The adult caretakers who reared the future sexual murderers either ignored, rationalized, or tried to normalize the behaviors that emerged in the boys. From their own personal problems, the distortions and projections occurring in their children were given support. In effect, the study approach was a developmental theory dealing with the parental impact on a child in the presence of parental conflict or preoccupation and the resultant distorted impact it had on the development of the child. It amounted to a theory with a developmental psychopathological perspective for the emergence of delinquent behavior in general. However, as a theory, it lacked specificity to predict an ultimate outcome of murderous behavior, let alone a sexual murder. According to this theory, these boys were not able to register the fact that their antisocial behavior should be punished because the behavior had been "normalized" in these families by generalizations such as "all boys get into trouble." This variable related to one's family background is frequently encountered in many delinquent youths.

To try to achieve more specificity, Ressler et al. proposed three factors that are formative events in the life of a child who has the potential for later becoming a sexual murderer. The first factor was having experienced either direct physical or sexual trauma or some indirect trauma (e.g., witnessing family violence). In such a situation, the child is viewed as not receiving the type of protection needed to deal with the impact such events have on him or her. From these frightening childhood experiences, memories emerge in the context of daydreams, fantasies, nightmares, and disturbing memories of the events. The unsuccessful resolution of these traumas leaves the child feeling victimized and helpless. As a response, he or she begins to use aggressive fantasies to achieve a dominance and control that has been absent in the real world. The abusive event may also induce a sustained emotional-physiological arousal that interacts with the child's thoughts about the trauma and alters his or her perceptions and patterns of interpersonal life.

The second formative event proposed by Ressler et al. was a developmental failure. This failure was a blocking of attachments that should have taken place between the child and his or her primary caretaker, which resulted in the adult lacking influence with the child. The authors did not offer any explanation of why this blocking occurred, although they acknowledged that they were not addressing any neurological or genetic factors.

The third hypothetical factor was the failure of an adult to serve as a role model for the child, such as a parent being absent or inadequately filling the parental role. It is unfortunate that the FBI study did not add a clinical dimension, for this could have provided other sources of knowledge about the individuals who committed sexual murders. Thus the clinical questions as to how or why such developmental failures occurred, and what diagnostic possibilities were present that specifically related to later sexual murdering remain unanswered.

The motivational model Ressler et al. proposed has a third level of patterned responses (after the ineffective social environment and formative events from childhood and adolescence) that includes two subcategories: critical personality traits and cognitive mapping and processing. The traits found in these men were related to their sense of social isolation. They would use fantasies related to autoerotic activities and fetishes as a substitute for human encounters. It is possible to argue that these men's sexual development was restricted from the lack of mutual caring, pleasure, and companionship they had experienced. The isolation experienced by these men led to their having a sense of being different from others; however, they also expressed anger at a society that they viewed as rejecting them. Other traits seen in the men were rebelliousness, aggression, chronic lying, and a sense of privilege or entitlement that they should get what they wanted.

Cognitive mapping and processing is the other subcategory of patterned responses. These refer to thinking patterns that give control and development to one's internal life and link it to the social environment. Such mapping and processing give meaning to events and control the states of helplessness, terror, and pervasive anxiety encountered in the course of personal development. In sexual murderers, the mapping and processing are seen as fixed, negative, and repetitious patterns that give an antisocial view to the world. The fantasies then stimulate these men and decrease their tension. Their self-image is terrifying to themselves and others because of the possibility that others could discover their fantasies.

Themes of control and dominance over others become a substitute for mastery of their own internal and external experiences. The men in Rester et al.'s study became aroused by high levels of aggressive experience that required stimulation. Themes of dominance, rape, molestation, power, torture, humiliation, and inflicting pain on oneself or others, or death itself became the main focus of their fantasies.

Another step in Ressler et al.'s model involved taking actions toward others that were seen as an effort to achieve a joyless dominance. Childhood behaviors to achieve such dominance are manifested in being cruel to animals, abusing other children, engaging in destructive play patterns, setting fires, and committing various property offenses. By adolescence, more violent behavior emerges, such as assaults, burglary, rape, and the commencement of sexual assaultive behaviors. However, once again, this is a background description that can fit many children who emerge into patterns of juvenile delinquency and perhaps later serious adult crime, as well. It lacks sufficient specificity to make predictions about who in such a group might actually emerge as a sexual murderer.

The last step in the model was a "feedback filter," in which these men's feelings of dominance, power, and control were increased. These feelings justified their earlier actions and helped them to sort out events to preserve the fantasies and avoid the external environment impinging on them.

Other Descriptive Studies of Sexual Killers

It is easy to assume that patterns of sexual aggression for more minor sexual offenses are the same as those present during sexual murders. Such patterns would seem more likely for killings that emerge during the course of sexual assaults. Whether the pattern also fits lust murderers is more problematic. To assume it is the same set of factors and fantasies for all sexual offenses leaves unresolved questions about why sexual murderers do not become even more prevalent than they seemingly are. Perhaps increased publicity of these cases seen recently will allow researchers to accumulate more knowledge about them. Unfortunately, because of the limited number of cases, researcher's knowledge base is still often focused on the few high-publicity cases, such as Jack the Ripper, Ted Bundy, David Berkowitz, or Dennis Nilsen. More recent notable cases include the still unidentified Green River Killer near Seattle; Arthur Shawcross, the strangler of 11 women around Rochester, New York; Bianchi in Los Angeles; Jeffrey Dahmer in Wisconsin; and Joel Rifkin around New York City. The clinical question, for which there is no adequate answer is, When do the fantasies and enactments related to more minor sexual deviancies extend or shift to those involving more ominous sadistic, if not murderous, components?

In one study of murders in England, 14% of the 306 murderers whose victims were females over age 16 years were classified as being "sexually motivated."[2] However, the authors of that study had previously screened out those legally classified as insane or having a diminished responsibility legal status. It could be presumed that the figure would be higher in the United States, given that the overall rates of violence and homicide are higher. Many of the individual studies in case reports appear to indicate that these individuals have severe disturbances in their personality functioning in a clinical sense. Many of them seem to be in the aggressive sociopathic type of group.

An early attempt at developing a profile of sadistic sexual murderers was done by Robert P. Brittain, who was both a forensic pathologist and a psychiatrist.[3] The profile of sexual murderers he developed was that of a male who was younger than age 35 years, introverted, and a loner, and having a rich fantasy life. A close, but ambivalent, tie with his mother existed in which she was seen as someone inordinately curious about his sexual life. A distant and punitive father gave rise to a difficult relationship between the father and son. The future murderer was seen as vain and sensitive to threats to his self-esteem, as well as having concerns about his sexual potency. Accounts of cruelties appealed to him, yet a mixture of kind acts would be recorded about him as well. A killing could occur in the course of a sexual assault, such as by strangulation. In some cases, sexual intercourse itself did not take place; masturbation might occur or some bizarre type of mutilation, dismemberment, or stabbing. The men Brittain studied were seen as having an intellectual grasp of the crime, but only showing a flat and superficial emotional response to it. Whereas some of the preplanning to their acts suggested cunning, they often returned to the scene of the crime and became upset if there was a lack of publicity.

West emphasized that it is often difficult to generalize about sexual homicides, given that there are often so many unique and distracting features to each case.[4] For some sexual killers, there is a pattern in which such aggression periodically breaks through, whereas for others the impulses remain on a fantasy level and then only break out in one violent and irrational act. In these cases, the usual defenses used against guilt and hostility have given way. Once the barrier is broken, the behavior seems more likely to recur and possibly become more extreme. However, this would correspond to cases where there have been long intervals between sexual murders in which the perpetrator remained dormant.

Sexual killers may share many of the characteristics with those who commit sexually sadistic acts in which violence is mixed with needs to dominate and degrade another. As noted, a recurrent and key question is what shifts matters from the level of fantasy to actual enactments of the sadistic sexual fantasies. A second question that applies to the subgroup of those who act on their fantasies is what shifts matters further into their becoming a sexual murderer. In between the fantasies and murder are a host of fantasies and activities in which sadistic behavior may occur in a legal or illegal context. Sexual homicides, in the sense of lust murders, are seen as having predisposing sexually sadistic fantasies that involve a sexually arousing component. The paramount feature is the persistent pattern of sexual arousal connected with images of pain and suffering inflicted on someone under the individual's control. However, the fantasies of pain and suffering need not have been present in their final form for years.

Dietz et al.'s study of 30 sexual sadistic criminals in the files of the National Center for the Analysis of Violent Crime revealed that 22 of the subjects were known to have murdered.[5] In fact, there were 187 murder victims, with five men responsible for 122 of the murders. Seventeen of the men were suspected of being serial killers. The ultimate cause of death could be established for 130 of the victims: 61% died by asphyxiation, whether through ligature manual strangulation, hanging, or suffocation; only 25% were killed by a gunshot wound. In the serial killings, there was usually an inconsistency in how the different victims were killed. However, even though only 3% of the victims died from a beating, 60% had been beaten before death. Fifty-seven percent of the perpetrators victimized only adults, whereas 43% victimized children.

Sexually sadistic individuals have some peculiar characteristics that accompany their offenses, including homicides when they occur. Details about their individual fantasies involving torture or arousing sadistic fantasies is important in trying to connect their thoughts with the acts of killing. Some of them engaged in what was referred to by Dietz et al. as excessive driving, in which they would drive long distances with a lack of any clear goal and then abruptly change direction or circle back. This behavior seemed to portray their need to feel free to do as they wished in contrast to the compulsive need to dominate and control others.

These individuals exhibited a type of pathological development in the quest for autonomy. Their fascination with police activities and paraphernalia similarly corresponded to their power needs and identifications. Before being killed, the victims may have been held captive for varying lengths of time to allow the perpetrator to exert further control on them or to inflict more pain and suffering. Victims may have been told to utter certain phrases to correspond to the killer's fantasies. Personal belongings of the victims might have been kept as trophies or souvenirs to signify conquests or to use at other times in recreating states of sexual arousal. This is congruent with 53% of the sexually sadistic offenders retaining records of their crimes, such as drawings, photographs, electronic recordings, or the victim's bones. Such practices suggest an unemotional, detached type of perpetrator who lacks empathy with other human beings. The narcissistic absorption would be seen as part of the psychopathy of the perpetrators.

The Case of David Berkowitz

The profile of one well-publicized sexual killer—Son of Sam—may be instructive at this point. Son of Sam was an individual who left notes signed with this appellation, seemingly either to challenge or baffle the police. Abrahamson, a New York psychiatrist, had the opportunity to investigate this killer over 4 years.[6] The case raised many issues that are still under discussion. Although eight young women were shot and killed in a year's time, none were sexually attacked as such. A sexual motive to the killings was hypothesized from the context of these shootings, in which many of the victims were in parked cars with their boyfriends at night. Some of the males were shot and killed as well. It was clear that these were a serial type of killing, but it could not be automatically inferred that these were necessarily sexual killings as distinguished from the killer's acting out of sexualized fantasies and conflicts. The killer was arrested shortly after the eighth killing and was revealed to be a 24-year-old male named David Berkowitz. He had given himself away by writing threatening letters to those who annoyed him. One note was to a neighbor whose barking dog upset him; he eventually killed the dog. Another letter to a neighbor referred to demons and the threat that he would light a fire outside the neighbor's door. Setting fires in old buildings or cars or rubbish heaps appealed to Berkowitz, and such arsonistic acts sometimes preceded the murders.

Berkowitz revealed a troubled childhood in which he had been adopted. Throughout his childhood he remained close to his mother, who indulged him, but he was resented by his father. When he was age 15 years, a major trauma occurred when his mother died of cancer. At that time, he became depressed. When the father remarried, there was a further estrangement between them. While in the U.S. Army, Berkowitz got into trouble with the authority structure. He later tried joining a fundamentalist religious group. His sexual views were strict, viewing sex outside marriage as a serious sin; however, he masturbated several times daily and remained shy of women.

A search for his biological parents upset Berkowitz even more. His mother was revealed as having been the mistress of a married man who had died, but most disturbing to him was that his mother had kept a daughter although she put him up for adoption. He described experiencing feelings of rejection and humiliation following this news, both of which were seen as the basis for a revenge type of killing. Berkowitz's first attempt at killing, when he stabbed a woman, failed. Later he planned to carry out the killings with guns. The process of seeking out young women, as if he were involved in a hunt, gave him an emotional high. After a shooting, he would return to his seemingly normal pattern of existence, such as going to work the next morning. At his trial, the psychiatric opinions differed between those who saw him as psychotic and driven by demons to commit violent acts versus those who saw the demons simply as a way of his expressing a bad side of himself. He eventually pled guilty to the killings and was sentenced to 547 years in prison.

■ Dismemberment Cases

Sexual killings need not be heterosexual in nature.

The Case of Dennis Nilsen

Dennis Nilsen was a homosexual government employee in London who killed at least 15 young males over a 4-year period ending in 1983.[7] The victims were mainly boys he would pick up in bars or on the street and who were under the influence of alcohol. He would offer them a place to sleep and subsequently strangle them. He would then dismember their bodies and dispose of them by putting some parts in garbage bins, burying other parts in gardens, and burning other parts. Later he boiled his victims' flesh and flushed it down a toilet. This eventually blocked the sewage system; sewer workers eventually found the human flesh. Based on his writings found after he was arrested, in which he described how attractive he found the bodies of dead young men, such as "the limpness of the movable parts . . . the texture of dead, cold skin to the touch," it was clear he had necrophilic interests.[8]

There is a striking similarity in the Nilsen case to one which I had the opportunity to evaluate in a legal setting after a man had been charged with the murder of his wife.[9] He had strangled her and dismembered her body and had begun to flush parts of her body down the garbage disposal. When it eventually became plugged, he had to stop. All of the dismemberment was carried out after the strangulation, in which trips were made from the bedroom where the killing had occurred and the kitchen where the garbage disposal was located. His mother, who lived with the couple, sat in the living room throughout all of these proceedings and said nothing. She was later charged as an accessory to the crime and convicted. He denied any previous sexual assaults or dismemberments.

The Case of Jeffrey Dahmer

The case of Jeffrey Dahmer in Milwaukee fits many of these behaviors as well.[10] Dahmer was charged with 13 counts of first-degree intentional homicide and two counts of first-degree murder after he confessed to killing 17 men. He was reported as having made the confession in a spirit of remorse and not in any spirit of bravado or satisfaction. Dahmer would kill his victim, undress and caress the dead body which he now possessed, and masturbate. He would then dispose of the corpses very quickly by using an electric saw and acid baths. However, he boiled the heads and saved several of them. The jury had trouble with the fact that Dahmer did not seem to enjoy torturing his victims while they were alive but obtained pleasure only when they were dead, a form of necrophilia.

Six years before his arrest for the homicides, Dahmer had been charged with disorderly conduct for exposing himself to children. He was found guilty and placed on a year's probation. Two years later he picked up a Laotian boy to pose for photographs, gave him a drink laced with a sleeping potion, and then fondled him. At the time he was charged with second-degree sexual assault and enticement of a child for immoral purposes and sentenced to 8 years in prison, but, after expressing contrition, the sentence was reduced to 1 year's detention with 5 years' probation. He was then to receive psychological treatment to deal with his sexual confusion and alcohol dependence.

Neighbors had seen Dahmer as a well-mannered, polite boy who kept to himself. At age 4 years, he had had a double hernia operation and suffered great pain, which he remembered all his life gave him the feeling that his genitals had been cut off. A high school teacher saw him as solemn and depressed. As a boy, he would kill squirrels and rabbits, skin and boil them, and preserve their heads for secret rites.[11] Colleagues at work and those who knew him in the Army described how he would become a dramatically changed, aggressive man when he became intoxicated. A 6.5-year period existed between his first killing and the second, but thereafter he began the pattern of serial sexual killings. Again, a significant clinical question is what permits these patterns to stay in check over many years, and what then promotes the beginning of a compulsive pattern of killing.

■ Children as Victims of Sexual Killings

Child sexual murders, which may be of a heterosexual nature, homosexual nature, or a mixture of both, are a topic in their own right.

Again, the same types of killings exist as with regard to adult victims: a sexual act may have taken place and the killing could have occurred in the context of the sexual act; the killing may have taken place to prevent a later discovery of the sexual acts themselves; or the killing could have been part of a planned act of lust killing. A distinction should be made between victims of a prepubertal age versus adolescents. Young children are chosen because they are seen as more vulnerable to being lured away and are therefore more helpless. Adolescent victims may come from a troubled family background and wander around the country, perhaps becoming caught up in a shiftless style of life in major metropolitan areas. Although some of these adolescents are reported missing, not all are. In contrast, young children are almost always reported missing, but some are never heard from again and may become victims of this type of sexual murder.

The moors murders in England achieved great publicity at the time when Ian Brady and his female lover tortured and killed several children and then buried them on the moors.[12] The perpetrators were eventually arrested and tried for the murders of a girl age 10 years and two boys ages 12 and 17 years, although it was felt that they may have been responsible for the disappearance of various other missing children.

Patterns cannot always be assumed to be fixed in nature, as is seen in the following case example.

Case Example

A 19-year-old male college student was charged with the death of an 8-year-old girl. He had first lured her into the basement of the store where he worked, stunned her by hitting her with a hammer, and then placed her in a box and driven to his parents' home, where he lived in the basement. A day later he took the girl, still in the box, to his brother's apartment, which he was watching while his brother was on vacation. There he began to sexually explore the girl with his finger, including her vaginal and anal areas, while in the shower with her. He paid great attention to her cleanliness.

His explanation for the killing was that it occurred in the context of debating within himself whether he should take her to a police station and tell the police what happened versus trying to hide the evidence. When he opted for the latter, it meant she would have to die. He filled the bathtub with water and laid on top of the girl until she drowned. He reported experiencing no sexual excitement while killing her.

In this case, the perpetrator had developed a fantasy of holding someone captive 9 months earlier, and, for 6 months, the fantasy had involved holding an adult woman captive. The fantasy then began slowly to shift to a young girl. Various combinations of fantasies were used and would recur before the final one was chosen. He described experiencing shifting personality states with different accompanying moods. One was an angry and irritable self that came to the fore when his fantasies were of abduction in contrast to his normal self, which was manifest when he went to school or work and was seen as a pleasant person. In the past, he had told male companions that he had thoughts of killing people, but they saw him as only joking.

■ Psychodynamics of Sexual Murderers

Almost everyone who has studied or assessed sexual murderers is impressed by the role that fantasy has played in their lives with respect to the eventual killing. One perspective is to see these murderers as basically exhibiting the hallmarks of a perversion or paraphilia, leading to a lust murder. Many of the primitive and polymorphous fantasies of the perpetrator as a young child are fused into the murderous act. Although the resulting sexual killing may not be an enactment of the preexisting fantasies, it usually occurs because the urge to act on the fantasies in some form eventually breaks through the perpetrator's ego defenses, with diverse outcomes.

Use of Denial

A mixture of tender behavior with brutal imagery may be present in sexual killers, with the balance tipping from one extreme to the other from time to time. The use of denial is often mentioned in connection with sexual murderers, as it is with sexual offenders in general. Caution is needed here because denial is often used on different levels of explanation.[13] For example, when denial is conscious, it refers to an individual simply trying to deny the acts outright. Sometimes denial is used to mean taking a position that the behavior was something justified, such as the perpetrator being provoked into the act or feeling that he or she simply became "carried away" and went a bit too far. Denial may also be used as a form of excuse, such as being intoxicated or on drugs at the time the attack occurred.

These types of explanations, in which denial is prominent, are quite different from the type of unconscious denial mechanism that is present in the sexual murderer. The unconscious denial in this group is more in the nature of a splitting mechanism in which one part of the perpetrator becomes horrified at the gruesome act that has been committed. Some experts have conceptualized this as a subsequent acting out of past childhood traumatic situations in which a screen memory has taken the place of actual events. The idea of various types of traumatic acts from childhood emerging in a distorted form in the adult is congruent with current theories about the effects of childhood abuse and deprivation.[14] The unresolved question is why such earlier abuse leads to an outcome of a sexual homicide in only a few individuals when child abuse appears so much more prevalent. Perhaps if there were opportunities to study and treat these individuals over a prolonged period of time, more answers would be available.

Role of Fantasies

What has been confirmed by clinical observations on sexual killers is that they are not usually outright psychotic. They are more likely individuals who periodically become obsessed with their fantasies. In contrast to the majority of individuals who have such fantasies, something promotes these particular people to literally act out their preoccupation, although often with embellishments. At times other than at the enactment of a brutal type of homicide, they lead what appears to be a normal life, engaging in work and other daily living activities, so that no one else notices anything unusual. It is also significant that the fantasies may not be acted on for years, although, in retrospect, if one had the opportunity to have worked with these individuals before a homicide, indications of the types of instabilities seen in certain personality disturbances would probably have been present. A question is then whether perverse fantasies have been present in those with certain types of personality disorders, such as borderline or narcissistic, which become expansive over time. When the sexual murder takes place, it is seen as an enactment in the external world of the internal situation that has been brooded about in the unconscious for some time.[15] When these fantasies break out by mobilizing themselves into action in the external world, it is something like an explosion or what was described several decades ago by Wertham as a "catathymic crisis."[16]

Splitting

The part of the person that carries out the torture, mutilation, and killing is not completely repressed in the sense of a dissociated state. It can more accurately be described as a splitting of the personality, in which one part of the personality is in the ascendancy, such as the part that carries out the acts, while the other, acquiescing part observes the events. However, it is the joint participation of these selves that allows the events to be recalled. The perpetrating part of the self that carries out cruel and sadistic acts of torture may ultimately be seen as the good part of the self carrying out these acts on another who stands for a projected, evil part of the self. Another possibility is that the evil or bad part of one or more of these others is introjected so that this part is in control of the self. Quite rapid alternations can occur between these parts, which explain puzzling acts of kindness or tenderness that get mixed in with acts of brutality and eventually homicide. Hence, this could explain such puzzling phenomena as the sexual killer who takes great pains to make a victim comfortable while he later tortures him or her or even in the act of torture wants the victim comfortable on pillows, such as in the following case example.

Case Example

A young woman was kidnapped and taken to an isolated area of a park during the middle of the night. She was tied down and beaten with fists over the course of several hours. At one point, she was told that she was to be offered as a sacrifice. The perpetrator then began cutting off her lower leg with a knife in an effort to remove her ankle.

Part way through the amputation, before any permanent damage had been sustained, he stopped in the middle of her screams and began to feel sorry for her. He proceeded to untie her and wrapped her in a blanket, expressing concern that she might be cold, and drove her to the emergency room of a hospital. After carrying her into the hospital and placing her in a wheelchair, he walked out. An alert nurse, sensing something was strange, copied down his license plate, which led to his later apprehension.

A variation of the splitting process occurs when certain aspects of the self are disowned or disavowed. An image of the potential victim to be selected emerges in the fantasy, which may initially be vague. For example, the perpetrator may first focus on the image of a young woman, then shift to the image of an older woman.

In other cases, the victim eventually selected is unknown and emerges on some chance basis of convenience, even though the fantasy and preoccupation with selecting such a victim may have been present for months or years. On occasion, the full fantasy has not been played out beforehand. For example, a child may be selected to be the projected depository for the hate, envy, and other feelings being experienced within the perpetrator; thus, later acts of torture or killing that child allows the perpetrator to permanently severe the bad aspects of the self from the individual. Or in the case cited above of the 19-year-old man who kidnapped the 8-year-old girl, the perpetrator's fantasy centered on knocking a girl unconscious by hitting her beforehand and then holding her captive for an indefinite time and engaging in sexual acts with her. The fantasy involved thoughts of treating her kindly when she was held as a captive, perhaps as a kind parent would, such as giving her a better home, food, and clothing than her own family had provided. At one point, the perpetrator tried out the fantasy.

It is this constant potential to shift out of this kind, nurturing role and allow another aspect of the self to become dominant that makes these situations so precarious. One of the disturbing things about these fantasies and enactments is that they serve complicated defensive and adaptive functions in which diverse types of psychopathology are present. Sometimes the fantasies may serve the function of keeping the person integrated and binding aggression.[17]

Dual aspects of cruel treatment mingled with compassionate concern are not confined to sexual homicides. They simply reflect the process of splitting. However, alternations between compassion and cruelty are significant clinical findings when working with any person who has paraphiliac problems. The potential for putting into another person the good or bad aspects of the self via a projective identification mechanism holds the potential for a miscarriage in either direction. The good self may be as likely a candidate for riddance as the bad self. Similarly, both homicidal and suicidal impulses may be simultaneously present. In the following case example, the interplay between the good and bad self is seen:

Case Example

While holding a woman captive who was tied in a chair, the perpetrator spent time washing her feet while crying along with her. He later recalled he was crying about her upcoming death, but at the same time did not want to hurt her. Because there was no way to kill her without hurting her, he could only undo the upcoming acts of molesting and killing up to a certain point by acting as her servant and joining her in crying. When these "reparations" ceased to be successful, a crisis point was reached and a homicidal act occurred.

Acts of cruelty to animals, including killing, may similarly be enacted in such a framework. If a pet is killed or tortured, a severe depression may later emerge accompanied by belated attempts at expiation.

Summary of Applicable Psychodynamic Hypotheses

Apart from innate aggressive tendencies that can fuse with the sexual, and which may vary biologically from person to person, there are some psychodynamic hypotheses that can be offered about the sexual murderer based on current knowledge. The following are summary points of these hypotheses:

1. In most cases, the victim is an unknown or anonymous person who is selected because of that fact.

2. The antecedents of a sexual homicide are present in quiescent form for a long period of time before a homicide occurs.

3. What finally precipitates a homicide is difficult to determine because homicides do not arise in the majority of those with sadistically perverse fantasies. In some cases, the incubated fantasy is primed and ready to be acted on whenever the right circumstances arise. In some cases, stalking behavior might have been involved in the fantasy, with multiple individuals being stalked who are unaware of being stalked or what might someday await them. Again, the prediction problem is present in not having the ability to predict if anything beyond stalking may ever occur. The research of Dietz on letters to celebrities and congressional representatives goes to the question of which individuals may be approached, but gives no predictive basis as to whether some type of attack might ever occur.[18,19]

4. Unresolved mixtures of love and hate exist in an amorphous state at different times in sexual killers; these mixtures are more characteristic of the mental life of a young child.

5. Themes of revenge and envy may become prominent as a danger period of action is approached.

6. The victim selected is often an innocent scapegoat for these tempestuous and unresolved feelings.

7. Acts of kindness and reparation may be carried out simultaneously with those of the utmost cruelty.

8. A displacement onto the victim of frightening internal images takes place, which seems to initiate destructive impulses.

9. Although sadomasochism is an essential part of normal sexual functioning, it can also present as a perversion. For those who attempt or commit a sexual murder, the behavior extends beyond the restricted perverse activities of simply deriving pleasure from inflicting or receiving pain as a condition for sexual gratification. A variety of different clinical types may be present in which aggressive components are acted out in the context of regression or disintegration of the superego, splitting, pathological grandiosity, and a loss of ego boundaries.[20]

10. Fetishistic objects may be used where ritualistic aspects accompany a sexual killing. The popular media often portray these as cult or

devil worship events, but they are more likely related to torturing the victims before death by use of instruments, electricity, beatings, burnings, or being tied up in painful positions.

11. In some cases, a childhood history of overt physical or sexual abuse may be present, but the lack of specificity for this finding mitigates it as a generalization. It is also possible to find terrifying images of authority figures that have been internalized from overindulgent parental figures.

12. Finally, without a resolution of these types of internalized conflicts and fantasies, serious questions remain about whether sexual killers will feel the need to repeat their violent behavior.

■ References

1. Ressler RK, Burgess AW, Douglas JE: Sexual Homicide: Patterns and Motives. Lexington, KY, Lexington Books, 1988

2. Gibson E, Klein S: Murder 1957–1968. Home Office Research Studies No. 3. London, HM Stationary Office, 1969

3. Brittain RP: The sadistic murderer. Med Sci Law 10:198–207, 1970

4. West DJ: Sexual Crimes and Confrontations. Brookfield, VT, Gower Publishing, 1987

5. Dietz PE, Hazelwood RR, Warren J: The sexually sadistic criminal and his offenses. Bull Am Acad Psychiatry Law 18:163–178, 1990

6. Abrahamson D: Confessions of Son of Sam. New York, Columbia University Press, 1985

7. McConnell B, Bence D: The Nilsen File. London, MacDonald-Future, 1983

8. Masters B: Killing for Company: The Case of Dennis Nilsen. London, Jonathan Cope, 1985

9. State v Hoffman, 328 NW2d 709, 1982

10. Masters B: The Shrine of Jeffrey Dahmer. London, Hodder & Stoughton, 1993

11. Norris J: Jeffrey Dahmer. London, Constable, 1993

12. Johnson PH: On Iniquity: Some Personal Reflections Arising Out of the Moors Murder Trial. London, Macmillan, 1967

13. Kennedy HG, Grubin OH: Patterns of denial in sex offenders. Psychol Med 22:191–196, 1992

14. Shengold L: Soul Murder. New Haven, CT, Yale University Press, 1989

15. Williams AH: The psychopathology and treatment of sexual murderers, in The Pathology and Treatment of Sexual Deviation. Edited by Rosen I. New York, Oxford University Press, 1964, pp 351–377

16. Wertham F: The Show of Violence. New York, Doubleday, 1949

17. Fogel GI: Perversions and Near-Perversions in Clinical Practice. New Haven, CT, Yale University Press, 1991

18. Dietz PE, Matthews DB, Van Duyne C, et al: Threatening and otherwise inappropriate letters to Hollywood celebrities. J Forensic Sci 36:185–209, 1991

19. Dietz PE, Matthews DB, Martel DA, et al: Threatening and otherwise inappropriate letters to members of the U.S. Congress. J Forensic Sci 36:1445–1468, 1991

20. Kernberg OF: Sadomasochism, sexual excitement, and perversion. Journal of the American Psychoanalytic Association 39:333–362, 1991

CHAPTER 11

Legal Versus Clinical Views on Homicide

Diagnosis and Voluntariness

In contrasting the viewpoints taken on homicide by psychiatry and the legal system, it must be realized that such a division is arbitrary to some extent and that diversities exist within each approach. For example, in both fields there is a dichotomy between those who take an academic perspective and those who are practitioners. The academic psychiatric critique is that legal jurisprudence has focused on arguing about philosophical questions that are at best of interest only to a small coterie of people. The questions are viewed as not having been resolved over the centuries and as, in fact, possibly not even being resolvable. In response, legal scholars may critique psychiatry as being devoid of understanding the necessity for philosophical and legal distinctions, an understanding they feel is necessary to grasp how a legal system functions in a society. These underpinnings pertain to opinions that, in an unacknowledged way, deal with matters such as free choice, lack of capacity, and the inability to understand the nature of an act, to name a few. These omissions are believed inherent in many psychiatric approaches, although the psychiatrists are often unaware of their absence.

On the practitioner side, the psychiatrist often finds that, in dealing with the perpetrator of a homicide, the attorney is often only seeking conclusory opinions, and that psychiatric opinions simply allow the plea bargaining process to begin or pressure to be brought on the other side for a resolution of the case. In turn, the practicing attorney finds the psychiatrist all too often just focuses on which psychiatric diagnosis to use and minimally concerned about understanding what the legal and societal dilemmas are for an individual who has committed a homicide and is charged with some degree of murder. The ultimate naïveté is seen in the position that a psychiatric opinion should be material in disposing of a case.

Whether the clinician has emphasized diagnostic classification or psychodynamic formulations, the contrast with the legal system is evident in both approaches. In this section, I exaggerate the contrast between the two viewpoints for heuristic purposes to illustrate the differences. In actual practice, the approaches may not be so diverse.

■ Issue 1: Societal Protection

Legal Perspective

The first and most striking difference is the emphasis the legal system places on the primary need to protect society and its citizens from threatening or dangerous people. Hence, the possibility of subsequent or repeated violence is seen as looming in all homicide cases unless a capital punishment is enacted, at which point it is believed total safety has been reached with regard to that particular individual. The theme of protection is preeminent over all other considerations. The presence of a mental disorder that may have possibly been operative in the crime, or what type of psychopathology may have contributed to a homicidal act, are both secondary considerations. The legal emphasis, then, does not emphasize the well-being of an individual or defendant. It is not even asked if the perpetrator acted on the basis of some type of derangement. Rather, the focus is a more utilitarian one of striving to maximize the safety of the larger group in a society against those who may or do commit acts of a homicidal nature.

Short of this utilitarian component, the legal emphasis might simply be seen as a perspective conforming to a theory of retributive justice, one of the traditional goals of criminal law. Only in more recent times has deterrence been considered as a goal. Rehabilitation was a late goal whose possible ascendancy was very short-lived; in fact, only sporadic, short-lived, and tenuous efforts at rehabilitation as a primary goal of the criminal justice system existed in the course of the twentieth century. The fragility of rehabilitation as a way of dealing with violent individuals is witnessed in its current downgrading and virtual eclipse. Correspondingly, the reemergence of just desserts as the guiding principle of jurisprudence in criminal law has changed how psychiatry participates in the process of dealing with homicidal people. This is seen most clearly in sentencing practices, which either reflect a shift to a determinate sentencing structure or simply view sentences as a version of "serving time" in which the perpetrator is prevented from committing further crimes. An accompanying assumption is that society is best served by the latter approach, with the presumption being that society's safety is better guaranteed by more frequent and longer incarcerations, if not executions. However, such an argument may be superfluous. It could simply be argued that just desserts demand such a solution.

Often it is felt there is no need to assess what happens to prisoners when they are released after many years of confinement for purely penal reasons. A long incarceration, or an execution, is morally justified as simply being the deserved punishment for an act of homicidal proportions. However, even in the emerging era of prolonged sentences for violent acts, the great majority of individuals are released after a set time period relative to their total sentence. Two issues are bypassed with equal frequency in assessing the effect of such confinement on the released perpetrators: their psychological and motivational status at the time of the homicide and their status at the time of their release. This begs the question as to whether the sources of their violent propensities have been dealt with at either end of the process. More profound is the question of whether one should care if they have been resolved, given that retributory ethics sees their imprisonment for the sake of removal from society as a just consequence of their actions.

Clinical Perspective

It may seem inordinately idealistic to say that a clinical perspective on the ultimate goals of dealing with homicidal individuals and community safety is needed. Yet, it could be argued, in the absence of confirmatory empirical data for either approach, that some type of preventive intervention to deal with the conflicts existing in individuals, their families, or in the social milieu that contributed to homicidal behavior might be a more optimal way to maximize community safety in the long run. The focus of such intervention would be to deal with the types of conflict that are present on a personal and environmental level. A more radical view would add that, without some fundamental changes occurring in the individuals and a social system that is seen as contributing to the vulnerability of individuals and groups toward violence, continued violence can be expected and predicted. Hence, efforts to increase societal protection only by way of increased lengths of incarceration may be doomed to failure.

■ Issue 2: Measuring Success of Attempts to Deal With Homicidal Individuals

A second major contrast between clinical and legal approaches to homicidal behavior is how each approach measures success in dealing with homicidal people and acts of homicide in a society.

Legal Perspective

Legal success is determined by low future rates of recidivism for such violence, irrespective of any other goals that might be pursued. However, because homicidal acts are usually connected with subsequent periods of long-term incarceration, it is difficult to evaluate what low recidivism actually means, given that a prisoner who had once committed a homicide is released at an older age after being incarcerated many years.

Studies in which comparisons are made between a low rate of subsequent reconvictions for homicides or other major assaultive crimes and other offenses have a built-in bias toward success and consequently possess little validity because the opportunity to recommit a homicide after a long incarceration is low. Those who have worked in the criminal justice system know that such data are relatively meaningless. Because adequate base rates for determining whether potential behavior has in fact been altered at all are lacking, it is likely that simply some chance variable, such as the passage of time, is the only variable in calculating recidivism rates. The only meaningful approach would be an empirical one in which released murderers are assessed at different follow-up periods and the results are compared. However, such empirical issues may be of little concern to those who believe such an approach may be interesting but unnecessary, given that their priority is community safety.

Defining success by reconviction rates also ignores diverse variables in a system, such as the different rates of apprehension and conviction or the impact of plea bargaining. Ultimately, success simply comes to mean incapacitating offenders for long periods of time in some custodial setting. Again, the underlying idea is that such an approach is either a just dessert for their behavior, or that more homicidal types of acts cannot be committed by these individuals within the community (except, perhaps, the prison community) while they are incarcerated. The neatness of such thinking, which amounts to incarcerating people for much of their adult life, ignores other criteria such as equity, notions of justice, the impact of incarceration on a prisoner's surviving family members (which often include children), and the attitudes of the general public. Such matters are considered interesting but somewhat irrelevant to the operational definition of success used in a retributionistic legal approach. For homicidal types of acts that do not result in a homicide, the fact that most of these people will be released after varying times is also ignored.

Clinical Perspective

In contrast to an approach stressing the supposed reduction of recidivism rates, a clinical viewpoint would define success in a different manner. It would inquire about a definition of success that goes beyond confinement. As a beginning, the conditions that gave rise to homicidal behavior would be considered. From a psychodynamic standpoint, there would have to be an attempt to resolve, or at least ameliorate, the conflicts that have existed either within an individual or between that individual and key people in his or her life. The underlying premise would be that such conflicts had something to do with what gave rise to such a murderous level of aggression in the first place. Thus, a clinical approach that emphasized interpersonal conflicts would require that these conflicts, whether within a group or in the individual's social environment, be detected and at least confronted. Success would be measured as the degree to which appropriate interventions lowered the individual's potential to continue behaving in the same way or, conversely, encouraged the individual to develop alternative ways of handling aggression.

A variety of theoretical stances could be taken for assessment purposes. From a behavioral approach, the goal would be to decrease violent behaviors. From a psychodynamic approach, emphasis would be added on resolving the conflicts predating the homicidal act and the subsequent impact such resolution would have on the individual's behavior. From a more idealized standpoint, the criteria for measuring success in either of these approaches would be whether attempts to actualize the potential of a person or help the individual attain some degree of emotional growth had been even partially successful. The difficulty in making such an assessment would be that, for it to be accurate, homicide rates for individuals who did not receive any intervention would have to be measured against those of a control group.

■ Issue 3: The Act Versus the Actor

Legal Perspective

A traditional distinction between the legal and clinical approaches to homicide has been the focus of the legal system on the act rather than on the actor. There is some merit in such an approach. Proponents of the legal approach are interested in the perpetrator's motives for a homicide only to the degree that intent can be proven. Intent is either used in the sense of common law case development or defined through the process of the legislative grading of offenses. Many of these legislative definitions of excuse, justification, and provocation have been based on the *Model Penal Code* of the American Law Institute.[1] The danger is that, by focusing excessively on the act by statutory analysis, the nature of criminal propensities within the individual are virtually ignored.

From a legal standpoint, the actor's mental state is subsumed under the concept of *mens rea* ("guilty mind"), which is used to distinguish degrees of culpability by degrees of pathological indifference to the societal norms. However, assessing mental culpability by the amorphous concept of recklessness on a continuum ranging from purposeful behavior to negligence not only ignores more complex intrapsychic conflicts but also ignores how acts are embedded in social situations. The following are some examples of the types of difficulties that arise when there is an excessive emphasis on the act:[2]

- Classifying driving while intoxicated that leads to a death as second-degree murder
- Assessing liability for murder based on corporate mistreatment of employees where intent has to be assessed in one or more individuals or for the "corporate entity"
- Minimizing the mental state required for homicide that can justify the death penalty

Other than when raised in the small number of insanity defense cases, motives and stresses on individual personality are customarily considered only at the point of sentencing after conviction or perhaps subsequent to imprisonment. Any interest in the actor as such is even less prominent under the determinate sentencing schemas that are now prevalent. Hence, the only time the perpetrator's motives are considered within the criminal justice system is when a defense of diminished responsibility allied to mental illness or insanity is used.

Clinical Perspective

In comparison, a clinical approach primarily examines the individual actor for a particular predisposing personality type of dysfunction or diagnosis. In this context, motives are seen as not simply a matter of curiosity, but as reflecting the personality traits and volitional aspects within an individual that need to be understood when a homicide occurs. When a broader inquiry into the mental state of a perpetrator is permitted, such as in a diminished responsibility jurisdiction, more tolerance is allowed for an inquiry into the actor as well as the act. Nor can it be assumed that the legal system is solely interested in the act. To determine *mens rea* requires an inquiry, at least in part, into the mind of the actor and a search for an intent or motive (which are not necessarily equivalent). It is inconceivable that the criminal law would operate in such a vacuum, and this is documented by the many references to such terms as premeditation, willfulness, knowledge, and recklessness of someone as well as his or her intentionality.

■ Issue 4: Normative (Legal) Versus Nonnormative (Psychiatric) Perspectives

A fourth contrast between the legal and clinical approaches has an academic overtone. Whereas criminal law is described as a normative enterprise, psychiatry is said to be amoral. In an oversimplified and exaggerated way, criminal law is seen as based on rule violations, whereas psychiatry's attitude toward rules is seen as laissez-faire. However, in practice, this seemingly neat theoretical distinction is largely invalid because normative, as well as moral, aspects are present in both clinical and legal approaches. For example, substantive criminal law obviously contains norms to evaluate transgressing behavior. Criteria had to evolve if a legal standard was to be created.

However, a psychiatric approach is not necessarily amoral. It has its own set of values as to what the norms of behavior should be. The difference is that a psychiatric approach does not confine itself to a "nothing but" assessment of violent behavior by the norms of preexisting criminal statutes. To do so would turn the psychiatrist into a quasi-prosecutor if not an outright moralist. As an example, an acquisitive or quite aggressive act may or may not reflect intrapsychic conflict. It could simply reflect an attempted solution to a problem—adaptive or maladaptive—in conjunction with certain personality traits or developmental arrests. Contrariwise, a psychiatric assessment could also see an acquisitive act as violative of community norms, which then requires the intervention of law enforcement agencies and the judicial system. There is always the hope that the more enlightened the criminal law system becomes, the more interested it becomes in how the human personality functions or malfunctions, rather than in merely categorizing by graded categories.

A less profound, but more prevalent, problem than homicide—that of lying or deception—illustrates the normative versus nonnormative arguments between the two approaches. A strictly ethical position might argue that actions violating the moral integrity of a person can never be justified. Presumably, this would mean that a difficult standard of absolute prohibition of lying or deceiving exists. The position hinges in part on the way prohibited acts are defined. For example, moral prohibition against killing per se does not extend to all types of killing. Self-defense is an example of killing that is accepted in almost all societies, as well as killings in war, for which, in fact, the killers may receive medals for their efforts. In an analogous manner, the prohibition against lying does not rule out all deception. Just as self-defense can involve aggression to the maximum point of killing when used to protect oneself against an aggressor, so it has been argued that an act of evasion or deception can justifiably be used to baffle a murderer or rapist to protect oneself or to aid in that person's apprehension.

Why lying or deception are unacceptable might be given different rationales from the legal and clinical perspectives. Customarily, they both would find the behavior undesirable. For example, the legal system might view lying as unacceptable because a system of justice is dependent on people telling the truth. Without such a foundation, or at least the perpetration of its mythology, the system is seen as totally unworkable. Psychiatry also views lying as unacceptable, but for different reasons. It raises questions about what the consequences of deception are in terms of the integrity of the self, as well as the effects of deception on human relationships. Not only are human relationships compromised by lying, but there is a distortion in the person's sense of reality.

Lying and deception have developmental components. In this context, children are studied to see how they begin to distinguish between truths and untruths. Part of the distinction lies in a cognitive ability to appraise reality and obey edicts to oneself not to lie. In more dynamic terms, this would be referred to as internalized prohibitions becoming operative.

There are also the descriptive approaches that have diagnostic significance when people engage in compulsive lying. For example, the symptom *pseudologia pathologica* is most often observed in those with hysteroid traits or borderline personality disorder diagnoses, and the question is how aware these personalities are of their distortions. In time, some of these people begin to lose their ability to distinguish truth from falsehood to varying degrees. Cases arise when someone has killed, or attempted to kill, another and subsequently totally denies the act. Because the act was witnessed by several people, at first blush one wonders if the person is either psychotic or an old-fashioned "cold-steel psychopath." Yet, on clinical evaluation it turns out he or she is neither, such as in the following case example.

Case Example

A woman stabbed her estranged husband several times in the parking lot outside his office. Afterwards, he managed to get to a nearby hospital and, following surgery, survived. His wife later appeared in the emergency room of the hospital saying her children told her their father was there. She flatly disclaimed any knowledge of the acts and alluded to the possibility he had done it as a move to help him get custody of their children and make it appear as though she had stabbed him.

There are individuals who lie, but deny they are lying, because they see their behavior as something that was not wrong. Alternatively, there are those with serious religious or political convictions who convince themselves that their lying was for a just cause, such as religious truth or the security of the country.

More profound clinical questions arise when people with paranoid delusional thought systems are not able to assess their beliefs that they are being persecuted by others and believe that they must act to protect themselves. On that basis, such distortions in truth may lead to violent actions. Is a person lying if they kill a loved one and firmly defend the act in the belief that it was a noble or altruistic act? What if similar thinking operates but in furtherance of sincerely held political convictions?

■ Issue 5: Explicit (Legal) Versus Vague (Psychiatric) Approaches

A fifth contrast between legal and clinical approaches is that criminal law relevant to homicide is a seemingly well-defined and explicit viewpoint, whereas clinical approaches to dealing with violent people is seemingly vague. The supposed definitiveness in legal approaches is exemplified in the criminal codes that define crimes in terms of the degree of a homicide based on factors such as premeditation, intent, negligence, reckless behavior, and the other factors discussed above. These amorphous distinctions are presumed to permeate into the public arena to allow citizens to make rational decisions about the consequences of their behavior. Supposedly, people can then know where they stand if they are contemplating a homicide or similarly violent act.

This is a position similar to the rational choice model advocated by some criminologists.[3] In a vastly abbreviated form, the rational choice model holds that people choose to commit crimes to satisfy certain commonplace needs rather than because they were driven by compelling internalized forces. The choice to act is viewed as requiring a different analysis for different crimes; consequently, crime specificity is a primary factor in the application of this theory. The costs, benefits, and opportunities vary with the different offenses. For a homicide, a series of distinctions would be made, ranging from the initial steps toward a homicide on to the culminating act. The actor's final choice would not necessarily be predicated on his or her having adequate information, but on whatever information he or she had, thereby implying a degree of limited rationality.

Such presumed rationality often flies in the face of reality. Legal terms and concepts may be at least as vague as any in the clinical realm, especially in their application to individual cases. Judicial opinions are not likely to provide clarity in delineating their nature. In fact, if all the legal codes and judicial rulings were crystal clear, there would be far fewer contested cases and little need for the endless stream of appellate rulings. Anything that deals with the vagaries of human behavior, be it in a clinical or legal context, necessarily has much attendant vagueness, even within the strict realm of legal concepts. For example, consider the vagueness inherent in discussions about the law regarding attempts at a homicide or the conceptual quagmire of legal and philosophical confusion about a conspiracy to commit a murder. Even though there are many difficulties inherent in determining a murderer's intent at the time of action, this remains a key element in bringing legal charges against murderers and deciding what type of plea bargaining might develop.

■ Issue 6: Formal Functions of Legal Versus Psychiatric System

In this next section, I contrast the formal functions of a legal system with the functions implicit in psychiatric approaches to a person who is homicidal or who has committed a homicide.

Definitions of Social Relationships

A primary formal function required in a legal system is a definition of relationships among the members of that society, whether a given individual, social group, or political entity is the focus. Within this framework, one function of a legal system is to define what activities will be permitted or not. The goal is to maintain an integration among the activities of people within that society.

Clinical approaches also require definitions. However, the definitions of the relationships among people within a certain group (e.g., a family, a broader social unit) are for different purposes. One primary purpose may be to control exploitative activities that can occur within the units. This model can then be extended to larger groups within a society, such as in social interactions, or to relationships within a group for someone who has deviated from the norms. Difficult cases become one of degree.

Legal systems need to deal with processes of ostracizing a deviator by way of the criminal process. In contrast, within the clinical approach, there is a type of social ostracism in which the person is labeled mentally disordered as a preferred explanation for the behavior, which also has an alternative mode of disposition.

Acceptable Levels of Aggression

A second formal function in a legal system is setting limits on how much open aggression a given society will tolerate at a given time. In this sense, the legal system is always directed toward the maintenance of law and order. However, it does not provide a way of allocating authority, or of determining who can exercise physical coercion on others, within a group. Some groups, such as the police or judges, are given the right or privilege to resort to physical coercion on others within certain set rules. Sanctions can be used in different ways to achieve particular social ends by coercive measures.

It is not that the field of psychiatry lacks an interest in how individuals display their naked aggression, be this in the violent form of committing a homicide or by one of the subtler means of power being used to coerce and manipulate others in interpersonal contexts. Its interest is rather in the diverse manifestations of aggression and the ego defenses present. Although the rules of interpersonal relationships do not have the same cogency and force of authority as those operating in a legal system, certain people frequently play out the game of controlling other people or groups. Coercive games of any type always carry the potential to go awry and lead to personal violence.

Mechanisms for Dealing With Violent People

A third formal function in a legal system is confronting and dealing with troublesome people in a society. One of the troubled groups includes those who commit a homicide. Certainly clinicians are interested in these troublesome people as well, but their interest primarily centers on obtaining adequate and valid diagnoses and treatment. With respect to treatment goals, psychiatry tries to address the conflicts that give these people trouble. It does this by addressing the capacities of these troubled people to live, work, and gain some gratifications in their lives and how these capacities have become impaired. Clinicians emphasize that their route of dealing with troublesome people is via treatment rather than by what appear to be chance factors. In contract, vague legal systems of assessing reckless or wanton behavior—either for the purpose of bringing legal charges or for fitting a person into a sentencing grid—seem, at best, like attempts to be pseudoscientific and, at worst, the manifestation of a politicized agenda. Explanations are given for an individual's behavior to determine the whys and wherefores, and how the effect of such an accumulation of unresolved conflict may lead to violent endpoints.

Redefining Relationships in Accordance With Changing Conditions

The legal system formally attempts to redefine and clarify relationships between individuals and groups under given social conditions that may be in a state of flux. Yet psychiatry may be attempting to do the same thing. In that sense, they are both required to adapt to change, and neither may be too successful at it. Such changes occur not only in family relationships but as an inherent part of development where individuals have to come to terms with a broader societal framework that impinges on them. An individual is expected to cope with many changes that may be biological and occur at critical developmental points. Other periods of flux interact with social and psychological variables at crisis points (e.g., graduating from college, entering marriage, dissolving a marriage, menopause, losing a loved one to death, aging). These social variables can lessen the resistance to a major mental illness and, in that manner, heighten an individual's vulnerability to violence.[4] There is also the need to deal with the ever-changing situations in people's lives, such as shifting jobs, economic changes, war, and the resurrection of old conflicts that periodically recur and continue to give trouble during the course of a life span. All of these stressful possibilities may require redefining relationships among people, and they can heighten stress and conflict of all types.

Interestingly, whereas the legal system derives its working principles by way of postulates developed from the past, as influenced by a particular culture, psychiatry has its own way of being preoccupied with the past. Psychiatry's concern with people is in terms of the ongoing influences of past events on them throughout their lives. Ultimately, it can be seen that legal, as well as psychiatric, approaches need to focus on the frustrations of individuals and their manner of response. How frustrations affect their relationships with others is often the key to homicides.

It may be desirable, albeit too idealistic, to think that relationships can be defined primarily in terms of rights and duties, privileges and responsibilities, and rights and powers of people. The history of human behavior is replete with innumerable examples that indicate the difficulties that arise if we simply limit ourselves to such attempted categorizations. When needed, a public resolution of the types of conflicts that emerge is one job of the legal system. Psychiatric expertise may be called into operation at points where something has gone awry in complex types of relationships. Ideally this is before they have become public, but it may be afterward, when the conflicts have been enacted in the public arena.

∎ The Use of Psychiatric Diagnoses in the Legal System

In addition to the judicial system and the other branches of government, many other disciplines have an interest in the subject of homicides. A question arises as to whether there is anything specific psychiatry can contribute to the problem of homicide.

Psychiatry has a long history of emphasizing that a valid diagnosis is important. Yet, some would question whether it matters if a diagnosis is made in homicide cases. Many articles and books have been written about diverse types of killings without any references to psychiatric assessment or diagnoses of the perpetrators whatsoever. Similarly, most homicide trials may take place without any reference to the psychiatric status of the perpetrator.

Diagnostic Labeling Versus
In-Depth Psychiatric Assessment

Some criticize limiting psychiatric contributions to merely providing a DSM-IV diagnosis.[5] Even within the confines of clinical work on homicide, it is surprising how much emphasis is placed simply on addressing the issue of whether the accused is psychotic or not, without appreciating the multiplicity of factors that overlap in diverse diagnoses. Discussions may wander off into specific legal or social contexts of the act, thereby ignoring psychiatry's understanding of causation, experience, classification, and therapy.[6] Unfortunately, such omissions are present in most reports to courts and attorneys in the assessments of homicidal defendants, and they are similarly witnessed in psychiatric testimony at trials. The need for careful thinking when applying psychiatric diagnoses to legal questions about homicides is clear. It is equally clear that an evaluation of individuals should never be viewed as complete simply when a descriptive diagnosis is rendered. There is also the principle that diagnoses are not diseases, which needs to be kept in mind in these situations.[7]

In any type of psychiatric assessment, it is implicit that a key variable is the capacity of the person to act, or to be able to refrain from acting, in certain ways. To exercise choice about one's behavior reflects a capacity to weigh alternative choices. Trying to reconstruct the mind of the murderer means that whoever is doing the reconstructing is almost always looking backward in time. (One exception would be if a researcher were attempting to assess a high-risk group and make predictions as to who might be subject to homicidal violence sometime in the future, or make predictions for some type of preventive assessment.) When legal questions are raised about an individual's mental state during the commission of a homicide, in the absence of guidelines, psychiatrists may take the liberty of expanding on their own ideas as to what the mental state of the person was. However, this historical state may or may not correlate with the person's existing or nonexisting incapacities.

A psychiatrist, analogous to other medical specialists, addresses the question of what limitations exist in the capacities of a given person and why they exist. In a broad sense, in every appraisal of an act of homicide, a moral question always lurks: whether, and to what degree, a person should and can be assessed as blameworthy. Of course, there are also clinical questions: Has a medical condition impinged on the capacity of a person? Has some adverse type of social situation been present? Have cumulative traumatic episodes been operative in the person's life in the prehomicidal period?

A common misconception among nonpsychiatric professionals, including some attorneys, is that the psychiatrist performs in a manner analogous to other medical specialists, in which the specialist (e.g., a surgeon, an internist) performs a procedure on a patient or assesses the patient's condition through inspection, palpation, or tests, after which the specialist arrives at a diagnosis. Apart from questions about the degree of validity of applying such thinking to other medical specialties, this approach bypasses the essential reasoning processes followed in psychiatrically assessing a patient. These processes include reviewing information from several sources, such as reports from places of employment, schools, and hospitals; medical histories; probation reports; statements of witnesses; psychological testing; investigatory reports by police officers and detectives; and so on. Only when the patient's reported signs and symptoms are put together with his or her social and historical background can the diagnostic impression, and possible incapacities contributing toward homicidal violence, be adequately assessed.

Limitations of a Diagnostic System in Legal Settings

In the situation of a person charged with a homicide, specific legal definitions operate apart from questions about the presence of syndromes, disorders, or diseases. Many times statutes or legal cases refer to the presence or absence of a mental disorder or disease without defining the terms. An insanity statute may require the presence of a mental disease and a "defect of reason" that may or may not be present in a particular mental disease. In addition, different jurisdictions have interpreted these medicolegal terms differently. Implicit in some definitions of mental disease may be the idea of limitations on the ability of a given individual to form an intent to carry out a certain act. The psychiatrist would then need to elaborate on what these limitations are. A common mistake encountered in the legal arena is to assume that every disorder listed in the DSM-IV is a disease. Even if a psychiatrist wants to take a position that a particular disorder is a disease, that disorder may not necessarily indicate an impairment in the capacity of a person to make choices. In and of itself, a diagnosis can never establish responsibility, or its lack, for a homicidal act.

When it comes to the junction between a clinical diagnosis and legal questions, confusion may be multiplied. First, the purpose of the diagnostic manuals, such as DSM-IV, is not to offer explanations for behavior. Only a few of the diagnostic categories are related to etiology, such as delirium, dementia, and amnestic and other cognitive disorders, which are presumed to be related to a medical condition and/or substance. Even with these few categories that imply an etiology, a particular behavior, such as homicide, is not explained without many additional intervening factors. To say that Mrs. Smith, who carries a diagnosis of a senile dementia, shot and killed her husband because she had dementia is an insufficient explanation at best. At its worst, it may also be a flatly erroneous opinion offered as a possible explanation.

For a particular diagnosis to be used as the explanation of a homicide, a step-by-step connection between the signs and symptoms of a particular diagnosis to the final act of a killing must be made. An explanation of homicide also means that various aspects of personality functioning must be assessed in terms of their functional capacities. These might be impaired in some areas of ego functioning but not in others. The dysfunctional areas, in turn, need assessment to determine whether, in fact, they are related to homicidal behavior. In making such an assessment, all sources of information need to be used. Even in legal cases not involving crimes as serious as homicide, examples of misattributions abound. As an example, a problem may arise with a series of lewd phone calls made in a neighborhood. The assumption may be that a rehabilitated former patient with a diagnosis of schizophrenic disorder is the culprit because, when he had once been in a psychotic state, he made threatening, although not lewd, calls to his family. If a homicide occurs, this type of slippery reasoning emerges in the search for a suspect; in fact, such thinking is pervasive in police investigative work. Another example is when a sexual homicide occurs in a neighborhood; in collecting suspects, the police gather not only the names of anyone who has ever committed a sex offense, but also those who have had a history of mental illness.

Diagnostic manuals have tried to make a disclaimer for their use in reaching legal conclusions by noting that the classification of mental disorders is simply a reflection of a consensus of current formulations in an evolving field of knowledge. They have referred to the clinical and scientific considerations involved in categorizing conditions as mental disorders as not being wholly relevant to legal judgments. Issues of responsibility, disability determination, and competency are not resolvable simply by having a diagnosis. On the other hand, if courts are to ask psychiatrists for their expert opinions about the state of mind of individuals who kill other people, it is unavoidable that some type of diagnostic nomenclature may be introduced.

Diagnosis provides a classification of mental disorders with criteria that certain people may meet. It is not an overall classification of people, nor does it offer precise boundaries for what is or what is not mentally disordered behavior. Such limitations further complicate the use of psychiatric nomenclature in legal work. The most a classification system can do is conceptualize a mental disorder as a clinically significant behavioral or psychological syndrome or pattern that is associated with pain, distress, disability, death, or loss of freedom, or that raises the possibility of such phenomena. Deviant behavior of a political, religious, or sexual nature, or conflicts that are primarily between individuals and their society, are not conceptualized as mental disorders. The goal is to conceptualize the behavior as reflecting a behavioral, psychological, or biological type of dysfunction.

Although a diagnostic manual may facilitate a classification to aid in the accumulation of scientific knowledge about a particular category, and perhaps the best related treatment, it does not address per se the question of capacities that have been mentioned as crucial to the operation of the legal system. However, the converse does not hold, in that if one starts with a basis for some incapacity, it presumptively raises questions about the possibility of a mental disorder contributing to such a state, but no more. Certain complaints about limitations on thinking may signify to a psychiatrist a differential diagnosis. For example, a retrospective history taken after a homicide, in which there have been antecedent behaviors of irritability, "flying off the handle," difficulties in relating to others at work or at home, brooding anger, and the expression of needs for vengeance and justice, may suggest that the significance of these behaviors be assessed from a psychiatric perspective. Similarly, specific past expressions of thoughts about carrying out a suicide or homicide indicate the need for assessment.

Listings of such complaints can only suggest possible descriptive diagnoses. For example, a limitation of functioning connected with a diagnosis of a bipolar or schizophrenic disorder may be suggested, but the diagnosis itself lacks specificity about what functions may be impaired. Achievement of specificity requires an individual assessment and determination. Many people carry ominous diagnoses of a psychotic disorder, yet they continue to function well in different areas of their lives. Such insights are as valid for schizophrenia as for any other diagnosis in which a false assumption is often made that an ominous-sounding diagnosis by itself carries an increased homicidal risk. Whether any such grouping, assuming valid diagnoses, carries such a risk is an empirical question. Sad to say, this question is only now beginning to receive the scientific scrutiny that has long been needed.[8]

What raises more complicated questions is the generic diagnostic grouping of personality disorders and their relationship to homicides. The diverse personality diagnoses cover a host of conditions, many of which are associated with unacceptable social behavior varying from impulsive acts to thefts to sexually conflicted acting out to being one of the factors contributing to a homicide. Even more troubling is when the diagnosis of posttraumatic stress disorder (PTSD) is offered as an explanation, or perhaps even as an exculpation, for homicidal violence (this issue has been discussed at length in Chapter 7). The ultimate expression of the posttraumatic situation is where the perpetrator of a homicide is portrayed as having been inadequate and helpless at some earlier point in his or her life, and the homicidal act is conceptualized as occurring because the person could see no other alternative available at that time except to destroy the person who was perceived as being the oppressor in his or her life. Such reasoning raises probing questions about individual responsibility. *Post hoc, ergo propter hoc* fallacious reasoning may surface. Whomever is retrospectively seen as having been the earlier oppressor is, after the homicide occurs, interpreted as the heretofore undisclosed cause of the violence. By this type of reasoning, it may be concluded that the person killed is the one actually responsible for the homicidal violence. The perpetrator would not be seen as responsible because of the preexisting trauma that had been inflicted on him or her. For example, an adolescent whose father had been beating him over a period of years is then seen as responding to the beatings when he kills his father at a later point.

A related problem is that, simply by virtue of applying a diagnostic label, the possibility for a harmful act may be suggested. The question becomes one of how far society and the legal system wish to go in accommodating the violent behavior of a person. Although the person may be idiosyncratically homicidal, it is treacherous to argue for a causal view that the person lacks the capacity to control his or her actions because of a particular diagnosis or because of some antecedent traumatic events.

The clinical error discussed above is sometimes referred to as the *diagnostic fallacy*. The fallacy consists of coming up with a diagnosis, whether valid or invalid, and then making a leap from it to an assumed explanation. The most frequent example occurs with some type of psychotic diagnosis, such as schizophrenia or bipolar affective disorder. For example, a presumption may operate that a proposed diagnosis, such as schizophrenia, paranoid type, by itself carries an obvious explanation as to why a killing took place. In fact, the diagnosis may not have any direct relevance to the killing any more than some other diagnosis might. In its crudest form, this chain of reasoning offers a conclusory opinion that someone has a schizophrenic diagnosis and, therefore, a causal relationship to an act of homicide exists. The result begs the question. Instead, what is needed is to examine the multiple factors that may be operating, rather than concluding that "Mr. Jones is schizophrenic, which is why he killed the intruder in his apartment building." One obvious possibility is that schizophrenic individuals may have burglars in their dwellings and may decide to shoot at them, just like any other citizen. Fallacious diagnostic thinking of this sort seems to arise more often in the context of hospital settings, where a diagnosis carries "excess baggage" in terms of seeming to explain all manner of things about a person, such as why the person does not eat

the food offered, objects to wearing a hospital gown, will not participate in group therapy, will not take medications, and so on.

■ Voluntariness

The question of the voluntariness of behavior in general is an old and
complex one for psychiatry and law and has preoccupied philosophers
over the centuries.[9] It has been debated for centuries without resolution, and recurs repeatedly with regard to some psychopathological
conditions. Contemporary psychiatrists and psychologists do not have
an answer to the free will problem anymore than do philosophers. The
most that can be argued is that certain types of mental disorders
impinge on the degree of freedom a person has about choosing between options. To conclude that a person has no choice in violent acts,
and that he or she had to kill someone, is an undemonstrable position.

The difficulty is that, when viewed from a clinical perspective, all
mental disorders, including the even broader area of conflicted behavior, can be seen to impinge on one's ability to make choices. The
striking example of a person with schizophrenia who has command
hallucinations from God to kill someone is one extreme. Individuals
with schizophrenia of the paranoid type, with delusional beliefs that
their thoughts can be read by others, can also be seen as having a
limitation on their choice options. Personality disorders offer enormous complexities in terms of assessing voluntariness. Factors such as
temperament, character, and traits limit the degrees of freedom. It is
interesting that, although clinicians often conclude that individuals
with a psychotic diagnosis have a compelled quality to their actions,
they are equally resistant to such possibilities for character problems,
particularly those related to a diagnosis of antisocial personality disorder. Instead, they more often assume that individuals with this personality disorder have total freedom of choice with respect to all rule
violations, including the most egregious self-destructive acts. Matters
become more complicated when individuals with such a diagnosis who
kill do so with some sense that the act was justified, even in a moral
sense.[10] The act of killing may be seen as a form of moral revenge for
someone having violated their rights or honor. Yet, in the absence of a

delusional system, the acts are interpreted quite differently.

When explanations for homicide are offered in terms of a causality-driven clinical model, the accompanying reasoning may more readily suggest exculpability for the person's acts. The fallacious leap from explanation to exculpation frequently operates in material presented in courtroom testimony. The converse also holds when a satisfactory causal explanation for a homicide is not available; the assumption may then be made that the act is either a rationally motivated act or that the killing is one without a motive, meaning it lacks an explanation. A person who kills another person at a gambling table when tempers flare is assumed to have acted out of anger; that person's action, however, is seen as a rational act, just like the myth of the cowboy heroes of the Old West who decided to draw and shoot during a card game.[11] However, if the killing seems to have an irrational quality, such as a person walking up to an unknown person on a street corner and plunging a knife in his or her back, the act is presumed to be irrational, and exculpatory modes of thinking quickly come into play.

The disciplines of psychiatry and psychology have no basis to partition motives for behavior into a rational or irrational dichotomy to assess responsibility. In fact, even to use such a dichotomy clouds the assessment of a person's functioning. For example, a young male wandering into his parents' bedroom and shooting them would seem irrational because most people do not behave that way. Yet, if logical reasons begin to be adduced for the behavior, the act may begin to seem more rational. Either way, a diagnosis per se cannot be the arbiter of culpability.

A caveat is needed when attempts are made to predict homicidal behavior from a particular diagnosis. The danger in such thinking is that it is made to seem as if the act flowed in a deterministic manner. Some researchers have attempted to show that certain diagnoses have a higher association with particular types of behavior than other diagnoses, such as depression with suicide or antisocial personality and bipolar disorders with higher risk-taking behavior. Therefore, questions arise about whether these diagnoses carry a greater likelihood of a homicide occurring. Again, analogical thinking is present in hypothesizing that, because suicide is self-destructive, then those who commit suicide also carry a greater propensity for other types of destructiveness. Are those who more easily violate norms or more often take risks more likely to kill as well? It could be argued analogously that certain states of despair, anger, and impulsivity give a person a greater disposition to act aggressively. Although such reasoning holds a degree of metaphorical appeal, great caution is needed when applying metaphors to prediction models in individual cases.

If valid actuarial data could be obtained, then correlations between diagnoses or certain traits and homicidal behavior could be made with higher probabilities. However, it would be treacherous to infer that any one member exhibiting such a diagnosis or set of traits would in fact behave in a homicidal manner. Yet that is exactly the position courts or legislatures have taken when they adopt rules that hold clinicians accountable, in retrospect, for making such predictions. Out of such thinking has come cases holding that clinicians have a duty to warn, or protect, others about the possibility of dangerous acts by patients. The *Tarasoff* case in California gave rise to a progeny of cases and legislation in this area.[12] Such treacherous thinking is also seen in the expanding area of malpractice cases against mental health professionals who are seen as having failed to predict a suicide or homicide; in those cases, it is alleged that the patient's standard of care was violated.[13] Although hindsight with respect to certain capacities in a person may be closer to 20-20, the diagnosis itself before a latent homicidal act can never be a highly reliable predictor as to a homicide; neither can the existence of certain traits in a personality.

One of the most difficult of all current areas is the burgeoning number of cases attributing a homicide to the past occurrence of some sexual or physical abuse (see discussion of PTSD model above and in Chapter 7). The original model focused on antecedent abuse in childhood but has now been extended to abuse occurring in adulthood as well, or to harassing behavior that may also be claimed to be a causal antecedent to the unavoidable outcome of an outburst of violence. The abuse or harassment is posited as the antecedent event that impairs the capacity of the person to control himself or herself in a subsequent act, such as murder of the abuser; hence, it is proposed that the subsequent act was not voluntary. It is interesting to note that, in DSM-IV, events such as simple bereavement, chronic illness, business losses, and marital conflict are not classified as traumas. These would, instead, be classified as factors that were leading toward an adjustment disorder diagnosis.

The stressor for the traumatic state in DSM-III-R was something markedly distressing to almost anyone and experienced with intense terror and helplessness. By the time of DSM-IV, it was expanded to a traumatic event in which a person experienced, witnessed, or was confronted with an event(s) that involved actual or threatened death or serious injury, or a threat to the physical integrity of the self or others, and a response thereto involving fear, helplessness, or horror. The symptoms involve reexperiencing the traumatic event, avoiding stimuli associated with the event, or experiencing a numbing of general responsiveness and increased arousal. A subsequent homicide is then explained with the reasoning that the previous trauma was of such a nature as to pose a serious threat to one's life or physical integrity. In the context of reexperiencing the traumatic event, the person may be reported as having recurrent dreams or intrusive recollections of the past event, or can enter dissociative states lasting from a few seconds to days in which the events are relived. Within this context, the person supposedly behaves as if experiencing the past traumatic event at the time of a killing. Among those changes the person experiences is a change in the degree of aggression felt, from increased irritability to fears of losing control.

In considering the connection between homicide and predating traumatic events or situations, one must consider that the great majority of people exposed to an event that is markedly distressing may show certain reactions for a brief period of time but no more. Subsequently, extreme degrees of responsiveness are present in only a small number who show the clinical picture of a PTSD.

When a homicide occurs in the absence of a psychosis, a host of possible diagnoses may be offered besides PTSD, such as multiple personality disorder, dissociative state, depersonalization, fugues, and a variety of what are claimed to be actions occurring in states of altered consciousness. In all of these, the implication is that the freedom to act otherwise has been lost. It could be argued that a spouse who kills her mate because she fears continued abuse from him is prevented to a degree in exercising free will and simply leaving the relationship because she fears her husband would find her later; to a woman in such a situation, killing might seem to be the only choice she could make to prevent her experiencing a harmful outcome.

When a person is involved in an emotionally painful relationship that is repetitious and not resolved over time, he or she may begin to think of homicide as the only solution. If this person is in therapy, the matter of exerting a choice may be stressed as part of the working-through process. Yet, once a homicide occurs, it is as though no choice had existed. The interpretation may then be offered that the person reexperienced an old situation in a dissociated state when he or she committed the homicide, as in the following case examples.

Case Example

A male is approached in a washroom by another man who is soliciting homosexual contact. The male claims that he became overpowered by fears from a previous, related situation and, feeling powerless, killed to protect himself. He later asserts that he had to kill the man because the scene in the washroom aroused the mental state he once had when he had been abused as an adolescent.

Note that in the above case, based on his own explanation, the man had sufficient control to make a choice of avoiding a state of powerlessness.

Case Example

A war veteran who had been exposed to killing in combat got into repeated fights in bars; these fights often, although not always, occurred when he was in an intoxicated state. He claimed that the fights occurred when he was reexperiencing the state as though he were once again engaged in combat.

These predicaments raise troubling questions. First is the validity of whatever diagnosis is used. Next is the difficulty in confirming what is alleged to have been the trauma. Although in some cases the trauma can be confirmed through outside evidence, in many cases it never can be. There is often an extreme degree of self-justification involved when such diagnoses are raised in court cases when they have not been diagnosed before a homicide, which is usually the case.

■ Conclusion: The Rationality of the Irrational

Where do these appraisals leave us with respect to psychiatric diagnosis, choice making, and acts of homicide? It means that rendering a valid and reliable diagnosis of a person is valuable, but has limitations in terms of explanations for homicides. Assuming that the components associated with a diagnosis can be confirmed as operating at the time of the homicidal act, what is still lacking is an explanation of how the mental impairments that were present actually contributed to the act of killing. The key is not only what past factors were operating in a particular person, and what was the person's disposition toward acting in a certain way, but what triggered the act of killing at a particular time. It ultimately comes down to the question of what psychological processes merged at the time of the homicidal act.

For some, such a formulation seems too rational. It implies that a person about to commit a homicide reflects, makes choices, and then carries out the act. In fact, this framework would neatly correspond to the legal definition of a premeditated first-degree type of murder. Although there are often rational components mixed in with the irrational in homicides, to understand an act beyond a superficial level requires much more than a determination whether or not someone could make a choice. It is not only that there are many perpetrators who cannot sincerely give a rational explanation for their acts, but there are also many who give sincere explanations that are not sufficient. In this setting, if the psychiatrist is to go beyond a layperson's level of explanation, he or she must look for impairments in personality functioning as well as unresolved conflicts and maladaptive solutions. Depending on how far one wishes to give license to hypotheses that cannot be disconfirmed, interpretations of behaviors are sometimes offered on a metaphysical level.

In the framework of ferreting out preexisting conflicts and maladaptive responses after a homicide occurs, the clinical investigator must seek a pattern of behavior that evolved into a homicide as a final outcome. A variety of choices may have been made by the person on such a pathway, with varying degrees of consciousness about the significance of each of these choices being operative at the time. I cite a few examples to illustrate this point.

In a pattern not uncommonly observed in dysfunctional marriages, the parties realize they have serious problems after an extended period of time has passed. They may have sought help from the usual variety of counseling services available and, perhaps, have had some separations. For a particular subset of couples, a sense of their being inextricably bound and not able to separate emerges.[14] Yet, they cannot continue to live with each other in any type of peaceful coexistence. In this setting, one of them kills the other—perhaps during an argument, while drinking excessively, or in the context of some comments being misinterpreted. The perpetrator is subsequently overcome with grief and remorse, and protests that he or she did not mean to kill his or her loved one. In this situation, an endless series of choices have actually been made by both parties without any conscious awareness that they were heading for a homicidal collision. It is not that they fully understood their motives and unconscious basis for some acts, but rather that they were aware of choices being made.

Another situation frequently arises in the context of a mentally ill person's laboring with some psychotic cognitive processes. This type of thinking manifests itself in regressive episodes where misinterpretations begin to be made, partial conclusions drawn, or an isolated event is seized on and given exaggerated significance. Such thinking is not always present, nor is it always fragmented. At times, it is kept in abeyance, perhaps when the person is maintained on appropriate medication. For a variety of reasons, many of these people elect to stop taking their medicine. In time, their cognitive disturbances recur and, on that basis, they begin to act on some of their misinterpretations, even to the point of a homicidal act. In these cases, questions arise about the mental capacity of these individuals given that they actually decided to stop taking the medication, which resulted in a series of other choices being made that ultimately resulted in a homicide.

In very few cases does anyone have more than a scintilla of knowledge about the long-range consequences of choices they are making. Some usually insist on a rational basis for all of their decisions. The more conflicted a person is in terms of psychological disturbances (e.g., having a gross impairment in his or her thinking, being disgruntled, having attentional problems, experiencing intrusive thoughts, making personalistic interpretations, having a lack of empathy with others' feelings, being preoccupied with needs for revenge, experiencing delusions, being caught in dejected moods with concomitant struggles), the greater is the predisposition to a violent outcome.

Events that involve individuals with such striking impairments in their functional capacities are the easier ones to reconstruct retrospectively. The more difficult situations are those in which individuals exhibit seeming rationality and intactness before a homicide, and perhaps afterward as well. It is not that they are attempting to feign being disturbed, but they have become convinced about the desirability, if not the necessity, of their behavior. One example is the person who harbors private delusional beliefs about a neighbor who is seen as somehow engaging in behavior harmful to him or her, and who, after years of such brooding, acts on that belief. The danger arises from processes in these individuals when they block out certain, more correct perceptions or deny that other interpretations are possible as to what the events in their environment mean.

What happens in these cases is similar to the following examples:

- A subtly paranoid individual denies information that would disconfirm inferences that are being made.
- A depressed patient becomes convinced that this is the worst of all possible worlds (turning *Candide* on its head) and, therefore, concludes that some action needs to be taken, perhaps to spare everyone more suffering.
- An obsessional person cannot stop focusing on how a realtor sold him a house, which he has concluded was not only overpriced but had many defects. Matters progress to brooding and depressive symptoms. After repeated efforts to gain relief from the realtor are rejected and his attorney tells him that his court case will come up in a matter of years, he feels that the only way to regain his sense of composure is to confront the realtor. The realtor is asked to sign a document that he will reimburse the buyer for a given amount of money. When he refuses to do so, the buyer shoots him.
- A helpless, senile individual gets word that his wife has devel-

oped a malignancy. He concludes that he wants to spare her any suffering. As a result, he immediately prepares to take action and shoots his wife.

- A manic patient with a bipolar disorder overcelebrates, becomes intoxicated, and proceeds to drive so recklessly that the car spins out of control onto a sidewalk and kills a pedestrian.

These examples all raise questions about the ongoing mental functioning of such people at the time of a homicide, and how the impairments involve cognition, perception, capacity to make choices, ego dominance over impulses, and volitional components to different degrees. In many of these cases, the person is distraught and suffering to some degree. Some remain convinced that they behaved in a rational manner given their situations. In some of these cases, psychiatrists would diagnose some type of psychotic disturbance, yet others have personality disorder disturbances, and some are comorbid. Although choices are still being made, these difficult cases raise profound questions about the choices not being made freely, or certainly not as freely as would someone without these handicaps. These examples raise fundamental issues and contrasts between the legal and psychiatric viewpoints when a killing occurs.

■ References

1. American Law Institute: Model Penal Code. §2.02. Philadelphia American Law Institute, 1962
2. Weisberg R: Criminal law, criminology, and the small world of legal scholars. University of Colorado Law Review 63:521–568, 1992
3. Cornish DB, Clarke RU (eds): The Reasoning Criminal: Rational Choice Perspectives on Offending. New York, Springer, 1986
4. Blugra D, Leff J (eds): Principles of Social Psychiatry. Oxford, UK, Blackwell Scientific Publications, 1993
5. American Psychiatric Association: Diagnostic and Statistical Manual of Mental Disorders, 4th Edition. Washington, DC, American Psychiatric Association, 1994
6. Littlewood R: Against pathology: the new psychiatry and its critics. Br J Psychiatry 159:696–702, 1991

7. Mindham RHS, Scadding JG, Cawley RH: Diagnoses are not diseases. Br J Psychiatry 161:686–691, 1992

8. Hodgins S (ed): Mental Disorder and Crime. Newbury Park, CA, Sage, 1993

9. Honderich T: How Free Are You? The Determinism Problem. New York, Oxford University Press, 1993

10. Katz J: Seductions of Crime. New York, Basic Books, 1989

11. Slotkin R: Gunfighter Nation: The Myth of the Frontier in Twentieth-Century America. New York, Harper, 1993

12. Tarasoff v Regents of the University of California, 17 Cal 3d 425, 551 P2d 334, 131 Cal Rptr 14, 1976

13. Beck JC (ed): Confidentiality Versus the Duty to Protect: Foreseeable Harm in the Practice of Psychiatry. Washington, DC, American Psychiatric Press, 1990

14. Cormier B: Depression and persistent criminality. Can J Psychiatry 11 (suppl):208–220, 1966

CHAPTER 12

Homicide in the Twenty-First Century

Where Knowledge Is Needed

To study violence only by way of the extreme examples of homicides may be too restrictive a concept for research purposes. In earlier chapters, I have noted many acts short of homicide that are equivalent in a psychiatric sense to the legal categories of attempted murder or aggravated assault. They not only involve the same external circumstances, but also the same intrapsychic factors. Further, diverse types of conflicts can lead to different types of violence in which one possible outcome could be a homicide. Conversely, a homicide can result from situations in which all the ingredients for a homicide seem lacking except the final end result. These are the types of acts that ordinarily do not result in a killing, yet a homicide results from a chance ingredient.

One major problem in understanding homicide is that efforts to study extreme violence have originated in several different disciplines. Although on the surface it would appear that the knowledge gained from all these perspectives would, when combined, give a more comprehensive, overall picture of homicide, in actuality there has been little integration of knowledge. Historically, homicide has been researched from legal and social perspectives; psychiatry's perspective is a relative newcomer. Researchers from the fields of physiology, biology, and the entire scope of the social sciences have all taken an increasing interest in homicidal violence.

Efforts to comprehend and develop research strategies for studying homicidal types of violence often seem to become so far extended that their focus becomes indistinguishable from a study of aggression. This blurring of the distinction between aggression and homicide can create confusion in interpreting results, given the wide variation that can exist between aggression per se and homicide.

■ Determining the Nature and Extent of Homicide in Contemporary Society

As mentioned in Chapter 1, one way to approach homicide is to study it using epidemiological methodology. However, criminologists have long been aware of the risks in using official statistics from diverse agencies as a basis for offering valid conclusions about the extent of any criminal behavior. This caveat also holds true for something as seemingly discrete as homicidal behavior. Homicidal behavior is more prevalent than the actual clearance rate of completed homicides, as noted in reports such as the *Uniform Crime Reports*. Some of the problems in obtaining valid statistical assessments on the incidence of homicidal violence are technical ones. In a perfect world of data collection, these obstacles could theoretically be overcome. However, there are other problems involving methodology that may not be solvable simply by improved techniques.

Reliance solely on law enforcement or legal classifications to assess homicidal behavior also proves insufficient. Part of the problem is that the focus is then on arrest rates or conviction rates and the different degrees of homicide that can be charged (e.g., first-degree murder, manslaughter). These approaches are insufficient from a research perspective—and from the community interest perspective—because it ignores many of the similar types of behavior that may not result in a homicide. As I have often noted in this book, the difference between a homicide and an aggravated assault is often a matter of an inch's variation in the path of a bullet. Hence, reliance on legal classifications for research is insufficient for understanding all the complexities of homicide. An expanded and reclassified approach would be needed, which would then raise a different set of problems. The nature and purpose of the research would determine whether such a reclassification, based on more than arrest and conviction rates and legal classifications, would be useful.

Almost all professional disciplines are interested in developing research strategies that could provide a more valid and reliable assessment of homicidal behavior than currently available. Different techniques have been used to compensate for existing deficits.

Self-Report Studies

One approach has been to use self-report studies, or victim surveys, in which reports are made about behaviors that could have resulted in a homicide or something close to it but did not. These are events that were never reported; why they were never officially reported, even as minor offenses, and how they might have been reported, are questions that need to be addressed. Clearly perpetrators are not motivated to report such incidents.

Another pervasive problem in studying homicidal violence from self-reports is that this type of violence has such a low base rate that it makes it seem impractical to use such methods. This handicap is specifically present when relying on surveys to seek out victims who could have been exposed to some level of homicidal violence.

Hospital Studies

One variation of this research strategy has been to use hospital data on individuals who have sustained various types of serious injuries in the course of altercations. A major limitation on these data is their unreliability in terms of being an accurate estimate of homicidal types of injuries. One area in which this type of data gathering has been helpful is in investigations of the incidence of physical abuse of children from early infancy through childhood. The goal has been to obtain a more reliable and broader estimate of the degree and kind of serious physical assaults that are perpetrated on children. In the early stages of this approach, assaults were classified solely on a medical basis, focusing on the type of physical injury received, without reference to etiology; this earlier system resembles the system used today for legal classifications of homicide. This hospital-based methodology could be extended to use data gathered from clinics and other health care facilities as well.

■ Victimology

The role of victims of homicide was originally studied within the framework of victim-induced homicides. This approach was later criticized as one that blames the victim. However, in the context of homicides occurring between intimates, it must be acknowledged that systemic behaviors in the relationship can give rise to homicidal behavior. Either party can often be seen as the perpetrator or the victim in the complex relationship that unfolds between two people, whether they be adults or an adult and a child.

Victims' roles in homicides need to be studied in greater depth than was done in the initial types of studies. In those earlier studies, events were simply portrayed in terms of victim provocation, involving one key person who later had an act of violence perpetrated against him or her. Although homicides can occur within relationships characterized to some degree as masochistic, certainly that does not sufficiently explain the complexities and possibilities inherent in the dynamic relationships between people where an unusual outcome such as a homicide results.

Another aspect of homicidal victimology research that requires more attention is clinical knowledge about the variety of interactions that may lead to violent outcomes between intimates. It is important to gain more knowledge about how some people seem to gravitate into a role of acting out violence in the complexities of their intimate personal relationships. If anything is known about relationships that have the potential to become violent, it is that neither party is a totally helpless individual in his or her interactions with others. Homicidal acts take place in the context of human interaction. It is also just as important to gain knowledge about why most people do not resort to violence in relationships, be they intimate or not. To address both of these questions, a multidisciplinary approach, rather than the segmented knowledge of one discipline, is crucial.

The context of an intimate relationship is really only one model of close human interaction that can lead to a homicide. Similar dynamics may operate in interactions with authority figures, such as larger or more physically powerful individuals, or those who are in authority over others, such as in workplace violence, or in interactions in which people provoke others they see as exerting control over them (e.g., the police). After studying the histories of individuals involved in these situations, a repetitious behavioral pattern appears in that they continually become involved in similar encounters that have the potential of turning into a homicide, with themselves as the victim. It can be fruitful to reconstruct what the consequences of their behavior have been in the past, and in the face of what factors those consequences rise to the level of their being seriously injured or killed.

Another area that needs investigation are those situations with the potential for erupting in a homicide in which a certain individual has played alternating roles at different times. Clinical work appears to indicate that some individuals actually alternate between the roles of victim and perpetrator. One phenomenon that needs to be examined is these people's past activities in which they have had violence directed against them, possibly by the person who later becomes their victim. These past activities often are found to have involved high-risk or illegal behavior, and include their threatening violence on others, such as threats of reprisal (either physical or social), or threatening some type of extortion regarding another's past violent actions. There may be a subsequent pattern of continued provocation, with the potential for the situation to become destabilized and evolve into violence. However, these are the types of clinical impressions that need empirical confirmation.

■ The Role of Instrumental Violence in Homicidal Violence

An operational viewpoint on homicide views such violence in terms of what is to be gained or achieved by the behavior. The gain in a homicidal type of assault is either the pleasure obtained in such an aggressive act or some type of retaliatory or self-protective mechanism. However, in some cases, such as a homicide taking place in the context of a robbery or rape, the explanation would be that killing was not the goal, but that it was simply instrumental to the main act. The initial goal was simply the burglary, but events got out of control so that the secondary violence of a homicide occurred. A derivative question then arises as to what are the key variables operating for events that seem to have "accidental" homicidal endings.

An instrumental model of homicide may only provide a partial explanation, at best. More evidence may be required to explain these types of human interactions (i.e., the homicides) than viewing them merely as being instrumental in achieving another end. On the other hand, attributing more elaborate motives (e.g., killing as a "release" of hatred, killing as incidental to some other criminal act) to people who express violence in this manner may be an inaccurate attribution. It also leaves unanswered questions about whether people carrying out other types of offenses, in which violence is instrumental, are not only unaware of the role that is being attributed to them, but the inferential processes for how a more complex set of motives is established, absent a type of intensive therapeutic investigation to unravel these complex questions. Some individuals would argue that the attribution of a role does not matter. Instead, they put forward the opinion that an individual's degree of conscious awareness regarding key variables (e.g., the degree of risk he or she is taking, the degree of force used in perpetrating a certain act, how a particular victim is selected) does indeed matter. However, to get into such specificity about the cognitive operations and motives of violent offenders on an instrumental level goes far beyond the obvious explanation offered in terms of their behavior simply being seen as instrumental to a main goal (e.g., a burglary). This does not mean that such research is not worth doing.

However it does mean that hypotheses need to go beyond the obvious operational explanation of the act serving some instrumental end. Whatever is learned about the instrumental aspects is then part of the overall story.

Some have suggested that instrumental models also may have application to studying the "legitimate" use of violence. Examples would be violence involving military personnel, violence in correctional facilities, or violence exhibited by police officers. In fact, the apotheosis of retribution—capital punishment—can be viewed as an instrumentalized type of violence that is not only legitimized but approved by a majority of the American public if we take as evidence that 37 American states have had their elected representatives enact death penalty legislation.[1] However, it is possible that such an inference is unwarranted. For example, in the United Kingdom the reverse occurred when 88% of public opinion polls were in favor of restoring the death penalty. However, 4 months later in 1994, the British House of Commons voted by a majority of 244 votes not to restore capital punishment for murder, and by a majority of 197 votes not to restore it even in the case of murdering a police officer.[2] In many of these situations, there is the assumption that extreme violence is an inherent, legitimate part of military or civil law-and-order occupations. This legitimacy model has also been applied to certain subcultural criminal groups, in which an analogy has been drawn between those groups and organizational groups in which violence is required to maintain discipline. The prime example is the consequences to someone who deviates within organized criminal groups by informing or cooperating with law enforcement agencies, such as in the Mafia. Even overzealous prosecutors may find their lives in danger.[3,4] It would be valuable to study these supposed situations in which violence is legitimized to discern what conditions must be present in order for homicidal acts to occur. One relevant question is the extent to which the justification of instrumental violence is seen as inherent in a role that promotes the use of violence. Such violence may, in turn, elicit counterviolence by the potential victims. Another question to be answered is what predisposing personality variables influence people to choose roles in which they may ultimately have to resort to extreme violence.

■ Social Meanings of Violence

Apart from the legal consequences, what particular social or moral meaning may an act of homicide have? This has been an important area for sociological investigation and philosophical speculation. The conceptual meaning of a homicide is often that determined simply by some type of official record keeping or the law enforcement process itself. However, the official meaning attributed to an act might be quite different from the meaning the act had for the perpetrator. To understand or explain such acts, it would be necessary to grasp the specific meaning of the homicidal act for the person performing it. Without this, explanations are likely to be at least inadequate or partially invalid.

Much research can be criticized for not seeking out the particular meaning of an act for the perpetrator. Worse yet, observers may rest content with the meaning given to homicidal acts by a particular agency that keeps official classifications, or by an agency whose job is social control. Too often the result is a set of stereotyped explanations that stifle further inquiry or offer rationalizations for the behavior in question.

The positivist approach, in which behavior is interpreted as being determined by outside circumstances, poses grave limitations for the researchers. However, research that would take into account the social meaning of particular acts would have to incorporate empirical as well as nonempirical approaches. For example, a preferred explanation could point out that an explanatory model might be viewed as causally adequate, yet have an insufficient level of meaning attached to it.

From a psychiatric viewpoint, taking account of the social meaning of an act is seen as necessary for research on extreme personal violence. In that sense, an examination of the social meaning of a homicide is an underlying necessity in any type of sociological research if it is to give cognizance to the psychiatric significance of the behavior. Joint psychiatric and sociological research on homicide—in which the construction of the social meaning of homicidal acts is addressed, along with the way people attempt to cope and make sense of their world via such constructions—is badly needed. There is something unsatisfactory in theorizing about violent behavior without making reference to the individuals involved and what meaning a particular act may have had for them.

Perceptions and motives that accompany the observed behavior are equally relevant. Although there have been detailed ethnographic studies of violence, what is needed is an attempt to forge a link between this type of work and more general theoretical constructs related to homicide. If that cannot be accomplished, the danger is that proposed explanations will be purely ad hoc or idiosyncratic. Theorists are aware of this dilemma, and they try to deal with it by resorting to approaches based on typing acts in terms of what meaning they seemed to have to the actor.

■ Social Control and Violence

The legalization of physical coercion and actual violence, as when used by the state to control or punish people perceived as deviant, is a process that has been going on throughout recorded history. However, the justification for such violence has never been sufficiently understood or adequately researched; it has simply been taken as a given.

The relationship between social control and the use of extreme violence is one of the single most important areas that cries out for further explanation. Social control is a very broad concept. Although part of this question has been examined by sociologists, there is a need for further investigation, such as into how individuals react when coercive power is exerted on them. The goal of such research is to elaborate on the distinction between what is described as legitimate force used to control others in contrast to the force connected with criminal violence. The question that should be addressed is whether there is a legitimate basis for the distinction and, if so, what validity such a distinction has. These questions are particularly germane to explanations put forward by state agencies that carry out social control via use of violence, such as when those authorities sanction a subgroup to carry out violence; for example, these groups could be set up for the purpose of regulating illicit drug distribution, setting up security units for those classified as dangerous in prisons, or acting as private security forces. The effects these approaches have on increasing the possibility of extreme violence by both the controllers and controllees needs careful investigation.

Relevant to this is how organizational changes may affect the perception of the enforcing agents in terms of their feeling a need to use increased force to achieve their mission. Different people may carry out these missions quite differently. A changed conceptualization of their role may mean that they start to perceive the nature of their interactions in such a way as to increase the probability of a homicidal act. If this occurs, it is more likely that those who see themselves as the recipients of such social control may strike out as a backlash because they perceive themselves to be potential victims of violence.

In this context, there is a need for more knowledge about the sociology of law, such as how law is used in society, and to integrate this knowledge with a psychiatric understanding of the dynamics of provocation. This would encompass investigating the legality of criminal violence carried out by agents of social control, how they perceive their mission, the origins of law about the use of violence, and how the processes of enactment of these laws influence their later application. Psychiatric input to these processes may well contribute to better understanding of confrontational types of violence and homicide.

■ Group Violence Leading to Killings

Attempts are often made to distinguish criminally motivated violent behavior from politically motivated violent behavior. It has also been argued that such a distinction is not totally valid. This does not mean that we should attribute a conscious intention to all so-called political activities that become violent. The fundamental position is that politics is one way of dealing with social conflicts in an effort to produce order. However, similar activities to secure such ends may also be criminal.

One implication is that it cannot be assumed that violent behavior should always be viewed as irrational. All too often, such an assumption is made when group violence occurs, particularly when accompanied by a homicide. Yet, violent acts that occur in a group setting often have great political or moral meaning for people. Whether the killings occurring between different ethnic and cultural groups are rational acts of patriotism designed to achieve legitimate ends or rather behavior that is closer to that engaged in by the criminal or insane mind is a debatable question. Perhaps that is why it is so difficult to understand, let alone stop, the killing occurring in the areas of Croatia, Bosnia, and Serbia. On a more specific level, homicides connected with assassinations or terrorism need psychiatric investigation and research. Some of these acts may be carried out based on long-smoldering hatred and needs for revenge that are important to understand in their own right but in distinction from acts more closely connected to the signs and symptoms of a mental illness. On a more specific level, homicides connected with assassinations or terrorism need psychiatric investigation and research in their own right.

Some violent situations can be described as "mob violence" that escalates and results in assaults and killings. The psychology of the mob is studied in the context of what different psychological and social factors coalesce with individual dynamics. The periodic eruption of these phenomena—in such diverse settings as sporting events, political rallies, and gang killings—are not understood in depth, even though they are often viewed as normative under the circumstances. Techniques for preventing group confrontations have worked only minimally. A related issue is some groups' social expectations that the way to solve problems is by direct confrontation and the avoidance of any type of compromise.

Another example of group violence is the slaughter of civilians carried out by military personnel. For some people, these acts of mass violence may be seen as instrumental to achieving a particular goal (e.g., fostering changes in society, punishing opponents, expressing deep feelings), and the perpetrators may be perfectly willing to pay the price that accompanies the commission of the crime. However, some of these individuals may also have varying degrees of psychopathology; it would be important to determine whether certain individuals who were carrying out the same act within the same agenda actually had quite different types of conflicts or personality traits. In this context, inquiry is needed about the social and political processes by which certain fostered behavior is defined as violent. The motives and consequences of using different definitions of violent acts is part of this.

Youth gangs, who ebb and flow in major American cities, may claim they are acting to foster a political agenda. Although this may be true for some, for others it is a rationalization for homicidal violence. Those who perpetrate mass killings or serial killings similarly need investigation on various levels (see discussion in Chapter 1).

■ Violent Individuals

The Predisposed Individual

A traditional and comfortable approach for psychiatrists researching homicidal violence is to focus on the individual perpetrators who have committed acts of violence. The focus may take either a neuropsychiatric or psychopathological direction in the search for factors that contribute to the personality structure of an individual. Apart from cases in which an insanity defense is raised with specific legal questions, the goal of such research is often to see what makes the person potentially vulnerable to commit homicidal types of violence. However, there may be an implicit assumption that previously violent individuals are the ones who later commit homicides, although this hypothesis has not been justified. Some individuals merely continue being violent in diverse ways, with a diminution in their violent behavior as they age.

Researchers who focus on social and environmental factors that contribute to violence often feel that clinicians overemphasize individual factors. The opposite type of criticism comes from those who feel that individual psychodynamic factors are too often ignored by those who compile sociological data. Many of these factors have been discussed in different chapters of this book and are simply noted here.

Researchers of homicidal individuals must necessarily acknowledge the diverse variables involved in those individuals' behavior. Some researchers have dealt with people's innate aggressiveness in an attempt to understand biological variables as a condition for the expression of violent aggressive impulses. Child development research has focused on the outcome of different child-rearing practices on aggressive behavior. However, to a great degree, the latter type of research has comprised more studies on minor types of aggressive displays than studies in which certain behaviors and traits are looked to for predictive significance for a person's later proneness to violent behavior. There is also the recurrent problem of the different socioeconomic statuses of families and what impact this has on types and kinds of aggressive behavior.

The Role of Punishment

The particular kind of punishment used in families is one variable that has been studied a good deal. Unfortunately, many of the studies comparing physical punishment with educational techniques as means of controlling behavior have focused on more minor types of overt aggression, such as behavior in classrooms, in contrast to serious assaultive violence. It is this latter outcome that needs to be studied to understand the relationship of punishment techniques to later homicidal types of behavior. The influence of disciplinary techniques with respect to the later occurrence of extreme violence is a very complex question. Long-range projections are also often fraught with low validity. A significant difference may exist between the conditions operating in experimental laboratory conditions in which punishment is administered in the form of mild electric shocks to humans or nonhuman species compared with the ways discipline is administered by parental figures.

Making any outcome predictions about a later homicide is quite precarious because of the multiplicity of variables that operate in homicidal situations and the relatively rare occurrence of homicide. The factor of living in a culture in which physical violence frequently occurs or is witnessed—directly or indirectly—cannot be ignored as having some influence on vulnerable people. The impact of the mass media and movies is now an inherent part of growing up in America. Often the histories of criminally violent juvenile and youthful offenders who eventually commit a homicidal act reveal that these individuals had been exposed to violence early in life. However, it would be precarious to suggest that the causal effects should be interpreted as linear. Much more specific longitudinal studies are needed to delineate the possible effects of these variables on an individual who later engages in homicidal behavior. Experiencing violence is also different than witnessing it. If experiments were run exposing children to witnessing violence in a laboratory setting, assuming it could be done ethically, it would still leave open many questions about the long-range effects of such viewing, particularly with respect to future homicides. Given the amount of serious violence in the United States, both experienced and witnessed, it would seem a safe conclusion that most of those exposed do not become that violent themselves or there would be even more homicides.

Physiological Variations

When discussing innate differences among individuals, the factor of conditioning that has promoted the expression of violence is often raised as a contributory variable. Arguments about the relative importance of such learning experiences versus the significance of physiological aberrations in the autonomic nervous system are currently impossible to resolve, primarily because these two kinds of variables interact to such a degree.[5]

For example, psychopathic individuals, or those clinically classified as having antisocial personality disorder, have been studied for different autonomic reactions, such as their lowered responses to certain kinds of stress or the difficulties in conditioning them for avoidance reactions. Along biological lines, the entire realm of genetic differences will play a prominent role in future research with this group. The possibility of seizure disorders or cerebral types of injuries—either prenatally or during the birth process—and infectious and traumatic processes are key antecedent variables in assessing a proneness to violence that will likely have a high research payoff. The theoretical framework is that such types of insults to young, developing humans predispose them to later difficulties in the control of aggression or to abnormal rage reactions of the episodic dyscontrol variety. The cyclicity of anger and rage in individuals with borderline personality disorder is just beginning to be understood in terms of these people's inherent instabilities and explosiveness.

Ego Functioning

As noted earlier, the basic approaches to the study of individuals who have committed some type of violent act is to focus either on their biological predispositions or preexisting psychodynamic conflicts. One hopes that this type of oversimplified dichotomy has had its day, for both approaches need to incorporate significant social variables in their explanatory models along with a study of ego functioning. Criticism of both approaches has largely been on methodological grounds because of difficulties in generalizing from one individual to another in ideographic approaches.

Nevertheless, the case history, or clinical assessment, approach can reveal immense details through gathering data on the developmental history and lifestyle of someone who has committed a homicidal act. It may reveal important information; for example, the types of intrapsychic conflicts operating and the psychological defenses that have failed, thus allowing the violent eruption of homicidal acts. What has contributed to the failure of defenses in such circumstances is a topic that also needs more detailed investigation. The failure of certain defenses with different types of killings, as correlated with different diagnoses, may prove quite fruitful.

Killings Without an Explanation

More bizarre types of killings, sometimes referred to as those lacking an explanation, call out for intense psychiatric scrutiny. These killings would include those that occur in the context of sexual encounters, random assaultive acts on unknown individuals that result in homicide, serial killings, mass acts of violence, and homicidal violence perpetrated on or by children. These unfortunate occurrences need to be studied to acquire knowledge about the propensities for such an outcome if they are to be better contained in the future. Acting out a delusional thought process that has been quiescent but then becomes activated in terms of taking a homicidal course merits investigation as to what factors finally tip the scales in these people compared with what allows the majority of people with such delusional beliefs not to take action.

Cases where an isolated and extreme violent act is committed by a person who, heretofore, had not shown any violent tendencies, is another group meriting research. A variation is the analogous situation where there is an eruption of violence under changed life circumstances. The most common is the person in a state of unresolved mourning who commits a homicide. Those who are in a state of severe depression are usually studied as suicidal possibilities, with homicide being ignored; this is a largely overlooked group in which these variables are missed.

Under military conditions, some soldiers may go beyond the norms of combat and begin to kill prisoners or civilians. A more refined version of this occurs when previously "normal," or at least nonviolent, individuals are working in a milieu, such as a prison or concentration camp, where they conform and adapt to the killing circumstances. Perhaps killings that occur in the context of being a guard or police officer are similar in that sanctions officially allow violence. Historical examples might be those who have functioned as hangmen or executioners. There is also the larger group who join in the activities as onlookers and receive some type of vicarious enjoyment from the activities, or those who silently acquiesce as passive participants, which is in effect a silent proxy. Related is the current onslaught in Africa, Asia, and Latin America from nationalist movements, ethnic rivalries, insurgent political groups, and regional conflicts in which civilians are the most frequent casualties.

Intoxicated States

Drug use and alcohol intoxication are well known to be contributing factors to severe violence. However, why they operate more prominently in some people to induce violent acts is the question. The usual explanation given for drugs and alcohol is that they facilitate violence by lowering the threshold for responding to provocation. Yet, this is more like stating the obvious. The acts may occur in a social milieu in which defenses have already been lowered. Indications are that things may not be that straightforward. For one, subtleties exist in terms of the effects of chronic drug and alcohol usage. For others, the violent behavior can accompany withdrawal syndromes when usage ceases. Diverse factors need to be addressed such as individual predispositions to the effects of alcohol or drugs, and the long-term effects of different combinations of drugs and alcohol that can contribute to violent acts. In essence, the role of drugs or alcohol as a contributory factor to a homicide involves a complex interaction between the pharmacological properties of the substance, the different individual reactions, and the precise social circumstances in which the act occurs. In addition, there is always the possible complicating factor of the presence of a comorbid disorder.

■ Violent Situations

Escalating Encounters

Considering situations shifts the focus to specific types of interactions that take place between individuals that eventually result in a homicide, rather than the behavior of individuals themselves (see discussion in Chapter 7 on masochistic phenomena and shifting victim roles). Tense interactions in which the potential for violence exists may occur between individuals over a prolonged period of time or may emerge from a combination of intense but brief interactions. When looked at more closely, these situations often can be assessed in terms of interactional processes that escalate because of slight miscues and misinterpretations that then begin to be perceived as serious threats. The aggressive responses become heightened on both sides, further retreats are made, and the probability of reaching a point of no return increases. If the tension does not subside quickly, there is the likelihood of an explosive and violent outcome.

A better grasp of the details of these interactions and escalating variables is needed, for they are the settings in which increased prevention will be possible for one large group of homicides. A process analogous to the "psychological autopsy" performed after a suicide can be fruitful in attempting to reconstruct what happened and what were the key variables. It is hoped that more knowledge of these processes can lead to better intervention by people who are either on site or who are called on to intervene in these situations. Not only the police, but individuals who work in clinical settings or in violence-prevalent areas, need to learn ways to diffuse such escalating encounters. It may be that bartenders and "bouncers" will become key preventive interveners, given that escalating scenes frequently occur in a drinking atmosphere, just as police are key people in the ubiquitous escalating domestic disputes.

Mass Media

The role of the mass media in heightening the potential for violence is similar to the impact of propaganda or advertising. The media is one contributory variable in a culture that already emphasizes such things as the "macho" way (e.g., through confrontation, reliance on weapons) to settle disputes. All too often, the media present this type of situation in a dramatic format; the subsequent relevance of modeling influences on the watchers is disturbing. It is difficult to confirm or disconfirm logically whether the mass media is one of the main culprits in contributing to violence reconstructing these events, let alone whether it can be part of the solution in curbing violence, for what occurs is a complex interaction that varies from one case to the next. However, the massive exposure to such types of modeling of aggression, via television and movies, that individuals receive from a young age on needs assessment.

Even more difficult to unravel are the effects of pornography. There are those who ardently advocate that seeing pornography contributes to violence and sexual murders. Of course, there are equally ardent critics on the other side of the argument.

There is also the phenomenon of individuals being willing to administer pain to helpless subjects, as has been demonstrated in social experiments using severe electric shocks. The conclusion is that individuals will conform to whatever environment is seen as acceptable at a particular time, especially when such behavior is sanctioned by authority figures. Further analysis is required to determine what individual variables cause some people to succumb in such circumstances. One interesting side question is whether there would be increasing participation by females in violent confrontations of this mode, given the blurring of boundaries in social roles of males and females. One hypothesis—which is perhaps more of a hope—is that males may not need to continue to rely on violence as a way of asserting their masculinity to the degree they have in the past because of the social changes in male and female roles that have taken place. If a decrease in violence does occur, one hypothesis is that it will be attributable to the increasing constraints placed on males to avoid violence against females. There is also the opposite possibility—that constraints on the use of physical violence by females will be lessened because that behavior has become more permissible for them—a paradoxical effect of equality. On a larger scale, the idea that more men and women need to arm themselves may override all these arguments in promoting more homicides.

■ Predisposition of Homicidal Individuals Within the Legal System

Among the usual problems and legal issues that arise in dealing with homicidally violent people in courts, many unresolved questions remain.

Capital Punishment

One issue is the effect of the increased prevalence of capital punishment statutes and those sentenced under those statutes and the effect it will have on all members of society. Although ever larger numbers of individuals continue to be convicted and take their place on death row to wait through years of the appellate process, the debate on the use and effectiveness of capital punishment from economic, moral, and deterrence points of view continues. What effect capital punishment will have in terms of aggravation or mitigation of violent behavior in the future remains largely speculative.

The usual forensic questions that are customarily discussed with regard to capital punishment, such as insanity defenses and competency issues, will undoubtedly continue to be raised, and even be expanded because of the increased reliance on capital punishment. The result is to use the most unreliable and least used approaches, such as insanity, in contrast to a society that is not bent on so harsh a retribution.

Perhaps one of the least appreciated consequences of capital punishment for first-degree murder convictions is that communities are lulled into thinking they have adopted a solution to control homicidal violence; instead, the case is simply that states are exacting retribution for increased homicidal violence on a few convicted killers.

Sentencing Trends

Similar questions arise in terms of the possible effect on homicidal behavior of different sentencing practices, such as the increased frequency with which people are being incarcerated for minor offenses and the increased length of sentences for most offenses. One hypothesis is that this removes violent individuals from society, and hence may lower the homicide rate. A contrary hypothesis is that increasingly punitive sanctions fosters the use of violence—either within the prison setting or within the civilian community, where individuals carry back the experiences of prison violence after they are released. Some offer an analogy between hardened criminals and a subset of veterans who return from combat in which they were exposed to violence and heavy drug use under certain conditions and who continue on such a pathway. Although these phenomena pertain to a minority of individuals, they raise questions about the need to examine crucial factors continually and come up with better explanations for why some individuals are homicidal as well as why communities that are attempting to control serious acts of violence are experiencing a sense of hopelessness.

Relationship of Other Offenses to Homicide

There is one criminological question to which psychiatry may be able to make its supplemental contribution. It deals with the relationship of other types of offenses (e.g., property offenses) to homicidal offenses in regards to what factors push an individual to become increasingly violent, if not homicidal, over time. The study of criminal careers in this context is the key to obtaining a better understanding of this group. One type of property offender may have an only occasional violent eruption, whereas others seem to progress to this seemingly inevitable endpoint, and the majority may confine themselves to property offenses. A study of reconviction rates and risks can focus on the assessment of progressive types of dangerousness.

Prediction tables have been constructed in relation to developing sentencing grids; developers of these tables have tried to rely on objective data such as previous convictions, age, marital status, socio-economic class, and employment record for the purpose of determining the crucial variables in determining the severity of the punishment. Unfortunately, in these grids, little weight is given to individual psychological factors. The question is whether explanations about such shifts in behavior can be better predicted if individual personality measures with clinical observations are also taken into account. Very little is known about the effect of treatment interventions on extremely violent individuals in terms of whether they elicit a changed outcome. This is partly because these individuals rarely receive such interventions, and, for the few who do, there have been no prolonged and controlled investigations to provide reliable conclusions. The types and durations of treatment need specification, as well as the theoretical basis for the treatment and the characteristics of those carrying out the treatment, before any conclusions about outcome are warranted.

Diagnostic Precision

Psychiatric contributions to understanding homicide are predicated on the validity of diagnostic classifications. Although reliability studies have multiplied, as well as the number of diagnoses with each edition of the diagnostic manuals, questions about the validity of the diagnostic entities remain. Despite attempts to use empirical testing for inclusion, acceptance of the diagnostic formulations rests with committees and advocates.

Inquiries about the validity of diagnostic frameworks is unfortunately often confused with philosophical conjectures. The latter asks whether diagnostic entities have a "real existence," meaning do they correspond to something that exists in nature. Put another way, do the diagnostic groups, to which those working in psychopathology give names, such as major depressive disorder, describe a set of signs and symptoms that exist even if never observed and given such a name by a psychiatrist? A scientific realist says yes, whereas a scientific fictionalist says no. However, this type of epistemological question should not be confused with the scientific question of how the signs and symptoms should be classified. This is basically an empirical problem to be solved ultimately by applied mathematics.[6] In the future, adopting such a more rigorous approach to diagnostic classification should allow substantive gains to be made in understanding certain homicides. By virtue of greater diagnostic accuracy, more specificity will occur to connect homicidal behavior with diagnostic categories. In the meantime, lacking a gold standard, the best we can do is to use a "boot strap" system of classification to imply the possibility of real classes by way of presumed indicators.

■ Conclusion

Each chapter in this volume contains the seeds for research sufficient to last well into the twenty-first century. What becomes more evident in studying homicidal people is the strain between those who believe that the emphasis should be on a greater academic sophistication in appraising the problem versus those who want more clinically attuned and forensically relevant output. In this book I have revealed how diverse topics overlap and actually continue to expand by virtue of the increased specificity that has occurred in psychiatric diagnostic processes.

The overall concern with violence bodes well for acceptance of the need for deeper research. At the same time, this concern is a sad commentary on the state of violence in many parts of the United States. Besides the contributions psychiatry can make toward improved validity and reliability in the diagnoses of homicidal individuals, it is hoped that psychiatry can also help researchers to achieve greater specificity in matching diverse kinds of homicides with specific diagnostic groupings.

The problem of homicide prediction continues to loom as large as ever. Increased knowledge from biological aspects of aggression will undoubtedly help us understand some aspects of homicidal behavior. One of the confusing elements in studying such violence is how much of the past work has focused not on homicide per se but rather on studies of aggression or at best on generalized definitions of violence. Such generalized studies on aggression and violence cover an enormous breadth of behaviors. They are all interesting in their own right, yet not all are germane to the problem of homicide. The result is a seemingly endless list of articles and books dealing with these topics. Sometimes the emphasis is biological, whereas at other times it is psychosocial, with an emphasis on social learning theory, the role of attachment, and similar factors. Yet other researchers believe the focus should rather be on sociological variables, such as the violence that continues to flourish among the underclasses. In the milieu of the inner cities in the United States, deterioration continues in the midst of a culture of poverty, drug use, and drug distribution. Accompanying this is the spreading incidence of juvenile homicides among younger and younger individuals, both as perpetrators and victims. The prevalence of handguns and hours of exposure children receive to television violence during their developmental years will likely see the continuation of extreme forms of juvenile violence and will merit increased scrutiny.

Given the societal emphasis seen in past work on homicide, a critic may wonder whether there is a place for a psychiatric perspective on homicide. The orientation of this volume has been that, regardless of what social hypotheses are offered, this does not bypass the need for correlating the acts of individuals with careful psychiatric assessment. If anything, the lack of such psychiatric work in the past has been a major deficiency in studies on homicide and violence. Whatever type of changes occur in the social milieu of people—be it in demographic changes, economic shifts, or governmental policy—there is always an individual actor who ultimately perpetrates a killing. A psychiatric perspective will continue to focus on these individual actors, much as will the legal system out of its need to assess blameworthiness.

Although the prevalence of violence among intimates has declined relative to violence perpetrated against strangers, it still accounts for a majority of the homicides occurring in the United States. The variety of biological predispositions and psychodynamic variables operating in the area of violence between intimates leading to homicides is much more complex than originally thought. This type of violence was once conceptualized around a few discrete situations: the occurrence of delusions of infidelity leading to a spousal killing, or a wife striking back at her husband after a long history of physical abuse. The context of such violence has now been widened considerably—for example, to children killing parents they allege have physically or sexually abused them, and battered wives who, because of the fear engendered in them by their spouse, strike out first and kill their spouse in the belief that this is necessary to defend themselves against a future homicide attack.

Questions about homicides in response to incest, marital rape, husband battering, abuse of the elderly, familicides, and the frequent role of drugs and alcohol in homicides all speak to the need for careful psychiatric appraisal in addition to an awareness of the social milieu in which homicides occur. Clearly, clinical fields, such as psychiatry, will continue to play a significant role in this important area of human behavior well into the twenty-first century.

■ References

1. Law enforcement and crime. Information Please: Almanac Atlas and Yearbook 1995, 48th Edition. New York, Houghton Mifflin, 1995, p 859

2. Rutherford A: Crime, law enforcement, and penology. Britannica Book of the Year 1995. Chicago, IL, Encyclopedia Britannica, 1995, pp 145–148

3. Jacobs JB: Busting the Mob/United States v Cosa Nostra. New York, New York University Press, 1994

4. Stille A: Excellent Cadavers: The Mafia and the Death of the First Italian Republic. New York, Pantheon, 1995

5. Volavka J: Neurobiology of Violence. Washington, DC, American Psychiatric Association, 1995

6. Meehl PE: Bookstraps taxometrics: solving the classification problem in psychopathology. Am Psychol 50:266–275, 1995

INDEX

*Page numbers printed in **boldface** type refer to tables or figures.*